On Glasgow and Edinburgh

On Glasgow

Robert Crawford

and Edinburgh

The Belknap Press of Harvard University Press

Cambridge, Massachusetts
London, England 〜 2013

Library of Congress Cataloging-in-Publication Data
Crawford, Robert, 1959–
On Glasgow and Edinburgh / Robert Crawford.
p.   cm.
Includes bibliographical references and index.
ISBN 978-0-674-04888-1 (alk. paper)
1. Glasgow (Scotland)—History.   2. Edinburgh (Scotland)—History.   I. Title.
DA890.G5C87   2013
941.3′4—dc23   2012020952

Book design by Dean Bornstein

for both
with love

Contents

Maps · ix

Prelude: A Treasured Rivalry · 1

Edinburgh

1. The Royal Mile: From the Castle to a Song · 43
2. The Royal Mile: From Story to Parliament · 74
3. Princes Street Gardens and the New Town · 100
4. Hill, Hwa-wu, and Port · 133
5. Medicine, Museums, Blood · 151

Glasgow

6. City Hearts · 179
7. Poverty and Wealth · 209
8. Street Life, Masterpieces, Tenements, Books · 231
9. Art, Learning, Arsenic, and Architecture · 261
10. Water · 295

Coda: The Falkirk Wheel · 311

Further Reading · 319
List of Illustrations · 322
Credits · 324
Acknowledgments · 326
Index · 329

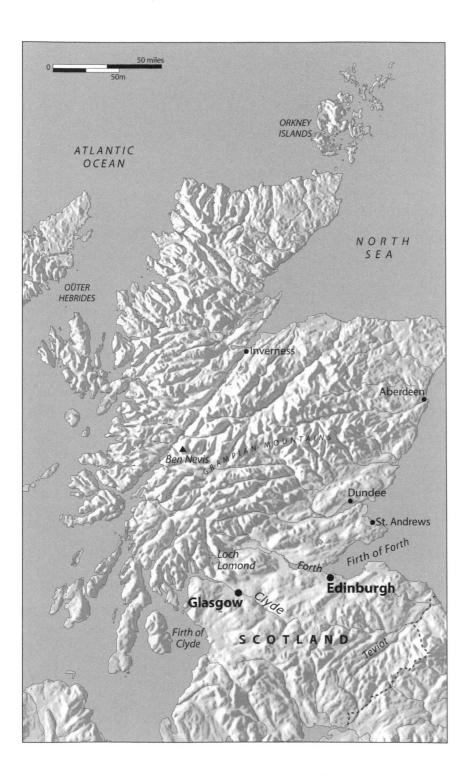

50 miles

50m

ATLANTIC
OCEAN

ORKNEY
ISLANDS

NORTH
SEA

OÚTER
HEBRIDES

•Inverness

Aberdeen•

▲
Ben Nevis

GRAMPIAN MOUNTAINS

Dundee
•

•St. Andrews

Loch
Lomond

Firth of Forth

Forth

Edinburgh

Glasgow

Clyde

Firth of
Clyde

SCOTLAND

Teviot

Edinburgh

1 Edinburgh Castle
2 Camera Obscura
3 St. Giles Cathedral
4 Museum of Childhood
5 Museum of Edinburgh
6 Canongate Kirkyard
7 Palace of Holyroodhouse
8 Scottish Parliament

9 Princes Street Gardens
10 Scott Monument
11 Royal Scottish Academy
12 Scottish National Gallery
13 Scottish National Portrait Gallery
14 Charlotte Square
15 Dean Gallery
16 Scottish National Gallery of Modern Art

17 Leith
18 Calton Hill
19 Royal Botanic Garden Edinburgh
20 Leith Walk
21 University of Edinburgh
22 Royal College of Surgeons Museum
23 Greyfriars Kirk
24 National Museum of Scotland

NW Circus Pl Circus Place
Great King St
Street
Dublin
Albany St
Northumberland
Abercromby Pl
Dublin St Ln S
York
St. James P
19
0.8 mile
Gloucester Lane
Heriot Row
Queen St
13
N St Andrew St
India St
Howe St
Heriot Row
Queen St
Gardens
NEW TOWN
St Andrew Square
St. Andrew St
15
16
0.9 mile
Queen St
Thistle St NE Ln
Thistle St
Thistle St SE Ln
Hanover
Thistle St NW Ln
Thistle St
Thistle St SE Ln
Hill St N Ln
Hill St
Hill St S Ln
N Castle St
George St
Street
Rose St
Meuse Ln
Princes
Young St N Ln
Young St
Young St S Ln
George St
George St
Rose St N Ln
Rose St
Rose St S Ln
Princes St
10
Charlotte Square
14
Hope St
Rose St N Ln
Rose St
Rose St S Ln
Rose St S Ln
Princes St
11
9
12
Waverley Bridge
Princes St
West Princes St
Gardens
The Mound
Market St
Mar
Cockt
Princes St
Mound Pl
N Bank St
Bank St
St. Giles St
High
3
King's Stables Road
Ramsay Ln
THE ROYAL MILE
2
Castlehill
Victoria St
George IV Bridge
Castle Terrace
Johnston Terrace
Cowgate
Candlemaker Row
Ch
King's Stables Road
Grassmarket
23
Spittal St
Lady Lawson St
West Port

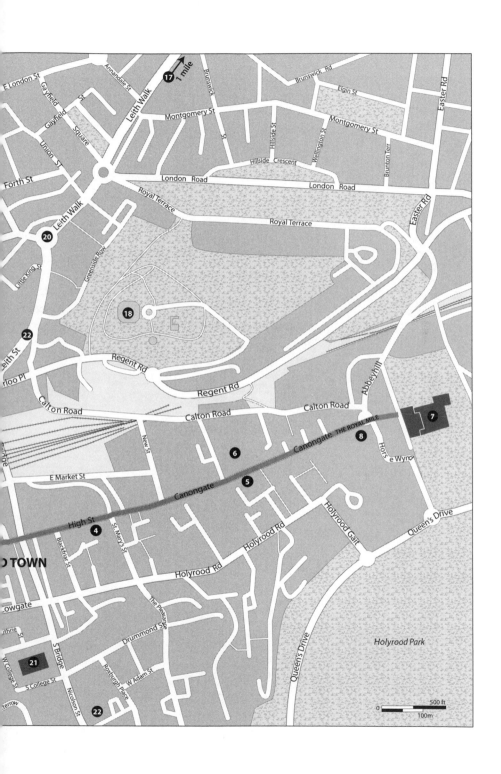

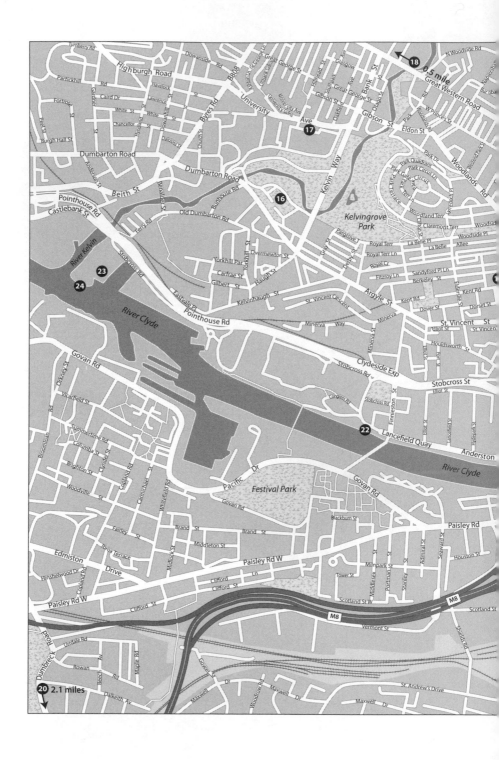

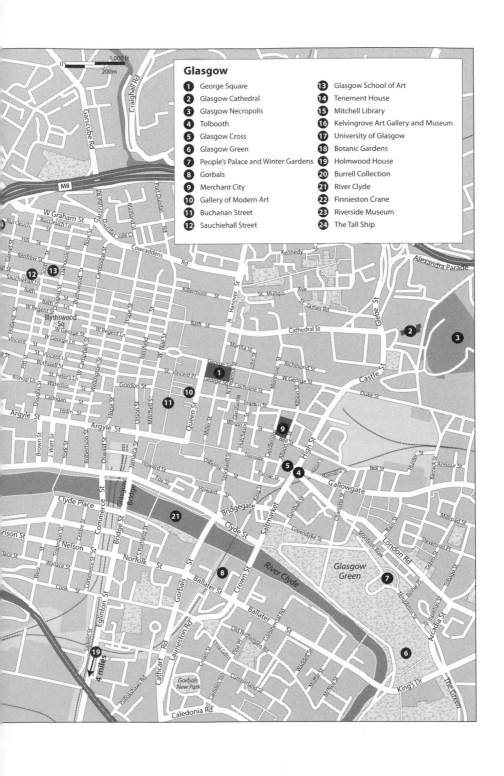

Glasgow

1. George Square
2. Glasgow Cathedral
3. Glasgow Necropolis
4. Tolbooth
5. Glasgow Cross
6. Glasgow Green
7. People's Palace and Winter Gardens
8. Gorbals
9. Merchant City
10. Gallery of Modern Art
11. Buchanan Street
12. Sauchiehall Street
13. Glasgow School of Art
14. Tenement House
15. Mitchell Library
16. Kelvingrove Art Gallery and Museum
17. University of Glasgow
18. Botanic Gardens
19. Holmwood House
20. Burrell Collection
21. River Clyde
22. Finnieston Crane
23. Riverside Museum
24. The Tall Ship

On Glasgow and Edinburgh

Prelude

A Treasured Rivalry

Like good and evil, Glasgow and Edinburgh are often mentioned in the same breath but regarded as utterly distinct. The rivalry between these cities, which is so long-standing that it has become proverbial, sets them alongside other urban centres—Los Angeles and San Francisco, Moscow and St. Petersburg, Rio de Janeiro and São Paulo—which like to jockey for supremacy within their nations. Though the two are almost comically diminutive when compared with Madrid and Barcelona, let alone with Beijing and Shanghai, Glasgow (population 600,000) and Edinburgh (population 500,000) are much smaller than most other internationally celebrated pairs of urban rivals. They are also absurdly closer together: only forty miles separates the two lowland Scottish cities; to travel by train from the centre of one to the centre of the other can take as little as forty-five minutes. In spirit, though, each considers itself far removed from its counterpart. Perhaps the most intellectually honest way to go from the west-coast city to the east-coast city would be to fly westward from Glasgow Airport over the Atlantic, crossing North America, the northern Pacific, Asia, and continental Europe, before descending over the Firth of Forth on the eastern seaboard of Scotland and then landing at Edinburgh Airport. That way, at least, one would arrive from Glasgow psychologically prepared.

There have been many books about each of these cities, but no one has ever written a serious volume exclusively devoted to both. To do so seems heretical but necessary. It is impossible to live life to the full in either place without occasionally thinking wistfully or smirkingly of the other, and no visitor can understand urban Scotland or the Scottish nation without comprehending these proud competitors. Beloved of tourists, Scotland is a small country of five million people, more than half of whom live in the area surrounding Glasgow and Edinburgh. This book is written for natives and guests alike. A tale of two cities, it focuses on twenty or so visitable sites

1

(usually specific buildings or clusters of buildings) in the historic core of each, and draws from those present-day locations aspects of the character and provenance of their municipality. Every chapter is constellated around several particular spots. The book does not aim to provide a comprehensive historical map, but strives to trace cultural leylines, some familiar, some long obscured.

The central feature here is a multi-chaptered account of each city; the present opening chapter sets out something of the background to their rivalry; at the volume's conclusion a short envoi gestures, optimistically, towards rapprochement. Having given Glasgow priority in my book's title, in ordering the contents I have placed Edinburgh first. In matters of arrangement, prioritizing, and protocol, where Edinburgh and Glasgow are concerned it is impossible to get things right. Yet in the midst of each city, when one eyes the surrounding high culture (which is what this book does), such concerns often drop away. "Look up!" generations of Glaswegian mothers have counseled their children, alerting them to the loftily ornamented Victorian glories of their urban heartland; in Edinburgh, the Castle and other hilltop monuments constantly encourage a raising of the eyes. Visually rich, the centres of both places are best seen on foot. These are not fast-paced metropolises like New York or Hong Kong, but slower, strollable European cities.

Most of this book is arranged sequentially in terms of space, rather then chronology: its core sections progress along streets and through parks. I have cast those chapters mainly in the form of town-centre excursions that use the visible fabric of the city—its built environment—as a gateway into the area's character and past. Architecture can function as social memory, and there are elements of architectural history in what follows; but more of the book concerns the people of each place. These cities are populated by folk with fascinating stories. To let readers relish some of the more notable achievements of the citizens of both places, I have written about women and children, as well as about famous and infamous men. Often, accounts of townscapes give the impression that cities have been lived in almost exclusively by adults; and it has been all too easy in a lot of Scottish historiography to assume that being Scottish means having two Y chromosomes.

Through attending to nodal sites in either place, then, the chapters that follow try to give the reader a sense of each city's history and people. Within the main "Edinburgh" and "Glasgow" sections, the principal locations are used often as points of entry into the city's story, and other notable attractions are mentioned in passing. A few chapters, like the one which discusses Glasgow's Burrell Collection and Holmwood House, focus on sites that are some distance apart; but often, as in the chapters on Edinburgh's Royal Mile, readers are invited to walk the route. I have tried to present an engagingly detailed continuous account, so that anyone who reads the book from start to finish will get a good sense of both cities and their famously scratchy relationship. Museums and galleries, Adam Smith and Walter Scott certainly feature—but so do small apartments, a poetry library, protean Madeleine Smith, and the entrepreneur Maria Theresa Short. Sometimes, partly for the sake of variety, I have chosen to view sites from unusual angles, looking, for instance, at one of Glasgow's best-known streets through the eyes of a Victorian child who grew up there, or noting how Edinburgh University was perceived by its most famous student from England. I have sought to mix novelty and familiarity in something like the way each of these great cities does, and to make both places attractive to a reader who may or may not have time to return.

The idea of portraying an entire municipality by means of a panoramic view reproduced inside a large cylindrical surface was first conceived on Edinburgh's Calton Hill by Irish artist Robert Barker, who patented the device in 1787 and soon had the temerity to exhibit his depiction of Edinburgh in Glasgow. Based around a particular selection of nodal points, this book cannot provide such a comprehensive wrap-round experience; but it does aim to exhibit revealing glimpses of each city to the other, and to a wider international public. Since Barker's day, each place, like most urban locations, has developed sprawling peripheral housing estates, often with insistent social problems. These, though occasionally alluded to, are not the preoccupation here. In concentrating mainly on city-centre heritage sites that present-day tourists may readily visit, I have adopted a necessarily exclusive focus. My choices can be disputed—another writer might have paid far more attention to football, folksongs, and food, far less to literature, gardens, and murder—but I hope that they work. Centering on permanent places that are open to the public throughout the year, I have given little space to such performance venues as halls and sports-grounds, privileging instead art galleries and historic homes.

At the start and at the heart of *On Glasgow and Edinburgh* is an extended, treasured rivalry. Competition between cities in a single country is a very ancient phenomenon, going back at least to Athens and Sparta, those famous city-states of classical Greece. Yet in the English-speaking world the rivalry between Glasgow and Edinburgh is foundational in that it precedes and to some extent prefigures all other fully developed, long-standing urban rivalries; those between New York and Boston, Sydney and Melbourne, Toronto and Vancouver come later. In England, London's overbalancing dominance has gone uncontested, and the jousting between Oxford and Cambridge is essentially between universities. Within Scotland, though, since at least the early eighteenth century, a sense of sparring and sometimes outright competition between the country's two largest cities has been a defining aspect of the nation.

It continues to be so. These two cities still look, feel, and sound markedly different. Each has its own accent: Glasgow's is guttural and (like the speech of some New Yorkers) enlivened by glottal stops; Edinburgh's is more singsongy, often rising towards the end of a sentence. Both places treasure their climate: Glasgow's is mild from the west-coast Gulf Stream, but damp; Edinburgh's, sunnier but whetted by east-coast winds off the North Sea. The two are so close that in a more sprawling country they might be seen almost as one conjoined metropolis, but each has its own municipal government, sports teams, universities, newspapers, and sense of direction. Glasgow has long liked to look westwards; I have heard it referred to as "America's fifty-first state." Its *Herald* newspaper, published under several different names during its long history, was founded in 1783, the same year as the Glasgow Chamber of Commerce, when the city was rethinking its commercial strategy in the wake of the American War of Independence; today the *Herald*'s owners are American. Asserting itself as a European capital, Edinburgh looks westward perhaps a little less often; that way it can avoid considering Glasgow. Edinburgh's resilient *Scotsman* newspaper, first published on Burns Night 1817, mentioned its native city several times throughout its first issue when pondering issues pertinent to culture, and alluded to Glasgow (once) in the context of gas lighting.

Often misunderstood, the rivalry between these two cities has a lively history. In his 1977 book, *Glasgow,* the scholar David Daiches argues that its first recorded flare-up occurred in 1656, as part of an argument over the standard of baking: "twa [two] honest men" from Edinburgh thought they could offer Glaswegians a higher standard of bread, and Glaswegians worried about their own "townes credit." At around the same time, a Cromwellian soldier described Glasgow as "not so . . . rich . . . yet a much sweeter and more delightful place than Edinburgh." However, the more substantial origins of mutual competitiveness lie in the years which followed the still-controversial 1707 Act of Union negotiated between Scotland and England. Edinburgh had lost its royal court to London in 1603, when King James VI of Scotland, son of the executed Mary Queen of Scots, succeeded Queen Elizabeth of England and moved south to become the monarch England calls James I. Monarchical union between the two kingdoms was followed by the 1707 parliamentary union, which sparked riots in Glasgow and Edinburgh when the independent parliaments of Scotland and England were replaced by one British parliament. For many Britons, since this new institution was based in the English capital city, it seemed very like the old English Parliament refreshed with an exotic sprinkling of Scottish MPs. For Edinburgh, however, the 1707 loss of the Scottish parliament, following on the seventeenth-century loss of the royal court, meant that Scotland's capital city was robbed of much of what had made it a capital in the first place. Edinburgh, then, was damaged in status by parliamentary Union, but the coming of a London-ruled United Kingdom provided opportunities for other cities, most notably Glasgow, to grow their trade. Commerce and banking, rather than baking, revved up the now centuries-old rivalry between Scotland's principal cities.

When the Bank of Scotland, Britain's oldest clearing bank, was founded in Edinburgh in 1695, only one of its subscribers came from Glasgow—which already had substantial mercantile discount houses of its own. Though the subsequent foundation of another Edinburgh-based establishment, the Royal Bank of Scotland, in 1727, trumpeted the capital city's economic dominance, in many ways it was Glasgow that made the greatest commercial advances. Edinburgh remained Scotland's cultural centre, a self-conscious capital of art. *The Edinburgh Miscellany,* a poetry anthology published in 1720, might include verses (such as "A Walk on Glasgow Green") depicting the beauties of the west-coast city, but the book's title says it all. Stylish and advanced, Edinburgh's Fair Intellectual-Club, founded by young women in 1718 and active for several years, demonstrated that women

5

as well as men might participate in intellectual improvement. During an era when *A Looking-Glass for Edinburgh Ladies* saw spinning work rather than brain power as belonging to "the true Character of a Good Wife," one of the Fair Intellectual-Club's members published verse in *The Edinburgh Miscellany.* This self-help group's nine teenage members (their number aligned with that of the nine classical muses) studied the *Tatler,* the *Spectator,* Shakespeare, Dryden, and other writers. They were, though, advised that "comedies should be read with caution," and their secret group was "discovered" when one of its members fell in love with a young man from a local "Athenian Society"—an early athenæum, or learned club, probably based on the Athenian Society of London.

Later—not least during the Enlightenment and the nineteenth century, when Edinburgh was home to major publishing houses, to encyclopædias such as the *Encyclopædia Britannica,* and to internationally influential periodicals such as the *Edinburgh Review, Blackwood's Edinburgh Magazine,* and *Chambers' Edinburgh Journal*—literary learning, as much as anything else, won Edinburgh its soubriquet "the Athens of the North"; and my discussion of the jostling between Glasgow and Edinburgh will be unashamedly bookish. The Scottish capital's Fair Intellectual-Club, along with more celebrated (predominantly male) "improving" societies and early eighteenth-century publications such as Edinburgh University professor Alexander Monro's 1726 *Anatomy of the Humane Bones,* contributed to the burgeoning of what is now called the Scottish Enlightenment. Yet it was at the much older University of Glasgow that Adam Smith's teacher Francis Hutcheson wrote the books and gave the lectures often seen as the clearest early indication of that surge in intellectual voltage.

Repeatedly, people are tempted to think of Edinburgh as Scotland's centre of learning, and to gender the Scottish capital as feminine, Glasgow as masculine. There may be lasting truth in such assumptions, but they need to be more subtly nuanced. In Glasgow, women as well as men took philosophy seriously, and sometimes women were at the forefront in commercial wrangling. When in 1725 Glaswegians rioted against the imposition of a Malt Tax, a published "Letter from a Gentleman at *Glasgow* to his Friend at *Edinburgh*" recorded that "a Woman, and a great many others with her, did make a Procession through the Town frequently through the Day, with a great many Children and Boys making a great Noise." This woman, exhibiting "great Majesty and Rage," was arrested, but was released next day when she quarreled with the city's Lord Provost and outwitted a force of more than eighty soldiers. If Glaswegian women could be formidable popular leaders, agitating about taxes and commercial threats, Glaswegian men were resolute too. In 1728 that same Glaswegian Lord Provost, Andrew Cochrane, presented £900 worth of Bank of Scotland notes at his local branch of the Bank of Scotland, and demanded coin for it. When the Edinburgh-based bank was unable to supply the cash, the Cochrane family took legal action, which eventually went as far as the House of Lords. The Glaswegians won. Private traders in their city led the way to the founding of Glasgow's first bank in 1750, followed by other similar establishments, one involving Cochrane himself. All of this indicates that the city in the west was beginning to flex its economic muscles. By the end of the 1750s, Edinburgh's financial institutions felt obliged to attempt to put their Glaswegian competitors out of business.

With growing commercial clout came civic pride. The first book-length account of a Scottish city was published in 1736 by "John McUre *alias* Campbel," a native Glaswegian who stated that his "great Age . . . long Experience and Employment" had given him thorough knowledge of Glasgow's "Antiquity, the Citizens Trade and Commerce, from what low and small Beginnings was rais'd here, and happily arriv'd once to such a Pitch, that we became the Envy of others." McUre does not mention Edinburgh at this point, but it is hard to imagine Glaswegians would have complained much if "others" in the Scottish capital had felt any "Envy." This historian's pride in his native place is palpable. His *View of the City of Glasgow* explains how there "stands deliciously on the Banks of the River *Clyde*, the City of *Glasgow*, which is generally believed to be of its Bigness the most beautiful City of the World, and is acknowledged to be so by all Forreigners that comes thither." That panegyric was not quite as improbable as it may sound. Already, three decades earlier, the well-traveled English spy and novelist Daniel Defoe had been impressed not just by the industry of Glasgow's merchants, but also by their town—"the cleanest and beautifullest, and best built city in Britain, London excepted." Even though he relished the capital of Scotland, Defoe had already noted Edinburgh's "discouragements and disadvantages."

For the Londoner Defoe and the Glaswegian McUre, the attractions of

1. Viewed from the south in this 1695 engraving by John Slezer, Glasgow is the city of spires and elegance praised by the Latin poet Arthur Johnston, by the English spy Daniel Defoe, and by the local historian John McUre, who described the way it "stands deliciously on the Banks of the River *Clyde*."

Glasgow were obvious. Yet McUre's problem, like that of so many subsequent West of Scotland observers, was the sheer *kudos* of Edinburgh as the northern capital city, albeit one that had lost both its royalty and its parliament. McUre faces up to this as best he can. He maintains that Glasgow "in respect of its Largeness, Buildings, Trade and Wealth, has been long, and justly reckoned the chief Town in the Kingdom next to *Edinburgh,* the Metropolis of *Scotland.*" That last qualification would become a familiar Glaswegian strategy. The preferred response of Edinburgh would be to avoid mentioning Glasgow at all, thereby confirming its own effortless superiority. Nearly a century and a half later, Robert Louis Stevenson, in his *Edinburgh: Picturesque Notes* (1879)—still the finest book about Scotland's capital—does mention "our rivals of Glasgow," but tellingly relegates them to a footnote. There he apologizes to his fellow Edinburgh citizens if he has said anything which displeases them or which pleases Glaswegians. Stevenson concludes, "To the Glasgow people I would say only one word, but that is of gold: *I have not yet written a book about Glasgow.*"

Ebullient Glaswegians always love to sing their city's praises. Edinburgh people usually reply with a lofty half-smile: you can tell that they once had their own royal court. For more than fifteen years after the publication of McUre's book about Glasgow, no one thought it necessary to counter with a matching tome about Edinburgh. Eventually, in 1753, William Maitland, a native of northeast Scotland who had already written a *History of London,* published his *History of Edinburgh . . . In Nine Books.* Comprising 551 large pages with small print and double columns, this magnum opus dwarfs McUre's more modest publication and marks the start of an ongoing "battle of the books" between the two cities. Over the centuries, well nigh 10,000 works have been published with the word "Glasgow" in their title, relentlessly outgunned by the more than 15,000 whose titles include the word "Edinburgh." Maitland wrote early in this vigorous *bibliomachia.* Invoking sources as old as Ptolemy, and asserting Edinburgh's unassailable status "from its foundations to the present time," his work is designedly monumental; but its very appearance coincides with—and perhaps in an overassertive way articulates—a certain anxiety in mid-eighteenth-century Edinburgh at a time when Glasgow was growing in confidence, wealth, and energy.

Maitland's way of dealing with Glasgow is to pretend it does not exist. The word "Glasgow" features nowhere in the index to his book, nor is it in the key to Hugo Arnot's even larger *History of Edinburgh* (1779). Written with support from the Town Council, these volumes were designed to bolster the Scottish capital's dominance, making the most of its regal antiquity. Conscious that "the History of *Edinburgh*" has been "hitherto unattempted," Maitland mentions "Romantic *French* Writers" who "about Five hundred Years ago" called the place "*Castrum Puellarum,* the *Maiden Castle,* from the Daughters of *Pictish* Kings said to have been educated therein." Though he goes on to say such tales "deserve not the least credit," he invokes them to boost Edinburgh's ancient allure, arguing that the settlement was probably founded around the year 626. This causes him some problems, since he has then to admit that "Edinburgh seems to have been but of little Note till about the Middle of the fourteenth Century" and that as late as 1400 "it appears to have consisted of mere Houses covered with Straw." Modern historians attach particular significance to the Northumbrians' capture of the settlement of Din Eidyn (the first word means "fort"; the second is a proper name) in 638, and its subsequent renaming as "Edineburg"— "burg" being Anglian for a town or stronghold. These historians go on to

9

highlight the place's tenth-century capture by the Scots of the MacAlpin dynasty, and how its castle passed several times between Scottish and English hands during centuries of warfare from the 1100s onwards. Maitland, however, spent relatively little time on the Middle Ages. For him, it was the coming of a parliament in 1436 that led the city "to be better looked on"; then, a couple of decades later, came "the Time of its Beginning to flourish, and of its justly being reckoned the Capital of the Kingdom." Maitland's foundational book-length study of Edinburgh makes much of King James III's granting of a charter in 1477 confirming the city's privileges to hold markets, and of quarrels with the neighbouring port of Leith on the Firth of Forth. Mid-sixteenth-century Edinburgh, a place where a hungry shopper could buy a dozen of "the best Laverock or Lark" for four Scots pennies, or "the best Swan" for five shillings, emerges as a capital city of food, but hardly of hygiene. Aware that this latter problem was still pressing two centuries afterwards, Maitland finds evidence that in 1553 "*Edinburgh* seems to have been greatly pestered with Filth and Dirt, by the Council's ordering all Dunghills to be removed from off the Streets, and Swine kept from coming thereon."

Though St. Andrews had been the ecclesiastical capital of later medieval Scotland, while Scottish kings had traditionally been crowned at Scone in Perthshire and had enjoyed residing at Stirling Castle, Edinburgh is presented in these and subsequent histories as *the* place most closely linked to Scottish royalty and to the nation's ancient parliament. After the disastrous Battle of Flodden in 1513, the building of Edinburgh's "Flodden Wall" confined the early Renaissance city within a protective barrier, strengthening the identity of a place that the Protestant Scottish exile Alesius (Alexander Alan) in 1550 compared to Prague, and whose houses he regarded as palaces distributed along its Via Regia, the street now called the Royal Mile. For Maitland, writing two centuries after Alesius, Edinburgh also featured as the key site of the momentous sixteenth-century Scottish Reformation. He recounts how on September 1, 1558, the feast day of St. Giles, "the tutelary Saint of Edinburgh," monks and priests found that "new Converts" to Protestantism were disrupting the traditional procession which in a "magnificent Pageant" carried a statue of the saint "in Triumph through the City." The Protestants "in derision" took a rival statue from Greyfriars Churchyard, nicknamed it *Young St. Giles,* and eventually tore it to pieces.

A few years later, during the reign of the Catholic monarch Mary Queen

2. Another engraving done by John Slezer in 1695 shows Edinburgh in the distance, with the village of Dean in the foreground. Edinburgh's castle, on its lofty rock, led the sixteenth-century writer Alesius to compare the Scottish capital to Prague.

of Scots, the now-dominant Protestant Reformers wanted a fresh identity for Scotland's capital: "The Reformation of Religion in *Edinburgh* being carried to such a Height, the Council . . . caused the Picture of *St. Giles* (by them called the *Idol*) to be cut out of the Town's Standard, and the Thistle to be inserted in its stead." Mary Queen of Scots had been welcomed home from France at New Year 1562 with a great Scots-tongued flourish:

WELCUM, illustrat Ladye, and oure Quene!
Welcum, our lyone with the Floure-delyce!   *fleur-de-lys*
Welcum, oure thrissill with the Lorane grene!   *thistle; Lorraine*
Welcum, our rubent roiss vpoun the ryce!   *ruby; rose; twig*

However, as Maitland's *History of Edinburgh* makes clear, Mary's later marriage to the overbearing Earl of Bothwell, accused of her first husband's murder, was seen by many as "to her eternal Reproach." Some Edinburgh people chanted "Burn the Whore!" Retelling this history in the mid-eighteenth century was a way of asserting that Scotland's capital, even without a resident monarch or parliament, was still the central city of Scottish life and continued to preserve a keen sense of its links to the national past.

Maitland's rhetoric makes this subtly apparent. He describes, for instance, how in 1579 Edinburgh greeted Mary's son, James VI, the last monarch of an independent Scotland, with a masque that included "a large polished Brazen Globe; from which, in a Machine, descended a *Cupid*, who presented him with the Keys of the City-gates, made of Silver, in a Silvern Bason, (which is lost: but the Two Keys, with a Silvern Chain, are still to be seen in the Town's Charter-house)." So modern Edinburgh, for Maitland and the city's successive historians, acts as a receptacle of treasures from the nation's past, rather than simply of items from municipal history. Moreover, this eighteenth-century chronicler implies that in some ways the city's glories have actually increased since the days when it hosted Renaissance Scottish monarchs. Commenting on late sixteenth-century medicine, Maitland in 1753 remarks that "the Art of Surgery was then but little known in *Edinburgh*, though at present it may justly vye with any other City in the Knowledge and Practice of that very useful and curious Art." In retelling Edinburgh's stories, Maitland also boosted the city's standing as an Enlightenment centre of "Knowledge." This is the city to which David Hume returned after writing his *Treatise on Human Nature* (1738-1740), and where William Smellie, local founder of the *Encyclopædia Britannica* (1768), later maintained that an English immigrant in the Royal Mile had told him, "Here I stand at what is called the *Cross of Edinburgh*, and can, in a few minutes, take fifty men of genius and learning by the hand."

Glasgow had not the same cards to play, and its first historian, McUre, knew it. Many of the western city's ecclesiastical records had been taken abroad at the time of the Reformation; committedly, McUre tracked them down. Not content simply to quote a Latin poem from William Camden's Renaissance survey, *Britannia*, which sings "Happy *Glasgow, Clyde's* chiefest Pride," he maintained that Druids had once lived in his native town "in Cells near the *Blackfryer* Church adjacent to the College." After this druidical rhetorical flourish, McUre saw Glasgow's early history almost entirely in terms of religious life: "The City owes its Rise and Progress to its antient Patron *St. Mungo*, who, some say, founded here an *Episcopal See.*" Drawing on John Spottiswoode's *History of the Church of Scotland* (1655), McUre retells legends of this saint, to whom Glasgow's "Cathedral Church was dedicated, and is called *St. Mungo's* to this Day." For all that McUre in 1736 appears to write as a Protestant, he records that Mungo's saint's day is January 13, "and that Day is the End of a Fair that holds in the Town for twenty

Days preceeding, and is commonly called the twenty Day of Yuill, or St. *Mungo's* Fair, (which is very beneficial to the People twenty Miles round *Glasgow,* resorting to the Fair)." For McUre, Glasgow's past is principally a religious one. Its beloved cathedral had been consecrated in the summer of 1136, in the presence of King David I of Scotland (who had also endowed the site of Edinburgh's Holyrood Abbey—though McUre makes no mention of that). A papal bull of 1172 had termed Glasgow a *civitas*—a city—and Archbishop William Turnbull is credited with the founding of Glasgow University in 1451. Too polite to point out that Edinburgh would have to wait nearly a century and a half before getting a university of its own, McUre does occasionally glance across at the Scottish capital when writing about his beloved native place—a city surrounded, he wrote, by "corn-fields, kitchen and flower gardens and beautiful orchyards."

Chronicling Reformation Glasgow, this Glaswegian writer is disturbed that its learned early sixteenth-century archbishop Gavin Dunbar, though "not of himself a Biggot," allowed two young men to be put to death as early Protestant martyrs. The archbishop, it seems, was in favour of sparing the youths' lives, "but these others who were sent to assist, told him expressly, that if he followed any milder Course than that which was kept at *Edinburgh,* they could not esteem him the Church's Friend, whereupon he was compell'd to give Way to their Cruelty; and these Innocents were condemn'd to be burnt alive." It is revealing to see McUre here directing his attention to the perceived vicious authoritarianism of the east-coast city, a sternness that curbs the more generous instinct of the west-coast archbishop. If Edinburgh chroniclers could simply ignore Glasgow, it was not so easy for Glaswegians to ignore Edinburgh. The latter, after all, was their capital city—and sometimes a good place to blame.

Yet this author of the first book on Glasgow was keen to show that local patriotism crossed sectarian divisions; he made it clear that the Cathedral of St. Mungo continued to matter as a civic icon to most Protestant Glaswegians after the Reformation. Whereas Edinburgh was a municipality often characterized by its awareness of its authority, in Glasgow there was a certain pride in the way the populace could challenge—even override—the wishes of those in power. This aspect of Glaswegian society is still treasured, and an early instance of it occurs in an anecdote which McUre recounts about an armed uprising by Glaswegians against their magistrates and their university principal, the learned Latin poet, iconoclast, and leading Presbyterian Andrew Melville, who had been educated at St. Andrews, Paris, and Poitiers, as well as in the Geneva of John Calvin's successor, Theodore Beza.

> It was while he [Thomas Crawfurd] was Provost that a Design was laid down to demolish the Cathedral, *anno* 1578, as Bishop *Spotswood* in his History tells us, and the Town hath the constant Tradition of it to this Day, that when Mr. *Andrew Melvil* the Reformer was the Head of the University, he and other Ministers of the Town plied the Magistracy with such Importunity, that at last they consented; several Reasons were adduced to it, viz. That it was a Resort for superstitious People to their Devotions in the Church; but the great Topick of all was, That the Church was a Monument of Idolatry, and the only unruin'd Cathedral in the Kingdom; but when the Masons were brought to take down the Building, the Crafts of *Glasgow* ran to Arms, and threatened immediate Death to them who should pull down the first Stone. Thus by the Bravery of the Trades of the City, the Cathedral, which is the greatest Ornament of the Kingdom was preserved.

Tellingly McUre writes here as an authority on his city and as a municipal official, yet also as a Glaswegian who sympathizes with revolt against authority. Such a combination came to characterize Glaswegian behaviour in later centuries and may be bound up with Glasgow's perception of itself both as powerful and as a perennial underdog. McUre's city must acknowledge from time to time that it stands second in status to Edinburgh, the capital, yet frequently its instinct is to resent the imposition of power. In the use of that phrase "the greatest Ornament of the Kingdom" one also senses that for McUre, as for other Glaswegians, their medieval cathedral was at least as important to their city's sense of itself as was the Castle to Edinburgh's folk. Eighteenth-century municipal historians drew on the past to assert civic importance in the Enlightenment present. They did so during shifting political and economic conditions which saw growth in Glasgow accelerating even as Edinburgh realized there was a need for citywide reconstruction.

The seventeenth and eighteenth centuries saw the burgeoning of Glasgow's power as a city of international traders. As early as 1647, when the city's population numbered only about 12,000 people, a Glaswegian ship, the *Antelope,* imported a cargo of tobacco from Martinique. By 1662, Englishman John Kay was describing the settlement on the Clyde as "the second city in Scotland." Caribbean and North American sugar and tobacco became traded commodities on which the city grew rich; after the 1707 Act of Union gave Scottish merchants official access to English colonies, Glasgow prospered as never before. In the second book devoted entirely to this emergent western commercial centre, John Gibson's *History of Glasgow, from the Earliest Accounts to the Present Time* (1777), "the prosperity of the city" is the paramount modern theme. Just a few years before Gibson wrote, Glasgow in one single year imported 47 million pounds of tobacco. Working with nearby ports farther down the Clyde at Greenock and Port Glasgow, the city's merchants and importers looked as if they might begin to monopolize aspects of Scottish trade.

Edinburgh, for all its tendency to ignore its western rival, began to realize that since the Union other parts of Scotland such as Aberdeen, Glasgow, and Dumfries had seen their trade grow, while that of the capital risked stagnating. In *Proposals for Carrying on Certain Public Works in the City of Edinburgh* (1752), Gilbert Elliot, Lord Minto, might note that "a trade has been opened from the port of *Leith* to the *West Indies*," but east-coast commercial engagement with those slave-dependent Caribbean colonial economies was not thriving to anything like the same degree as that of Glasgow. Minto makes cursory mention of Glasgow, but prefers to align Edinburgh with its fellow capital city, London, albeit to the Scottish capital's disadvantage. Complaining of "neglected arts and industry" in Edinburgh, he is proud of that place as "the metropolis of SCOTLAND when a separate kingdom, and still the chief city of NORTH BRITAIN," but he worries that its situation, "placed upon the ridge of a hill . . . admits but of one good street" (the historic Royal Mile), while "narrow lanes leading to the north and south, by reason of their steepness, narrowness, and dirtiness, can only be considered as so many unavoidable nusances." Glasgow, relatively close to the spectacular scenery of Loch Lomond and the Highlands, increasingly relished its fine situation. Historically trapped by its old Flodden Wall, Minto's Edinburgh is stymied because it is boxed in.

> Confined by the small compass of the walls, and the narrow limits of the royalty, which scarcely extends beyond the walls, the houses stand more crouded than in any other town in *Europe*, and are built to a height that

15

is almost incredible. Hence necessarily follows a great want of free air, light, cleanliness, and every other comfortable accommodation. Hence also many families, sometimes no less than ten or a dozen, are obliged to live overhead of each other in the same building; where, to all the other inconveniencies, is added that of a common stair, which is no other in effect than an upright street, constantly dark and dirty.

The phenomenon of these twelve-storey tenements would lead to Edinburgh's being described in a later century as a precursor of Manhattan, but this eighteenth-century observer noted only that "several of the principal parts of the town are now lying in ruins" while "many of the old houses are decayed." For Lord Minto in 1752, "The meanness of EDINBURGH has been too long an obstruction to our improvement, and a reproach to SCOTLAND." He suggested ways "to enlarge and beautify the town, by opening new streets to the north and south, removing the markets and shambles, and turning the *North-Loch* into a canal, with walks and terraces on each side." In "*Turin, Berlin,* and many other cities," he argued, "what is called the *new town,* consists of spacious streets and large buildings, which are thinly inhabited, and that too by strangers chiefly, and persons of considerable rank; while the *old town,* though not near so commodious, is more crouded than before these late additions were made." Today Edinburgh's New Town, laid out from the 1760s onwards, is seen as the world's greatest surviving example of large-scale Georgian town planning. Yet when Minto was writing in 1752, many observers in search of urban beauty perceived it not in Edinburgh, but forty miles west on the prosperous banks of the Clyde, a place surrounded (as McUre had pointed out sixteen years earlier) by "open and large streets" with "a pleasant and odoriferous smell."

Still, proposing that Edinburgh had to be redeveloped, Minto looked for models everywhere but in Glasgow. In Dublin he found that "manufactures and commerce" had grown as a result of the city's being "enlarged"; in England he saw commercial and urban expansion. The growth of Edinburgh, he was convinced, would help to promote a "UNITED BRITAIN." This Scottish lord's Unionist dreams show how much Edinburgh's nascent New Town was a political project designed to cement a sense of the United Kingdom.

Others in the Scottish capital were more down-to-earth about practical solutions. Today we may think of mid-eighteenth-century Edinburgh in terms of its great atheist philosopher Hume or its kirk-dominated university and lively Enlightenment debating clubs; but in a 1752 pamphlet, judge and historian David Dalrymple, Lord Hailes, described the townscape as primarily a place of human excrement. Poor sanitation, he argued, was the reason "that so few people of rank reside in this city; that it is rarely visited by strangers; and that so many local prejudices and narrow notions, inconsistent with pleasant manners and growing wealth, are still so obviously retained." Dalrymple's solution to the stench of Edinburgh was simple: the city needed a new castle in the form of a great public toilet. Building more "necessary-houses" or "houses of office" (restrooms) would enable the Scottish capital to become "*the centre* of all possible refinement." In touch with Maitland (who was then at work on his pioneering *History of Edinburgh*) and an avid reader of Minto's *Proposals* for urban improvement, Dalrymple tetchily put Edinburgh's still-medieval sanitary arrangements down to a residual anti-Englishness in the Scottish capital.

> Every art cultivated, every blandishment of life invented, or improved, by the *English,* has by our deluded countrymen been held in utter abhorrence. Among their other prejudices, that at *houses of office* has not been the least inveterate. And indeed the situation of the *necessary-house* erected upon the wall of the castle of *Edinburgh,* might induce many of the lower sort among us to imagine, that our independency was annihilated, by a standing army's being maintained, to sh-te down upon the faces of the much injured *Caledonians.* That ærial *necessary-house* seems to lord it over our capital.

In the sixteenth-century, Alesius had written of Edinburgh Castle as a place from which "enterprising youths" were lowered in baskets to rob the nests of vultures on the rock below; later ages would see the Castle solely in terms of romance and heritage; Dalrymple here regards it, with Aristophanic gusto, principally as a source of shit. Edinburgh's eighteenth-century nickname, "Auld Reikie" (Old Smoky), may relate to the smelly smoke from the town's chimneys glimpsed from afar, but also calls to mind the stench evoked in many accounts of the place written by its inhabitants. Such folk were used to the quaintly frenchified cries of "Gardieloo!" (a Scots version of *Gardez l'eau!*—"Watch out for the water!") shouted by residents of tall "lands," or

3. Arthur's Seat (an extinct volcano) and the cliffs of Salisbury Crags dominate the Edinburgh skyline in this view from the New Town's Princes Street, looking over Waverley railway station towards some of the spires and tenements of the Old Town. In the eighteenth century, residents of the Old Town would yell "Gardieloo!" ("Watch out for the water!") as they flung the contents of chamber pots from upper-storey windows.

tenements, as they emptied the contents of their chamber pots from an upper storey onto the roadway below. When Robert Fergusson (1750–1774) wrote the greatest of all Edinburgh poems, "Auld Reikie" (1773), he was, like Maitland, singing the glories of the place:

> AULD REIKIE, wale o' ilka town   *best of every*
> That *Scotland* kens beneath the moon!   *knows*

But Fergusson soon moves on to calling attention to the "morning smells" unleashed by vigorous housemaids who, with an "inundation" as big as eighteenth-century Edinburgh's central lake, the North Loch, emptied their chamber pots brimming with what the poet euphemistically terms "Edina's roses"—"To *quicken* and *regale* our *noses.*"

True to the spirit of the often bookish rivalry between the two cities, Fergusson's blazoning of Auld Reikie's glories and stink called forth a rival Glaswegian poetic production a decade later. Writing three years before

Robert Burns published his first book, John Mayne begins his "Glasgow" with an opening whose "ilka thing" parallels Fergusson's "ilka town" and so seems like a sly, competitive wink towards "Auld Reikie":

> Hail, GLASGOW! Fam'd for ilka thing
> That heart can wish or siller bring . . .   *silver*

Mayne's poem uses "Standard Habbie," a stanza form different from the one Fergusson used in "Auld Reikie." But Standard Habbie (which some later called the Burns Stanza) was then often associated with the Edinburgh poets Allan Ramsay and Fergusson; so in form as well as content the work can be read as asserting Glasgow's importance in the face of Edinburgh's cultural productions. In addition to its rotting housing stock, Edinburgh may have had its own decaying monarchical palace, but in Glasgow, Mayne insists, "the houses here / Like royal palaces appear." In the western city, "bus'ness is brisk" and the arts are flourishing "wi' gowd [gold] galore." Alert to the value of his city's situation on the "bon[n]y Clyde," Mayne knows and celebrates with a Scots accent the source of Glasgow's prosperity; he offers a vignette in which traders with the British Empire's colonies and former colonies parade at the start of a town-centre afternoon at Glasgow Cross:

> 'Tween ane and twa, wi' gawsy air,   *one and two; handsome*
> The MERCHANTS to the Cross repair;
> And tho' they shine like Nabobs there,
>   Yet, weil I wat,   *well I know*
> Commerce engages a' their care,
>   And a' their chat:
>
> Thir wylie birkies trade to a'   *These wily men*
> The Indies and America . . .

Transatlantic trade had made Glasgow great, even though commerce had been damaged by the recent "American War." The city's traditional motto—"Let Glasgow flourish by the preaching of the Word"—was later abbreviated to simply "Let Glasgow flourish." The place certainly flourished commercially, and the arrival of manufacturing associated with the Industrial Revolution (a development to which Glasgow-based men such as Adam Smith and James Watt contributed much) enhanced the city's growth and standing. Edinburgh ("not a manufacturing town," as Robert Forsyth put it in 1805) scarcely invested in heavy industry; Glasgow did so with a vengeance. Glaswegians were keen to protect their commercial interests, and eager to ward off any economic challenges from Edinburgh and its hinterland. Hugo Arnot's 1779 *History of Edinburgh* had complained, for instance, that although there were "four sugar-houses on the east coast of Scotland," including one in Edinburgh and another in Leith, "these, at present, are mostly supplied from Glasgow." Arnot's use of the phrase "at present" was carefully judged; he argued that, in future, Edinburgh's port should compete more vigorously for trade with the West Indies, so that sugar could come as direct "consignments to the port of Leith."

Such Edinburgh efforts to curb or compete with Glaswegian enterprise were not appreciated in the west. Just three years after Mayne's poem praising the way "A' hands in GLASGOW find employ," the Town Clerk of Glasgow helped to arrange for the publication "in the Edinburgh and Glasgow newspapers" of resolutions designed to fend off a perceived threat from landholders in the area around Edinburgh known as the Lothians. These men of the east sought to alter laws governing the importation of meal and grain into Scotland in ways that the Glaswegians regarded as a challenge. First of all, Glasgow's merchants resolved that "manufacturing" depended on stable, affordable food prices.

> *Secondly,* That the method proposed at a meeting of some Landed Gentlemen, lately held at Edinburgh, as the standard for opening and shutting the ports, would tend to advance the price of grain in this and the neighbouring Western Counties.
>
> *Thirdly,* That it is well known the price of meal in Glasgow and its neighbourhood, is always higher than in the Lothians; and if the price of meal and grain in these counties is to be the standard for opening and shutting the ports in Scotland, this great manufacturing district, which, even in plentiful seasons, requires importation from other counties, can never expect to see the medium price of meal as low as it has heretofore been.

Glasgow guarded its commercial assets, determined to fuel its strength as a manufacturing and trading centre. Often this led to east-west disputes.

The 1790 opening of the Forth and Clyde Canal, which allowed vessels to cross Scotland for the first time, marked the culmination of a scheme that had been envisaged more than a century earlier and that had led to tension between the two cities. Proposals drawn up in the 1760s by engineer John Smeaton had outraged Glasgow entrepreneurs because Smeaton planned for the canal to bypass their city entirely. Edinburgh worthies had scorned Glaswegian counter-proposals for reducing the projected waterway to "a ditch" or "a mere puddle," and insisted that "the fools of the West must wait for the Wise Men of the East." Further wrangling had followed. If the canal's opening created a physical link between Glasgow and Edinburgh, arguments over its route and specification also intensified the mutual wariness between these traditional competitors.

The rivalry took in commerce and engineering, but flourished especially in the written word and the field of culture. In his posthumously published *Autobiography,* Edinburgh-connected Alexander Carlyle, who had studied in 1740s Glasgow, wrote that the west-coast city was "far behind" in "taste." Brought up in a zone of "warerooms" and "trade," its females, he claimed, were "entirely without accomplishments," since "there was neither a teacher of French nor of music in the town." Glasgow, for this east-coast writer, could be summed up in the phrase "coarse and vulgar"—a snooty Edinburgh perception of the place which has not entirely vanished today. To many in nineteenth-century Edinburgh, Glasgow seemed anxiously provincial. The Scottish capital's literary lion, Walter Scott, wrote about "St. Mungo's favourite city" briefly in his 1818 novel, *Rob Roy,* giving a warm-hearted portrait of a fictional Glaswegian civic "dignitary," the sagacious Bailie Nicol Jarvie, who is first introduced as "breathless with peevish impatience." From Edinburgh's point of view, Glaswegians could appear not just peevish but nervously full of themselves. In the early 1800s, Glasgow-educated, Edinburgh-domiciled Robert Forsyth contended that this attitude stemmed from a yearning for status:

As the rise of Glasgow has been very rapid, its inhabitants have not yet entirely lost the sentiment usually found among those who reside in small towns, of a great fondness for their own town, and a patriotic zeal for its respectability, and for the fame of whatever is connected with it. Hence the people of Glasgow seem much more anxious than those of

21

the more ancient city of Edinburgh, to exhibit to strangers their public buildings and the beauties of their city, and are much more anxious that it should obtain applause.

Some Glaswegians still exhibit such zeal—and Edinburgh continues to respond with an amusedly superior silence.

As the eighteenth century ended and the nineteenth began, the nature of each municipality and its self-perception subtly altered, further emphasizing differences. The building of Edinburgh's New Town reinforced the capital's sense of itself as Scotland's metropolis; the speedy growth of Glasgow's population (66,000 by 1791) made it one of the most rapidly expanding cities in Britain, adding to a pride in its own energy. Yet the development of cotton mills and (thanks to James Watt) steam-powered industrial manufactories, as well as chemical plants like the vast Tennant's St. Rollox bleachworks, which employed more than a thousand people and was considered the largest concern of its kind in the world by the 1830s—all these changed Glasgow from the idyllic area noted by earlier travelers into something altogether darker.

At one point in the nineteenth century, Glasgow could claim to be Europe's fourth-largest city; its population growth, which eventually peaked at a little over a million, was phenomenal. In 1834, out of Scotland's 134 cotton factories, almost all were within a twenty-five-mile radius of the city centre. It is conventional to demonstrate the changes in the urban environment through statistical tables and sociological accounts, but relatively early the metamorphosis of the place was registered shrewdly by local writers of verse. In his 1824 "Verses Composed While Walking on Gadshill, on the North Side of Glasgow," William Harriston was excited to see that

> By Glasgow's enterprising race,
> Changes daily still take place,
> Where late were fields and gardens green,
> Lofty tenements are seen.

But as Harriston also noted,

> Chemistry proficient here
> New triumphs wins from year to year—

Here funnels of majestic size,
Ascend, and mingle with the skies,
Tow'ring like spires of pop'lous town,
Of metropolitan renown;
They vent the smoke aloft in air,
For passing clouds away to bear . . .

Reaching a height of more than 460 feet, the tallest tower of the St. Rollox works, nicknamed "Tennant's Stalk," was erected in 1842—the highest chimney on earth. Yet decades earlier, other Glaswegians had been quite aware that not all of their city's pollution was being borne away on "passing clouds." The Romantic poet Thomas Campbell was born in Glasgow in 1777; by the time he reached the age of fifty, he was anxiously writing his "Lines on Revisiting a Scottish River." He began with a telling question:

And call they this Improvement?—to have changed,
My native Clyde, thy once romantic shore,
Where Nature's face is banish'd and estranged,
And heaven reflected in thy wave no more;
Whose banks, that sweeten'd May-day's breath before,
Lie sere and leafless now in summer's beam,
With sooty exhalations cover'd o'er;
And for the daisied green-sward, down thy stream
Unsightly brick-lanes smoke, and clanking engines gleam.

Glasgow is one of the first cities in the world to beget a poetry of industrial pollution. There is even an 1842 poem by John Mitchell written in Standard Habbie and spoken in the voice of the city's newest northern chimney, or lum: "St. Rollox Lum's Address to Its Brethren." In a contemporary engraving of the great lum of the St. Rollox Works, a further eighteen chimneys are visible in the background. This "PREMIER LUM" may boast of "how on upper air / I spread my smoke"—but for those working below, the city could take on apocalyptic resonances. James Macfarlan, a working-class Glaswegian pedlar-poet and weaver's son who died at the age of thirty, wrote in "The Wanderer" of a place of demonic "mighty furnaces," of "deaf'ning anvils," and of forges "like great burning cities" amid the urban "thoroughfares of tumult."

Toiling there the poor boy-poet, grimed, within a dismal den,
Piles the fire, and wields the hammer, jostled on by savage men;
Burns his life to mournful ashes on a thankless hearth of gloom,
For a paltry pittance digging life from out an early tomb.

Resentfully, Macfarlan complained how, destitute, he had written to Edinburgh publisher Robert Chambers for help, and had "proceeded to Edinburgh" in search of assistance: "For three successive days did I call at that gentleman's office, but on no occasion had an answer been left." Edinburgh had its own poor, and its own social problems, but those of Glasgow were regarded as worse, and even at times as untouchable.

Not just for boy-poets, but for many of its male and female, adult and child inner-city workers as well, Scotland's western industrial hub was Old Testamentally hellish. Yet its citizens felt pride in the resolution and big-heartedness that, sometimes apparently in spite of itself, the place might produce. This is palpable in a sonnet entitled "Glasgow," published by Mary Macarthur, widow of a local merchant, in the year that the great St. Rollox chimney was constructed.

I trod thy streets, proud city of the Clyde!
    Great mart of commerce! And on every hand
Were sights and sounds to trade alone allied,
    Yet fraught with dreams of many a distant land.
Thou art,—as cities from remotest time,
    Tyre, Sidon, Babylon, and all have been,—
A very world of wretchedness and crime;
    At once rich, poor, magnificent, and mean:
Still, there are human hearts within thy walls,
    So purified, so broadly stamped with "Heaven,"
That thou—'tis known on high, what'er befalls—
    Not wholly to idolatry art given;
And works of mercy have been done in thee,
That towns and nations might repent to see!

What emerges here alongside the note of piety is something very Glaswegian: a generosity of spirit that comes from shared endurance of an often adverse urban predicament. Other nineteenth-century Glasgow women

4. The cupola of Holmwood House, designed by Alexander Thomson in the late 1850s, is an arresting emblem of the Victorian wealth of Glasgow, known in those days as the "second city of the Empire." Above this spacious villa's main staircase, the cupola is supported by sculpted chimeræ. Its curved glass is etched with stars, but its paintwork is troubled by damp.

were more straightforward about the conditions. "Wanted a filter, to filter the Clyde, / After some hundreds of people have died, / Chancing to fall in its poisonous tide," wrote Marion Bernstein in the 1870s; the river that had once been an emblem of the city's beauty now epitomized Glasgow as a place of industrial filth. An 1842 report by Edwin Chadwick considered the city "possibly the filthiest and unhealthiest of all the British towns." A popular soubriquet—"Workshop of the World"—asserted local industrial eminence but glossed over the darker side of things. Another phrase, much prized by Victorian Glaswegians and still uttered today, was "second city of the Empire." This formulation acknowledged the commercial and heavy-industrial strengths of Glasgow in a way that let it leapfrog over Edinburgh: the first city of the British Empire was patently London; then came Glasgow, Birmingham, and other manufacturing giants, with Edinburgh lagging far behind. Yet the Glasgow which had been seen in the eighteenth century by John McUre as Scotland's "chief Town in the Kingdom next to *Edinburgh*" was fated to exchange its Scottish second place only for another (albeit greater) status as the imperial number two.

For the Victorian poet Alexander Smith, who worked at various times in both cities, the differences were extreme. Smith's "Glasgow" sees its urban subject in terms of "the tragic heart of towns"; here is a zone of apocalyptic "Terror! Dream!" where "Black Labour draws his weary waves" and where the person who dwells "within a gloomy court, / Wherein did never sunbeam sport" longs to escape to the beautiful surrounding countryside. Smith finds in Glasgow a new kind of impressiveness: "In thee, O City! I discern / Another beauty, sad and stern." Yet the speaker of his poem also urges on this place's enormous energy and seems to feel for Glasgow familial love, as well as awestruck fascination:

> Draw thy fierce streams of blinding ore,
> Smite on a thousand anvils, roar
>   Down to the harbour-bars;
> Smoulder in smoky sunsets, flare
> On rainy nights, with street and square
>   Lie empty to the stars.
> From terrace proud to alley base
> I know thee as my mother's face.

Smith did know Glasgow well, but Edinburgh (where he later worked as Secretary to the University) was gloriously exotic. If his western city is invariably "smoky" and even hellish in aspect, throughout his poem "Edinburgh" the Scottish capital is glimpsed "high in heaven"; Smith is struck by the east-coast city's unpolluted "mistless firmament." This urban landscape shines rather than smoulders: "Thou hangest, like a Cyclops' dream, / High in the shifting weather-gleam."

In the twentieth century, Hugh MacDiarmid, a poet with no great love of either Glasgow or Edinburgh, would rewrite Smith's line as "Edinburgh is a mad God's dream"; but the Victorian Smith, from the west of Scotland, delights in orientalizing Edinburgh as "a very Persian tale," a marvellous hallucination: "Mirza's vision, Bagdad's vale." In this Scottish capital, the recently erected Scott monument still "gleams," not yet blackened by smoke from the nearby railway; the delicate, fair "Great City" calls to mind

"Venice, 'neath her mellow moons," and, like Venice, is a tourist venue satu-rated with the allure of its own history:

> Within thy high-piled Canongate
> The air is of another date;
>   All speaks of ancient time:
> Traces of gardens, dials, wells,
> Thy dizzy gables, oyster-shells
>   Imbedded in the lime—
> Thy shields above the doors of peers
> Are old as Mary Stuart's tears.

Smith's Edinburgh is a wonderful museum of itself; his Glasgow, a working industrial city. This contrast perceived by a poet of both places was true to the self-image of each. It hints, too, at ways in which Edinburgh (not just Glasgow) had had to reconcile itself to coming second.

No more the capital of an independent country, and no longer even a great city of the Enlightenment, nineteenth-century Edinburgh increasingly mined its own past. Walter Scott, its greatest writer, showed it how to do so. In fictions like *The Heart of Midlothian* and *Chronicles of the Canongate,* or in his antiquarian researches (such as his discovery of Scotland's ancient crown regalia, hidden in Edinburgh Castle), he rebranded history for eager consumer culture and Romantic æsthetic taste. Soon the magnificently in-ventive Scott became, himself, a monumental part of Edinburgh's cityscape; and in the decades that followed his death, the Scottish capital made itself a great *polis* of museums—the National Museum of Scotland, the Scottish Na-tional Portrait Gallery, the Museum of Edinburgh—all of which helped to enhance its national significance, but also increased the sense that it was a city averting its eyes from the here and now. Whatever else, Glasgow was very much a site of the heavy-industrial and commercial Victorian present. If the Edinburgh of the book you are reading is essentially inflected by its En-lightenment and Romantic cultural inheritance, then this volume's Glasgow is a city crucially shaped by the Victorian British Empire.

Edinburgh's soubriquet "the Athens of the North," first bestowed in 1762 but popularized in the nineteenth and twentieth centuries, also speaks of pastness. A place of antiquities, Edinburgh might have its own acropolis, its own partially completed replica of the Parthenon, monuments based on smaller Athenian temples, and even, in its Art College, a fine collection of plaster casts of classical sculptures which, developed from the late eighteenth century onwards, remains splendid; yet Edinburgh was Athenian, too, in the sense that it had been surpassed by a more modern imperial metropolis. If the Pax Romana of the ancient world empire had given way to the Pax Britannica of Victorian imperialism, then London was the new Rome. Edinburgh, so proud of its northern memorials and long-gone independent past, liked to claim the sort of relationship with London that perhaps Athens had had with the capital of the Roman Empire. Like ancient Athens, Edinburgh prided itself on its intellectual nimbleness. Calculating that in 1805 it contained as many as 3,000 lawyers and 1,500 academics, Robert Forsyth maintained that there was "probably no city in the world of the same extent in which so great a proportion of the inhabitants consist of well-informed persons." Glasgow's professional class was much smaller: by 1883 it made up just 4 percent of the Glaswegian workforce, whereas the comparable figure for Edinburgh was 12 percent. The east-coast "modern Athens" rightly thought well of itself as a city of the mind, but increasingly what once-great Edinburgh possessed was a kind of secondary, already historical allure; it could not claim to be the second city of the modern empire, but could assert the distinctiveness of its lost independent heritage. Edinburgh never called itself a "second city"—it left that to Glasgow—but its status as "Athens of the North" announced it not just as second to the Athens of Greece, but also more subtly as a cultural centre of curious and noble antiquity now rendered politically redundant by modern imperial London.

In addition to an eighteenth-century canal, a nineteenth-century railway linked Scotland's two Victorian second cities. Opened in 1842, this railway came with its own published *Guide* hymning "the extensive and rapidly increasing intercourse between Edinburgh and Glasgow, and their intimate commercial and social relations." Valiantly, even breathlessly, the *Guide* set forth the splendours of both places, and of everywhere in between. Edinburgh was given the first twenty-five pages of descriptive coverage, which were headed by an epigraph from the national bard, Robert Burns, and emphasized the importance of the city: "As the metropolis and principal seat of the legislative and executive estates of the kingdom, it appears to have enjoyed an eminent celebrity from an early period of our national history." At the far end of the line, Glasgow came last and was afforded nineteen pages, which were headed by an epigraph from someone called Bell (who?) and explained: "Glasgow derives her principal claims to high consideration among the cities of the British Kingdoms, from the extent and enterprise exhibited in the manufacturing and commercial undertakings which are conducted by her adventurous sons." This was the railway *Guide*'s way of saying what Alexander Smith would put more magniloquently in verse. Soon, and predictably, the railways, rather than simply increasing "intercourse" between Glasgow and Edinburgh, provided a new outlet for their mutual competition. Rivalry developed between the Caledonian Railway Company, which used Glasgow as a hub, and the North British Railway Company, which ran trains from Edinburgh to Carlisle. As each company tried to muscle in on what was perceived as the other's territory, their jousting led to some of the greatest engineering projects of the age, culminating in the construction of the Forth Rail Bridge during the years 1883–1890.

By then, resurgent Glasgow-Edinburgh rivalry had spread to the sports field, but not in quite the way modern observers might expect. Historically, sports in each city have always been numerous—from the inner-city bowling greens of an eighteenth-century Edinburgh, where a fencing teacher called Machrie extolled the glories of "cocking" (cockfighting), to the 1930s, when Glasgow boasted 131 tennis courts, nine cricket grounds, and seventeen hockey pitches. Scotland claims to be the birthplace of golf, and in recent times Scots have excelled at cycling, curling, and tennis. Yet, perversely, many of today's Scots assume that the great national game is soccer, a sport whose familiar modern, fast-flowing style of play may have been pioneered in the later nineteenth century at Glasgow's Cathkin Park by Queen's Park Football Club (founded just outside the city in 1867), but in which Scotland has shown little international distinction within living memory. Cheered on with good humour and patriotic fervour, the national football team has never won a World Cup, and no Scots have snatched the European Cup for almost half a century. Though Edinburgh and Glasgow each have several soccer teams, by far the most famous are Glasgow's Rangers (founded in 1872 and placed in financial liquidation in 2012) and Celtic (founded 1888); from their beginnings, as the twenty-first-century historian of Glasgow, Irene Maver, puts it, "As a large percentage of their revenues came from playing each other, it came to be realized that there was commercial potential in exploiting religious and ethnic differences, with Rangers representing an assertive "true-blue" brand of Scottish Protestantism and Celtic the Catholic Irish." To this day, these clubs (collectively known as "the Old Firm") and people claiming to support them are often associated with sometimes violent Protestant-Catholic sectarianism; unwary visitors to Glasgow might be wise to avoid their sometimes toxic rivalry. As well as giving rise to brutal high passions (domestic violence in Glasgow escalates markedly after Old Firm matches) and even to sectarian murders, football in Glasgow has had other tragedies. At Ibrox Stadium, home ground of Rangers, a stairway collapsed on January 2, 1971, killing and injuring many supporters. Edinburgh football, in comparison—even the ongoing struggle between long-term rivals Heart of Midlothian ("Hearts") and Hibernian ("Hibs")—is a tamer, sometimes lamer, affair.

Fortunately the internecine sectarian rivalries often visible around Glaswegian soccer, in a city which struggled ineptly and sometimes vitriolically to come to terms with substantial nineteenth- and early twentieth-century Irish Catholic immigration, did not infect the older rivalry between Glasgow and Edinburgh when it first progressed to the sports field. On November 23, 1872, in "miserable weather" on a West-of-Scotland winter Saturday, the first "inter-city football match" between Glasgow and Edinburgh took place. The "football" was rugby football, rather than the soccer which later came to be the most eagerly followed sport in both cities. The *Glasgow Herald,* which thought the contest "truly splendid," registered something of the excitement with which the game was greeted, and managed to be magnanimous in declaring "the Edinburgh team the winners of one of the best matches we have ever seen played." From the Edinburgh end, the *Scotsman,* used to sunnier east-coast climes, rather relished making much of the Glaswegian "heavy rain falling during the morning, and continuing at intervals all day, several drenching showers descending during the progress of the game," covering in mud the Glasgow players' "snow-white jerseys." Teams still compete for the 1872 Challenge Cup in the twenty-first century. Edinburgh boasts the national rugby stadium, at Murrayfield; and Glasgow, the national soccer arena, at Hampden Park. Today's Challenge Cup players comment that "there is rivalry between the two teams because of the history of the fixture, but there is also rivalry between the cities on the whole as far as any sport is concerned."

For all that its origins lay in the eighteenth century, by the later Victorian era that rivalry was a subject of international attention—and sometimes slightly patronizing amusement. Reprinting a piece from the London *Times* on September 18, 1881, the *New York Times* regaled its readers with an account entitled "Edinburgh and Glasgow, Wherein and How Widely the Two Scotch Capitals Differ." The ordering of the names here may be significant, but more shocking is the designation of Glasgow as a western "capital" to match Edinburgh—seen here as "capital" only of the east. No one in Edinburgh would dream of calling Glasgow a "capital." Regarding Edinburgh as having grown from "feudalism," but Glasgow as having prospered through "trade," the anonymous 1881 writer enables readers to discern fairly easily where his sympathies lie; equally revealing is the way he takes it for granted that "there has always been a rivalry between the neighbors." In this piece, Glaswegians, characterized by their city's "riches, energy, and liberality," seem the people of the present and future: "While spending their gains freely, they have never been addicted to show: they have lived within their means, and laid money by, and so they are likely to go on flourishing." Damned with faint praise, Edinburgh people, on the other hand, are a bunch of the "eminently steady and respectable"—lawyers, professors, doctors, and clergy; "there are no colossal fortunes and few really wealthy men." This sounds like a city ever so genteelly on the slide. "Scotch people, like Swiss and Savoyards, love to end their days in the land of their birth; but those who have been exceptionally fortunate seldom care to settle in Edinburgh." A city sometimes berated for its macho values, Glasgow comes over as modern, even in terms of gender; Edinburgh, with its retired Scottish civil servants from British-Empire India and its struggling widows, seems bound to the polite past. "In Glasgow it is nothing unusual to see the door of an imposing mansion opened by a trim maiden. In Edinburgh one man, at least, in decorous black appears to be insisted on as a voucher of respectability."

If a North American audience was expected to smile at the rivalry and divergence between the two cities, in Scotland itself those differences intensified, permeating diverse areas of life. Stereotypically, Glasgow has gone on being regarded as more vulgar than Edinburgh, but in terms of coarseness it would be hard to beat the epithet of the eighteenth-century Edinburgh legal grandee Lord Kames when he bade his last adieu to his judicial colleagues: "Fare ye a' weel, ye bitches." Glasgow's supposed vulgarity can emerge as radical artistic vitality, a spirited challenge to the status quo. So, for instance, in the late nineteenth century the generally conservative artists of the Edinburgh-based Royal Scottish Academy regarded with some scorn painters who were unprepared to work in the capital—particularly, upstart artists from Glasgow. Attracted to modern French *plein-air* landscapes, a group of younger Glasgow artists mocked their staid Royal Scottish Academy antagonists in Edinburgh, bestowing on them, and on the West-of-Scotland artists who respected them, the nickname "Gluepots" because of the way they attempted to give their works a spurious patina of age by applying a thick "megilp" varnish. Though locally a few people denounced them as "a coterie of self-idolaters," the ambitious, unapologetic young "Glasgow Boys" achieved international success, exhibiting in cities ranging from Munich and Paris (where they were described as "making art history") to St. Louis and Philadelphia. Their bold brushwork and sense of light also appealed in London, where their work seemed closer to Impressionist painting than to the much more conventional pictures associated with Edinburgh's Royal Scottish Academy.

Some found it hard to understand how such work could emanate from artists linked to Scotland's grimiest and reputedly coarsest industrial city. English writer Israel Zangwill suggested in 1896 that "Glasgow is all glorious within and its inner artistic aspirations make up for and are perhaps inspired by its outer unloveliness." Admittedly, and perhaps revealingly, few landscapes by the commercially and artistically successful Glasgow Boys picture Glasgow itself; most are of rural scenes. Exceptions are John Lavery's series of oils portraying fashionable society at the 1888 Glasgow International Exhibition, and his elegantly contemporary canvas (now in Aberdeen Art Gallery) depicting a middle-class tennis party on the grounds of a wealthy solicitor's house in the Glasgow suburb of Cathcart. Such scenes have dash, poise, and energy; they give the lie to reductive attempts to define Glasgow simply through a perceived coarseness or "unloveliness."

Trade had made this western city at once parochially proud and internationally minded—not a bad combination. Mercantile links to America went back to the seventeenth century; connections with Japan prospered in the second half of the nineteenth. Admirers alike of Japanese prints and of the art of James McNeill Whistler, the Glasgow Boys helped persuade Glasgow Corporation to become the first public collector to buy a painting by that American artist, who later arranged for some of his best work to find a permanent home in the city. Two Glasgow Boys, Edward A. Hornel and George Henry, were financed by local shipping magnate William Burrell and art dealer Alexander Reid to make a fruitful 1894 painting tour of Japan, even if the *Glasgow Herald,* complained: "Why Mr. Hornel should seek inspiration in Yokohama or its neighbourhood we are at a loss to understand." Pictures such as Hornel's adventurously coloured canvas *The Balcony, Yokohama* (now in the Yale Center for British Art) or Henry's exquisite *Japanese Lady with a Fan* (painted in Tokyo in 1894 and now in the Glasgow Art Gallery at Kelvingrove) are among the Boys' more surprising triumphs, and are fascinating to contemplate alongside the uncharacteristically industrial mural *Shipbuilding on the Clyde,* painted by Lavery on the wall of the Banqueting Hall of Glasgow City Chambers—a picture which shows in detail the construction of a warship for the Imperial Japanese Navy.

Such was the international fame and appeal of the Boys that even the place they called the "Edinburgh Academy" could not resist them forever, however hard it might try. When the Academy's new president pontificated in February 1892 at the Glasgow School of Art, apparently speaking dismissively of Impressionism as "an 'ism' with a devoted band of followers in Glasgow," the visitor from Edinburgh was pilloried in the "Letters" columns of the *Herald* for having "sneered at Glasgow art." His having come to "cosmopolitan Glasgow" to "speak words of wisdom to the West" was particularly resented: "The West has developed its art independently of the Academy's power to fetter or to blight, for Glasgow enterprise, without an Academy, has grown its new notable 'Glasgow school,' which is recognized throughout the art world—a thing that the chartered Academy has not yet been able to do for its parish."

Ever prickly about its east-coast rival, this confidently cosmopolitan Glasgow was the city that produced the architect Charles Rennie Mackintosh and the designer Margaret Macdonald. At times, it seems to have enjoyed asserting its own fierce local pride by implying that Edinburgh and Edinburgh's supposedly national institutions were in fact rather more provincial in outlook. As the nineteenth century passed into the twentieth, there was indeed some truth in this. Though from 1885 Edinburgh had hosted the Scottish Office, an outpost of the British Civil Service tasked from London with the job of administering Scottish affairs, the Scottish capital could strike visitors as oddly powerless and spectral. Convalescing there during

World War I, the English poet Wilfred Owen noticed in Princes Street not so much the Castle or the Scott Monument as a newspaper seller standing in the gutter, a "pale rain-flawed phantom of the place." Orkney-born Edwin Muir, who saw Glasgow as a hell on earth, regarded Scotland in the 1930s as having at its heart "a blank, an Edinburgh." This was the early twentieth-century capital which nationalist poet Hugh MacDiarmid regarded simply as "too stupid yet / To learn how not to stand in her own light."

Edinburgh's age of Enlightenment glory was now long gone. For all that it was not nearly as hard hit by the Great Depression as industrial Glasgow (many of whose shipyards stopped all production), drab, underpowered Edinburgh nonetheless seemed fated to be depressed. Its careful but restrictive Presbyterian prudence made it the city that Scotland's greatest twentieth-century novelist, Muriel Spark, simply had to get out of. She wrote of it with devoted attention in her autobiographical *Curriculum Vitæ* and in her celebrated novella set during the 1930s, *The Prime of Miss Jean Brodie;* but it became for her the place, as she put it, "that I, a constitutional exile, am essentially exiled from."

Arguably, what saved Edinburgh was high culture—but not, on the whole, its own. The coming of the Edinburgh International Festival in 1947 was part of a postwar British effort to rebuild political bridges through the arts, and to counter the lingering austerities of World War II rationing. A picturesque historic city, Scotland's capital was selected as a suitable British venue for a cultural jamboree; perhaps it could even become a Salzburg. First dreamed up by the director of the British Council in Scotland, Harry Harvey Wood, the ambitious festival of high art—opera, symphonic music, drama, ballet—brought fresh cosmopolitanism and vigour. Rightly complaining that the Festival eschewed Scotland's own greatest art forms, such as poetry and traditional song, local writers, artists, and others set up rival events which can be seen as ancestors of today's Festival Fringe. Though the early mélange of official and unofficial events sometimes evolved uneasily, it grew into a triumph. Held each August and September, the Edinburgh International Festival and its Fringe now constitute the world's largest, most successful arts festival. There are satellite festivals, too—from the International Book Festival (again, the biggest of its kind) to the annual "Edinburgh's Hogmanay" celebrations, billed as "the World's Best New Year

Party." Today most outsiders regard Edinburgh, rather than Glasgow, as Scotland's cosmopolitan city of art. In the twenty-first century, it is the people of the east-coast city and the surrounding area who buy more than half of the Festival's tickets. Yet in the earlier decades of the 1900s, no one would have thought of the modern capital of Scotland in terms of global festivity. In the city itself, until relatively recently, there was an assumption that all this cultural splash was mainly put on for visitors. At Festival time, locals departed on holiday (perhaps renting out their apartments to tourists), or simply went off by themselves to hide in what Wilfred Owen had once termed "their quiet home."

A sense of the subdued, rather downtrodden city that persisted even during the early decades of the Festival can be gleaned from Sylvain Chomet's 2010 animated film *L'Illusionniste,* an extended cinematic love letter to Edinburgh. Set in a 1950s milieu of dark buildings whose grimy, uncleaned sandstone seems to invite louring skies and rain, this modern classic of cinematography draws on the Gallic legacy of Jacques Tati as it tracks the progress of a fading music-hall performer around the Scottish capital, featuring depictions of famous buildings as well as visually stunning panoramas. Touching, beautiful, and amusing, *L'Illusionniste* offers many glimpses of still utterly recognizable landmarks, but its loveable Edinburgh is quirky, small-town, provincial—at quite the other end of the spectrum from the city of the glitzy International Festival.

One can only imagine the effect that the success of that Festival over many decades has had on Glaswegians. They have hit back with smaller-scale and distinctive carnivals of their own, from the popular "Celtic Connections" music extravaganza to "Glasgay," a celebration of gay and lesbian arts, and the "Aye Write!" festival of literature. Some may take solace from the realization that to this day no song about Edinburgh is as well known as a composition by the early twentieth-century music-hall artiste Will Fyffe —a lyric of benign Sauchiehall Street intoxication entitled "I Belong to Glasgow." More controversial (in Glasgow because it was boycotted by some local writers and artists, in Edinburgh simply because it seemed so astonishing) was the selection of Glasgow in 1990 as European City of Culture. This followed hot on the heels of a clever advertising campaign that deployed a smiling "Mr. Happy" logo and proclaimed from 1983 onwards, "Glasgow's

Miles Better" (the words "than unsmiling Edinburgh" were never included), and that was part of a strong strategy for what planners term "culture-led urban regeneration."

Yet at the start of a decade when unemployment hit 30 percent in some of the city's surrounding housing estates and almost 40 percent in the central district, and when nearly 30 percent of Glasgow's social housing (the largest such concentration in western Europe) suffered problems with damp, the 1990 designation "European City of Culture" seemed to some a bad joke. Ironically, this title owed not a little to the prominence of Glaswegian novelists, who soon resisted being co-opted by what they saw as a public-relations exercise. In *Lanark* (1981) and in a series of fictions beginning with *The Busconductor Hines* (1984), Alasdair Gray and James Kelman, respectively, gave Glasgow its most convincing (usually male and bleak) fictional voices. Each of these very different authors writes of working-class urban culture in ways perhaps more attuned to American than to English literary sensibilities. In Gray's 1977 ink, watercolour, acrylic, and oil portrait of Kelman, the books on the bookshelves behind the writer include texts by Kafka, Beckett, Joyce, and Henry Miller: works which have mattered to both of these authors and which signal a re-energized cosmopolitan sophistication in west-coast Scottish writing. Stylistically, Gray's imaginative use of Glasgow itself and Kelman's fusing of the narrative voice with the speech of his largely working-class characters have been influential for a younger generation of fiction writers including, at times, the Glasgow-based Janice Galloway and A. L. Kennedy, as well as the Edinburgh novelist Irvine Welsh. Welsh, the most commercially successful of these, has certainly learned from Glasgow writing, though much of his work lacks the strong ethical and political commitment of Gray, Kelman, Galloway, and Kennedy. Simply because of the story's gritty subject, people sometimes mistakenly assume that the internationally acclaimed film of Welsh's distinctively Edinburgh-centred, heroin-fuelled *Trainspotting* must be set in the badlands of Glasgow.

Occasionally trying on each other's artistic clothes, Glasgow and Edinburgh continue to be markedly different, as well as mutually competitive. Their personalities are still part of their street life, and insistently seep into print. Among recent nonfiction books that best give a flavour of these cities are Alasdair Gray's *A Life in Pictures* and the Edinburgh parts of Candia McWilliam's memoir, *What to Look for in Winter*. If Glasgow writing has tended to win most of the artistic plaudits over the past few decades, Edinburgh fiction has enjoyed the greater popular success. From J. K. Rowling to Alexander McCall Smith, authors based in the Scottish capital have become international celebrities. Though individual writers may eschew the old Glasgow-Edinburgh rivalry, their cities have hardly done so. No sooner, it seems, had the twenty-first-century capital been designated UNESCO's first City of Literature than Glasgow followed up a few years later by bagging the title UNESCO City of Music. Glaswegians, after carving motorways brutally through parts of their downtown area in the 1970s and securing money to upgrade their much-loved underground railway system (the world's third-oldest), have taken quiet pleasure in the recent utter mess that Edinburgh has made of trying to re-install an inner-city tram line.

Central Edinburgh, the Edinburgh dealt with in this book, can seem something of a splendid stage set, even a museum exhibit. In a city of grand, often riverless bridges, some historic streets are windswept in their elevation, others oddly and fascinatingly sunken; among the latter, the sixteenth-century Mary King's Close (whose remains now lie beneath the Royal Mile's City Chambers) has a haunted, museum-like stillness. "It is hard to think of another British city that has changed so little," writes its twenty-first-century historian Michael Fry. In this, as in so much else, Glasgow might seem Edinburgh's antithesis: areas of central Glasgow—near the north end of the Kingston Bridge, for instance, or down by the Science Centre—are almost completely and exuberantly of the late twentieth and early twenty-first centuries. It is now nearly a hundred years since the great tower of the St. Rollox complex was demolished in 1916, and a long time even since the young Alasdair Gray was fascinated by the site of the derelict north-Glasgow chemical works nicknamed by locals "the Stinky Ocean." Though there remains shipbuilding on the Clyde, and there is still some manufacturing, Glasgow was traumatized by the loss of its heavy industry and by social problems so persistent that some might wonder why anyone would want to visit Edinburgh's western rival. Glasgow has a significantly higher murder rate, more acute addiction problems, lower life expectancy, one of the world's highest obesity rates, and a lot more unemployment. Yet, for all its history of social inequality, Glasgow retains a sense of protean energy, and I have never met anyone (including people from Edinburgh) who did not assert that it was the friendlier of the two cities, or who failed to be impressed by its architectural and artistic treasures. "Edinburgh," the *New Yorker* essayist Alastair Reid once wrote, "seems too leisurely to be a proper city." No one would write that about Glasgow.

Overall, Glasgow has managed the often painful metamorphosis from a past dominated by heavy industry to a largely postindustrial present more successfully than almost any other comparable city in the world. Vast tracts of Detroit and areas such as Highland Park in Michigan have become venues for urban "ruin porn"; but in the one-time Scottish capital of heavy industry, iconic modern buildings such as the strikingly carapaced Scottish Exhibition and Conference Centre have given the city a confident new identity—and, despite the serious social problems that it continues to wrestle with, a sense of continuing prosperity. For Glasgow, much of the twentieth century involved painful and momentous metamorphosis. In Edinburgh, with the exception of the coming of the Festival and the university's construction in the George Square area of what Michael Fry denounces as "a concrete desert of dreary, shabby buildings from an era at the nadir of British architecture," it would be easy to think that relatively little had happened. Glasgow, the Glaswegians' narrative might claim, adjusted to modernity and even fell too much in love with modernist ideas of redevelopment, boldly punctuating its skyline with high-rise buildings; Edinburgh dreamed through its Festival and slept.

Yet Glasgow—which has since razed several of its tower blocks with characteristically "gallus" (bold) vigour—has no monopoly on stories of change. For the end of the twentieth century and the start of the twenty-first was also the era when Edinburgh, apparently against the odds, became once again the seat of a Scottish Parliament. In its historic heart it built a confident new legislative building—the most stunning contemporary architectural statement in the nation. Edinburgh started awake, proud of its past, and suddenly realized that it was part of a country ready to look to the future. Today it is the capital city, playing host to a pro-independence Scottish government, which seems linked to ideas of major political change; while Glasgow, more politically conservative (with a small *c*), saw little alteration in the complexion of its Labour-dominated socialist municipal politics for more than half a century. Only in the Scottish parliamentary election of 2011, when the western city elected several representatives committed to Scottish independence, did its politics significantly shift.

During recent times, rebirth has come to these two cities in very different ways. Edinburgh has begun to rediscover what it means to be a capital, albeit one of a still-dependent country. It has lived through the financial woes of 2008, when on October 14 the *Scotsman*'s front-page headline read simply, "The Downfall of the Scottish Banks," and a leading article spoke of "catastrophic failure" as the Royal Bank of Scotland and Halifax Bank of Scotland, both headquartered in Edinburgh for centuries, were "forced to collapse into government ownership." The east-coast city, which had been marketing itself with the slogan "Inspiring Capital" and had relished its status as Britain's leading financial centre outside London, could only lick its wounds. Glasgow, perhaps more used to traumatic upheavals and always with a fondness for grand-scale, somewhat Stalinist planning, drew breath; eighteen months later, it published proposals to transform itself into one of Europe's greenest hubs, with schemes ranging from hydro power generation by means of urban canals and rivers to a series of wind farms on brownfield former industrial sites, new trams, a network of urban woodlands, congestion surcharges for motorists, and biogas plants. A senior advisor for climate adaptation at the U.S. Environmental Protection Agency stated that "the Sustainable Glasgow Initiative is a model for cities around the world." However, this plan to reduce the city's carbon emissions by 30 percent by the year 2020 assumes investment from the private sector of almost £1.5 billion, an amount that seems ambitious during an economic recession. Successful in its bid to welcome the 2014 Commonwealth Games (which Edinburgh has already hosted twice in the past half-century), Glasgow has been an ambitious place for hundreds of years, and shows no sign of stopping now. For centuries, too, its (usually undeclared) aspiration has been to live up to one of its traditional soubriquets as "the dear green place"—and to outsmart its sly rival, Edinburgh.

Since 1995, Edinburgh's Old and New Towns have been listed as a UNESCO World Heritage Site. The area's twenty-first-century assets range from its Parliament to its pandas, the latter presented to the city's beautifully situated zoo on Corstorphine Hill in 2011 by the People's Republic of China. Fiercely proud Glasgow may be destined always to be Scotland's second city, especially now that there is no British Empire to allow it to outflank its nation's capital. But the rivalry between these urban stalwarts has run for more than three hundred years and shows refreshingly little sign of abating.

39

In Glasgow not long ago I bought a joke book by Ian Black called *Weegies vs. Edinbuggers: Why Glasgow Smiles Better than Edinburgh;* later the same week I saw in an Edinburgh bookshop *Edinbuggers vs. Weegies: Why Edinburgh Is Slightly Superior to Glasgow.* It was the same paperback book, which can be turned upside down and reversed to show whichever "front cover" is appropriate to the city in question; revealingly but unsurprisingly, there are almost twice as many Glaswegian jokes about Edinburgh people as there are jokes by "Edinbuggers" about "Weegies."

An appetite for the jousting between these two cities is ultimately a hunger for life itself. Their prickly, often jokey relationship offers a metaphor for human vitality. Yes, worthy institutions assure us that the two urban centres must collaborate to win more attention, greater investment, and enhanced opportunities in a globalized economy—but that is marketing-speak. Would the world really be so interested in Glasgow and Edinburgh if they merged into one neat corporate alliance? It is in part the centuries-old rivalry, the differences, the splendidly distinct flavoursomeness of these almost-but-never-quite neighbours that constitutes their enduring yet dynamic allure. Edinburgh, say Glaswegians, is all "fur coat and nae [no] knickers"—gorgeous, but suspect. Edinburgh chooses not to reply to that. In both cities, there is the assumption that Glaswegians are rough diamonds whose hospitality, especially to those in need, is legendary; whereas in Edinburgh, folk wisdom has it, at whatever time you arrive on someone's doorstep you may be welcomed with the words, "You'll have had your tea"—meaning that the visitor will have already eaten and so the host will not need to provide any nourishment. Such caricatures are unfair, yet far too much fun to jettison. Only people from Edinburgh could dwell in a universe without Glaswegians; only Glaswegians could live on an Edinburgh-less planet. Everyone else may enjoy this pair of stubborn cities; no one can understand Scotland without paying attention to both. I hope this book gives a necessarily partial but nonetheless rich sense of each entity, occasionally winking across at the other. To love these two places feels like bigamy. It is.

→ Edinburgh ←

The Royal Mile:
From the Castle to a Song

The Castle Rock called Edinburgh into being. Ever since the first few houses clustered round the Castle, no city in the world has had a more spectacular medieval centrepiece. Once crucial for defence, surveillance, and maintaining order, the Castle remains a British military barracks but is now principally for looking at. Unfailingly photogenic, it still appears, as England's John Taylor put it in his *Pennyles Pilgrimage* of 1618, "so strongly grounded, bounded, and founded, that by force of man it can never bee confounded." Yet by day its visual dominance owes more to dark basaltic geology than to architecture, while by night what highlights its antiquity is electrical floodlighting. Singing the praises of Edinburgh, the Renaissance Scottish Latin poet Arthur Johnston thought "nowhere more deserves a sceptre." Above all, the Castle makes Edinburgh's capital-city bossiness seem easy: a product of terrain as much as of human ingenuity.

Thanks to its eminence on the massive, craggy rock, Edinburgh Castle looks ancient and unchanging. It is neither. What so impresses the modern eye is only the most recent version of a fortress whose earliest incarnations were swept away long ago. Some of the first poetry associated with the territory we now call Scotland mentions the tribal settlement of Eidyn, or Din Eidyn, its band of warriors drinking mead in a noble hall. Gold-torqued, their swords flashing, fighters galloped southwards to do battle. Their sixth-century leader was named Mynyddawg, and they called themselves the Gododdin—the double *d* being pronounced *th*. This is the tribe the Romans termed the Votadini. A fragmentary heroic poem, *The Gododdin*, records their deeds in Old Welsh, a language once spoken around Edinburgh. That poem's mention of Eidyn and its hall may be the first literary record of what is now Edinburgh Castle, built atop a long-extinct volcano. Remains of prehistoric hilltop forts survive in the surrounding area, but the original hall of the Gododdin is no more. What survives is their commanding view from

5. Edinburgh Castle rises high above Princes Street Gardens on its craggy, basaltic rock. Pictured by twentieth-century photographer John Bethell, it still looks as described by John Taylor in the early seventeenth century: "so strongly grounded, bounded, and founded, that by force of man it can never bee confounded."

the windswept Castle Rock, north over the Firth of Forth to the Kingdom of Fife and the Grampian Mountains beyond, south towards the bare Pentland Hills.

By the eleventh century, the rock again boasted a royal residence—as well as a Christian chapel. Yet modern tourists approaching the Castle see something very different. Gone are the days when Victorian children scaled the rock face, finding it (as George Borrow writes in *Lavengro*) rich in "strange crypts, crannies, and recesses, where owls nestled, and the weasel brought forth her young." Today's visitors would face arrest if they attempted to climb up the fortress's surrounding cliffs. Instead, having strolled up Castlehill at the end of the great street called the Royal Mile, they cross the Castle Esplanade, an expansive parade ground. Here each summer night during the Edinburgh Festival, audiences on steeply raked seating applaud massed bands of pipers with dancers, army vehicles, soldiers in dress uniform, and other performers in the Edinburgh Military Tattoo. This popular amalgam of highly orchestrated armed-services nimbleness is all kilted march-pasts, bagpipes, and impressive brass-band shine. Beyond the Esplanade loom the Castle portals: a convincing late-nineteenth-century drawbridge with a castellated gatehouse of the same vintage, and twentieth-century statues of Robert the Bruce by Thomas J. Clapperton (who also sculpted figures for Liberty's department store in London's Regent Street) and William Wallace by Alexander Carrick of the Edinburgh College of Art.

If this sounds touristically phoney, it does not feel so. The stone ensemble of the Castle looks massively monumental simply because it is. Today's Castle complex—part barracks, part visitor attraction—is a mélange of structures from different eras. Earlier buildings were demolished, succumbed to furious assault, or gradually and gracefully subsided. Everything in the Castle is a replacement. Fourteenth-century structures were substituted for older ones. The sixteenth-century Portcullis Gate, now a portal within a portal, took the place of the previous Constable's Tower, destroyed by a bombardment of English artillery in 1573. The Portcullis Gate itself was soon scheduled for partial redevelopment, designed in Victorian times to recreate, centuries afterwards, aspects of the long-gone Constable's Tower. Edinburgh Castle is the product of many people's ideas of just how a monumental Castle ought to appear. Made up of everything from a prison to a dogs' cemetery, it works magnificently. In 2011 a new temporary structure seating 8,700 people was developed to be installed on its Esplanade, making that venue all the more suitable for the Military Tattoo, rock concerts, and theatrical extravaganzas. Walking through the Castle itself is at times like strolling up a lane through a stage set of well-nigh impregnable solidity, or ascending through a conglomeration of stacked archæological levels.

One of the Castle's most spirited restorers was Jean Hippolyte Blanc, born in Francophile Edinburgh in 1844, the son of a French immigrant who sold ladies' shoes. Blanc designed several local churches and a brewery, but this enthusiast for photography, architecture, and antiquarianism set his sights loftily on the Castle. On February 10, 1886, the *Scotsman* reported his plans to restore the Portcullis Gate and Tower, along with parts of the twelfth-century St. Margaret's Chapel. Blanc had sought advice from another Edinburgh Castle restoration enthusiast, Professor Daniel Wilson of Toronto, as well as from local public bodies. His head full of Gothic elaborations, details filched from British Museum manuscripts, and other historical Scottish buildings, Blanc pressed ahead with the aid of his associate William Nelson. Conscious of the desirability of having something good to show "tourists visiting the forthcoming International Exhibition," Blanc soon after gave the Castle's Renaissance Great Hall a makeover which involved a Late Gothic door, a substantially new south elevation, and, except for much of the splendid hammer-beam roof, a new interior. Such "restorers," operating with one eye on supposed antiquarian sources and the other on tourists' tastes, are easy to mock, but the Castle is in their debt. It still thrives today by mixing carefully monitored historical stewardship with the Tattoo's spotlit glitz. Visitors in search of authenticity may find fragments of the medieval St. Mary's Church kept as museum pieces, but most prefer to be overawed by the arsenal of weaponry flaunted in the Great Hall, or to relish the staircase Blanc added to improve access to what Victorians called "the Mons Meg battery."

It says something about traditional local attitudes toward women that Edinburgh Castle has two contrasting Margarets—one a saint, the other (since "Meg" is short for "Margaret") a cast-iron femme fatale. Mons Meg is the Castle's toughest survivor. Arrayed with other ordnance high on the ramparts, as if about to bombard Princes Street below, this huge late-medieval gun from the town of Mons in Belgium is a weapon of mass destruction which has long since become a bulky good-luck charm. One of the world's oldest surviving cannons, it is six thousand kilograms in weight—so heavy that, mounted on wheels, it would have been hauled across Renaissance Scotland at a rate of about three miles a day. Firing 150-kilogram cannonballs, Mons Meg was used as a roving siege gun in the fifteenth century, but by the 1540s was retired to Edinburgh Castle to blast out ceremonial salutes. One of these celebrated the marriage of Mary Queen of Scots to the French dauphin in 1558, but Meg's birthday greeting to the future King James VII in 1681 was her last full-throated outburst. The gun's great mouth —or "muckle mou"—burst, occasioning the later Edinburgh poet Robert Fergusson to exclaim in Scots,

Oh willawins! MONS MEG, for you,   *woe!*
'Twas firing crack't thy muckle mou;

What black mishanter gart ye spew	*mischance made*
Baith gut and ga'!	*both; gall*
I fear they bang'd thy belly fu'	*full*
Against the law.	

In the 1600s John Taylor, who climbed inside, was told the gun's barrel was "so great within that a Childe was once gotten there," while in late nineteenth-century California Robert Louis Stevenson met a man who "remembered his father putting him inside Mons Meg." The Castle's modern guardians have long since placed a grate across the muzzle so that it is no longer possible to insert even the smallest human being. The great gun still excites visitors, though. I remember my infant daughter performing a gleeful *pas-de-bas* on meeting her, dancing in the cannon's mouth.

This ancient weapon is a favourite Edinburgh emblem, though it is a nearby, far more modern piece of ordnance which is fired daily at one o'clock to alarm visitors and summon the city's residents to lunch. Today's Castle is

6. Mons Meg, used as a roving siege gun in the fifteenth century, is one of the world's oldest surviving large cannons. Meg has been admired by visitors to Edinburgh Castle since the 1540s, but was last fired in 1681.

47

a spectacular showpiece. Tourists hear how the citadel changed hands several times under sustained attack during the late-medieval Scottish Wars of Independence. Often besieged—and once bombed by a 1916 German Zeppelin—this architectural icon is a doughty symbol of Scotland's refusal to be subjugated by centuries of (mainly English) attackers. Yet its story is also one of complex Scottish infighting. During the sixteenth-century Reformation, it was held by a local garrison commanded by Sir William Kirkcaldy. For all his Protestantism and friendship with John Knox, Kirkcaldy was loyal to his Catholic sovereign, Mary Queen of Scots. Mary had given birth to her son, the future King James VI of Scotland, in Edinburgh Castle in 1566, and for three long years after her imprisonment in England by Queen Elizabeth, Kirkcaldy held the Castle for his exiled sovereign. Eventually it fell to a combined English and Scottish force. In "Ane Ballat [Ballad] of the Captane of the Castell," Kirkcaldy defended Mary as his rightful "prince" and denounced all who "Abused hir, accused hir / With serpent wordis fell [evil]." He was hanged for his trouble. Modern visitors to the Castle's Palace area can see a cartouche bearing the date 1566 and the monogram "MAH" (for Mary and her then husband, Henry, Lord Darnley) above a door close to the small room where James Stuart, James VI, that last king of an independent Scotland, was born. This room has a medieval ceiling and, high on the walls, ornamentation incorporating the Latin initials "MR" and "IR"—for Maria Regina and Iacobus Rex—painted in 1617. Fourteen years earlier, James had headed south to succeed Queen Elizabeth I of England at the time of the Union of the Crowns of the Scottish and English kingdoms. An enthusiast for the divine right of kings, he relished being the first monarch of all Britain.

If Edinburgh Castle is most usually associated with royal struggles, titled people, and battling kingdoms, it is also a place bound up with the city's largely forgotten insurgent democratic energies. The Edinburgh democrats David Downie and Robert Watt were held there after their arrest in 1794. Inspired by the ideals of the French Revolution, after the British government's suppression of the radical Friends of the People in Edinburgh, Watt and Downie were involved in a plot to manufacture pikes for use in a popular insurrection. Edinburgh Castle was to be captured, the town's judges and magistrates seized, public banks taken over; then the king in London was to be ordered to end war with France. Downie, a goldsmith, and Watt, a bookseller's clerk in his thirties, had hoped to storm the Castle as if it were a Scottish Bastille. Instead they found themselves arrested and incarcerated there. Drawn with a dignified countenance by the celebrated Edinburgh miniaturist John Kay in 1794, Downie was banished and died in exile. Wrapped in a greatcoat and wearing a red nightcap, his stockings hanging loose, a wretched-looking Watt was hauled from the Castle on a black-painted hurdle drawn by a white horse and heavily guarded by soldiers. He was executed farther down the Royal Mile for what was called in court "one of the wildest phrenzies that ever entered into the heart of man."

Such democratic conspiracies are seldom mentioned by the Castle's present-day guardians, but are as much part of the history of Edinburgh as the sufferings and machinations during the era of Mary Queen of Scots or the exciting moment in 1818 when the arch-royalist Walter Scott (who had helped beat up democratic radicals as a young man) discovered in Edinburgh Castle the forgotten crown jewels of King James VI's Stuart dynasty. Today the royal regalia are proudly displayed behind glass. Scott's Castle was a Romantic treasure trove: feudalism in stone, timber, and metalwork. The Castle of Watt and Downie represented oppressively antidemocratic authority. High on its dark rock, hiding its prison cells and dominating the city, this great fortress evokes not just the Bastille but also Kafka's castle above Prague. For hundreds of years it served as a gaol for notable Scots. Imprisoned there in the fifteenth century, poet and Latinist Gavin Douglas (translator of the *Æneid*) complained it was "wyndy and richt [right] unplesand."

With all its violent past and imposing architectural hodgepodge, Edinburgh Castle still provides dignity, as well as panoramic vistas. At the Castle Rock's highest point stands a small chapel dedicated (probably in the twelfth century) to the memory of St. Margaret. A revered immigrant, that Hungarian-born and English-reared queen of Scotland died in 1093 after reigning with her Scottish husband, King Malcolm Canmore. Her *Vita* (Life), written in Latin soon after Margaret's death by her confessor, Turgot, is the first biography of a Scotswoman. It celebrates her learning, piety, and determination, presenting her as saintly but tough: she delights in books, meditates frequently on "the terrible day of judgment," and tells the governor who looks after her children "to whip them when they were naughty." For all that the architecture of St. Margaret's Chapel has been modified over the centuries, and measures only around thirty feet by fifteen, it has a stateliness enhanced by its stained-glass windows. Designed by Douglas Strachan in 1922, these depict Scottish saints and warriors, Margaret being the only woman amongst them. Her presence in this small space, like her association with the founding of the grander Holyrood Abbey at the other end of the Royal Mile, asserts that Edinburgh is a city whose physical structure speaks of femininity as well as masculinity. The Royal Mile runs from Margaret to Margaret. Close to her chapel on the Castle Rock, the much more masculine space of the Scottish National War Memorial, planned by Sir Robert Lorimer and built in the 1920s to memorialize Scottish troops killed in World War I, is not without its own female figures. Interior bronze reliefs by Alice Meredith Williams memorialize the Women's Services. Lorimer's shrine has a paved floor of Ailsa Craig granite out of which bursts the bare rock on which the Castle sits. This chapel articulates a sense of sacrifice, but of endurance too. It appears ancient, but is also modern—like the Castle itself.

This present chapter (like Edinburgh, some would say) is very much about appearances; it is about modes of looking and control, and about the city's official and unofficial view of itself. Anyone who strolls down the north side of Castlehill, a little below the Esplanade, can enjoy fine views over the city as well as down the Royal Mile; but the best vantage point—sanctioned by generations of locals and tourists alike—is from the pinnacle of the nearby tall, curious building known as the Camera Obscura which now houses a popular "world of illusions." Here, just a few hundred yards from the venerable Mons Meg, are twenty-first-century holographs, what is billed as our planet's "largest plasmasphere," and a host of other high-tech optical devices. On the top storey sits an older invention: a camera obscura, which is a large flat circular screen more than twenty feet in diameter onto which a complex periscope-like arrangement of lenses and mirrors projects real-time images of the surrounding city—from the Castle portcullis to Princes Street and the distant hills of Fife. If Edinburgh is sometimes regarded, not least by Glaswegians, as a city whose superior surfaces mask inveterate nosiness, the top floor of the Camera Obscura wholeheartedly confirms this. When I last visited, its "megascope," touted as "probably the world's most powerful public telescope," was strategically placed to snoop on passersby. Tourists are asked politely not to point the building's surveillance equipment at neighbouring windows. Indoors, though, wholly unobserved under cover of the small, tower-top dome, the traditional camera obscura lets adults and fascinated children spy with gleeful abandon: zooming in on soldiers with rifles guarding the entry to the Castle, on couples strolling among the grassy slopes of Princes Street Gardens, or on shoppers with carrier-bags walking along the Royal Mile. Few can resist this quintessentially Edinburgh plea-sure—a citywide intelligence gathering that rings changes on the traditional Scottish Calvinist's anxiously invasive search for signs of saving grace. To survey the Camera Obscura's own little-known history and the lives of its founders reveals much about the mores of Scotland's capital. Familiar in the mid-nineteenth century as "Short's Observatory," the building's lower sto-reys once formed part of a seventeenth-century tenement; they were remod-eled in 1853 under instructions from the redoubtable entrepreneur Maria Theresa Short.

Thought by some to have been an impostor, this lady appears to have returned from the West Indies in 1827, declaring herself the daughter of local optician Thomas Short, who had helped to establish an observatory on Ed-inburgh's Calton Hill in 1776. James Craig, planner of the city's New Town area, had designed an octagonal observatory for Calton Hill. His scheme had been modified by the celebrated architect Robert Adam, eager for the observatory to resemble a fortress. Building commenced, but when money ran out Thomas Short turned the structure into his family home, erecting a little observatory nearby. After Thomas's death, a family feud involving combat with blades and guns led to the abandonment of the observatory, but the campaigning Maria Theresa got hold of its great telescope and was allowed to set up a new, wooden building not far off. A popular Calton Hill alternative to the neighbouring, much grander Royal Observatory, this wooden structure was controversial; Maria Theresa Short, a feisty woman with markedly Catholic forenames in a male-dominated Protestant society, was soon subjected to criticism.

For all that it contained powerful scientific instruments, her observatory was unashamedly crowd-pleasing. It had sideshows, statuary, and what the polite Edinburgh bourgeoisie saw as a "peep show." Accused of being be-hind the "teasing and pestering" of walkers on Calton Hill, Short main-tained: "All I have ever done has been simply to point out the Observatory to strangers." In 1834 Lord Cockburn scornfully described her observatory, then in its planning stages, as "a wooden show-box about thirty feet high and as many in diameter, in the form of an inverted punch-bowl, which was to rest on a rim of wall six feet high, and to be open night and day for a *camera obscura,* telescopes, and all manner of optical exhibitions." Cockburn persuaded the Town Council to rescind permission for the observatory's construction, but Maria fought back. So, Cockburn complained, the "abominable edifice" was built. In 1836 the *Scotsman* was advertising its "SPLENDID CAMERA OBSCURA . . . of 12 feet focal length . . . adapted for displaying the magnificent scenery around the Calton Hill." A decade later, advertisements proclaimed that "for one week only" the observatory would host a public explanation of the principles underlying "THE ELECTRIC TELEGRAPH, which is creating a sensation in the Scientific World at the present period." Attempts to turn the nearby Nelson Monument into "a place of exhibition" by installing a *camera obscura* inside it drew the ire of the Town Council. A local councillor suggested facetiously that this optical device should be used to monitor church attendance on Sundays, with policemen noting down details of "carriages, cabs, and other vehicles" conveying people to their kirks. Maria Theresa Short unsettled Edinburgh. A petition was got up against her. One prominent citizen complained of "the annoyance to which the Council had for so many years been subjected from the proprietrix of the Observatory."

By 1850, despite Miss Short's having mounted three appeals, the Town Council voted by twelve votes to six to have her observatory removed. Dr. William Glover, one of the dissenting members, complained that this "was neither just nor honest." Author Samuel Laing lamented the banishing of Short's "good solar microscope, models of various interesting machines, such as the atmospheric locomotive engine, and the electric telegraph, showing their working"—not to mention the telescopes and displays which nourished the imagination: "For the small sum of three pence the intelligent school-boy or the reading artisan could realize in his mind the aspects of the moon, of Jupiter, of Saturn." Laing complained that "a great educational means, honourable to the city" had been "swept away one morning by order of the provost, baillies, and town council, because the proprietrix's servant had insulted the dignity and disturbed the quietude of a town councillor's digestive walk on the esplanade, by thrusting into his hand a bill of the wonders of animalculæ exhibited by the microscope in a drop of water." Laing's colourful denunciation of a zealous Council who had made sure the finest telescope was "thrown out on the green" and the observatory's "roof and walls torn down" was disputed, but carries conviction in its defence of the enterprising "proprietrix."

Short was not a woman to be suppressed. After she married Robert Henderson in 1849, she and her husband purchased property on Castlehill and converted that into a reborn "Short's Observatory." After rebuilding the side and rear walls of the old tenement in ashlar (squared stone), the new owners added two storeys topped by fortress-like battlements surrounding a wooden octagonal domed structure. By the 1860s, advertisements were proudly proclaiming "TO STRANGERS VISITING EDINBURGH" that "the only Point from which [one can obtain] a complete View of the entire City, with the surrounding Country, is from the Tower of SHORT'S OBSERVATORY, CASTLE HILL." If Maria Theresa Short had lost her battles on Calton Hill, on Castlehill she erected her tower of victory. Along with the camera obscura, she advertised "Grand Solar and Compound Microscopes." Visitors were given maps of Edinburgh "in which every place of interest is clearly marked"; these complemented the "pictorial effect" of the camera obscura itself.

The view from the top of the tower is still breathtaking. After Short's death in 1869, her establishment was taken over by W. D. Hart, a "philosophical instrument-maker," who lived in it with his family. His business interests including fitting newly fashionable electric bells to Edinburgh properties, ranging "from Mansions to Stables." Hart kept the name "Short's Observatory," and the tower remained a popular family attraction in the Victorian city. Renovating and refitting it, he incorporated a lecture room and set up telescopes alongside "beautiful working models of machinery which are wrought by electricity." These included a model railway, pumping engines, and telegraph instruments "which the visitors are allowed to work at pleasure." In the 1890s, after Hart's death, most of his observatory's contents—from a "galvanic machine" to a large barrel organ—were sold off and the property was taken over by an imaginative polymath, Patrick Geddes. An enthusiast for microscopes and all kinds of science, Geddes kept the camera obscura, but carried out a remarkable reorganization of the building, changing its name to the Outlook Tower. Its uniqueness was now boosted by Geddes's own far-reaching vision.

Born in Aberdeenshire in 1854, Geddes had studied briefly with the

Darwinist T. H. Huxley in London, and had helped to regenerate old properties in the Royal Mile. A product of Edinburgh's tradition of encyclopædism (in his twenties he had written for the locally produced *Encyclopædia Britannica*), he sought a renaissance in Scottish culture. As a young man in the 1880s, the charismatic Geddes gave daring public "Lectures to Ladies" on "The Elements of Biology." Dashing and brilliant, when he established his Outlook Tower in 1892 he was best known as the co-author of *The Evolution of Sex*. Seeking to relate biology to human behaviour, Geddes was often controversial, but also a conservationist. In Edinburgh he helped to restore houses near the Castle at Ramsay Gardens, today one of the city's most exclusive addresses, where he took up residence close to his Outlook Tower. Ramsay Gardens incorporated the old home, nicknamed the "Goose Pie," designed by eighteenth-century poet Allan Ramsay, whose anthology *The Ever Green* had collected and revived glories of older Scottish poetry. From the Outlook Tower, Geddes ran summer schools for men and women that offered courses relating to his interest in social evolution. Drawing on much older traditions of the "auld alliance" between Scotland and France, he helped to found a modern Franco-Scottish Society. He set up the Edinburgh Social Union. He produced his own new magazine, *The Evergreen*, calling for a "Scots Renascence" and questioning the anglicizing of Scottish education and customs. Geddes wanted nothing less than a fresh synthesis between culture and democracy.

In 1895 he wrote about the need to "express the larger view of Edinburgh as not only a National and Imperial, but a European city—the larger view of Scotland, again as in recent, in mediæval, most of all in ancient times, one of the European Powers of Culture—as of course far smaller countries like Norway are to-day." His invocation of Norway, which was then seeking independence from Sweden, signals a Scottish nationalist aspect to his thought, and he was inspirational for Scotland's greatest twentieth-century poet, Hugh MacDiarmid, who championed the cause of political independence as well as a Scottish renaissance in culture. Like MacDiarmid, Geddes saw Scottish nationalism and internationalism as interdependent.

At the Outlook Tower, Geddes established what has been seen as the world's first sociological museum. A 1906 booklet, *A First Visit to the Outlook Tower*, sets out his unsettling ideas. Visitors were first of all rushed up a spiral staircase to the very top, "because the exertion of climbing makes one's blood circulate more rapidly, thus clearing the fog out of the brain and preparing one physically for the mental thrill of these outlooks." People contemplated life through the camera obscura. Then they sat in a darkened "in-look room," encouraged to ponder the significance of what they had seen. Next, they descended via different floors of the building given over respectively to Edinburgh, to Scotland, to language, to Europe, and to the world. Loving holistic views, Geddes sought a synthesis of the arts and sciences, including what he had learned in Paris to call "La Science Sociale"; across his lifetime, his correspondents ranged from Charles Darwin to Bengali poet Rabindranath Tagore. Convinced that "physics and æsthetics, economics and ethics are alike steadily recovering their long-forgotten unity," Geddes emphasized repeatedly the need to begin with the local and move towards the universal. The man who had taken over Short's Observatory was an enthusiast for Edinburgh as a city of encyclopædic vision. He was sure that "the studies of sun and stars, of rock and flower, of beast and man, of race and destiny are becoming once more a single discipline."

If his talk of "race and destiny" now sounds worrying, Geddes's work on environmental studies, "civics," and town planning was nonetheless influential. Having set up a small Environment Society in Edinburgh with a local teacher, he went on to help shape the establishment of the British Sociological Society in 1903, and had a viewpoint that, like his Outlook Tower, was productively eccentric and visionary. "This is a green world," wrote this biologist, town planner, and environmentalist, "with animals comparatively few and small, and all dependant on the leaves. By leaves we live. Some people have strange ideas that they live by money. They think energy is generated by the circulation of coins. Whereas the world is mainly a vast leaf colony, growing on and forming a leafy soil, not a mere mineral mass: we live not by the jingling of our coins, but by the fullness of our harvests."

Geddes's words have been quoted by twenty-first-century Edinburgh campaigners from the "People's Republic of the Canongate" and by environmental activists in the United States. He saw his Outlook Tower as a national resource helping to set forth a vision of human ecology; he held some of his summer schools at the nearby sixteenth-century Riddle's Court, while to further his vision he sought to establish a linked series of national museums and exhibition centres in Edinburgh and internationally. Though these ambitious schemes failed, they fed into his books *City Development: A Study of Parks, Gardens, and Culture Institutes* (1904) and *Cities in Evolution* (1915), which incorporates his sketch of the Outlook Tower. Geddes coined the term "conurbation," but emphasized, too, the importance of regionalism and the understanding of local historic environments—whether in Edinburgh, India, or Palestine. His staging of a large urban exhibition in the Scottish capital brought an invitation to contribute on a grand scale to town planning in India, while his work was taken to the United States by admirers like Lewis Mumford.

It was the Old Town of Edinburgh and the Outlook Tower which inspired Geddes. They were the laboratory for his developing "Science of Cities." He rejoiced that "amid what was and is the most dense and dire confusion of material and human wreck and misery in Europe, we have every here and there some spark of art, some strenuous beginnings of civic sanitation, some group of healthy homes of workman and student, of rich and poor, some slight but daily strengthening of Democracy with Culture; and this in no parliamentary and abstract sense, but in the civic and concrete one." The present-day structures at the Outlook Tower, Ramsay Gardens, and elsewhere are among the local legacies of this visionary.

Geddes imagined an Old Town renaissance bound up with "towers of great observatories" such as his own. In Edinburgh, the Outlook Tower has been seen both as a forerunner of the mid-twentieth-century "Mass Observation" project and as an eccentric tourist attraction. Familiar today as the commercially oriented Camera Obscura, the building survives as an emblem of Geddes's town-planning ideals, and of the earlier scientific populism of Maria Theresa Short. Both were imaginative stagers of exhibitions, though Geddes's Outlook Tower was not financially self-sustaining. The twenty-first-century Camera Obscura, with its popular scientific optical illusions, telescopes, and exhibits, is closer to Short's vision. Yet few who climb the flights of stone stairs to the rooftop camera obscura can fail to see Edinburgh as a jewel of the town planning which so fascinated and inspired Patrick Geddes.

Not far from the Camera Obscura is Lady Stair's Close, where Robert Burns lodged in 1786 on his first visit to the Scottish capital. Today, small exhibitions about Burns, Walter Scott, R. L. Stevenson, and others connected with literary Edinburgh are part of the alluring, low-lintelled Writers' Museum housed in seventeenth-century-style premises within the Close.

7. Surmounted by a round white wall and small dark dome, the Camera Obscura is a landmark on the Old Town skyline. Here viewed from the north, it rises beyond the imposing towers of New College and the Church of Scotland's Assembly Halls. This photograph was taken from an upper-storey window in the New Town's Princes Street, with Princes Street Gardens in the foreground.

Outside, in "Makars' [Poets'] Court," quotations from Scottish literature are carved into flagstones. Higher up the hill, from the airier vantage point of the Camera Obscura, you can see the nearby towers of Edinburgh University's divinity school (New College) and the Assembly Halls on Mound Place that host the meetings of the Church of Scotland's General Assembly— its annual ecclesiastical parliament. The New College and Assembly Halls complex of buildings is celebrated for its imposing bronze statue of that sixteenth-century leader of the nation's Protestant Reformation, John Knox (c. 1513–1572), who championed the educational ideal of having a school in every Scottish parish. The long-bearded Knox stands on the left, with one arm raised, just inside the courtyard of the college.

New College was new in 1846. During that year, it was established as an educational arm of the strictly Presbyterian Free Church of Scotland, whose ministers had staged a mass walkout from the established Church of Scotland three years earlier, protesting against aristocratic interference in the democratic rights of their congregations. Other spires cluster around, including that of the Tolbooth Church on Castlehill (now headquarters of the Edinburgh International Festival) and the Tron Kirk, remodeled in each of the past four centuries, and still upright, if disused, in the part of the Royal Mile known as the High Street. Yet no Edinburgh ecclesiastical building is more striking than the High Kirk of St. Giles, which stands surrounded by a courtyard farther down the High Street's south side. St. Giles and the surrounding buildings constitute a rich nexus of Scottish culture. In the cobbled roadway outside, several stones are patterned in a heart shape, indicating the site of the Old Tolbooth prison featured in one of Walter Scott's finest novels, *The Heart of Midlothian*. When that gaol was demolished, the obsessive antiquarian Scott looted its ancient door, which still survives with a hoard of spoils in his mansion at Abbotsford in the Scottish Borders. Not far from the cobblestone heart beside St. Giles, trampled by tourists and parked on by cars, is John Knox's grave. It is marked only by a small plaque on parking space 23. Few people recognize its significance, but—charismatically stern, egotistically masculine, iconoclastic, and vigorously democratic —Knox still holds a place of ambivalence in Edinburgh's heart, while the High Kirk where he once preached remains a flourishing place of worship.

Beside St. Giles are the Law Courts, a complex of buildings including the old Parliament House (where the pre-1707 Scottish Parliament met), the

High Court, and attendant legal quarters, as well as several law-related libraries. Architecturally noble among these, though generally closed to the public, are the grand Signet Library (used by lawyers known as "Writers to the Signet") and the Advocates' Library, which appointed philosopher and historian David Hume as its Keeper in 1752. The National Library of Scotland, a less æsthetically distinguished newcomer built mainly in the 1950s, backs on to these older book hoards, but there is no through-way for the general public. Visitors have to enter the National Library from round the corner on George IV Bridge to see a free public exhibition of its world-class John Murray Archive (manuscripts of Byron, Darwin, Jane Austen, David Livingstone, and many others) or to apply to consult its millions of books. The law requires that one copy of every volume published in Britain be sent there.

Books have long mattered in Edinburgh. The city was an important centre for publishers and printers in the nineteenth and twentieth centuries; but its most scandalous book-related incident is reputed to have taken place much earlier, in 1637—not in a library or a printing house, but in St. Giles. Having had a new Parliament House and law courts built over the church's old graveyard, the London-based King Charles I decided that unruly Scots Presbyterians should be subject to a new, Anglican prayer book. Its rules presumed that worshippers would kneel at Communion, venerate saints' days, and engage in other threateningly Romish and thoroughly un-John-Knoxian practices. Legend has it that when this prayer book was introduced at St. Giles on July 23, 1637, an old woman named Jenny Geddes, who sold vegetables in the street nearby, was sitting on a wooden stool in the congregation. As the Bishop of Edinburgh encouraged a public reading from the new prayer book, Jenny yelled with biblical vehemence, "Out, thou false thief, dost thou say mass at my lug [ear]?" and hurled her stool at the preacher. A riot ensued. Whether or not she existed, Jenny Geddes, female and feisty in a man's world, iconoclastic and resolutely egalitarian, embodies something dear to a great many Scots, whatever their religious beliefs. Few people today could identify the life-size equestrian statue outside St. Giles in Parliament Square as that of Charles II, son of the prayer-book-toting Charles I; but for generations, almost all Scots knew who Jenny Geddes was. Robert Burns, poet and horseman, named his mare after her. The horse threw him.

When Edinburgh was founded as a burgh around 1130, St. Giles was to be its large-scale parish church. Almost nothing of the twelfth-century structure remains. Medieval Scottish chroniclers record that it was burned by the English when they sacked the city in 1385. The following century saw extensive building on the site, and the distinctive crowned Scottish Late Gothic spire, still one of the glories of Edinburgh's skyline, was in place by 1500. Knox became minister of St. Giles in 1560, the most decisive year of the Scottish Reformation. The church's shining weathercock arrived in 1567, crafted by skilled smith Alexander Hunyman. Long before that, rows of timber-fronted booths, or lock-up shops—the "luckenbooths"—had been built by silversmiths and other traders nearby, partly blocking the roadway. The name "Luckenbooths" was later applied to tall tenements on the High Street, built to overlook the lock-ups, but the original Luckenbooths were demolished in 1817. "Luckenbooth brooches," once sold by silversmiths from their booths, are still designed for sale in local jewellery shops. These small silver love tokens often feature two intertwined hearts ornamented with precious stones. Traditional, wish-laden, often delicately elaborate, they are Edinburgh at its most romantic.

The demolition of the Luckenbooths was part of the early nineteenth-century rebuilding of Parliament Square and St. Giles. In the later eighteenth century, the church's minister had been Hugh Blair, whose blandly eloquent sermons were read across the English-speaking world; but St. Giles decayed after Blair's death. In the 1820s it was still functioning as a kirk, but it also housed police offices and provided stabling for a fire engine. The Victorians rebuilt most of the external walls, and in the 1870s—spurred by Edinburgh's Lord Provost, William Chambers—made the kirk's interior dourly grand. Shortly before World War I, architect Sir Robert Lorimer added the tall, elongated, Gothic-style Thistle Chapel, but the overall interior remains what *The Buildings of Scotland: Edinburgh* calls the nation's "finest piece of late medieval parish church architecture." People who enter St. Giles today see an uneasy stand-off between its original Catholic cathedral-grandeur and its later Protestant heritage. They may also realize that it has a resonant bookishness that grandly outdistances Jenny Geddes's spirited critique of the Anglican prayer book. Though there is no poets' corner, the Moray Chapel bears an inscription by Scotland's great Renaissance poet George Buchanan, while the South Aisle has bronze reliefs of Robert Fergusson and of

8. This view of the Royal Mile looks eastward down the High Street toward the distinctive crowned spire of St. Giles Cathedral, with the Firth of Forth visible over the rooftops beyond.

9. The interior of St. Giles, photographed in 1948 during the second year of the Edinburgh Festival. Today the renovated interior is little changed, and the imposing High Kirk is used not only for religious services but also as a venue for Edinburgh Festival performances.

the nineteenth-century novelist Margaret Oliphant; not far off is Augustus St. Gaudens's life-size bronze of Robert Louis Stevenson reclining on his chaise longue. Stevenson, who trained nearby to be an advocate, would have been surprised to find himself lolling for all eternity in St. Giles, so close to the courts where he spent many boring hours observing Edinburgh lawmen and learning "to breathe dust and bombazine, to feed the mind on cackling gossip, to hear three parts of a case and drink a glass of sherry, to long with indescribable longings for the hour when a man may slip out of his travesty and devote himself to golf."

Around St. Giles, lawyers come and go as they have done for centuries. Yet for a few weeks each summer since 1947, the Edinburgh Festival has put a very different complexion on things. Once the Festival was all opera and high culture; several of T. S. Eliot's plays were premiered there. Gradually, however, the official Festival has been engorged by its huge "Fringe," which features all sorts of performances, ranging from stand-up comedy to students' Shakespeare. Almost every public space in the city, including the High Kirk, becomes a venue for artistes. I remember being taken as a child in the 1960s to see a rather solemn procession entering St. Giles for a religious service to bless the Festival's commencement; more recently, I have stood with my son, perched on a low stone wall near the High Kirk's door, watching an Australian juggler delighting the crowd, and a fire-eater manœuvring a unicycle taller than a man. He cycled away, oblivious to any disrespect, neatly over John Knox's grave.

Another John—John Scott, Master Wright to the Town of Edinburgh—designed the magnificent hammer-beam roof of the old Parliament Hall, built in the 1630s. Its sculpted Danish oak is now more than matched by the great beams of the debating chamber in the new Scottish Parliament at Holyrood, but Parliament Hall conjures up its own telling sense of museum-like emptiness. Here, about a hundred steps back from the Heart of Midlothian patterned in the cobbles outside, is where the old Scottish Parliament died. Most of the statues around the walls (Walter Scott, the judge and diarist Lord Cockburn, Francis Jeffrey, law lord and founder of the *Edinburgh Review*) portray nineteenth-century Unionists. Yet it is impossible not to reflect on the pre-1707 bustle which made this room the centre of Scottish political wrangling, before parliamentary power in Scotland's capital was killed off for almost three centuries. However much British Unionist historians and commentators have tried to defuse its eloquence, the account given by George Lockhart of Carnwath, a Jacobite member of the old Parliament, remains utterly compelling:

> And so the Union commenced on the first of May 1707, a day never to be forgot by Scotland. A day on which the Scots were stripped of what their predecessors had gallantly maintained for many hundred years—I mean the independency and sovereignty of the kingdom. Both which the Earl of Seafield so little valued that when he, as Chancellor, signed the engrossed exemplification of the Act of Union, he returned it to the clerk, in the face of Parliament with this despising and contemning remark: "now there's ane end of ane old song."

If Parliament Hall remains as a reminder of a parliament that was almost lost forever, then the libraries that surround it show something of the book culture that helped to maintain Scottish identity. That self-image was reinforced by the country's legal, ecclesiastical, and educational institutions, whose distinctiveness survived the Union and still continues. Walter Scott, an Edinburgh-trained lawyer, read in these libraries. His late-Victorian successor, R. L. Stevenson, a less eager law student, pointed out with novelistic glee that beyond Parliament Hall "you may see Scott's place within the bar, where he wrote many a page of Waverley novels to the drone of judicial proceeding." Accessible from Parliament Square, the Signet Library was being constructed when Scott's first novel, *Waverley,* went on sale in 1814. This library is on two levels, the upper particularly notable for its long, light, book-lined extent, and a central dome thronged with images of ancient and modern poets, philosophers, historians, the god Apollo, and the nine Muses. By 1821, when Thomas Stothard painted these, many a "drone of judicial proceeding" had been heard, and Scott, Edinburgh's most famous lawyer, had published thirteen major novels in seven years.

In their extant architectural form, the surrounding book rooms such as the Solicitors' Library and the Advocates' Library are nineteenth-century structures. Originally founded in 1689 by novelist and lawyer Sir George Mackenzie (later nicknamed "Bluidy Mackenzie" for his persecution of the fundamentalist Protestant Covenanters), the Advocates' Library began as a collection of specialist texts for Edinburgh's legal fraternity, but soon some poetry, theology, and even fiction were added. The library was used by

Edinburgh Advocates such as the eighteenth-century biographer and diarist James Boswell, who became one of its curators. Its most famous librarian was the great philosopher David Hume, who held what he called the "genteel office" of Keeper of the Advocates' Library from 1752 until 1758. During Hume's tenure, there was some controversy over *"indecent Books"* such as *L'Histoire amoureuse des Gaules* (The Amorous History of the Gauls)—a work promptly expunged from the Library's catalogue. The Francophile Hume, then at work on *An Enquiry Concerning Human Understanding* (1758), seems to have been uncomfortable in his post; he is rightly remembered as an incisive Enlightenment thinker who explored ways of knowing and interrogated theories of causation, rather than as a law librarian. His emphasis on the value of the imagination in perception and comprehension accords with his remark in his work on "human understanding" that in the perfect republic "music, poetry, and contemplation" would be the "sole business." Articulating this ideal, he does not mention the business of lawyers.

Today frequented by prosperous-looking legal professionals, most of whom are male, the area around and especially behind St. Giles can seem Edinburgh at its most exclusive. It is also rich in strange stories from the past. Just after Hume left the Advocates' Library, inside the Parliament House eighteenth-century entrepreneur and author Peter Williamson set up Indian Peter's Coffee Room, sadly no longer extant. Kidnapped from Aberdeen at the age of ten, Williamson had been taken to America where he was sold for sixteen shillings as an indentured slave to a fellow Scot in Pennsylvania. Not long afterwards, he was captured and tortured by Native Americans; he escaped and thereafter served with the British army at the siege of Fort Oswego. His autobiographical *French and Indian Cruelty* (1757) records his "kidnapping" and his progress—"bruis'd[,] cut, mangled and terrified"—across eastern North America. The Edinburgh hangman ordered that this book be publicly burned because of its accusations against Williamson's Scottish abductors, but Peter won legal actions against them and became one of the capital's most colourful Enlightenment characters, setting up not just his Coffee Room and a newspaper, the *Scots Spy,* but also the city's first street directory and penny postal service. For this last accomplishment he was awarded a substantial pension, and he would stroll past St. Giles looking rather different from the 1759 engraving which depicts him smoking a very long pipe and wearing the attire of a Native American of Delaware. Frequently republished, tales of Williamson's kidnapping and adventures were popular far beyond the Parliament House, and, more than a century later, were surely familiar to the future Edinburgh author of *Kidnapped*.

Tellingly, R. L. Stevenson points out in *Edinburgh: Picturesque Notes* that the Parliament House, built on a slope, presents one storey to the north, but many to the south, "and range after range of vaults extend below the libraries." The Victorian writer takes his readers "by the flicker of a match" through "a labyrinth of stone cellars" below ground, under "the interminable pattering of legal feet," down past the cells, past a lumber room full of artefacts—"lethal weapons, poisoned organs in a jar, a door with a shot hole through a panel, behind which a man fell dead." Eventually, now with the aid of "a peep of yellow gaslight," his readers pass an engine and "gear of the steam ventilator," then exit through the engineers' door into what was then Edinburgh's "Irish quarter," associated with the notorious murderers Burke and Hare: "broken shutters, wry gables, old palsied houses on the brink of ruin, a crumbling human pig-sty fit for human pigs."

Disconcertingly, Stevenson has passed in one short walk from respectable legal tedium to dire squalor, where the poor "will return at night and stagger to their pallets." This city of closely compacted contrasts is the Edinburgh which underpins *The Strange Case of Dr. Jekyll and Mr. Hyde,* as well as the imagination of Stevenson's Edinburgh admirer Arthur Conan Doyle: both men set their most celebrated crime fictions in London, but it was a London nourished by the Scottish capital. In the twenty-first century, the narrow, below-street-level stacks where the National Library of Scotland stores some of its many tomes recall Stevenson's words about "range after range of vaults," while the dark chasm of the Cowgate at night, seen vertiginously from George IV Bridge as it tunnels along the back of the Law Courts behind St. Giles, can still echo with taunts and druggy yells very different from the Parliament Square lawyers' billable, measured tones by day.

Parts of the Royal Mile were once thronged with children. In the 1760s, according to Burns's Edinburgh publisher, William Creech, "Young ladies might have walked, unattended through every street in the city." By 1783, however, it seemed to him that "the mistresses of boarding-schools have found it necessary to advertise, that their young ladies are not permitted to

10. Old lodging houses in the Cowgate, painted by James Riddel for the 1912 edition of Robert Chambers's *Traditions of Edinburgh* (1824), the world's first study of urban folklore.

go abroad without proper attendants," since "boys, from bad examples at home, and worse abroad, are become forward and insolent." This certainly struck the sharp-eyed forty-two-year-old English traveller Sarah Murray when she observed the street children of the Royal Mile at the end of the eighteenth century:

I never saw any thing like the swarms of children in the Canongate. I believe they do every thing but sleep in the street. It may be truly said that they are fat, ragged, and saucy: and it is not to be wondered at; for what can be expected from an education begun and ended in the street. I was one fine evening walking up this *inviting* Canongate, nicely dressed, in white muslin: an arch boy eyed me, and laid his scheme;—for when I arrived opposite a pool, in the golden gutter, in he dashed a large stone, and, like a monkey, ran off chuckling at his mischief.

Just over a hundred years later, farther up the Royal Mile, near the Castle, Castlehill School—today the premises of Scots Whisky Centre (the school's teachers might or might not have approved the change)—counted more than a thousand children on its roll. In the twenty-first century, adult tourists predominate all along the Royal Mile, though bus parties of school students regularly visit the Castle and other sites, eager for toys and souvenirs. "If you could bring a humming top to me I would like to have it," four-year-old Robert Louis Stevenson, known in his family as "Smoutie," wrote to his father, who was then away from the family home at 1 Inverleith Terrace in the New Town. The young boy also wanted "a kind of Swiss cottage that won't break." As a child, Stevenson (whose ancestors' business was lighthouse building) was fascinated by mid-nineteenth-century street life, especially by the man who came with his ladder each evening to light the gas lamps. One of these stood outside the front door of the Stevensons' house. "The Lamplighter" became the most famous poem in Stevenson's deft poetic kindergarten of 1885, *A Child's Garden of Verses*:

My tea is nearly ready and the sun has left the sky:
It's time to take the window to see Leerie going by;
For every night at teatime and before you take your seat,
With lantern and with ladder he comes posting up the street.

Now Tom would be a driver and Maria go to sea,
And my papa's a banker and as rich as rich can be;
But I, when I am stronger and can choose what I'm to do,
O Leerie, I'll go round at night and light the lamps with you.

Stevenson was an infant in the 1850s. Later in life, as cities were beginning to install electric lighting, he penned "A Plea for Gas Lamps," praising

their "warm domestic radiance." Electric street lighting had reached Edinburgh's principal thoroughfares by the early twentieth century, but the future novelist Muriel Spark, growing up as Muriel Camberg at 160 Bruntsfield Place in the 1920s, still lived on a gas-lit tenement street. In her day, the
street lamps had pilot lights. A lamplighter carrying a long pole came in the
evening to turn each one on, and Muriel, like Louis in the previous century,
waited at her window to watch him. One of her favourite toys was her capacious toy pram. Made for twins, it had a folding hood at either end. Her
dolls, Red Rosie and Queenie, sat facing each other.

Like the Muriel Spark who so relished her childhood toys, Stevenson
spent his childhood in Edinburgh and often walked past the historic tenements of the Royal Mile. One of his early books was called *Virginibus Puer-
isque* (For Boys and Girls), and he knew that his home city could captivate
infants as well as impress adults. Fittingly but also innovatively, in the mid-
twentieth century Edinburgh opened the first museum in the world devoted
exclusively to the history of childhood. Now situated in tenements on the
south side of the High Street, a little farther down the Royal Mile, this institution was started in 1955 by a town councillor, Patrick Murray. He used
some of his own boyhood toys, such as his model railway set, as its nucleus.
An eccentric, balding, bespectacled bachelor optician, Murray had a preoccupation with UFOs. Almost as soon as he started his museum, donated playthings flooded in. Within two years it had moved to an eighteenth-
century tenement in the High Street. Three years after that, Murray left the
Town Council and became the museum's first full-time curator. Insisting
that the new institution was "not aimed at children" but was "about them,"
he did a brilliant job, but it is unlikely he would have been hired today. Once,
when asked if he liked children, he retorted, "Not between meals." More
controversially, he encouraged a proposal to have a memorial window placed
in his museum's entrance hall showing "Good King Herod" and the infants
whose slaughter that monarch had ordered. Murray's captions for his exhibits became notorious. One, beside a display of tiny toys, read:

The Maniacal Cult of "Smallness"
The love of extremely miniature work is probably an aspect of some ob-
scure mental disease, but it's great fun nevertheless. In its minor form it
broke out in the construction of small models which can be set in match-

boxes or nutshells. But when it becomes really virulent it can only be expressed by such outrages as dressing fleas. Naturally, doing a "Flea's Wedding" calls for extreme care as nothing reflects so badly on all concerned as a woman turned out carelessly on her wedding day.

Politically incorrect, even at times sinister-sounding, Murray was an utterly inspired curator. Today the free museum he founded occupies five storeys, crammed with everything from puppet shows, automata, and dollhouses to phenaktiscopes, zoetropes, stereoscopes, magic lanterns, and a robot donated in the 1970s by locally born sculptor Eduardo Paolozzi. If you want to see a wooden miniature nineteenth-century butcher's shop with more than forty joints of meat hanging in it, this is the place. If you simply choose to sit down with your children and play snakes and ladders on a very big board, you can do that too.

Though it may be that more of today's youngsters clamour to visit the nearby fairground horrors of the Edinburgh Dungeon on Market Street, or to be taken to that abandoned, reputedly haunted underground street called Mary King's Close, the Museum of Childhood is the best reminder that the Royal Mile is not just a place for adults. The tenement which houses the present-day museum was formerly the childhood home of three famous eighteenth-century Edinburgh beauties, Catherine, Jane, and Eglintoune Maxwell. All were tomboys, and there is a famous story of how young Jane (later a patroness of Robert Burns) rode a pig along the Royal Mile, with her sister Eglintoune running along behind, spurring the creature on with a stick.

While they come from several countries, many of the toys in the Museum of Childhood were made for well-off middle-class children such as Stevenson and Spark. Stevenson remembered that one day when he was a little child, in Howe Street, just round the corner from his house, he was sworn at vehemently by "a lame boy of rather a rough and poor appearance" when he asked the lad if he would like to play. Edinburgh class barriers were and are sensed even by the very young. Spark was taken to preschool children's parties wearing a simple white-silk knitted dress adorned with feather stitching. The little kilted middle-class boys she met there were quite different from the "rough boys" she would see playing "Scotch or English?" in streets and playgrounds. This game involved tying a stone to a piece of string and swinging it round, while challenging other lads to say which country they belonged to. In her autobiography, *Curriculum Vitæ,* Spark recalls that though all the boys she saw playing the game were Scots, most, when challenged, would shout back "English!" and run away, trying to dodge the whirring stone. Much earlier, the famous Edinburgh mathematician and autobiographer Mary Somerville (after whom Somerville College in Oxford is named) remembered participating with other eighteenth-century girls in a game called "Scotch and English." It "represented a raid on the debatable land, or Border between Scotland and England, in which each party tried to rob the other of their play-things. The little ones were always compelled to be English, for the bigger girls thought it too degrading."

Since he was too sickly, and probably too middle-class, to play street games with rough lads, Stevenson, who termed some of his favourite novels "romances," regarded childhood games of hide-and-seek as "the well-spring of romance." Some of his greatest fictions—*Kidnapped, Treasure Island, The Strange Case of Dr. Jekyll and Mr. Hyde*—are games of hide-and-seek: stories to play at, as well as to read. Like the Museum of Childhood, where you can see spinning tops and other toys from the Victorian era, Stevenson's work, so much of which is rooted in his Edinburgh upbringing, is a great celebration of the vital links between play, imagination, and art.

Today a good deal of children's play in Edinburgh, as elsewhere, takes place indoors in front of electronic screens. Yet the heritage of street games is not entirely forgotten. A cinematic classic is the short black-and-white film *The Singing Street.* Made in 1951 by Edinburgh's Norton Park Group, a team of schoolteachers turned filmmakers, it features the children—mainly the girls—of Norton Park School, in the city's working-class Abbeyhill district, not far from the east end of the Royal Mile. In a smoky city of grime-coated tenements and alongside dark, spiked railings near back-courts where white blouses and shirts hang pegged to washing-lines beside the railway, young girls, a few in headscarves and many in mid-length woollen coats, dance and sing of sweethearts and a bonnie bunch of roses. Many of their rhymes, not least the skipping songs, are designed to identify romantic partners. Stressing the regular metrical beat of the words as two girls swing the skipping rope for a third to jump over—or as they dance in a circle, hands joined and arms raised, around a girl in the centre—they sing:

> The wind, the wind, the wind blows high,
> The snow comes falling from the sky.
> Audrey Fraser says she'll die
> For the want of the golden city.
>
> She is handsome, she is pretty,
> She is the girl of the golden city.
> She is handsome, one, two, three,
> Come and tell me who shall be . . .

Then come verses spelling out the sweetheart's name. The girls' skipping to their songs is sometimes elaborate, as they tap "Heel, toe; heel, toe; / All the way to Jericho." Dancing, they beat time on each other's shoulders, or weave in and out of a circle of singers chanting, "In and out of the dusty bluebells." Though trams and buses and cars pass, they have a confident sense of their own territory. "Come on, away ye go, this is a lasses' game," one tells a group of boys who have come to play marbles where the girls have chalked on flagstones the markings for a game of "peever" (hopscotch). The Edinburgh filmmakers' mid-twentieth-century movie may be choreographed to some extent, but its impetus clearly comes from the children. Touching tenement doorways as she goes, a dark-haired lass rollerskates excitedly downhill in black-and-white. Fittingly, this film is sometimes screened at the Museum of Childhood. One of the movie's creators, mathematics and science teacher James T. R. Ritchie (1908–1998), went on to write modern classics of Edinburgh children's lore, including the book *The Singing Street* (1964).

Song as well as spoken narrative for children remains part of the area, not least thanks to the work of the Scottish Storytelling Centre, opened during 2006 on the Royal Mile—next to the fine sixteenth-century museum known (traditionally but inaccurately) as John Knox's House—in property owned by the Church of Scotland. Designed by distinguished local architect Malcolm Fraser and linked to the associated Scottish Storytelling Forum, the Centre aims to give every child in the nation the experience of live storytelling. Sustaining oral culture in Scotland and beyond, so as to enable old traditions and values to flourish in new ways, this institution presents a great range of offerings, from puppet labs and "tiny tales" for people younger than three, to workshops on Scots ballads, to spoken narratives that accompany painted scrolls illustrating Bengali chants. Vibrantly international while rooted in Edinburgh's centuries-old inheritance, the Centre is a wee twenty-first-century castle of whispering, oral history, and song.

The Royal Mile:
From Story to Parliament

Edinburgh's greatest linear narrative, the Royal Mile is itself a magnificently strollable story. Beyond the Castle Esplanade, one enters it via Castlehill and the Lawnmarket, the latter named after an ancient market that took its own name from the "land," or country, outside the medieval burgh. From St. Giles, the High Street, part of the Royal Mile, with the much-modified eighteenth-century City Chambers on its northern side, runs gently downhill until, past the intersection with St. Mary's Street (where you can see an 1867 tenement that was the first fruit of Edinburgh's Victorian Old Town improvement), it becomes the Canongate. This chapter invites the reader to stroll along the medieval *vicus canicorum*—"street of the canons"—where Augustinian clergy walked westwards from their abbey at Holyrood. Beside the royal buildings opposite the foot of the Canongate, the ruined Holyrood Abbey can still be visited as part of a tour of the Palace of Holyroodhouse. Or the walker can turn right toward the modern Scottish Parliament and the Dynamic Earth environmental centre, or left along Abbeyhill, where 1950s schoolgirls twirled skipping-ropes and sang their songs.

So freighted with stories, history, and souvenir shops, the Royal Mile changes its name as it goes, and can seem to alter, too, according to the season and the time of day. Walk down the Canongate just after dawn on a sunny spring morning, before there is much traffic: you will hear seagulls mewing on its high chimneys, and glimpse the glitter of the sea beyond its eastern end. At such times birdcalls, a few pedestrians, and the early-morning absence of cars all function as reminders that this is, in origin, a medieval street. Yet shiver along it on a foggy winter's night, then veer off down one of its shadowy closes, and you can see this roadway as the spectral thoroughfare of eighteenth- or nineteenth-century Edinburgh—a place for dark deeds and mayhem. In 1736, during the tense times after parliamentary Union with England, the Porteous Riots brought combat to the Royal Mile when British troops opened fire on a crowd after the hanging of a Scottish smuggler. Nowadays, thronged with tourists on a summer's afternoon, its traffic calmed in parts by wide pavements, the street appears almost a twenty-first-century simulacrum—a film set built to entice photographers. Yet its buildings, some scuffed and others renovated, are authentic and tell true tales. The People's Story, a museum of Edinburgh's popular history, located in the sixteenth-century Canongate Tolbooth (a former gaol) imaginatively conveys information about pubs, dungeons, and protests since the eighteenth century. A little farther up the hill, on the same side of the Canongate, the twenty-first-century Storytelling Centre mingles its own fictions and facts. Yet the grand narrative of Edinburgh is also silently present on housefronts nearby, on plaques and inscriptions above doorways, in finials, even in cobbles.

Entered across the Canongate, just opposite the People's Story, the Museum of Edinburgh, like the better-known, sixteenth-century "John Knox's House," is a fine place in which to relish more of the city's past. The cluster of buildings housing the museum is itself impressively historic, incorporating sixteenth- and seventeenth-century dwellings. If you walk through the adjoining arched passageway from the Canongate, you can see high on a building on your left what remains of the crest of the Acheson family: a cock perched on a trumpet. Nearby, above upper-storey windows, are the date 1633 and the monogrammed initials of Margaret Hamilton and her husband, Sir Archibald Acheson. Among Sir Archibald's honorific titles was Baronet of Nova Scotia, though he never set foot in that Canadian maritime province. Fronting the Canongate on the triple-gabled property which makes up a substantial part of the museum and was traditionally known as "Huntly House" are several Latin inscriptions, replicas of earlier originals. Allowing the building to speak to posterity, the three central inscriptions were confidently and subtly addressed to readers (like us) in the implied future:

HODIE MIHI CRAS TIBI CUR IGITUR CURAS 1570

Today belongs to me, tomorrow to you, so why be anxious?

UT TU LINGUÆ TUAE SIC EGO MEAR[UM] AURIU[M] DOMINUS SUM

As you are master of your speech, so I am master of my listening.

CONSTANTI PECTORI RES MORTALIUM UMBRA

Mortal affairs are a shadow to a constant heart.

As at John Knox's House, so here the reader is aware of one of the great lapsed languages of Scotland: Latin. To serve "mortal affairs," the buildings now housing the Museum of Edinburgh have been reinvented over the years as everything from a dwelling for the sixteenth-century master of the Scottish Royal Mint to a nineteenth-century hairdressing salon. In Victorian and Edwardian times, the shop of printer and stationer W. Sanderson at 148 Canongate, which specialized in poetry, song, and sheet music, was known as the "Poet's Box"; it also sold for a penny translations of the Latin inscriptions on the premises. Where youngsters once peered at song lyrics through the window of the Poet's Box, they now troop instead up the hill to the Scottish Storytelling Centre or are bused in school groups to the People's Story to learn something of oral culture.

Yet the old, creaky-floorboarded Museum of Edinburgh, with its atmospheric succession of dark, wood-panelled rooms, conjures up good stories too, tales that touch repeatedly on the problem of good and evil. This chapter will call attention to some aspects of Edinburgh's night side—including dark secrets, prostitution, murder—before concluding in the full glare of present-day politics. From the Museum of Edinburgh's upper-floor windows you can look out on nearby stone inscriptions and memorials belonging to a *polis* of the dead; inside the museum are everything from gleaming municipal silverware to a gloomy-looking sedan chair. In the early seventeenth century, one of the Achesons who lived on the site was charged with investigating "witchcraft, sorcerie, inchantment and utheris develische and detestable practizeis." It is hard to prowl round today's Museum of Edinburgh without being conscious of the city's penchant for wicked double lives. Executed in 1670, Major Weir was an Edinburgh merchant burgess who had commanded the burgh guard. Loyal to the fundamentalist Presbyterian Covenanters, he lived with his sister, Jean, in a property (long since demolished) in the West Bow. A tall man with "a grim countenance and a big nose," Weir wore a long dark cloak, carried a staff, and was nicknamed "Angelicall Thomas." In 1670 the city was scandalized by the revelations made at his trial for "Incests, Adulteries, Fornications, and Bestialitys." Accused of a long-running incestuous relationship with his sister, he was said to have

11. The Museum of Edinburgh, on the south side of the Canongate, part of the Royal Mile. On the right is Huntly House, whose Latin inscriptions allow the building to speak to posterity in Scotland's most ancient literary language.

slept also with his stepdaughter, to have had sex with a mare in Ayrshire, and to have committed other heinous crimes. Hugo Arnot, who declined to publish full details in his 1785 *Celebrated Criminal Trials,* thought Weir in the courtroom was simply "delirious." Others were sure he was a sorcerer. Found guilty, he was strangled, then burned at the stake; Jean Weir, having confessed to sorcery as well as incest, was hanged nearby in the Grassmarket.

Major Weir's story, the tale of an outwardly respectable merchant who was actually a monster, haunted Edinburgh, and was in some senses replayed just over a century later when local town councillor Deacon William Brodie, a cabinetmaker who had inherited £10,000 and taken over his father's highly respected business in the Lawnmarket, was extradited in 1788 from Holland. Brodie had fled there in an old blue coat "out at the arms and elbows," intending to escape to New York. At his trial in Edinburgh's High Court, where he cut a much more dapper figure dressed now in "a new dark blue coat, and a fashionable waistcoat, black satin breeches, and white silk stockings," it emerged that he had been responsible for a spate of crimes. These ranged from bank robbery to a raid on the Excise Office and the theft of the ceremonial mace from Edinburgh University, for whose Divinity Hall Deacon Brodie had recently crafted handsome bookcases. Father of several illegitimate children, he had also kept two mistresses. Evidence produced at his trial ranged from respectable business communications with Philadelphia merchants, to a crowbar, pistols, and pick-locks. One servant testified that she had seen the Brodie gang playing dice, and noticed Brodie come in one night dressed in old-fashioned black clothes to meet with his friends; after she had cleared up their meal of cold fowl and fresh herring, she saw the gang come back in from the Edinburgh darkness; now Brodie was attired differently, in light-coloured clothing. This tale of dark and light, respectability and scandal, grew long-lived, fascinating the city. Deacon Brodie's trial took place the year after Burns's poems were first published there; both the poet's printer and his publisher were among the forty-five men from whom the jurors were selected. Burns's publisher, William Creech, was chosen as a juror, and soon published his own *Account of the Trial.*

Brodie pled not guilty. Even when condemned to hang from the Tolbooth gallows, he was convinced he would somehow escape. He did not. One of only two surviving examples of his cabinetmaking is a handsome, four-drawered mahogany clothes press inscribed "Made by William Brodie for Jean Wilson spouse to John Carfrae, Coach maker in the Canongate, 1786." This Carfrae may have been related to James Carfrae, one of Creech's fellow jurors at the Brodie trial, and to the Mrs. Carfrae who was Robert Burns's landlady when he lodged off the High Street in 1786. The Museum of Edinburgh has displayed to generations of visitors the Brodie family Bible. The entry for William Brodie's birth has been removed from it—probably by his sister, Jean, after the shame of her brother's hanging.

Stories of Weir and Brodie fed into Edinburgh's mythology. In the early nineteenth century James Hogg wrote a tale based on legends of Weir and surely drew on the "Angelicall" old sorcerer in *The Private Memoirs and Confessions of a Justified Sinner,* his account of duplicity, fundamentalism, and murder, partly set in Scotland's capital. Robert Louis Stevenson, an admirer of Hogg's novel, was fascinated by a piece of Brodie-made furniture (now in the Writers' Museum) that stood in his own childhood home. When he was in his teens, Stevenson began to write a play about this notorious "respectable man" Brodie; he then collaborated with W. E. Henley on the failed drama *Deacon Brodie; or, The Double Life,* before reconfiguring elements of the tale as the London-based *Strange Case of Dr. Jekyll and Mr. Hyde.* In the twentieth century, Muriel Spark's Miss Jean Brodie makes quite clear that she knows the significance of her surname, and interpretations of Edinburgh's facts and fiction—from the Old and New Town division to the modern crime novels of Ian Rankin—frequently invoke tropes of scandalous doubleness. Yet this complex city is much subtler than these iconic binaries allow—more resolutely heterogeneous.

Particularly in recent years, the Museum of Edinburgh has made efforts to portray not just the nuanced history of local men, but also that of Edinburgh's women and children. Emblematic is a photograph of Bessie Watson. Taken when, like Bessie herself, the twentieth century was nine years old, this picture shows a girl dressed in tartan and holding a set of bagpipes. On her sash is emblazoned the slogan "VOTES FOR WOMEN." Early nineteenth-century Edinburgh had only thirty-three people (all men) who were eligible to elect the local Member of Parliament, but the city was seldom short of political agitation. Born in the 1830s out of the antislavery movement, the Edinburgh Ladies' Emancipation and Freemen's Aid Society had encouraged an interest in women's politics. So did the later Edinburgh National Society for Women's Suffrage, founded in 1867. The latter's pacifist Quaker secretary, Eliza Wigham, had made what was surely the most important intervention by a British woman in the American Civil War. Her 1863 book, *The Anti-Slavery Cause in America and Its Martyrs,* highlighted the role of women in the struggle against U.S. slavery, vehemently urging Britain to avoid any alliance with "a Confederacy having for its corner-stone American Slavery, the deadly enemy of the poor slave, and of Righteousness and Freedom throughout the world, and the impious rejecter and opposer of every law and attribute of Almighty God."

Living almost all her life at 5 South Gray Street in Edinburgh's Newington district, Wigham seems never to have visited the United States. Yet her writings, such as the letter she published in the *Scotsman* on November 11, 1863, show just how well she could argue her abolitionist case. In 1870, when the radical MP Joseph Bright, speaking in Edinburgh, compared the subservient position of Britain's married women with that of the "negro" before Lincoln's presidency, the eloquent, unmarried Wigham might have understood. She was a stalwart campaigner for liberal causes, including women's rights. Campaigns she supported were denounced locally as "hysterical" preoccupations of the "shrieking sisterhood," but few would call them that now. Though she died ten years before the great suffragist procession of Saturday, October 9, 1909, in which the girl piper Bessie Watson strode along Princes Street, Eliza Wigham's tenacity prepared the way for that march. As a southerly breeze blew banners with slogans such as "What's guid for John is guid for Janet," the sun shone on a long line of women, most walking but a few on horseback, led by their "general," the redoubtable, flat-capped Flora Drummond, who, as the *Scotsman* noted two days later, "rode astride" rather than sidesaddle like the other ladies. Fascinated but impassive, a significant part of the city's population lined the route, climbing on lorries or stationary tram cars to view the march. It would take the First World War and many more protests, arson attacks, and other campaigning acts before the franchise was gradually extended to the marchers; but the "Votes for Women" sashes still to be seen in the Museum of Edinburgh, along with other suffragette artefacts, are a fine indication of the city's part in that story.

Near the museum, a little farther down the same side of the Canongate, is the gateway to the Canongate Kirk, its grassy graveyard running right to the edge of the pavement, with only a low wall topped with iron railings separating the living from the dead. After King James VII of Scotland (known in England as James II) had the nave of Holyrood Abbey converted from serving as parish church to the old burgh of the Canongate, and turned it instead into the chapel of Scotland's chivalric Order of the Thistle, he gave orders for a new Canongate Kirk to be built on the Royal Mile. Construction started in 1688, when the churchyard was also laid out. Its much-remodeled interior now painted in pale blue and white, the kirk, erected in the shape of a Latin cross, has a design unusual for a Scottish church. This layout may have been intended by the Catholic king to lend itself to "Romish" worship. Canongate Kirk was dismissed by a 1798 *Traveller's Guide* as having "nothing remarkable about it," but it is a beautiful space. On the flagstoned floor of its apse are the names of all its ministers, from 1560 until the present. Occasionally visited by members of the British royal family because it remains the "Kirk of Holyroodhouse," it is now most famous for the population of its graveyard.

Adam Smith is buried just to the left of the entrance gateway. He lived for a time in the nearby seventeenth-century Panmure House, which still stands with its crow-stepped gables, just along the road close to some beautiful public gardens at Dunbar's Close. Author of *The Theory of Moral Sentiments* (1759) and *The Wealth of Nations* (1776), Smith was interested in kinds of exchange—of language, sympathy, and understanding, not just of money. Nowadays superstitious economists sometimes throw coins on his grave, but Robert Burns, alert to Smith's wider interests, versified a passage from *The Theory of Moral Sentiments* when he wrote in his poem "To a Louse": "O wad some Pow'r the giftie gie us / *To see oursels as others see us!*" Cast in bronze close to St. Giles, Alexander Stoddart's twenty-first-century statue of Adam Smith now gazes down the Royal Mile towards the philosophical economist's old home—though if he could see himself as others see him, Smith might realize that his expression is forever unflinchingly grim.

The sympathetic poet Burns was an admirer of Smith's work, but even more enthusiastic about the poetry of Robert Fergusson (1750–1774), who is laid to rest not far from Smith in the Canongate Kirkyard. Though Burns never met Fergusson, he read his poetry avidly, and wrote to local officials when he arrived in Edinburgh in 1786, complaining that Fergusson, a "justly celebrated Poet, a man whose talents for ages to come will do honor, to our Caledonian name," was lying in an unmarked grave. Commissioning a tombstone for Fergusson, Burns wrote the inscription for it which is still there today. He loved the vernacular vivacity of Fergusson's Scots-tongued verse, which celebrated Scottish folklife in Edinburgh and elsewhere, but he was haunted by Fergusson's fate: the twenty-four-year-old poet had died raving on a bed of straw in Edinburgh's madhouse. In a book of Fergusson's work, Burns wrote around an engraved portrait of the poet heartfelt English-language lines which serve as a great plea to society to support its artists:

Curse on ungrateful man, that can be pleas'd,
And yet can starve the author of the pleasure.
O thou my elder brother in misfortune,
By far my elder brother in the muse,
With tears I pity thy unhappy fate!
Why is the bard unpitied by the world,
Yet has so keen a relish of its pleasures?

The local pleasures which Burns enjoyed included a dalliance with Edinburgh-domiciled Glaswegian beauty Mrs. Agnes McLehose, known as "Clarinda," who is also buried in the Canongate Kirkyard; a goddess to Burns, in old age she was remembered by the publisher William Chambers as "short in stature, and of a plain appearance, with the habit of taking snuff." Fergusson's grave has attracted more attention. Writing eagerly from Samoa in 1894, the author of *Treasure Island* wished to have added to it the words, "This stone originally erected by Robert Burns, has been repaired at the charges of Robert Louis Stevenson and is by him rededicated to the Memory of Robert Fergusson as the gift of one Edinburgh lad to another." These words remain carved on the stone, memorializing the men whom R. L. Stevenson at the end of his life called "the three Roberts." Modern pedestrians on the street outside the entrance to the Kirkyard can salute Robert Fergusson where, carrying a book and cast in twenty-first-century bronze by sculptor David Annand, he strides purposefully away from his grave.

Fergusson is the consummate poet not just of the Royal Mile, but of Edinburgh's Old Town, summing it up even as the New Town was being planned. His poem "Auld Reikie" opens with a dawn scene in which, racily, "morn, wi' bonny purple smiles,/ Kisses the air-cock o' St. Giles," and the poet lets us glimpse "servant lasses" and "barefoot housemaids" who empty shit and urine from their stinking chamber pots. At noon in this eighteenth-

12. On the Royal Mile outside the Canongate Kirkyard, the poet Robert Fergusson (1750–1774) clutches a book and strides away from his grave. David Annand's bronze statue of the laureate of "Auld Reikie" was commissioned to mark the 250th anniversary of Fergusson's birth.

century cityscape, "the trader glours" and gowned lawyers "toss and air" their "wings." Come night, thieves, whores, and carriers of sedan chairs throng the Royal Mile and adjacent streets. Drunks stagger by as "feet in dirty gutters plash" and further "clarty [dirty] odours fragrant flow." Fergusson celebrates such Edinburgh drinking clubs as the Pandemonium and the Cape: "Mirth, music, porter deepest dy'd,/Are never here to worth deny'd," even if the resultant hangover gives the reveller a look like "a painted corp[se]."

This is the Old Town of licence and revelry which Burns experienced about fifteen years later, when he lodged there. The friend with whom Burns boarded on the site of what is now Lady Stair's Close was, like Fergusson, a lawyer's clerk. Rising as tall as fourteen storeys, Edinburgh's Old Town tenements stacked the eighteenth-century social classes: lowest at the bottom, middle classes halfway up, nobility rising to the top. A water supply flowed down the Royal Mile from a cistern on Castlehill, and gallons of it were carried "in barrels, on the backs of male and female porters, up two, three, four, five, six, seven, and eight pairs of stairs, for the use of particular families— Every stor[e]y is a complete house, occupied by a separate family; and the stair being common to them all, is generally left in a very filthy condition; a man must tread with great circumspection to get safe housed with unpolluted shoes." From his first-floor lodgings, Burns heard through the badly plastered ceiling all the shenanigans of the wild "Daughters of Belial" partying above—"when they are eating, when they are drinking, when they are singing, when they are &c." Mrs. Carfrae, Burns's strict, "staid, sober, piously-disposed, sculduddery-abhoring" Edinburgh landlady, assured the young poet: "We should not be uneasy and envious because the Wicked enjoy the good things of this life; for these base jades who lie up gandygoing with their filthy fellows, drinking the best of wines, and singing abominable songs, they shall one day lie in hell, weeping and wailing and gnashing their teeth over a cup of God's wrath!"

Such "gandygoers"—fornicators—could be laughed at or mocked, but the female poor of the Old Town increasingly worried respectable locals. The High Street had been associated with whoring for centuries before phrenologist William Tait, who had worked as surgeon to the midwifery dispensary in the nearby High School Yards, wrote his 1842 study of Edinburgh prostitution, *Magdalenism*. Fifteen years after the murders carried out by

Burke and Hare, Tait was concerned about impoverished hookers boarding and lodging in Edinburgh's nearly two hundred Old Town public brothels.

> The infamous dens in which these beings lodge, are principally situated in the High Street and Grassmarket, with the adjoining closes; and they are so much dreaded by every one, that they sometimes get the whole close to themselves. This is the case with North Fowlis and Geddes' Closes, Halkerston's Wynd, and North Gray's Close. The apartments which they occupy are of the most deplorable description, and generally without one article of decent-like furniture. Their beds consist of a little straw, and a piece of old carpet forms all their covering; and they are so lazy and indolent, that their apartments are seldom put in any thing like comfortable order. The same marks of slothfulness are obvious in their own dress and appearance. They rarely wash themselves, and their clothes are hardly ever changed till they rot off them with dirt.

The Old Town of Fergusson and Burns had been filthy. In the nineteenth century it got steadily worse. Yet people recalled, too, the area's Enlightenment vitality. It had been a place of good wine and hearty songs, but also, as the novelist Tobias Smollett had put it in 1770, an intellectual "hotbed of genius." In 1771, Benjamin Franklin had come to visit David Hume and Adam Smith, though Hume, who had lived at several Old Town addresses with his "regular family: viz., myself . . . a maid, and a cat," moved the following year to the fledgling New Town. Remembering the Old Town in its Enlightenment heyday, the natural historian William Smellie—Robert Burns's printer and one of the founders in 1768 of that greatest of all Edinburgh encyclopædias, the *Encyclopædia Britannica*—recalled those words of a visiting Englishman which will bear repeating: "Here I stand at what is called the *Cross of Edinburgh*, and can, in a few minutes, take fifty men of genius and learning by the hand." Dated January 26, 1776, a list of members of Edinburgh's Poker Club, one of the city's many convivial societies, includes the names of Smith, Hume, the chemist Joseph Black, dramatist John Home, philosopher and pioneer of sociology Adam Ferguson, rhetorician Hugh Blair, historian William Robertson, and mathematician William Robison, along with other Scottish Enlightenment luminaries. By that date, Robert Fergusson had been dead for two years, but it would be another decade before Robert Burns would take Scotland's capital by storm. Hatted, tailcoated, shrewd, all of these men once walked past the Canongate Kirk, where the bronze statue of Fergusson now clutches a hardback volume.

If that book-carrying poet is going anywhere in the twenty-first century, it is surely with the intention of crossing the road to walk down Crichton's Close to the Scottish Poetry Library. For despite all its Enlightenment history and Old Town memories, the Royal Mile is also attuned to contemporary culture. The Scottish Poetry Library Association was founded in 1982 after local poet Tessa Ransford (later the Poetry Library's first director) heard an American voice asking, "Where is the poetry library in Edinburgh?" By 1984 the library was occupying premises farther up the Royal Mile, at Tweeddale Court—poets Naomi Mitchison, Sorley MacLean, and Norman MacCaig read at its opening party as celebrants dined on a recently devised novelty: vegetarian haggis. Today's light, serene, purpose-built library in Crichton's Close was designed by Malcolm Fraser and opened in 1999. Though relatively small, the building serves as Scotland's principal focal point for the art of verse; as well as lending books, its staff help to organize many publications, readings, talks, and other events throughout Scotland. Across one and a half millennia, poetry has been Scotland's greatest art form, and Scottish writing is at the heart of the library's collection. Yet from 1985, when, working with *Verse* magazine, it brought together for the Edinburgh International Festival Scottish Gaelic poet Sorley MacLean and French poet Michel Deguy to read in the Cowgate's historic St. Cecilia's Hall (built for the Musical Society of Edinburgh when Robert Fergusson was eleven), the Poetry Library has been international in scope; it has involved itself in gigs from Kolkata to Brussels, and brings to Scotland poets from every continent. Few countries can boast such a resource; the library is a national treasure. Farther down Crichton's Close are the cramped Edinburgh offices of the BBC and, across Holyrood Road, the more expansive headquarters of the *Scotsman* newspaper. Such media organizations are based in this area to be close to the Scottish Parliament, but the Poetry Library speaks of an abiding discourse subtler than the arguments of journalists or political committee rooms and more enduring than any of the dynasties which have inhabited the nearby royal palace. No book lover who travels down the Royal Mile to Holyrood should fail to acknowledge it with gratitude.

Pronounced "Hollyrood" but spelled "Holyrood," the name of the area

13. The Scottish Poetry Library, in Crichton's Close (entered off the Canongate, roughly opposite the Canongate Kirk), is one of Edinburgh's noblest institutions. A focal point for Scotland's greatest and most abiding art form, the library's current premises were designed by architect Malcolm Fraser and opened in 1999.

at the eastern end of the Royal Mile means "holy cross." It is a word whose significance has changed over recent years. "Holyrood" always used to refer to the monarchs' "Palace of Holyroodhouse" at the foot of the Royal Mile. Now more commonly it designates the Scottish Parliament built opposite the Palace at the start of the twenty-first century, on the site of a former brewery. Architecturally and ideologically, Palace and Parliament confront each other in a striking stand-off. Associated with privilege and Britain's hereditary monarchy, the Palace is a traditional stone dwelling, while the Parliament, bastion of today's Scottish democracy and occupied by republicans as well as monarchists, is a thoroughly postmodern structure. Whereas the Parliament is very much a working building despite its stunning interiors, the Palace—occupied by the reigning, London-based monarch for about one week each year—is more of a beguiling museum-piece.

Picturesque in itself and romantic in its setting, the Palace of Holyroodhouse stands in a landscape that has been settled for millennia. The surrounding Holyrood Park has extended roughly to its current borders since the mid-sixteenth century. This great green space contains traces of four substantial prehistoric forts, some perched high on an extinct volcano whose remnants—the mountain known as Arthur's Seat and the cliffs called Salisbury Crags—provide a dramatic backdrop to the Palace, the Parliament, and the modern Dynamic Earth geological and ecological exposition. For geologists, this is iconic terrain. It was James Hutton, the Enlightenment Edinburgh pioneer of modern geology, who first examined a dramatic hiatus in the geological deposition of rocks on Salisbury Crags (where his Huttonian Section is still marked for walkers to admire), and this scrutiny led him to extremely unsettling conclusions. His 1795 *Theory of the Earth* stated that, when it comes to the planet's history, "we find no vestige of a beginning,—no prospect of an end." More interested in rocks than in mythology, Hutton did not comment on the name "Arthur's Seat," which suggests at least a wish to invoke those early medieval times when Welsh, the language of *The Gododdin* and the tales of King Arthur, was spoken in Edinburgh. The city's place names can be hard to date or fathom, but we know that Holyrood Abbey was founded in 1128 by King David I of Scotland, son of St. Margaret who was said to have brought to her adopted country a fragment of the true Cross—the holy rood—on which Christ was crucified. Attached to this Abbey were royal chambers favoured by later medieval Scottish kings, who hunted deer in the adjacent Holyrood Park. By the start of the sixteenth century, King James IV (later killed by the English at the disastrous battle of Flodden) had erected his palace, its structure now overlain by the quadrangle of the present building. A map, said to have been drawn by an English spy in 1544, shows a square dwelling which has towers at its corners and which is marked "the kyng of skotes palas;" nearby are sketched the larger abbey and wooded parkland at the foot of the broad Royal Mile.

King James V remodeled the Palace. His French queen, Madeleine of Valois, died there after just forty days in Scotland; James then married another Frenchwoman, Mary of Guise, and their daughter Mary Queen of Scots succeeded to the Scottish throne when only days old. Attacked by the English army of Henry VIII, who sought to obliterate Edinburgh completely, the Palace suffered serious damage in the 1540s. Amid fears for her life, the six-year-old Scottish queen was evacuated to France, where she later married the young dauphin, heir to the French throne. George Buchanan, the great poet who afterwards lived in Holyrood Palace, wrote a splendid Latin poem hymning these nuptials. His epithalamium longs for a day when Scotland and France might be joined in an era of peace "æquæva æternis cœli concordia flammis"—"tuned to the endless concord of the stars."

The sudden death of Mary's French husband dashed such hopes, and in 1561, just after the Protestant Reformation in Scotland, the youthful, staunchly Catholic queen returned to her native land. Stepping ashore at Leith, the port of Edinburgh, she took up residence at Holyrood. Mary fascinated leading Scottish Protestants, including the scholarly George Buchanan. He read the Roman historian Livy with her and addressed her in verse as "Nympha" (Nymph). That resolute Calvinist John Knox also seems to have sensed her charisma, both sexual and intellectual; in his self-aggrandizing *History,* he recorded that Mary complained of finding in Scotland "nothing . . . but gravity," for, Knox sternly explained, "she was brought up in joyousity." The Scottish Reformer thought her a "Roman harlot." He demanded that she be subject to the discipline of his democratically minded fledgling kirk. She fought him off, not least with irony: "Well, then, I perceive that my subjects shall obey you, and not me; and shall do what they list, and not what I command: and so must I be subject to them, and not they to me."

Mary's refusal to kow-tow to her subjects, and her liking for continental favourites, enraged many. On March 9, 1566, pregnant with the future King James VI, she was dining in "a narrow private Room" in Holyrood Palace with some of her ladies and her Italian secretary David Rizzio when several armed men burst in. One of them was her second husband, Henry Darnley, jealous of Rizzio's influence. Buchanan, who knew several of the people involved, described how, as the men tried to drag Rizzio away, "the Queen presently rose, and sought to defend him by the Interposal of her Body; but the King took her in his Arms, and bade her take Courage, they would do her no hurt, only the Death of that Villain was resolv'd on." Though Buchanan maintained the attackers wanted to take Rizzio "to hang him up publickly, as knowing it would be a grateful Spectacle to all the People," what happened was that, having hauled the Italian out to a nearby room, they all stabbed him until he bled to death. This is the most dramatic incident in the history of the Palace of Holyroodhouse, and the rooms where it happened are a "must-see" for visitors, even if the guides no longer assert with full confidence that the floor remains indelibly stained with David Rizzio's blood.

The young Italian's murder was part of a chain of events which led, Buchanan asserted, to the queen's plotting with the Earl of Bothwell (whom she soon married) to kill her husband, Darnley. According to Buchanan, Mary "resolv'd to go to Glasgow" with her baby son, so that she would not be accused of plotting in Edinburgh. Meanwhile, it was arranged that Darnley, who had been ill, would be carried in a litter to "an House uninhabited for some Years before, near the Walls of the City, in a lonesome, solitary Place, between the Ruins of two Churches, where no Noise or Outcry could be heard." As Buchanan tells it, Mary had returned to Holyrood. "The Queen had deferr'd the Murder till that Night, and to seem perfectly easy in her mind, she would needs celebrate the Marriage of *Sebastian,* one of the Musicians, in the very Palace, and then the Evening was past in Mirth and Jollity, then she went with numerous Attendance to see her Husband; she spent some Hours with him, and was merrier than usual, often kissing him, and giving him a Ring, as a Token of her Affection."

Buchanan, a distinguished dramatist as well as a poet and historian, next has Mary remind Darnley "*that* David Rizio *was killed the last Year, just about that Time,*" before she leaves him and returns to Holyrood "to dance that Night at the Wedding of Sebastian." After she goes, Darnley is strangled and the house where he has been staying is blown up.

The extent to which Mary, who soon afterwards married the Earl of Bothwell, was involved in the killing of Darnley is hotly debated. Buchanan, who had admired the queen up to this point, clearly turned against her and thought her guilty. He collaborated on writing the *Detectio,* an early detective narrative which helped to seal her eventual fate: she was beheaded by her English cousin, Queen Elizabeth, who was convinced Mary was plotting against her. Later, in an ironic turn of events, the Protestant Buchanan took up residence at Holyrood, where, after helping to have Mary condemned, he became tutor to her young son, King James VI. Unsurprisingly, James detested him.

Dramatized in Germany by Friedrich Schiller in *Maria Stuart,* sung of in Scottish ballads, and often filmed in Britain and America, the story of Mary Queen of Scots, more than anything else, makes Holyroodhouse the iconic palace of the Stuart dynasty, which ruled in Scotland, and later the whole of Britain, for more than four centuries. After James VI succeeded Elizabeth as the monarch of England in 1603 and moved to London, the Palace of Holyroodhouse was little used. Scotland had lost its resident royalty, and Edinburgh's regal residence suffered centuries of neglect, punctuated by occasional bursts of restoration and very infrequent royal visits. The most famous of these was in 1745, when Bonnie Prince Charlie, the exiled "Jacobite" Stuart monarch, sought to retake the British throne from the rival Hanoverian monarchy, which had seized power in London. Ensconced briefly at Holyrood, the Catholic Stuart "Pretender" (as the Protestant Hanoverians dubbed him) held a grand ball in the largest room in the palace, the Great Gallery, and rode in the parklands outside, where the dramatist John Home was an onlooker.

> The Park was full of people, . . . all of them impatient to see this extraordinary person. The figure and presence of Charles Stuart were not ill suited to his lofty pretensions. He was in the prime of youth, tall and handsome, of a fair complexion: he had a light coloured periwig with his own hair combed over the front: he wore the Highland dress, that is a tartan short coat without the plaid, a blue bonnet on his head, and on his breast the star of the order of St. Andrew. Charles stood some time in the park to shew himself to the people; and then, though he was very near the palace, mounted his horse, either to render himself more conspicuous, or because he rode well, and looked graceful on horseback.

Eager for weapons, Bonnie Prince Charlie sent a letter, dated "Palace of Holyroodhouse, 25th September 1745," to the Provost of Glasgow, asking for hard cash and "two thousand broadswords." The Glaswegians resisted such importuning from Edinburgh; but it was a time when, as the Jacobite Gaelic poet Alasdair mac Mhaighstir Alasdair put it, in a language which neither Prince Charlie nor most of the Scottish capital's fifty thousand or so substantially pro-Hanoverian citizens would have understood,

> 'S iomadh armunn, lasdail, treubhach
> An Dun Eideann, ann am bharail.

> [There's many a valiant, daring hero
> In Edinburgh, well I know it.]

14. The Royal Palace of Holyroodhouse, now the monarch's official residence in Scotland, stands at the eastern end of the Royal Mile, beside the imposing ruins of Holyrood Abbey, which was founded in 1128. There has been a royal residence at Holyrood since at least the fourteenth century, and the palace has been inhabited by monarchs as different as Mary Queen of Scots and Queen Elizabeth II. Here David Rizzio was murdered and Bonnie Prince Charlie danced.

At Holyroodhouse the handsome Stuart prince and his heroes danced, surrounded by images of his actual and his invented ancestors, all 110 of them, whose restored portraits still adorn the walls.

Though these paintings survive *in situ,* the prince, defeated at the decisive Battle of Culloden near Inverness in 1746, was forced to flee his kingdom; Hanoverian troops, soon billeted at the Palace and welcomed by many in the Scottish capital, slashed at the Stuart portraits with their swords. Prince Charlie's forces might have occupied Edinburgh briefly, but the Hanoverians had always kept control of the Castle. The Palace at Holyrood was left to moulder. Nominally looked after by the Duke of Hamilton, the Abbey's roof collapsed in the 1760s; and soon afterwards Edinburgh's laureate, Robert Fergusson, who liked to walk to Arthur's Seat and "Holyrood-house," complained in the Scots tongue,

> O HAMILTON, for shame! the Muse
> Wad pay to thee her couthy vows,   *Would; kind*
> Gin ye wad tent the humble strain,   *If you would attend to*
> And gie's our dignity again: *give us*
> For O, waes me! the Thistle springs   *woe is me!*
> In *domicile* o' ancient kings,
> Without a patriot to regret
> Our *palace* and our ancient *state.*

At Holyrood Abbey debtors could seek sanctuary, free of their creditors until they left its precincts. During the 1790s the Palace was home to post-Revolutionary French aristocratic refugees. English traveler Sarah Murray noticed there "the unfortunate Duc de Serrent . . . still weeping for his murdered sons, his only children." Thirty years later, Walter Scott choreographed a gaudily daft visit to Edinburgh by the Hanoverian King George IV in 1822, when the monarch (adorned in supposedly Highland couture made from sixty-one yards of satin, thirty-one yards of velvet, and seventeen yards of cashmere) wore below his kilt what Scottish artist David Wilkie, who painted His Majesty processing into Holyrood, described as a "kind of flesh-coloured pantaloons." By that time, the king was the first reigning British monarch to visit Scotland in almost two centuries, and Holyroodhouse was tidied up enough so that, although as a residence it was no longer fit for a king, at least receptions could be held there. The Palace was dilapidated again by the mid-nineteenth century, when Queen Victoria, who stopped off en route to Balmoral, gave orders for its restoration. In 1850, sumptuous apartments such as the Morning Drawing Room were renovated for her; and to ensure that she would not have to gaze on the ample buttocks of a female nude painted above the fireplace, Jacob de Wet's seventeenth-century picture was covered over with mirror-glass. That mirror-glass has since been removed.

Today's visitors to the Palace of Holyroodhouse can pay to enjoy its many splendours, from a cat and mouse embroidered by Mary Queen of Scots to the nearby Queen's Gallery, opened in 2002 to celebrate the Golden

Jubilee of Queen Elizabeth II and showcasing selections from the superlative royal art collection. One of the most atmospheric experiences is simply to stand in the soaring medieval remnants of Holyrood Abbey. This is the hallowed ruin which in the early nineteenth century inspired sightseeing German composer Felix Mendelssohn to write his Scottish Symphony, and which was painted in heady, Gothic moonlight by the remarkable Frenchman Louis Daguerre, later a pioneer in the field of photography. Shattered and splendid, the Abbey might have been configured for ardent Romanticism.

Opposite the Palace of Holyroodhouse, built in a very different style and long campaigned for, the Scottish Parliament, Scotland's greatest piece of contemporary architecture, was designed by the Catalan architect Enric Miralles. When the forty-five-year-old architect died from a brain tumour in 2000, the building of the Parliament was supervised over the next four years by the architect Benedetta Tagliabue (his wife) and the Edinburgh-based architectural partnership RMJM. Brilliant, determined and charismatic, Miralles is said to have visited Edinburgh as a teenager learning English, and to have made eighteenth-century Edinburgh architect William Adam the starting point for his academic thesis. Miralles was fascinated by the way buildings relate to topography. His early drawings drafting the Scottish Parliament emphasize the sculptural flow of terrain and express his wish for the Parliament to be like the land, built out of it and carved into it as part of a "gathering situation: an amphitheatre, coming from Arthur's Seat." The conglomeration of buildings is most impressive when viewed from Salisbury Crags, from Arthur's Seat, or from Calton Hill, all of which afford a view of its leaf-like, flowing shapes—Miralles sketched the complex while using a collage of stalks and leaves as a model. The finished structure is at once monumental and village-like, an assembly of shapes in apparently organic dialogue with one another, as well as with the wider geology of Edinburgh. To enter the Parliament is to enter a great work of the imagination.

Blending a tracery of branches with bulky, castellated forms, but also with what can seem like aspects of an airport terminal, this modern Parliament building often nonplusses visitors. Many remain uncertain as they pass through the relatively dark concrete vaults of its entry hall, whose low ceiling with its abstracted saltire crosses feels vaguely medieval. Yet most people are won over by the structure's ability to surprise and delight as they move on

15. Officially opened in 1999, the Scottish Parliament had to wait five years for the completion of its striking new building at Holyrood, designed by the Catalan architect Enric Miralles. He saw it as part of a "gathering situation: an amphitheatre, coming from Arthur's Seat." This photograph looks over the Parliament site from the rocks of the mountainside above, towards Calton Hill beyond.

into its garden lobby, where a flow of twelve sculpturesque, leaf-shaped roof lights made of stainless steel, glass, and oak struts allows natural light into an area substantially floored with polished Aberdeenshire granite and from which stairs ascend gently towards the debating chamber. Finished in oak, sycamore, and glass, this airy chamber, about 1,200 square metres in area, has a stunning oak and steel-beamed roof free of supporting columns. Openness characterizes the space. Its 131 seats and desks were all designed by Miralles, and each has its own microphone on a long, flowing, plant-like stalk. The seats are arranged in a semicircle, rather than (as at Westminster) confrontationally. To sit there feels like being inside a wooden ship—a ship of state.

Individual committee rooms in the Parliament are particularly beautiful, sculpted as much as built. Attuned to his building as an ensemble, Miralles designed everything from its dark external panels (said to be based on the shape of Henry Raeburn's famous painting of a "skating minister" in

Edinburgh's National Gallery) to the debating chamber's patterned carpets and the furniture for the parliamentarians' individual rooms. These offices incorporate "thinking pods" with nest-like window seats. The larger Parliament complex encompasses older structures, particularly the historic Queensberry House—associated with the Act of Union which abolished the ancient Scottish Parliament in 1707. Yet with its broadcasting galleries, visitors' crèche, and spaces for wheelchairs in the debating chamber, Miralles's is assuredly a contemporary building. On the Scottish Parliament's website you can find everything from a list of the literary quotations worked into the legislature's Canongate Wall to details of expenses claims made by each elected representative.

The Scottish Parliament has a long, disrupted history. First mentioned in the thirteenth century, it survived King James VI's move to London in 1603. An ill-advised Scottish colonial venture in Panama—the Darien Scheme—and the refusal of England to allow Scottish merchants access to English colonial markets led to economic problems around 1700. Soon, thanks not least to a substantial dose of bribery, the Treaty of Union was concluded in 1707. According to its terms, the English Parliament in London remained little changed, except for the addition of forty-five Scottish seats to what was now called the British House of Commons. Despite riots in towns across Scotland, the old Parliament in Edinburgh was extinguished. More than three-quarters of a century later, Robert Burns, in a famous song, complained that his country had become "England's province" and denounced the signatories of the Union Treaty: "We're bought and sold for English gold / Such a parcel of rogues in a nation!"

Though many, many Scots, including leading figures of what we now call the Scottish Enlightenment, were happy to relish the economic gains of Union and to participate to the full in the colonial projects of the British Empire, there were continuing concerns about a perceived loss of Scottish identity. For all his celebration of "Britishness" (an awkward cultural fiction which has inspired no major English authors), Edinburgh's Walter Scott was alert to this in the Romantic era. By the early twentieth century, there were pressures to grant "Home Rule" to Ireland and Scotland; but whereas Ireland seized back its independence through revolution, Scotland simply waited. In part inspired by Yeats's Irish cultural Renaissance, the poet Hugh MacDiarmid and other enthusiasts founded the National Party of Scotland (later the Scottish National Party, or SNP) in Glasgow in 1928. Their aim was to regain independence for Scotland, and the most remarkable development in Scottish politics over the past century has been the growth of the SNP. For decades its members were regarded as eccentrics; now more than a third of Scottish voters support them. The other main parties in Scotland—Labour, Liberal-Democrats, and Conservatives—remain staunchly Unionist, defending the unity of the British state while supporting devolution of power to Edinburgh. Curiously, since it seems to have little to gain from London rule, the Scottish press is Unionist too. Yet support for the SNP has increased steadily over the past half-century, and the main political contest in the Edinburgh Parliament is not (as in England) between the Labour and Conservative parties, but between the Unionist parties and the pro-independence parties, by far the largest of which is the SNP.

After many decades of discussion concerning an assembly or parliament for Scotland, a referendum on the issue was held in 1979. A majority of those who voted cast their votes for a Scottish Parliament, but the Unionist Labour government at Westminster had stipulated that the establishment of this would require the endorsement of at least 40 percent of the Scottish electorate. That threshold was not quite crossed. Defeat led only to greater pressure, which took a variety of forms. Protesters such as the Old Town artist Kenneth Skeel mounted a day-and-night vigil at Calton Hill; poets published significantly titled books such as Douglas Dunn's *St. Kilda's Parliament* (1981), Edwin Morgan's *Sonnets from Scotland* (1984), and my own collection *A Scottish Assembly* (1990); politicians, clerics, and others set up a Scottish Constitutional Convention which published a *Claim of Right for Scotland* (1989) and *Scotland's Parliament, Scotland's Right* (1995). A further referendum, granted by the Westminster Labour government of Tony Blair (who had been educated at Edinburgh's elite private school, Fettes College), was held in 1997: of those who voted, 74 percent supported the establishment of a Scottish Parliament enjoying powers devolved from Westminster. Without its own building, the Parliament met for the first time on May 12, 1999, in the Church of Scotland's Assembly Halls on the Mound. There the show was stolen by its chairperson, Dr. Winnie Ewing of the SNP, when she announced with dignity and delight that "the Scottish Parliament, which adjourned on 25 March 1707, is hereby reconvened."

Officially opened by Queen Elizabeth II on July 1, 1999, the Parliament had to wait five years until its new building at Holyrood was completed—at a reported cost of £431 million, considerably less (Glaswegians might note) than the money spent on Edinburgh's skimpy new tram line. Just over a year after the Parliament's royal opening, the inaugural First Minister of Scotland—widely admired Glasgow Labour politician Donald Dewar, who had been to the fore in commissioning the new building—became fatally ill. So, by the time the Holyrood Parliament building opened in 2004, both its Scottish political overseer and its Catalan architect had been dead for several years. In supporting the establishment of the Parliament, Labour and other Unionist parties had deliberately arranged its voting system to try to ensure that no single party could gain an outright majority. This scheme was designed to frustrate pressures for Scottish independence, and the Unionists assumed that the new Parliament's existence would help curb the rise of the SNP. They were wrong. In the Scottish election of 2007, the SNP returned as the largest party, though without an overall majority. Led by First Minister Alex Salmond, they formed a minority government, and quickly changed the title of the legislative body from the "Scottish Executive" (a form favoured by Westminster) to the "Scottish Government"—a term now used by all parties but long resisted by London. At the following Scottish election, in 2011, the SNP won a landmark victory, gaining the first overall majority in the Parliament, and the re-elected First Minister Salmond declared that Scottish independence was now "inevitable." Whoever forms Scottish Governments in the future, that issue seems central to the modern political landscape.

Before the re-establishment of the Scottish Parliament, Edinburgh was a lapsed capital city. The renaissance of the Parliament at Holyrood has gone hand in hand with a rebirth of Scotland's capital, one that even recent banking disasters have failed to stop. Increasingly confident and mature, Holyrood's Scottish Parliament has 129 members, about two-thirds of them male. Members of the Scottish Parliament (MSPs) are elected every four years by a single transferable vote system. Some represent immediate local constituencies; others, wider geographic areas. Though the Parliament can legislate on Scottish issues—including education, health, housing, transport, culture, sport, social work, and policing—it was set up so that powers over significant issues such as taxation, defence, aspects of public finance, and authority over constitutional issues were retained by Westminster. This has led to political tussles in a United Kingdom where the implementation of political devolution has meant that Scotland, Wales, and Northern Ireland have their own parliaments, but there is no parliament specifically for England. A consequence is that much of the time of the British Parliament at Westminster is taken up with predominantly English issues, and Westminster seems remote, antiquated, unduly controlling to significant numbers of people in other parts of the United Kingdom. On the other hand, for all it introduced free personal and nursing care for elderly people and has resisted charging fees to Scottish university students, the Parliament in Edinburgh during its first decade produced comparatively little distinctive legislation. It may be that it has still some developing to do before it lives up fully to the deep and complex imagination behind its building at Holyrood.

Princes Street Gardens
and the New Town

Stretching out to the north of the Castle Rock, Princes Street Gardens was once a forest. In the fifteenth century, King James III ordered it to be flooded, creating the Nor' [North] Loch to strengthen the Castle's defences. Soon this lake became a useful place to get rid of witches: the ones who sank beneath the surface and drowned were judged innocent, while survivors were burned nearby at the stake on Castlehill. When they had run out of witches, Edinburgh's townsfolk boated on the loch in summer or skated on it in winter if it iced over. By the eighteenth century, the Nor' Loch was so full of the overcrowded Old Town's sewage that the authorities decided to drain it and develop a sweet-smelling New Town beyond its northern banks. Digging the New Town's foundations and making other urban improvements produced heaps of broken stone and detritus. These were piled up in part of the loch to create "the earthen mound," now known simply as "the Mound."

Several times this vast spoil heap sank, but Edinburgh's labourers just kept chucking on more earth and rubble. By one 1792 estimate, "there must have then been 1,305,750 cart loads thrown upon it." That year, fine dwellings were being constructed along Princes Street—"a long line of modern houses, built of white stone, upon an elegant and uniform plan," observed English visitor John Lettice. For all he thought Edinburgh a "second order" capital, Lettice found it "brilliant." The New Town's "air of lightness, elegance and splendour" was "probably not to be surpassed, if equalled, in any other city in Europe." Parallel to Princes Street on its northern side, the equally new Queen Street also consisted "of a single line of houses." With uninterrupted views across the Forth to Fife, the vista from Queen Street "beats all the other parts of the town," declared Sarah Murray a few years later. Yet today it is Princes Street, with its southerly outlook across Princes Street Gardens, which is the city's most famous New Town thoroughfare.

No roadway could be more appropriate for this chapter, whose prominent topics include social class and (self-)representation.

Princes Street is supremely spectatorial. Since its inception, flâneurs have flocked to it. "All the lads and lases besides bucks and begars parade there," wrote seven-year-old Marjorie Fleming in 1810. In the early twentieth century, locals called it "the Strand," joking that, like an entertainment venue, it had a "Shilling Side" and a "Half-crown Side." In 1904, Rosaline Masson catalogued its "constant stream of traffic . . . cable cars with noisy bells, motor cars, carriages, bicycles, electric broughams, station lorries, hansom cabs, and the crawling 'char-a-bancs,' with their scarlet-coated drivers." The sensation of crossing the street at its west end was brilliantly captured by Scottish artist Stanley Cursiter in an experimental, quasi-Futurist 1913 oil painting—a welter of geometrically intercut trams, sunny, dark-hatted figures, and a proudly striding white dog. By the 1950s, when Teddy boys and Teddy girls in Edwardian-inspired garb were strutting their stuff— even in Edinburgh—one of the street's nicknames was "the Talent Walk." Nowadays, beggars mix with elegant young women from the New Town, the heirs of poet Edwin Muir's graceful Ann Scott-Moncrieff. Memorialized as having "the air of an early muse," she died in 1943 at the age of thirty-nine.

> Yet "the world is a pleasant place"
> I can hear your voice repeat,
> While the sun shone in your face
> Last summer in Princes Street.

The sun shines right along this tramlined east-west artery, the lofty acropolis of Calton Hill at one end, the less lofty road to Glasgow at the other. Yet the most stunning spectacle to be seen on Princes Street is not so much its people as its general outlook. This thoroughfare is a mile-long window onto one of Europe's finest urban vistas—encompassing not just the Castle on its rock and such imposing buildings as the 1902 Balmoral Hotel with its bulbous, nigh-200-foot clock tower, and the Greek-temple-style Royal Scottish Academy at the foot of the Mound, but the whole long skyline of the Old Town, which makes, as the twentieth-century Edinburgh poet Norman MacCaig put it, "a Middle Ages in the sky." All of this looks utterly beguiling from ground level. It is even more striking from a few storeys up—say, by day from an upper floor of Jenners department store, that grand 1890s emporium sacred to traditional upscale Edinburgh shoppers; or, even better, floodlit by night from the lofty balcony of the New Club, a concealed and almost comically exclusive private members' association whose slabbed concrete 1960s interior resembles a James Bond villain's lair. Cramming together characterless modern chain stores and a medley of older buildings, the architecture of Princes Street is now a mishmash. This only emphasizes that what matters is looking away from the buildings, southwards across perhaps the world's most beautifully situated city park, that ex-loch called Princes Street Gardens.

After the Nor' Loch was drained, the Gardens arrived slowly. Sarah Murray noted "nauseous scents" there in the 1790s, while the author of *Scotland Delineated* (1791) complained that Princes Street fronted on to a "deformed marsh." If only it could be "converted into a smooth meadow and sloping bank, it would contribute not a little to the beauty of its situation." Several decades later, around 1820, Robert Louis Stevenson's "ardent, passionate, practical" grandfather, the engineer Robert Stevenson, helped to lay out the Gardens just west of the Mound. These new Gardens extended round the Castle Rock as far as the back of the Grassmarket, though later nineteenth-century building projects reduced them to their present extent. In 1830, the East Princes Street Gardens were planted on the Mound's other side. Originally designed as private plots, the land was designated a public park in 1876; increasingly it became a sculpture area, a place not just for grass, paths, and flowers but for statuary celebrating Scotland's—and especially Edinburgh's—great and good. Except for several war memorials, all of the monuments in the Gardens are to eighteenth- and nineteenth-century male writers, though some of these (such as missionary David Livingstone, or midwifery pioneer James Young Simpson) are best remembered for their achievements outside the covers of books.

By far the most famous memorial here is the Gothic-style Scott Monument, a magnificently odd sandstone space-rocket parked just off Princes Street. One of the most influential writers in the worldwide history of the novel, Walter Scott was born in Edinburgh in 1771. He grew up to practise law in the New Town. Scott was initially a best-selling poet, but later defected to even better-selling prose. His historical novels, such as *Waverley, Rob Roy,* and *The Heart of Midlothian,* helped to consecrate Scotland for

16. Seen here from the north, with St. Giles to its left and the Bank of Scotland buildings on the Mound to its right, the Scott Monument in Princes Street Gardens was designed by George Meikle Kemp. Its foundation stone was laid in 1840. Commemorating Edinburgh's most influential writer, the Scott Monument is surely the world's most elegantly substantial literary memorial, even if to modern eyes it looks ready to blast off at any moment.

the Romantic sensibility. Scott's imagination ranged from India to Orkney, and he was the first novelist to write for a global audience. His fiction's society-wide sweep excited and influenced such different admirers as Balzac, Dickens, Mazzini, and Tolstoy; in America, James Fenimore Cooper was styled "the American Scott." Though many of the Edinburgh-born author's novels, such as *Ivanhoe* and *The Talisman,* are set outside the country of his birth, it is with Scotland that he is forever linked. "Breathes there a man, with soul so dead,/Who never to himself hath said,/This is my own, my native land!" exclaims an excited voice in *The Lay of the Last Minstrel,* making clear that Scott's own native land was "Caledonia! Stern and wild,/Meet nurse for a poetic child!"

When Scott died in 1832, there was a wave of national mourning. "Scottland," as the Victorian poet Alexander Smith put it, craved a splendid memorial to her greatest novelist. Embarrassingly for Edinburgh, Glasgow got there first, but in the Scottish capital an 1836 competition to plan a monument led, eventually, to the commissioning of a design from George Meikle Kemp. This shy, bushy-haired, poetry-quoting joiner with a passion for Gothic architecture had dreamed of restoring Glasgow Cathedral. His blueprint for a Scott monument drew on his experience making meticulous drawings of Melrose Abbey in the Scottish Borders, and his structure was originally intended as a centrepiece for Edinburgh's grand Charlotte Square. Fundraising brought early gifts of money not just from the Scottish capital, but from as far away as St. Petersburg, where Scott was much admired. Eventually, on the afternoon of Saturday, August 16, 1840, more than 3,000 people (each of whom received a special commemorative medal) attended the laying of the foundation stone in Princes Street Gardens. Even the mason's trowel, specially made for the ceremony, was inscribed "in honour of The Immortal Scott." With civic pomp, a glass jar containing such items as a copy of the day's *Scotsman* newspaper and "Plans of the City and County of Edinburgh" was buried solemnly in the foundations, though the Edinburgh Tee-total Band, stationed on a lower slope at the centre of the Gardens, discomfited the Lord Provost when it commenced playing in the middle of his long speech celebrating Scott, "genuine patriotism, . . . high morality and virtue."

Founded on rock sixteen metres below ground level, the 200-foot-high monument was opened six years later. Perfecting it took longer, and small-scale statues were still being added as late as 1882. It incorporates more than fifty characters (mainly fictional) who appear in Scott's work, and at its base sits Sir Walter himself, carved from a thirty-ton block of Carrara marble by Sir John Steell, whose similarly solemn marble Queen Victoria was hoisted atop the Royal Scottish Academy in 1844. A dog lover as well as a writer, Scott is accompanied by his lanky deerhound, Maida.

The Scott monument surpassed James Craig's great Stirlingshire obelisk to George Buchanan as Scotland's most noble literary memorial, and is said to be the world's largest literary monument. Its 1840s construction was pictured by pioneering photographers D. O. Hill and Robert Adamson, who recorded the masons crowbarring sculpted sections of the carved pale sandstone into place, and working in their nearby Princes Street sheds. The resulting memorial was and is a triumph, but its making involved tragedy. As they worked the sandstone, the masons inhaled its dust. The most famous of them, Hugh Miller, wrote that "few of our Edinburgh stone-cutters pass their fortieth year unscathed, and not one out of every fifty of their number ever reaches his forty-fifth year." Before the great structure had reached its full height, and not long after he was photographed by Hill and Adamson sitting astride an unfinished block of masonry, Kemp, the monument's designer, fell into a local canal and drowned. The last stone was formally placed near the sky-high pinnacle by his ten-year-old son, Thomas.

Visitors who climb the Scott Monument's 287 steps are rewarded with wonderful views of the city, but the ascent is not for the claustrophobic. If you are tall, some of the monument's lintels are disconcertingly low, while descending from the top of its narrow spiral staircase feels like squeezing yourself awkwardly into an antique Gothic tube. Four circular viewing galleries are sited at different levels. The impressive Edinburgh City Art Centre collection in Market Street includes Joseph Woodfall Ebsworth's panoramic watercolours showing vistas to the north, south, east, and west from the top of the monument in the mid-1840s, the pale sandstone of Edinburgh's new buildings gleaming in the sun. Yet as soon as the monument was erected, railway lines were cut into the base of Princes Street Gardens, and smoke from coal-fired trains, along with intensifying Victorian smog, gradually blackened many structures, including the monument itself. Its sandstone contains a residue of shale-oil, which binds with soot and atmospheric pollution. Removing the dirt damages the surface of the stone, which then

17. This photograph from the 1840s shows masons at work on carvings to be added to the Scott Monument. The picture was taken by the pioneering photographers Robert Adamson and David Octavius Hill, whose studio was for a time in Rock House on Calton Hill.

deteriorates badly. That is why, though repairs using Binny sandstone from the original West Lothian quarry were made in the late twentieth century, plans to clean the substantially blackened monument were soon abandoned. Today, a little patchy in its discolouration, the Scott Monument looks even more louringly Gothic than its architect originally intended.

No nearby monument contrasts with it more completely than the small, low, pale stone set in a grove of slim silver birches in West Princes Street Gardens. Commissioned in 1987, this little memorial reads simply: A MAN OF LETTERS. It is dated 1850–1894, and is carved with three letters— *R, L,* and *S*—the initials of Robert Louis Stevenson. Nowadays, far more people in Scotland and elsewhere know Stevenson's work than Scott's. The witty, elegant, and modest RLS tribute is characteristic of the work of its designer, the poet, artist, and gardener Ian Hamilton Finlay (1925–2006), a unique figure in twentieth-century Scottish cultural life whose own sculpture garden at Stonypath, south of Edinburgh, is now a national treasure.

Other monuments in the Gardens include the Ross Fountain, a gilded Parisian celebration of female nudity. Purchased by Edinburgh gun maker Daniel Ross in the mid-nineteenth century, it was condemned by local kirk minister Dean Ramsay (himself later memorialized nearby) as "grossly indecent . . . disgusting . . . and disgraceful to the City"; more recently, the New Town wit Sara Lodge has called it "an ashtray with acromegaly." Among the Gardens' war memorials, the most noticeable is an equestrian bronze of a soldier in the Royal Scots Greys. Wearing his tall bearskin hat and mounted on his horse, Polly, this figure was sculpted by Birnie Rhind in the early twentieth century to commemorate the dead of the Second Boer War. Of special interest to North American visitors may be the Scottish-American War Memorial, a little west of the Royal Scots Greys monument. Featuring a stone frieze of marching soldiers and a larger sculpted figure of a kilted warrior with his eyes on Edinburgh Castle, it carries the inscription "The Call—1914—A Tribute from Men and Women of Scottish Blood and Sympathies in the United States of America to Scotland." This is followed by an Old Testament quotation from Judges 5:18—"A people that jeoparded their lives unto the death in the high places of the field."

Scottish losses on World War I battlefields were disproportionately high. Evoking the late-medieval battle of Flodden, in which a Scottish king and his nobility were slaughtered, one speaker at the inauguration of the Scottish American Association in 1919 asked, "What was Flodden for Edinburgh, compared with the years 1914 to 1919?" Killed at Cambrai in 1917 fighting for the 4th Seaforths, the poet Ewart Alan Mackintosh is author of the verses quoted on the Scottish American War Memorial's frieze. Its sculptor, Robert Tait McKenzie, was born in Ontario of Scottish parents in 1867 and taught at the University of Pennsylvania. He served in the Royal Army Medical Corps during World War I, and works by him are to be found in Ottawa, Cambridge (England), and Washington; in the collection of the Metropolitan Museum, New York; and in the Harvard Art Museums.

When McKenzie died in 1938, his wish was for his heart to be transported from the United States to Edinburgh, for burial in front of the memorial he had designed. No sooner had this encased human organ been brought for interment than Edinburgh Corporation explained that, under existing regulations, it was not in their power to grant his wish. His heart was buried nearby in the churchyard of St. Cuthbert's, a few days before the annual service at the Scottish American War Memorial in September 1938. The following year's commemoration was cancelled because of the outbreak of World War II, and before long, air-raid shelters were dug in the upper levels of the Gardens. Sandbags placed around the Scottish American Memorial were removed in 1942 to mark America's entry into the war. Four years later, General Dwight Eisenhower laid a wreath at this site while two kilted pipers played a lament. He praised Scotland's fierce sense of democracy: "While I cannot claim to be of Scottish blood, I am certainly in that other category—of Scottish sympathies."

Though time brings its ironies and reversals to Edinburgh, as it does everywhere else, in Princes Street Gardens it is measured with particular beauty. One of the best-loved features of the West Gardens, just at the corner of Princes Street and the Mound, is the Floral Clock. First laid out by the "enterprising and energetic City Gardener" John McHattie in 1903 (when it had only an hour hand), it was developed further the following year when, thoughtfully, a minute hand was added. The clock face is regularly planted out with bright flowers. The hands, also covered in flowers, are turned by a mechanism concealed in the base of the nearby statue of Allan Ramsay; an eighteenth-century poet with a fine sense of humour, he probably would not have minded.

The Floral Clock was the first of its design in the world, and has been widely imitated. In summer, children and adults crowd the surrounding balustrade waiting for the little mechanical bird that appears from below Ramsay's statue every quarter of an hour. Now powered by electricity, the clock is replanted every year with up to 35,000 plants; each new design celebrates an anniversary or notable event, and this botanical timepiece has long since become as loved an Edinburgh institution as the Botanic Gardens or the Castle. The city's infants peer through the stone balustrade at the clock's spring blooms; adults glance at it as they pass down the steps on their way into the Gardens to eat lunch in the June sunshine, to read, or to kiss; the old bring their grandchildren, pointing towards the spot where the bird will soon reappear.

To the east, Princes Street Gardens look towards the great clock tower of the Balmoral Hotel, where J. K. Rowling completed her Harry Potter series of novels; to the west, they extend towards St. Cuthbert's Church, and wind round the edge of the Castle Rock in the direction of Edinburgh's grandest concert venue, the circular Beaux Arts–style Usher Hall on Lothian Road. Built just before World War I thanks to a donation from a distiller, this structure was extended in the early twenty-first century with the addition of a sleek, free-standing glass wing, described by filmmaker and cultural critic Murray Grigor as a "herniated tumour." The Usher Hall is now part of a designated cultural quarter that comprises the Royal Lyceum and Traverse theatres, the Edinburgh Filmhouse (the city's leading arts cinema), Festival Square, and the nearby Edinburgh International Conference Centre.

More visually prominent cultural landmarks are the two neoclassical temples of art at the foot of the Mound between the East and West Gardens. Both were designed by William Playfair; erected decades apart, they form a satisfyingly integrated scheme. First to be constructed (beginning in 1822) was the Greek Doric building now known as the Royal Scottish Academy, but originally called the Royal Institution. It was commissioned by the Board of Manufactures and Fisheries to house the Royal Society of Edinburgh, the Institution for the Encouragement of the Fine Arts, and the Society of Antiquaries. Edinburgh's Royal Society, which (unlike the Royal Society of London) encompasses the arts as well as the sciences, was founded, like the Society of Antiquaries, in the late eighteenth century. Its Fellows have included Walter Scott, Scottish physicist James Clerk Maxwell, and (more recently) Edinburgh's most famous present-day resident, the aforementioned J. K. Rowling; it now occupies premises in George Street, close to Clerk Maxwell's big twenty-first-century bronze statue. Over the years, all of the Princes Street Royal Institution's initial occupants moved elsewhere, and, from 1835 onwards, the artists of the Royal Scottish Academy began to make themselves at home.

Edinburgh's first artistic academy had a well-liked local poet as one of its founders. Allan Ramsay—he who now presides over the Floral Clock—started the city's earliest circulating library on the eighteenth-century High Street. A staunch enthusiast for Scottish culture in many forms, Ramsay built himself the distinctive octagonal house nicknamed the "Goose Pie" near the Castle, in what is now Ramsay Gardens. In Edinburgh he collected verse for *The Ever Green*—his 1724 anthology of "Scots Poems, Wrote by the

Ingenious before 1600"—whose title was later borrowed by the polymath Patrick Geddes. Sometimes high-toned, Ramsay's own verse could also celebrate Edinburgh lowlife: Old Town brothel madam Lucky Spence advises each of her hookers to wait until the client is "asleep, then dive and catch / His ready cash." Ramsay's son, also Allan, was, at his best, one of the shrewdest and most sympathetic painters of women that Britain has produced. He portrayed men, too, drawing his bulbous-nosed father wearing a soft hat in 1729, the year the older man signed a document to establish the Academy of St. Luke in Edinburgh, for the "encouragement of these excellent arts of Painting, Sculpture and Architecture &c and the Improvement of the Students."

The economic consequences of the Unions of 1603 and 1707 encouraged several of Scotland's finest painters—including the younger Allan Ramsay, and that assured painter of the Scots poor and English high society Sir David Wilkie—to move to London. Scotland's greatest portraitist, Henry Raeburn, however, remained ensconced in Edinburgh, where he had been an orphan since early childhood. There he painted Enlightenment luminaries such as thirty-eight-year-old Walter Scott, po-faced James Hutton, and the Reverend Professor Hugh Blair, but also others such as David Hunter of Blackness and kilted Colonel Alastair Macdonell, who are remembered now principally because Raeburn so stylishly depicted them. Like the National Gallery of Scotland's famous poised, black-coated figure of the skating minister, the Reverend Robert Walker, Raeburn's Hunter and Macdonell are hatted. This artist loved to paint such figures, the brim of the hat casting its shadow on the sitter's forehead, heightening the brightness of eyes and face. Raeburn's handling of oil paint was as masterly as his psychology. In the National Gallery of Art in Washington, Scottish sunlight catches the white bonnet of Miss Wedderburn, listening to her niece Betty Johnstone chatting as the young woman's uncle, John Johnstone of Alva, smiles slightly, his balding head—surprisingly hatless—glowing like a moon. Though the portrait of the young Margaret Macdonald in the National Gallery of Scotland is strikingly voluptuous, Raeburn often liked men and women with older, slightly potato-shaped faces that communicate immemorial sagacity.

A canny businessman as well as an artist, Raeburn was central to the founding of a Scottish exhibition society which, in 1826, led to the establishing of the Royal Scottish Academy, heir to the Academy of St. Luke. Thanks in part to the guidance of the artist, photographer, and administrator David Octavius Hill—the RSA's famous, long-serving nineteenth-century secretary—the academy was flourishing when it moved into its new residence at the foot of the Mound. The building, topped by a sculpture of Queen Victoria, continues to be its home. Its artistic and financial fortunes have fluctuated over the years, and some (not least in Glasgow) have found it an over-exclusive club. In 1971, when there were just twenty-nine academicians and attitudes were a little different, artists who showed their work at the RSA's Festival Exhibition still published their private addresses in the exhibition catalogue. Sir William MacTaggart, the past president, had the swankiest address (4 Drummond Place in the New Town), and you could buy a picture by Sir William Gillies, one of the modern masters of Scottish landscape art, for as little as £40. Today the academy stages shows of its members' work and hosts international exhibitions during the Edinburgh Festival. Its prices have gone up.

Behind the RSA, built in an impressively austere neoclassical style, which saved money and led to æsthetic clarity, stands the National Gallery of Scotland. Its high-ceilinged spaces house pre-twentieth-century splendours; more recent artwork in Edinburgh is held at the Scottish National Gallery of Modern Art, the Dean Gallery (sometimes now called the "Modern Two"), the Scottish National Portrait Gallery, the Edinburgh City Art Centre, and elsewhere. Finished by the Victorians in 1854, the National Gallery gained a subtly integrated glass-fronted underground extension in the early twenty-first century. Called the Weston Link, this connects the Gallery with the Royal Scottish Academy and affords pleasant views along East Princes Street Gardens. The gallery's treasures now include Titians, El Grecos, Poussins, Rembrandts; a splendid group of French Impressionist pictures by Monet, Van Gogh, Gauguin, Degas, Pissarro, and others; as well as what has become the gallery's signature piece, the aforementioned skating minister. The painter Allan Ramsay's own collection of eighteenth-century French art was incorporated into its holdings, as was the very fine 1900 Vaughan bequest of Turner watercolours, sparingly exhibited (according to the donor's terms) each January—an Edinburgh treat.

One of the gallery's directors complained a little peevishly in 1911 that "unlike the Glasgow Gallery, which owes so much to the generosity of citizens, who have bequeathed, or gifted to it in their life-time, valuable collec-

18. The pillared National Gallery of Scotland (on the left) and the Royal Scottish Academy (on the right) are set below the white houses of Ramsay Gardens and the might of Edinburgh Castle. East Princes Street Gardens lie in the foreground, with West Princes Street Gardens beyond. Bordering the right-hand side of this photograph, Princes Street runs the full length of the gardens.

tions, . . . the National Gallery of Scotland has received no great numerical addition from any Scottish collector." It remains true that several of the National Gallery's greatest treasures are on loan from the Duke of Sutherland (one of his Titians, *Diana and Actæon,* was transferred to the gallery's ownership in the early twenty-first century for £50 million), but few visitors would complain that the collection is less than superb. A favourite picture, Titian's *Three Ages of Man,* foregrounds a clothed, garlanded girl suggestively fingering two flutes as her almost naked lover gazes besottedly into her eyes. On the right, some putti sleep and play; farther off, as the landscape expands towards the sea under blue yet clouding skies, an old man holds and contemplates two skulls. Edinburgh people are brought to stare at this as children, wander past it as courting couples, and gaze on its unchanged magnificence in their eighties, as they lean on their sticks. It is, despite its title, a painting without middle age.

The National Gallery's elegant, octagonal ground-floor rooms are a fine setting for Thomas Gainsborough's full-length masterpiece *The Honourable Mrs. Graham*. Standing tall and slender, her hair up and her silvery bodice matching a silvered hat from which extends a tall, equally silvery feather, she is all sophisticated verticality. Utterly different is El Greco's small, gaunt, hauntingly illumined head of Christ, *The Saviour of the World;* or, in another area of the gallery, Gauguin's dramatically geometric red-and-black vision of Jacob wrestling with an angel, *The Vision after the Sermon*. Yet visitors often look for Scottish landscapes—and although the Scottish art is somewhat uneasily displayed in the basement, the National Gallery holds a fine collection. Several of its treasures are among the best works of William Mac-Taggart (1835–1910; grandfather of the Sir William mentioned above), who lived in Edinburgh for a time but painted almost exclusively scenes from the west coast of Scotland, where his Gaelic-speaking ancestors had dwelt for generations. Independent of French Impressionism, he evolved a breathily atmospheric brushwork which caught the weather, colours, and grandeur of the Scottish coast. Three paintings in the National Gallery's collection illustrate his development: *Spring* (1864) is a Victorian genre piece with children, a daisy chain, a straw hat, and a summer field; *Machrihanish Bay* (1878) is all minimalist atmospheric laterals—brushstrokes denoting dark seaweed, translucent breaking waves, a streak of headland, sky, and masterfully little else; *The Storm* (1890) is passionately impasto paint, boldly wind-blown, full of spray, dark clouds, and a few tempest-tossed seagulls. In this last picture, the artist's children, whom he loved to sketch in oils and who were photographed capering at the tide's edge on MacTaggart's beloved west-coast beach at Machrihanish, have been almost entirely subsumed into the landscape. If wild Scottish weather could paint, it would paint like this.

Edinburgh holds great pictures, but there are few superlative pictures of Edinburgh. The best artist to attempt to capture it was an Englishman, J. M. W. Turner. An admirer of Walter Scott's works, Turner painted the classic outlook from Calton Hill and made the city look a little like a North British Rome, if not quite a northern Athens. A few years later, in 1825, Burns's friend Alexander Nasmyth also painted the view from Calton Hill, as well as *Edinburgh from Princes Street with the Royal Institution under Construction;* but his finely detailed panoramic topographies lack the release of genius. More modestly appealing are works by the short-lived William Crozier—his 1928 oil paintings of Princes Street Gardens and nearby streets under snow, some of which are in the collections of Edinburgh City Art Centre and the Scottish National Gallery of Modern Art. For a photographic overview, nothing matches the ærial view of Edinburgh taken by ex–World War I reconnaissance photographer Alfred G. Buckham. Snapped around 1920, this image is held in the collections of the National Galleries of Scotland. Seen from an unusual northwesterly angle, the Castle on its dark rock dominates the foreground, while smog or fog encircles Arthur's Seat beyond the city streets. The National Gallery itself is clearly discernible, its great westerly stone pillars smaller than matchsticks, while high above in a dramatic sky circles an early Royal Air Force biplane.

If Scotland's landscape paintings are sometimes uneasily displayed in Edinburgh, and are distributed across the city's galleries, then portraits of the nation's great and good are splendidly exhibited and mainly concentrated in one remarkable site. Ideas for a national collection of Scottish portraiture had been discussed as early as 1778, but more than a hundred years passed before John Ritchie Findlay, proprietor of the *Scotsman,* wrote a confidential letter to Sir William Fettes Douglas on December 7, 1882, arguing "that no modern country of like limited area and population has produced so many men of far more than local eminence in literature, science, art, and arms; yet Scotland has no National Portrait Gallery." Findlay pledged to fund one, provided that others came up with matching cash.

He wrote his letter before the Home Rule controversy of 1886, when the *Scotsman,* founded by his great-uncle and originally a radical and Liberal newspaper, moved to the staunchly British Unionist line it still maintains. The establishment of the Portrait Gallery in the New Town's Queen Street was bound up with debates over whether the Scots and Irish should be allowed by the Westminster Parliament to have Home Rule. Championing "our national history," Findlay wanted this visual articulation of heritage to stand among what he termed (misquoting Robert Burns at the building's opening on July 14, 1889) "Edina's palaces and towers." Even the newspaper he owned complained the next day that "Scotland has been neglected, and is at this moment neglected, by the Imperial [Westminster] Government." It denounced Scottish politicians' refusal to focus on the arts; but at the same time, condemning those politicians' "grievances [as] more or less imaginary," it implied that agitation for Home Rule was foolish. In conception and design, the Scottish National Portrait Gallery is a Victorian assertion of national identity; its origins are also meshed with aims to foreground Scotland as a principally cultural, rather than political, entity—part of a tendency in British Unionism to use Scottish culture as a safety valve to release or rechannel energies that might otherwise find expression in desires for Home Rule or independence.

Complexly political, and refurbished in the early twenty-first century during the tenure of Scotland's first ever pro-independence government, the gallery is quirkily magnificent. Its collections were built up with energy by its comparatively young first director, John Miller Gray. Having written about its eye-catching assembly of white vitreous paste cameos of Scottish Enlightenment luminaries made by James Tassie, Gray died of a brain hæmorrhage before his forty-fourth birthday, leaving almost all of the money he possessed to purchase more portraits for the gallery. The building's architect, Robert Rowand Anderson (who had already designed Mount Stuart, a sumptuous west-coast island palace for the eccentric Marquis of Bute), described his new creation as built in "the Secular Gothic of the latter half of the thirteenth century, a style that lends itself readily to the style of the building, and secures the greatest amount of light to those rooms that must be lighted from the side only." Anderson's red-sandstone Portrait Gallery seems to make architectural homages to the Doge's Palace in Venice, to the Gothic residences of the medieval French hill-town of Cordes-sur-Ciel (which Anderson had sketched), and to other alluring structures on the Continent.

Yet nothing could be more Scottish than the fresco friezes of Caledonian notables high above the building's entrance hall. They were painted in the years 1897–1900 by the popular English-born, Edinburgh-educated artist William Brassey Hole, whose sundry other works included canine illustrations for *The Dandie Dinmont Terrier* (1885) and etchings of Edinburgh University professors. As the visitor looks up, Hole's gloriously crowded procession extends north, south, east, and west round all the walls. It features everyone from Tacitus (Roman author of the first book to pay significant attention Scotland) to Sir David Brewster, inventor of the kaleidoscope. Nearly every figure is Scottish, and, unlike the vast job-lot of kings at the Palace of Holyroodhouse, almost all actually existed. Hole has done his best to include several women among his predominantly male panoply. One is Flora Macdonald, who famously rowed Bonnie Prince Charlie to safety as he fled from British redcoat troops; another, kind-faced in her brown head-

19. William Brassey Hole's frieze of illustrious Scots covers the walls high above the entrance hall of the Scottish National Portrait Gallery in Queen Street. Designed by Robert Rowand Anderson and opened in 1889, the "Secular Gothic" building is elaborate, luminous, and quirky.

scarf, and just visible over the left shoulder of her red-bearded, helmeted, dirk-clutching husband, is the eleventh-century queen Gruach, wife of Macbeth.

For anyone interested in Scotland, the Scottish National Portrait Gallery is a must-see. From its earliest days, its most-discussed paintings have been those depicting Robert Burns. His friend Alexander Nasmyth painted a portrait of him as a confident outsider in 1787, soon after Burns had first come to visit Edinburgh. It was immediately engraved as the frontispiece to the Edinburgh edition of Burns's *Poems, Chiefly in the Scottish Dialect,* so that, as its subject joked, "I will appear in my book looking, like other fools, to my title page." Nasmyth's other, full-length portrait of Burns (also in the Portrait Gallery) was painted decades after the poet's death. It shows him robust in knee-high boots and, as a contemporary pointed out, "very tight buckskin breeches." Nasmyth's farmer-bard is wearing what looks like a cowboy hat.

Here in this splendidly lit art museum are the famous folk of Scotland, many linked to Edinburgh, some caught in less familiar poses. Though now regarded as an idealized female figure personifying the spirit of France, Ponce Jacquio's delicately regal bust of a young woman was long thought to depict the eighteen-year-old Mary Queen of Scots. It dates from around 1560, shortly before the poet-queen's first husband, the French dauphin, died, and around the time that she expressed her "hard pain" in a French poem describing how her brightest day had darkened: "Et n'est rien si exquis,/Qui de moy soit requis" ("And there is no fine thing/That I now desire").

Very different is Hugh Douglas Hamilton's eighteenth-century portrait of Mary's Stuart descendant Bonnie Prince Charlie: an aging, alcoholic exile with bags under his eyes, he contemplates loss of his throne, his country, his wife, and his mistress. Iconic images of David Hume (by Allan Ramsay), Walter Scott (by Raeburn, whose big-windowed studio was just down the road at 32 York Place), of Byron (by Kentucky's William West), and of J. M. Barrie, author of *Peter Pan* (a stunningly bleak oil by William Nicholson) are among the collection's highlights. You can see dour, bookish Thomas Carlyle trying to keep warm indoors in his hat, and leggily elegant Muriel Spark fiddling with her formidable glasses. Traditionally, it is the paintings which have attracted visitors—but more recently and deservedly, the photography collection has achieved greater prominence. This enormous hoard, which deserves its own museum, includes what is by far the world's finest collection of Hill and Adamson calotypes, most taken in Edinburgh in the 1840s, as well as much more recent photographic portraits, such as experimental works by Calum Colvin.

The Scottish National Portrait Gallery in Queen Street is at the heart of New Town life, and emblematizes Edinburgh's—and Scotland's—pride in its past. It is also a Gothic anomaly surrounded by a masterpiece of resolutely neoclassical Georgian town planning—the finest such townscape on earth. The neighbouring streets are laid out in a grid plan of almost Glaswegian regularity, very different from the Old Town's crowded topography. Now regarded as a great Enlightenment project, the New Town was made possible by the feudal system. An arrangement for "feuing" land, used in Scotland for centuries, allowed a landowner to get money ("feu duty") for his ground, yet keep control over what would be built on it. As A. J. Youngson explains in his second (1988) edition of *The Making of Classical Edin-*

burgh, this meant "Scots landowners could plan large areas in a unified way without having to pay for the development themselves; and this made coherent planning easier." While Edinburgh's New Town expanded, strict conditions were laid down about such matters as the height of buildings, encouraging both architectural regularity and pleasantly Romantic scenic vistas.

The original New Town was planned by an avid young reader of poetry named James Craig, though his plans were much modified. Craig was apprenticed as an Edinburgh mason in the year of Robert Burns's birth, and a portrait of this dog-loving town planner is part of the Portrait Gallery's collection. In 1766, at the age of twenty-seven, Craig won the gold medal in a competition to design a "New Edinburgh." His plan, which may originally have involved streets laid out in the pattern of a Union Jack, was clearly political. The Unionist Craig soon dedicated it to the king as a scheme for "His ancient CAPITAL of NORTH BRITAIN"—as Scots eager to be seen as Unionists often termed their country. The effort involved in perfecting his designs at his drawing board made Craig ill. Unfortunately, for all that the New Town development progressed successfully, winning admiration from some, its original planner struggled to secure further work: "In a solitary walk last night . . . I have had much leisure indeed to ponder the various turns of fortune, which so often chequer human life," he wrote in 1782. After pawning his gold medal, he died insolvent at the age of fifty-one in 1795, a year before Burns, and was remembered by his obituarist in the *Scots Register* as "unfortunate."

Today's principal streets and squares between Princes Street and Queen Street follow Craig's layout, but no individual New Town building by him survives. His neatly symmetrical Grecian Physicians' Hall in George Street was demolished in 1844, and nowadays the only extant structures in Edinburgh designed by him are the 1780 gateway to Leith Fort in North Fort Street, and the Observatory House on Calton Hill. Robert Adam advised Craig on the latter, but it is as much Gothic as neoclassical. Nineteenth-century critics such as John Ruskin were snooty about Craig's regimented New Town; R. L. Stevenson, who grew up there, defended its "draughty parallelograms," helping to bring about a change in attitude. Today the whole area is regarded as a gem of town planning.

It is in part literary in inspiration. Craig was obsessively proud to be related to the early eighteenth-century Scottish poet James Thomson, whose long poem *The Seasons* helped to foster a taste for the picturesque and for wild weather. Craig's surviving 1767 plans quote several lines from the fifth part of Thomson's "Liberty," a work attuned to ideas of post-Union Britishness and improvement. The poetry hymns "august . . . public works" that include "stately Streets," "Temples," and "Squares that Court the breeze," along with "Long Canals" and a sense of "the encircling Main." Craig's New Town was built without the long canal he planned for the foot of Princes Street Gardens, but the breezy urban squares, streets, and "temples" do give glimpses of the Firth of Forth, and so offer a refreshing sense of "the encircling Main." Schooled by the poetry of Thomson (author of "Rule, Britannia," and praiser of landscape views), Craig had a taste for what he later termed "picturesque and elegant" scenery. At the king's command, he changed his original street names to make them less local to Edinburgh and even more regally British.

If the New Town articulated British Unionist politics, it also spoke of the politics of class. In the decades after the parliamentary Union of 1707, the Royal Mile gradually began to rot. Professional men continued to work near the parliament-less Parliament buildings, but generally aspired to reside somewhere markedly less smelly. At first, some of them moved southwards to newly built residences. As early as the 1730s, Argyle Square had been laid out south of the Old Town, followed by Brown Square in the 1760s. Both were demolished in the nineteenth century, but part of their grander cousin George Square survives close by. These squares south of the Castle were projects designed to allow professionals to live in fresh, neoclassical houses close to their work in the Old Town, yet free of its malodorous aspects. Still, if the academic rhetorician Hugh Blair lived in Argyle Square, and Walter Scott grew up at 25 George Square, Edinburgh's future lay northwards. Soon the New Town, where the adult Scott lived in Castle Street, took over as the destination of choice for Edinburgh's ambitious professionals.

Though earlier generations had considered building to the north, a turning point was the 1752 publication of Lord Minto's *Proposals for Carrying on Certain Public Works in the City of Edinburgh*, which looked to the great example of London and a vision of a "UNITED BRITAIN" in planning a "new town" principally for "People of fortune, and of a certain rank." A few years before Craig won his gold medal, Edinburgh's ambitious Lord Provost George Drummond gazed northwards out of an Old Town window and remarked to his younger acquaintance Thomas Somerville: "Look at these fields . . .; you, Mr. Somerville, are a young man, and may probably live, though I will not, to see all these fields covered with houses, forming a splendid and magnificent city."

Part of the New Town's splendour and magnificence depended on its being planned for the well-off. Polite shopkeepers, and even the occasional genteel business (such as Isbister's Ladies' Straw Hat Manufactory), moved in; servants' quarters were provided in smaller, lower mews terraces where stables were built behind the principal roads. But the prevailing tone of these streets, which expanded northwards after the French Revolution and Napoleonic Wars, was resolutely that of the North British upper middle class. By 1832, it was being pointed out to the British Parliament's sanitation enquiry that although the New Town had Christian philanthropic societies "for the conversion of the Jews and the negroes, and other similar purposes," nevertheless "there exists not one for the far more necessary and desirable object of gradually cleansing out the wretched dens of the Old Town." The smelly, voteless poor were left to multiply in their "miserable habitations," where they experienced the horrors of murderers Burke and Hare. At a safe distance, just across Princes Street Gardens—and soon, like the rest of polite Europe and America, captivated by the splendidly costumed feudal fictions of Walter Scott—Edinburgh's feu-duty-paying, prosperous, and enfranchised middle classes held dinner parties in their elegant apartments in the New Town's salubrious streets.

As part of Craig's vision of British Unionism, a square named after Scotland's patron saint, Andrew, was to be laid out at the eastern edge of the New Town, counterbalanced by a further square named after George, patron saint of England, to the west. Neat political complementarity of this sort does survive in today's New Town, where two parallel streets, Rose Street and Thistle Street, are named after the national flowers of England and Scotland, respectively; but Craig's planned St. George's Square was renamed Charlotte Square (after the British queen) when it began to be built in 1792. The architect of this square's grand buildings was Robert Adam, a Scot who once complained, as his ambitious Unionist countrymen often did, that "Scotland is but a narrow place," claiming he needed "a greater a more extensive and more honourable scene I mean an English life." Adam is buried in Westminster Abbey, and designed great houses for English aristocrats; yet his finest public buildings are in an Edinburgh he never quite appreciated to the full. Though modified during construction, his vast, domed Register House still stands on the New Town side of North Bridge, where it was erected around 1774 to preserve the ancient manuscript records of Scotland from being eaten by the Old Town's "ratts, mice and other vermine." In the 1790s, Adam was also responsible for designing the city's new Bridewell Prison, part of a complex of buildings with large yards, low on Calton Hill, that included the "fellons' jail" and the "debtors' jail." Even as Adam was accommodating these felons, he was also redesigning Edinburgh University. Impressive, but just a little gaol-like, it looms round a yard of its own just south of the Old Town.

Charlotte Square, though, is Edinburgh's most splendid and best-known Adam design. It is neither square, nor exclusively Adam's work. Like Craig and other architects, Adam produced grand plans for large swathes of Edinburgh (including the Old Town), but the plans were never used. For Charlotte Square, he was asked by the Town Council to design house frontages in considerable detail, to encourage uniform planning, and to submit plans for a church. Craig, when he had outlined his New Town, had envisaged a place of worship at the square's western side. True to the spirit of the 1752 New Town *Proposals* and a wish at that time "To grace *EDINA* with majestic Domes," Adam proposed a great domed Grecian-temple kirk for Charlotte Square. It looked a bit like a shortened version of his Register House, but was to be adorned with statues of graceful, arm-swinging, terpsichorean lasses in long flowing skirts. Perhaps predictably, the kirk-dominated Town Council later substituted a cheaper, plainer, and wholly un-terpsichorean domed design by Robert Reid. Reid also planned the layout of New Town roads north of Queen Street, but most of the rest of Charlotte Square remains Adam's. His sense of elegant magnificence is clear in the high, columned frontage of Number 6, now called Bute House and used in the early twenty-first century as the official residence of the First Minister of Scotland. The proportioning of Charlotte Square, with its large central octagonal lawn and high kerbs incorporating mounting blocks for carriage passengers, is imposing. So are some of the grand interiors. The drawing room in Bute House has a delicately plastered ceiling; its fireplace is decorated below the mantelpiece with a Grecian reclining female nude. She looks as if she has been bound with seaweed.

20. Spacious Charlotte Square is surrounded by New Town houses designed by Robert Adam in 1791. To the west is Robert Reid's domed St. George's Church (later West Register House) of 1811. The Albert Memorial on the square's central lawn was unveiled in 1876. During the late summer of each year, the Edinburgh International Book Festival erects its many capacious tents on the grass.

Adam died the year after he designed Charlotte Square. It was several decades before all of its houses were completed and occupied. One of the first families to move in were the Grants, a well-off couple who had met in Glasgow. They lived at Number 5, and their daughter Elizabeth, born in the house in 1797, played with the children who lived on either side. She remembered shutting one of them in a cupboard and stealing his drum. Elizabeth fought with the red-jacketed boy next door at Number 6, son of the improver Sir John Sinclair, first president of the Board of Agriculture and initiator of the multivolume *Statistical Account of Scotland.* The red-jacketed boy's little sister, Catherine Sinclair, went on to write *Holiday House* (1839), one of the first works of modern children's fiction.

Lawyer Henry Cockburn, who lived at Number 14 from about 1816, once asked for peat (not "to be got easily here") to be sent to his house by coach. He remembered when north and west of Charlotte Square lay nothing but open fields: "I have stood in Queen Street, or the opening at the north-west corner of Charlotte Square, and listened to the ceaseless rural corn-craiks, nestling happily in the dewy grass." Cockburn liked New Town life, relishing "a glorious . . . Godlike booze . . . surrounded by Greek scenes, with two fireplaces." His house, like several others in the Square, now belongs to an investment fund linked to a Ukrainian property tycoon. Once the territory of Edinburgh's notables (some years after Field Marshal Douglas Haig, World War I commander, was born at Number 24, Victorian landscape artist William MacTaggart moved in), Charlotte Square was colonized by legal and financial firms in the twentieth century. Now most of these have left for more modern offices elsewhere.

Visitors who wish to see inside one of the original dwellings can enter Number 7. First occupied in 1796, this property is now a museum known as the "Georgian House," owned by the National Trust for Scotland. Though its interiors largely lack the ornate decorative plasterwork found in several grander properties in Charlotte Square, its chandeliered upstairs drawing room is where the Lamont family, the first inhabitants, danced the polonaise with their guests. They were looked after by six servants, but their home had been built without running water: a water barrel in the kitchen was replenished at a cost of a penny a day. John Lamont had his portrait painted by Raeburn, and his house, today beautifully furnished with period pieces and hung with paintings of luminaries such as Edinburgh lawyer and man of letters Henry Mackenzie (whose *Man of Feeling* was the young Robert Burns's favourite novel), transports locals and tourists alike back to late-Enlightenment Edinburgh. Just across the Square is Robert Reid's St. George's Kirk, while an elegant hotel occupies the southeast corner opposite. Many of Charlotte Square's other properties have been bought as long-term investments by trusts, said to be hoping to lure back financial firms. The people of Edinburgh live in streets nearby, but the grand Square, sometimes oddly deserted, is for much of the year a little icily set apart.

The exception is during the late-summer weeks of the Edinburgh International Book Festival, when Charlotte Square Gardens are given over to what is now the world's most jam-packed literary jamboree. Unlike the Frankfurt Book Fair, which is designed entirely for publishers and agents to do deals, Edinburgh's Book Festival is all about authors entertaining audiences. Throughout the event, Edinburgh folk and visitors throng the Square. Marquees are erected around the equestrian statue of Prince Albert (unveiled in the gardens by Queen Victoria in 1876); Victoria and Albert, lovers of Scotland and of books, might have been surprised but not unamused.

Developed since the 1980s by such directors as Jenny Brown, Faith Liddell, and Catherine Lockerbie, all of whom were influential in getting Edinburgh designated the world's first "City of Literature" by UNESCO, the Book Festival attracts writers from across the globe. Many of its events are sellouts. The town whose nineteenth-century literary entrepreneurs once published Walter Scott, George Eliot, Joseph Conrad, the *Edinburgh Review,* and *Blackwood's Magazine* may have lost most of its publishers, but it attracts more authors than ever. While the best-known among those who live in Edinburgh are writers of genre fiction such as J. K. Rowling, crime writer Ian Rankin, and popular novelist Alexander McCall Smith, the Book Festival brings poets, fiction writers, dramatists, biographers, and scientists from all parts of the planet. Tending to avoid celebrity hacks, the Festival's centre of gravity is spectacularly literary. Highlights have ranged from lectures and readings by Margaret Atwood, Seamus Heaney, and Harold Pinter to performances for children by the author of the *Harry Potter* novels and by Britain's Poet Laureate, Glasgow-born Carol Ann Duffy—surely the only Glaswegian ever to be credited with the words, "Edinburgh is my favourite city."

Arguably the Book Festival's tastiest event was a special supper held in 2000 in honour of the 250th birthday of Robert Fergusson. Newly commissioned poems were read by Scottish poets, and many "caller" (fresh) oysters were consumed in the spirit of Fergusson's lively celebration of local marine produce from Newhaven and the Firth of Forth:

> AULD REIKIE's sons blithe faces wear;
> September's merry month is near.
> That brings in Neptune's caller cheer,
>   New oysters fresh:
> The halesomest and nicest gear
>   O' fish or flesh.

Now so big that its hundreds of events have begun to spill out of the tented city erected annually in Charlotte Square Gardens, the Book Festival accommodates its visiting authors in nearby hotels. After their readings, they stride, stroll, or stagger through streets built on the fields where corncrakes sang hoarsely two centuries earlier. Farther down the hill are splendid residential roads like the circular Moray Place, laid out in 1822, and the smaller India Place, built on land owned by the eventually wealthy artist Raeburn; the beautiful Ann Street, just west of the Water of Leith, is said to be named after his wife.

Marriage to Ann made Raeburn wealthier, and from 1813 onwards he began to feu ground, creating a new, village-like development northwest of Charlotte Square. While most of the New Town is made up of tenements or apartment blocks, albeit ones far more genteel than the Old Town's tenements, Ann Street has lower Georgian houses with elegantly kept front gardens. Like so many of Edinburgh's roads, it is steeped in literary history. R. M. Ballantyne, author of *The Coral Island* and hero to his younger fellow townsman, the future author of *Treasure Island,* was born at Number 25. Robert Chambers, publisher and author of the world's first collection of urban folklore, the classic *Traditions of Edinburgh* (1824), lived for a few years at Number 28. *Traditions of Edinburgh* takes the Old Town as its focus; genteel Ann Street is a different milieu. To live in it is now beyond most people's means; to drift along it on a warm summer day is one of the free delights of Edinburgh.

Westwards and northwards, as the nineteenth century progressed, further suburbs were added. When the ailing Frédéric Chopin visited to play a recital in Queen Street in October 1848, he stayed not in the classical New Town but north of it, in Canonmills, at 10 Warriston Crescent, in those days the home of a Polish-born Edinburgh doctor. At the very foot of the New Town, close to where a tannery stopped the finest streets' prosperous progress, artisans of the 1860s moved into the eleven parallel roads of flatted cottages known as the "Colonies." One of these is named after the depressive writer and stonemason Hugh Miller, who had shot himself a few years earlier. In the nineteenth century, it was a long way in terms of social class from Charlotte Square to the Colonies, where carved emblems of tradesmen's tools adorn the keystones of some ground-floor windows. Today the literary descendants of writers like Robert Fergusson and the ill-starred Miller return each year with pens and laptops to re-occupy Charlotte Square.

When Robert Adam laid out the Square, it seemed a splendid terminus to development. Instead, the Square and nearby streets incited further construction. Around 1830, the celebrated Scottish engineer Thomas Telford had a great bridge designed to carry a road about a hundred feet above the

Water of Leith, allowing for more building on that river's northern side. Soon streets of houses ran northeastwards, but to the northwest green spaces remained, impressively punctuated by an architecture of youth and death. Youth predominated. Daniel Stewart's and Melville College, a Victorian stone fantasia on Elizabethan and Jacobean themes, is still a private school, but two other impressive educational establishments have since been overpowered by art. The Dean Orphanage, or "Orphan Hospital," designed by architect Thomas Hamilton in 1831–1833, is now known to locals as the Dean Gallery (though designated by its managers as the "Scottish National Gallery of Modern Art 2"); the plainer John Watson's School opposite is today the Scottish National Gallery of Modern Art. Alongside the former orphanage runs the Dean Cemetery, a moody necropolis under whose parkland lies artist and photographer David Octavius Hill, memorialized by a fine bronze bust sculpted by his wife, Amelia Paton, Scotland's leading woman artist of the nineteenth century; her bronze of David Livingstone stands in East Princes Street Gardens. Also in the Dean Cemetery, within easy shouting distance of the Victorian orphans, were laid to rest such Edinburgh worthies as memoirist Lord Cockburn, architect William Playfair, and *Edinburgh Review* editor Lord Francis Jeffrey.

Though nowadays this part of Edinburgh seems tranquil, its serenity was achieved at some cost. The dwellings of the poor in the original Dean Village were cleared away to make stables, and homes for servants of the well-off in Belgrave Mews. The name "Dean Village" was then superimposed on the originally medieval settlement of Water of Leith Village, with its mills and, later, its tannery. A rebuilt mill and granary can still be seen in the Dean Village, but many of its buildings are picturesquely Victorian. The alluring riverside hamlet, so close to the city centre, is dominated by the lofty Dean Bridge and, at the bridge's northern end, by the Victorian Holy Trinity Church, unobtrusively converted for a time, in the late twentieth century, into an electricity transformer station.

Modern technology also fills the former Dean Orphanage. Where once its separate corridors for boys and girls were thronged with small scampering humans, now the centre of the building is dominated by a vast robot-like welded steel sculpture, created in 1999. Twenty-seven feet tall, striding below a ceiling inlaid with resin reliefs from 1973 that look like designs for semiconductors, this sculpture depicts the Roman god Vulcan. Its maker was Edinburgh's most astounding modern artist, Sir Eduardo Paolozzi (1924–2005), who grew up in Leith and attended Edinburgh College of Art, before pursuing a career that took him to London, Paris, New York, Venice, and Munich. Paolozzi's achievements range from the redesigned riverfront in Cologne to mosaic decorations for London's Underground station at Tottenham Court Road. Yet, bequeathed by the man himself, the greatest concentration of his œuvre—from graphics and collages to monumental bronzes—is in Edinburgh.

If Scotland's capital is a Burke-and-Hare city haunted by gruesome memories of medical dissection, then some of Paolozzi's most arresting works—huge public bronzes such as *The Wealth of Nations* (outside the Royal Bank of Scotland's headquarters at Gogarburn, on the city's outskirts) or *Manuscript of Monte Cassino* (beside St. Mary's Roman Catholic Cathedral in Broughton Street)—look like assemblies of cut-up body parts, often spliced with mechanical or architectural elements. Proud of its historic Surgeons' Square, where cadavers were dissected, nineteenth-century Edinburgh was a centre not only for surgeons but also for phrenologists, who believed that the shape of the human skull gave indications of character. Frequently, Paolozzi's sculpted heads exhibit cuts and slicings. Darkly unsettling, his late, cyborg-like bronze figures—one upside down, designed in 1997 for Edinburgh University's King's Buildings site (which housed the Faculty of Science and Engineering and the Institute of Cell Biology)—look as if they are being tortured or ruthlessly modified.

Owing debts, perhaps, to Italian Futurism, this relentlessly intellectual sculptor, who grew up eager for popular comic books, model æroplane kits, and American films, was obsessed with the machine age. Paolozzi was a child in an era when Edinburgh boys were preoccupied with mechanical construction; his near-contemporary Muriel Spark remembered her older schoolboy brother making a model of the Forth Railway Bridge with his Meccano set. Many of Paolozzi's collages can be aligned with the Pop Art movement, and with the poetry of his Glaswegian contemporary Edwin Morgan; but the sculptor was fascinated, too, by the grimmer aspects of technology. There can be humour in some of his work, which is preoccupied with bunk, rubbish, computers, and recycling, but there is often a sense of brutality. Familiar with Fascist ideology from an early age, he made or planned pieces with titles such as *War Games Revised*, *The Crucified Robot*, and *Why We Are in Vietnam*. In Paolozzi's sculptures, his "metallization of a dream" grew monumentally disturbing, featuring interrogations of male violence, incursions of technology into the organic (particularly the human form), and a wish to connect these with his early experience in Leith and Edinburgh. His creations and de-creations speak to and from a city fascinated by body modification, from the Enlightenment anatomy schools and Burke and Hare to cloning and that most famous ovine product of Edinburgh science, sad-eyed Dolly the Sheep.

Yet, for all the unsettling aspects of Paolozzi's work, the Dean Gallery, which has become his monument, also houses the Scottish capital's most child-beguiling interior. This is a re-creation of the Leith-born sculptor's studio: a marvellous clutter that includes an æroplane propeller, shelves of plaster heads, bags, musical instruments, a bunk bed, tools, charts, posters, books, a ladder, and pieces of unfinished sculpture. Here Paolozzi's sophisticated yet also small-boyish imagination seems caught forever. Though you cannot walk into the studio and pick things up, its sheer madcap array is unforgettable—a glimpse of a great artist's workshop. Children are always impressed by the vast striding figure of Vulcan, but the studio room with its worktable's invitation to sculpt and its bunk bed's prompt to dream is a reminder that Paolozzi's blacksmith Vulcan is both a "metallization" of the sculptor as colossal maimed imagineer, and, more straightforwardly, a cumbersome, jumbo-size toy.

It may not be entirely contrary to the sometimes transgressive spirit of this sculptor's work if you contribute to a recent tradition as you leave his museum. Outside, on the path that leads towards the Scottish National Gallery of Modern Art across Belford Road, is Paolozzi's sculpture of Isaac Newton, grandly entitled *Master of the Universe*. This work, which dates from 1988–1989, is partnered by a variant now in Hong Kong. Each is subtly different, as is the later, larger figure of Newton in the courtyard of London's British Library. Deriving from an illustration by William Blake (who disliked Newton), the sculpture depicts the scientist, as Paolozzi put it, "crouched in a position reminiscent of Rodin's *Thinker*." While this may be true, there is also something beetle-like about the bent-double figure, whose back seems a plated carapace. If you put a bronze penny in the small space underneath Newton's downward-pointing finger, it transforms the monumental bronze thinker into a tramp bending awkwardly to pick up a minuscule coin. No

21. *Master of the Universe* is the title of this bronze sculpture of Isaac Newton by Eduardo Paolozzi (1924–2005), Edinburgh's greatest sculptor. This figure marks the approach to the Dean Gallery, one of the buildings of the Scottish National Gallery of Modern Art, which boasts a superlative Paolozzi collection.

doubt a Glaswegian started this modern tradition of subverting Edinburgh's Master of the Universe, but it is surely worth encouraging. From time to time, the coin is removed; so please replace it if you visit.

Beyond Newton, across the parklands, is the Scottish National Gallery of Modern Art (now sometimes termed "Modern Art One"). First founded in 1960 in a different building, since the mid-1980s the twentieth- and twenty-first-century collection has occupied what was once a school endowed for the fatherless sons of the city's professional classes. The plain interior of its building, designed in Greek Doric style by William Burn in 1825, makes a handsome exhibition space. Among the museum's treasures—many of them undisplayed—are brightly coloured landscape paintings including those of the "Scottish Colourist" painters. Foremost among these artists were Samuel John Peploe (1871–1935), who went to school in Charlotte Square, Leith-born John Duncan Fergusson (1874–1961), Leslie Hunter (1879–1931), and Francis Campbell Boileau Cadell (1883–1937), who painted fashionable women in elegant New Town interiors. The Scottish capital took some time to develop a taste for the Colourists' work (arguably, there is a better hoard in Kirkcaldy), but it is now eagerly collected. These Francophile painters visited Paris, where they were influenced by Henri Matisse and André Derain. Though Derain's sunshine-exuding 1905 oil painting of the southern French village of Collioure was not purchased by the Gallery of Modern Art until 1973, local taste for such pictures was encouraged by the Colourists' example. A small selection of their canvases now holds its own among paintings by Matisse, Picasso, Léger, and other Continental masters.

Later twentieth-century Scottish painters, such as the now underrated abstract artist William Gear (who, encouraged by Paolozzi, exhibited alongside Jackson Pollock at the Betty Parsons Gallery in New York in 1948), W. G. Gillies (who taught at Edinburgh College of Art), and John Bellany (who once hung his vibrant expressionist oils on the railings near the Royal Scottish Academy in a public show countering the exhibition within), are also represented in this collection. Ranging from Oskar Kokoschka to Aristide Maillol, and Josef Beuys to Damien Hirst, it is a fine gathering of work. Among its brightest Scottish stars is Joan Eardley. This English-born artist's wild seascapes and northeast Scottish field scenes, where pollen has blown onto the canvas and been left there as part of the painterly act, are among the gallery's best-loved modern pictures, though recently some of her work has migrated to the halls of the Dean across the road. Running spectacularly downhill under a grey-skied, pre-decimal sixpence of a moon, Eardley's row of cottages in the northeast coastal village of Caterline affords a wintry half-rhyme with Derain's high-summer, orange-roofed cottages tilting down to Collioure's purply, South-of-France sea.

"The Vigorous Imagination," the most famous show held at the Scottish National Gallery of Modern Art, took place in 1987. It focused attention on a new generation of Scottish artists, most of them men and many from the Glasgow School of Art. Several went on to find international fame. Fife's David Mach (who had already built a Centurion tank out of books and a Parthenon out of car tyres) sculpted a room-sized, avalanche-like flow made out of glossy magazines; but most of the exhibitors were painters. Glaswegian Stephen Campbell, fresh from exhibiting in New York, showed enigmatic postmodern figurative compositions with ludic titles such as *English Landscape with a Disruptive Gene* or *Buildings Accusing the Architect of*

22. The modern "landform" by Charles Jencks, born in Baltimore in 1939 and long resident in Scotland, provides a flowing contrast to the Greek Doric architecture of a school designed in 1825 by William Burn. The school has been converted to form one of the buildings of the Scottish National Gallery of Modern Art.

Bad Design; Ken Currie and Peter Howson depicted powerful scenes of working-class Glasgow life, bringing heroic west-coast dossers (homeless people) into Edinburgh's politest parkland; Stephen Conroy delighted in beautifully executed compositions with dark-suited males; Calum Colvin made photographic collages, often involving elements of kitsch. Gwen Hardie, whose work had been acquired by the Metropolitan Museum in New York, exhibited large-scale studies of parts of the female body, such as clenched fingers; Kate Whiteford, yet another Glaswegian, showed work based on Celtic symbols, and in the same year made vast "land drawings" of a fish, a spiral, and concentric circles, cut into the earth on Calton Hill and filled with white marble chippings. Now joined by a younger generation of conceptual artists such as Glasgow's Douglas Gordon and Karla Black, a number of the exhibitors at "The Vigorous Imagination" are among the best-known figures in contemporary Scottish art.

Outside the gallery, part of the lawn has been laid out in a spectacular

and harmonious "landform" mound sculpted round a water feature. Designed by Charles Jencks, a Scottish-based maker of cosmological gardens,
its loops and terraces are calm and attractive. Such attention to imaginative
gardening is a nice link to the landscaping around the nearby Water of Leith,
where a succession of bronze male nudes by Anthony Gormley was installed
in 2010, and where, surrounded by birdsong, one can walk along a wooded
riverside path in the direction of the older sculptural form above St. Bernard's Well. There, in 1788, Alexander Nasmyth designed a small circular
Roman temple on the riverbank site of a medicinal spring. Inside was placed
a statue of Hygeia, goddess of hygiene and good health; the original was replaced by D. W. Stevenson's Victorian version in 1888. Sturdily curative
and feminine (though apparently with a broken nose), Hygeia still stands—
recently restored, under her cupola of diminutive stars—so different from
Paolozzi's Vulcan.

✣ FOUR ✣

Hill, Hwa-wu, and Port

Edinburgh's true acropolis is the Castle on its commanding rock. Yet in the Romantic era, when the city became known as "the Athens of the North," local visionaries seem to have thought two acropolises would be better than one. Soon after shipping the Parthenon Frieze from Athens to London, the Scottish nobleman Lord Elgin (he of the Marbles), along with Sir Walter Scott, Lord Cockburn, and other influential persons, came to the conclusion that what Edinburgh needed was a hilltop temple of its own. Their chosen site was Calton Hill, whose steep slopes dominate the view towards the east end of Princes Street. Here, a memorial to the dead of the Napoleonic Wars would be raised—"a restoration of the Parthenon." Planned to occupy much of the summit and to sit on a vast, pillared base runneled with its own catacombs, this crowning glory of the Scottish capital would be even grander than its Athenian precursor. Edinburgh being Edinburgh, it might also double as a kirk.

All went well until the money ran out. By 1829, twelve columns topped by an architrave had been erected. To this day, those columns are all that stands of the "National Monument," designed by William Playfair as "a splendid addition to the architecture of the [British] empire." It catches the eye, but more as a doomed Romantic fragment than a neoclassical triumph. Also in 1829, Thomas Hamilton's Scottish Greek Revival, Doric-columned Royal High School was completed at the foot of Calton Hill. Yet Playfair's unfinished Parthenon above it, that imposing might-have-been, remains dominant. In 1907, there were suggestions it might be completed to celebrate the bicentenary of the Act of Union between Scotland and England. In 2007, when a pro-independence Scottish Government came to power, nobody was suggesting that. Curiously, the partial Parthenon had been earmarked in 1908 as a potential site for a Scottish Parliament; and so, in the later twentieth century, had the Royal High School. Edinburgh took a

23. Among the buildings on Calton Hill (here viewed from the south) are the tall Nelson Monument with its "time ball," William Playfair's Parthenon-like National Monument, and, on the lower slopes, the Doric-columned Royal High School designed by Playfair's rival Thomas Hamilton in 1829.

long time to come to terms with the fact that its second acropolis (which some people had nicknamed "Edinburgh's disgrace") was destined to remain forever unfinished, succeeding as a magnificent mistake.

This unrealized Parthenon was neither the first nor the last classicizing monument in the Calton Hill area. The coalescing of Romanticism and Classicism in Edinburgh will be prominent in this chapter. In the Old Calton Burying Ground, Robert Adam's 1777 cylindrical monument to David Hume, the sky starkly visible through a circular aperture in its roof, takes its inspiration from the tomb of Theodoric at Ravenna. Higher on Calton Hill's slopes is the Robert Burns Monument, which Thomas Hamilton modeled on Athens's Choragic Monument of Lysicrates and which was built in 1830, just after construction of the would-be Parthenon stopped. Cheekily, in the following year Hamilton's neoclassical rival, William Playfair, took the same Athenian original as the template for *his* nearby monument to Burns's patron, Dugald Stewart, a professor at Edinburgh University and an Enlightenment philosopher. Building these neoclassical structures at the height of the Romantic era may seem odd to us, but terms such as "Scottish Enlightenment" (first used in 1900) and even "Romanticism" are later academic labels. Just as Scott, the mighty novelist of the High Romantic era, was very much a son of the Enlightenment, so what we term the Scottish Enlightenment was shot through—from James Craig's Rock House on Calton Hill onwards—with Gothic and Romantic dreams. Architecturally as well as in terms of literature and art, Enlightenment and Romantic forms in Edinburgh and elsewhere are not distinct but fused. The New Town was built to provide calmly neoclassical regularity, but also to enable residents to enjoy Romantic vistas of the Castle, Calton Hill, and the Firth of Forth. To stand on the summit of Calton Hill is to be surrounded by neoclassical fantasies, and to sense Edinburgh not just as "the Athens of the North" but as what Walter Scott called "mine own Romantic town."

Calton Hill can seem, too, a glorious architectural junkyard. The 1807 Nelson Monument, its tallest building, is a quirky Scottish tribute to the victor of Trafalgar whose most famous naval signal opened with the words "England expects." Rising six storeys above ground level, this slender, battlemented tower is surmounted by a "time ball," designed to be raised and lowered at noon as a signal to ships on the Forth. Not far off, the old City Observatory lies derelict. By night, Calton Hill can be dangerous; Ian Rankin, Edinburgh's most famous contemporary crime writer, sets one of his fictional murders there. By day, the Hill commands some of Edinburgh's finest views. Amateur and professional photographers follow artists such as Turner and Nasmyth, who chose it as their vantage point; after dark, it is distinctly wilder, and of late it has become a venue for the celebration of the ancient Celtic Mayday rites of Beltane. As part of this relatively recent reinvention—Edinburgh's wildest festival—hundreds of young folk, mostly students, dance around with flaming torches, wearing little more than body paint.

In the nineteenth century, Calton Hill boasted an observatory, a camera obscura, and marvels of optical science, and in the 1840s it was also briefly home to the most famous partnership in the history of photography. At Rock House, Edinburgh artist David Octavius Hill and Robert Adamson of St. Andrews set up their studio. Adamson was a chemist and engineer with a taste for Gothic and Romantic fiction; Hill knew no chemistry, but had a reputation as an artist. Many of their early photographs were associated with that mass walkout of kirk ministers in 1843 known as the Disruption. Refusing to be subject to the patronage of local aristocrats and landowners, those clergymen who gave up their homes and salaries rather than compromise their democratic principles were regarded as "modern martyrs." Adamson and Hill used the recent invention of "calotype" photography to document them in portraits. The two calotypists also photographed Edinburgh contemporaries, from Hugh Miller and anatomist Robert Knox to their own families and friends. Often beautifully composed, their pictures have been described as among the incunabula of photography.

If Adamson's St. Andrews was the first town in the English-speaking world to have its people, buildings, and natural environment thoroughly documented through the new medium, then the Edinburgh Calotype Club was the world's first photographic society. Adamson's early death in 1847 put an end to the partnership, though the Rock House studio was later taken over by photographer Thomas Annan, before he moved west to Glasgow. More than half a century later, some of Hill and Adamson's photographs were featured by Alfred Stieglitz in his influential journal *Camera Work*. These Scottish pictures of the fisherfolk of Newhaven near Leith, gunners at Edinburgh Castle, and memorials in the city's Greyfriars Churchyard became eminently collectible. Examples can be found in major museums, from the Getty in Los Angeles and the Metropolitan Museum in New York to the Scottish National Portrait Gallery and the extensive photographic collections of St. Andrews University Library.

While working at Rock House, Hill and Adamson photographed the erection of one of Edinburgh's most important monuments, the Political Martyrs' Memorial. Their picture shows a vast scaffolding surrounding the ninety-foot stone obelisk on its square plinth, whose foundation stone was laid in the Calton Hill Cemetery in 1844. Planned during the same period as the monument to the Tory Walter Scott, this very different memorial commemorates his political antagonists. It bears the names of five Scottish democratic republicans who had been jailed or transported abroad in the years after the French Revolution. One of them, Glasgow lawyer Thomas Muir, became Australia's first political prisoner. Muir's rhetorically forceful words, spoken at his trial in Edinburgh's law courts on August 30, 1793, are among the inscriptions in capital letters at the base of the monument: "I HAVE DEVOTED MYSELF TO THE CAUSE OF THE PEOPLE. IT IS A GOOD CAUSE—IT SHALL ULTIMATELY PREVAIL—IT SHALL FINALLY TRIUMPH."

In a late eighteenth-century Scotland, where monarchists and Unionists controlled all the channels of power, expressing sympathy for French Revolutionary liberté, egalité, and fraternité was dangerous. A republican sympathizer, Robert Burns feared he might share "Muir and Palmer's fate": transportation to the Australian prison colony of Botany Bay. Thomas Fyshe Palmer, William Skirving, Maurice Margarot, and Joseph Gerrald are the other radical "martyrs" this Calton Hill memorial commemorates. Skirving (said to have christened his son "Citizen" and to have lived on or close to the site of today's Scottish Parliament) spoke defiant words at his Edinburgh trial: "I know that what has been done these two days will be REJUDGED." These words, too, appear on the monument.

By the 1830s and 1840s, increasing pressures to democratize society meant that such men, condemned as criminals when "democracy" was a dirty word in Britain's corridors of power, might be celebrated by the Friends of Parliamentary Reform in Scotland and England. In the years leading up to the Chartist democratic demonstrations of 1848, this group organized the monument's construction. The *Scotsman* reported that a crowd estimated at 80,000 people had assembled on Bruntsfield Links in 1832 to greet the passing of the Parliamentary Reform Bill, which (to a relatively small degree) extended the right to vote. By 1837, when the radical *Tait's Edinburgh Magazine* ran a long review headed "Memoirs and Trials of the Political Martyrs of Scotland," a public meeting of the Reformers of Edinburgh was being told that the "political martyrs" of the 1790s were heroes: "The real offence committed by these unfortunate victims of judicial iniquity consisted in their having combined to obtain, by constitutional means, a Reform in the Representation of the People."

As pressure for a monument to these earlier victims of "rancorous Tory persecution" grew, money was raised, and by August 1844 the Complete Suffrage Association, only four hundred strong, processed in black clothes "through the Parliament Square (passing the courts where those patriots received their hard and unmerited sentences)" and down the High Street to Calton Hill. Recalling his days as an Edinburgh student during the martyrs' trials, the radical Scottish MP Joseph Hume complained that "we see monuments to their persecutors." He quoted Muir's courtroom speech, which mentioned Thomas Paine, and praised the "glorious cause" of "timely reform." Hume dedicated the new, radical monument to "the cause of public liberty," and the public cheered. Three thousand people on Calton Hill heard the Presbyterian minister Patrick Brewster, himself one of the recent Free Kirk Disruption "martyrs," maintain that "the Government which depended on an aristocracy never could stand."

All this was far removed from the ideology of Walter Scott, that staunch admirer of the feudal system, but it is the Chartist-supported democratic monument in the Calton Burial Ground, rather than the far better-known Scott Monument, which heralds modern democracy. Soon after its erection, a legal challenge against its tribute to "sedition" was brought by Edinburgh worthies, including the trustees of William Blackwood (late publisher of the widely read Tory periodical *Blackwood's Edinburgh Magazine*). Eventually, they lost. Of all the memorials on and around Calton Hill, none is more redolent of Scottish democracy than the one devoted to the political martyrs.

Fittingly, this starkly democratic monument stands close to the life-size bronze statue of Abraham Lincoln which was unveiled by the tellingly named Wallace Bruce, Edinburgh's American Consul, in 1893. Europe's first memorial to the murdered president (one of whose sons was christened William Wallace Lincoln), this monument was created by New York sculptor George E. Bissell. Commemorating Scots who fell in the American Civil War, and sometimes called the Emancipation Monument, it shows a freed slave looking up beseechingly to President Lincoln. In a city where race is discussed far less than religion or politics, this is Edinburgh's only public statue featuring a black man. The contemporary Scottish poet Jackie Kay, whose portrait bust is one of the herms around the loch at Edinburgh Park, may be the only black woman so honoured.

Glaswegians are often suspicious of Edinburgh because its official rhetoric tends to stress the city's sense of links to royalty, money, pomp, and grandeur, rather than its heritage of radicalism or political martyrs. Yet, despite the fact that one of the Scottish capital's favourite green spaces is formally entitled the "Royal Botanic Garden," hardly anyone in Edinburgh calls it that. Locals refer simply to "the Botanics." Officially, the "Royal Botanic Garden Edinburgh" now extends to four Scottish sites, and together these green spaces hold the second-richest collection of plant species in the world. Three of the sites, however, are elsewhere in Scotland; the main and muchloved Edinburgh garden—"the Botanics"—is at Inverleith, where the herbarium alone, developed from 1839–1840 onwards, includes around three million specimens. These represent between half and two-thirds of the flora on earth. Beautiful, and alive with birdsong, the gardens were recently voted by international botanic gardens professionals as among the world's top four of their kind, along with the New York Botanical Garden, Missouri Botanical Gardens, and Kew Gardens. Edinburgh's "Botanics" contain a light and elegant art gallery, located in the 1774 mansion of Inverleith House, where invited exhibitors have included Louise Bourgeois, John Cage, and Merce Cunningham. In the surrounding seventy-three acres of grounds, you can forget you are in a city—but every so often, gracefully framed by trees and shrubbery, there are beautiful views of the historic urban skyline. The Botanics are a haven of horticulture and other arts. Their story is bound up, too, with Edinburgh's place in modern science.

The city's first Botanic Garden was founded in the seventeenth century by James Balfour and Robert Sibbald, two cousins whose interests united medicine and botany, encouraging the development of Enlightenment thought in Edinburgh and beyond. Working as a physician in St. Andrews, Balfour is said to have "first introduced into Scotland the dissection of the human body." With Sibbald, he helped to found Edinburgh's Royal College of Physicians around 1680, and in 1685 Sibbald became Edinburgh University's first medical professor, publishing his *Pharmacopœia Collegii Regii Medicorum Edinburgensis* as well as a survey of Scottish natural history, *Scotia Illustrata.* Balfour had been fascinated by natural history since his student days at St. Andrews; he went on to collect what was judged Scotland's finest library of that subject. An eager traveller, he was impressed by the gardens at Blois belonging to the Duc d'Orléans, whose Scottish superintendent Robert Morison was later regarded by Linnæus as the principal pioneer of botanical classification. Morison and Balfour became lifelong friends. When Balfour returned to Edinburgh, he and Sibbald seem to have collaborated on establishing a botanical garden at Holyroodhouse around 1667, though Balfour soon moved many of his plants to a larger "physical garden" on the site of the present-day Waverley Station. That garden's curator, James Sutherland, dedicated his 1683 catalogue of plants, the *Hortus Medicus Edinburgensis,* to Edinburgh's Lord Provost.

Civic-minded, yet also contemplating "other Gardens abroad," Sutherland was confident that Edinburgh's garden "runs up with most of them, either for Number, or Rarity of Plants," some of which he had obtained from as far afield as the *"east and west Indies."* Happy among his "Virginian spiderworts" and "great bastard spleenworts," Sutherland was likewise interested in plant classification: "To make the thing easier for Beginners, I have Planted in One corner of the Garden, the Dispensatory Plants in an alphabetical Order." Like the work of Balfour and Sibbald, Sutherland's earthy seventeenth-century enthusiasm involved developing, in Edinburgh, physical and intellectual institutions which these men wished to be regarded as proud aspects of their city's life. They were enlightened before the Enlightenment.

Beginning in the 1720s, the academic Charles Alston also developed Edinburgh's botanical strengths, though he attacked Linnæus in his *Tyrocinium botanicum Edinburgense* (1753). By the mid-eighteenth century his successor as the university's botanical professor, John Hope, was one of the first people in Britain to teach the Linnæan system. In the gardens, now removed to a five-acre site of light sandy soil "on the west side of the road to Leith," Hope set up a monument to Linnæus commissioned from Robert Adam. Much transplanted and a little cracked, but still inscribed "LINNÆO POSUIT I. HOPE 1779," this carved stone memorial now stands among a complex of greenhouses and science buildings at Inverleith. Hope was another Fellow of the Royal College of Physicians. With Adam Smith, David Hume, and others, he had set up the Select Society, one of Enlightenment Edinburgh's several debating clubs. Through teaching, collecting, and correspondence, Hope ensured that botany and natural history as well as medicine were at the heart of the Scottish capital's Enlightenment learning. Advised by Benjamin Franklin and others, he increased Edinburgh's plant holdings and built up a school of botanists whose influence stretched as far as India. Through his lectures, he linked botany to physiology and anatomy. He is buried in Greyfriars Churchyard, and a genus of tree is named after him: Hopea.

After Hope's time, in the early 1820s, when summer botanical lectures were given in its greenhouses, there were plans to move the gardens to a nine-acre site southeast of the Palace of Holyroodhouse; but in 1824, the year before Charles Darwin came to Edinburgh as a student, a twelve-acre site at Inverleith had been taken over. The gardens have since expanded but still include this original ground, which was developed to contain "a commodious well-lighted apartment, but perfectly plain," where Professor Robert Graham, later first president of the Botanical Society of Edinburgh, gave lectures. Along with John Hope's son (an eloquent Edinburgh chemistry

professor), Graham was one of Darwin's teachers. Darwin's Edinburgh ex-
ploits included the dissection of geraniums and plants from a collection now
in the Edinburgh herbarium, and it is probable that while a young medical
student he visited Inverleith. He and Professor Graham each made botanical
excursions with Robert Greville, whose *Flora Edinensis; or, A Description
of Plants Growing near Edinburgh, Arranged According to the Linnæan System* was published in 1824, and whom Darwin called "the great Botanist"
two years later. While working on his *Scottish cryptogrammic flora*, Greville
was accompanied by the teenage Darwin on a voyage to the Isle of May in
the Firth of Forth. The teenager found it so funny when the Edinburgh
plantsman was discomfited by the screeching of kittiwakes that a fellow student recalled he had "to lie down on the greensward to enjoy his prolonged
cachinnation."

The greensward at today's Edinburgh Botanics has known many famous
visitors. Just over a century after Darwin's student years, the young Muriel
Spark and her childhood friend Frances Cowell liked to roam there. They
once buried a jointly written short story full of Celtic Twilight motifs, but it
has never been found and the authorities take a very dim view of anyone
who digs for it. Even the modern surface of the Botanics has historical interest. Topsoil used to fill some of the 1960s greenhouses was taken from the
building site of the Forth Road Bridge, while the earth in the gardens' oldest glasshouse, a handsome octagonal 1834 Tropical Palm House whose design was supervised by Robert Graham, supports a *Sabal Bermuda* palm
tree which was already mature when transplanted from the Leith Walk site
in 1822.

Among the loveliest areas of the Botanics are the Chinese gardens, their
pathways bowered with foliage and affording lyric glimpses—a bathing
blackbird or a droplet-flecked duck perched in summer under white blossoms by a waterfall below a small wooden bridge. Inverleith has more Chinese plant specimens than any site outside China. Today it boasts strong
links with Yunnan Province and with botanists elsewhere in the People's Republic, but its treasured Chinese connections have a longer history. Close to
where the Scottish plant collector George Forrest once brought back specimens from China, Chiang Lee, known as the "silent traveller," wrote several
poems in the gardens one spring during World War II. Watching a shaft of
sunlight striking rhododendrons and azaleas in bloom, he saw a thin layer

24. The Royal Botanic Garden at Inverleith, blending elements of Scotland and China, affords beautiful glimpses of the central Edinburgh skyline to the south. Including graceful Chinese gardens, it has more Chinese plant specimens than any other site outside China.

of coloured mist above the blossoms—a beautiful phenomenon the Chinese call "Hwa-wu." Chiang Lee thought of lines by Robert Burns: "Common friends to you and me,/Nature's gifts to all are free."

The gardens are rich in such moments of scot-free, priceless respite. Modern wanderers can enjoy not merely the alluring vistas over the Chinese Hillside, the Rock Garden, the Woodland Garden, or the recently installed Queen Mother's Memorial Garden, but also (just in case it is raining) the John Hope Gateway, an indoors centre for botanical information. Opened in 2009 and designed by Edward Cullinan Architects, this fine postmodern pavilion with its light and airy first-floor restaurant includes a "Real Life Science studio," where visitors can see and hear how experts from Edinburgh's Botanic Gardens are now working with people in more than forty countries, ranging from Afghanistan to New Caledonia and from China to Iraq. An exhibition on the importance of biodiversity looks out through a sixty-metre-long curved window over tiered ponds onto a specially planted garden.

If John Hope, Charles Darwin, or other botanists and naturalists from Edinburgh's past returned in the twenty-first century, they would not be disappointed. They might share, though, the frustration of the twenty-first-century Regius Keeper, Professor Stephen Blackmore, who writes in the introduction to his popular book *Gardening the Earth: Gateways to a Sustainable Future:* "Everything in the world has its name and its place. Everything has its way of growing and living. Some people know the names and way of things, but most don't. Strange—they remember the colours of every football team but can't tell kingcups from buttercups."

Over the centuries the Botanic Gardens at Inverleith have delighted many who can't tell kingcups from buttercups, as well as all who can. One of the latter was certainly Robert Moyes Adam (1885–1967), appointed an assistant gardener in 1903. Adam had studied science at Heriot Watt College, as well as drawing at the Edinburgh College of Art and botany at Edinburgh University. His first job at the gardens was to assist in preparing drawings for lectures by the professor of botany, but he soon began to photograph plants. Much of his work was scientific and commercial. Yet by photographing locations ranging from Edinburgh to the remote Scottish island of Mingulay (which Adam visited in 1905, just before its evacuation), he established himself over several decades as one of his country's most important photographers. From quiet snapshots of back gardens in pre–World War I Portobello to detailed images of plant specimens, birds' nests, and scenes in the Botanic Gardens, Adam had a shrewd eye for the natural environment in Edinburgh as well as elsewhere. As an old man, chatting with Edinburgh friends such as John Anthony, author of the *Flora of Sutherland,* he enjoyed a quiet glass of sherry after Sunday morning kirk service, but he died decades before the best of his work came to be recognized in the twenty-first century for its keen sense of ecology. Today's visitors to Inverleith may like to do what Adam occasionally did: wander out into the Botanic Gardens and point a camera lens up towards an interesting passing cloud.

Walkers with time and energy to spare may choose to meander all the way along the Water of Leith footpath, which runs through green, wooded parklands filled with birdsong from Inverleith to the city's port. The word "Inverleith" means "basin of the [Water of] Leith" and refers to the river which runs close to the Botanic Gardens on its way to join the Firth of Forth. It flows into the Forth at the coastal settlement of Leith, now dominated by blocks of contemporary waterfront apartments, a massive Scottish Government civil-service building, and the dockside Ocean Terminal shopping mall. Yet the sight of a ship berthed at a quayside, or the anchor of a historic transatlantic ship set like a sculpture in a modern urban forecourt is enough to remind onlookers that this area (separately administered until 1920) was once a very different place. From at least the fourteenth century, Leith served as Edinburgh's port, populated by mariners, brewers, traders, and merchants. Out of it flowed exports such as wool and hides; in came commodities ranging from roof tiles and the national supply of claret to books, fine clothes, and people. In the nineteenth century, when Leith was a very substantial port indeed, passersby could still see on its waterfront the palatial, crumbling house of one of its great patrons, Mary of Guise, the Catholic mother of Mary Queen of Scots. She ruled briefly from the port, which at one point threatened to rival Edinburgh, but her citadel was besieged by Protestant reformers in 1560, and Leith's walls were demolished. Edinburgh regained, and has since kept, the upper hand.

Today most of Leith's older waterfront structures have succumbed to developers. Gone are not just Mary of Guise's grand house but also the vast, funnel-like towers of the Glassworks, an early twentieth-century landmark. Surviving properties such as the privately owned sixteenth-century Lamb's House (where Mary Queen of Scots was welcomed when she sailed back from France to claim the throne of Scotland), and fragments, including a stone at Trinity House inscribed for the "MASTERIS AND MAREN-ERS" in 1555, are reminders that Leith was sixteenth-century Scotland's busiest port. It and its mariners were hymned by Renaissance Latin poet Arthur Johnston as proud and independent. Even in the mid-eighteenth century, large sections of the shoreline remained open grazing. A 1750 watercolour shows a windmill standing surrounded by coastal fields nearby, some of which formed the Leith Links golf course, while a few years later Robert Fergusson rejoiced in attending popular horse races on a sunny July day, watching "on Leith-Sands the racers rare." We even know the names of some of the eighteenth-century horses: Best-at-the-Bottom, Land-ladie, Cavers.

In the early nineteenth century, there was a competition to lay out a further "New Town between Edinburgh and Leith"—the existing New Town was clearly not enough—with roads running around, then north of, Calton Hill. William Playfair won the competition, and the building of such streets as Leopold Place commenced. Where once trees and fields had bounded Leith Walk—still today the main thoroughfare to Leith—imposing, often neoclassical thoroughfares sprang up around it. By Robert Louis Stevenson's time, you could look from the north of Calton Hill's grassy slopes, "tessellated with sheets and blankets out to dry," and see "suburbs run out to Leith . . . with her forest of masts."

Despite those forests, or perhaps because of them, Leith was not always salubrious. Its twentieth-century tower blocks of social housing mark pockets of economic deprivation not far from sleek twenty-first-century apartments built by speculative property developers eager to regenerate the area and profit from its now substantially postindustrial docks. Not all of these speculations have succeeded. For centuries, Leith has enjoyed mixed fortunes. The future Lord Provost of Edinburgh William Chambers, a bankrupt's son and the author of a volume of "autobiographic reminiscences," wrote of how he had gone "trudging down" there looking for a job as a grocer's delivery boy in 1813, the year before Scott published *Waverley*. Stopping for a moment opposite a public fountain, he sized up the shop from the outside.

> The windows exhibited quantities of raw sugar in different varieties of brownness, hovering over which were swarms of flies, in a state of frantic enjoyment. Sticks of black liquorice leaned coaxingly on the second row of panes, flanked by tall glass jars of sweeties and peppermint drops; behind these outward attractions, there were observable yellow-painted barrels of whisky, rows of bottles of porter, piles of cheeses of varied complexions, firkins of salt butter, and boxes of soap. At the counter were a number of women and children buying articles, such as quarter-ounces of tea and ounces of sugar; and the floor was battered with dirt and debris.

Traditionally, Leith Walk was a haunt of prostitutes, and Leith was considerably more edgy than central Edinburgh. Of the carriages, or "chaises," heading down Leith Walk to the eighteenth-century races, Fergusson commented, "Some chaises honest folk contain, / And some hae mony a *Whore* in." Though the late nineteenth-century port had known great prosperity, it was subject to large-sale slum clearance; and almost two centuries after Chambers watched flies in a grocer's window, its association with rot was strengthened when Irvine Welsh made Leith the setting for parts of his notorious 1993 novel of heroin junkies and urban violence, *Trainspotting*. That book's bleakly ironic title refers to the then-derelict (now demolished) Leith Central Station, with its huge railway shed where trains no longer ran.

Living a little to the south, off Leith Walk, in a one-bedroom, ground-floor flat at 7 South Lorne Place, the unpublished single mother J. K. Rowling completed *Harry Potter and the Philosopher's Stone;* her flat was broken into and stoned in a neighbourhood where violence, crime, and addiction were rife. Yet recently the port, its early nineteenth-century docks infilled but its Victoria and Albert Docks remaining, has become increasingly gentrified. In 1833, extensions to the port facilities at Leith temporarily bankrupted the City of Edinburgh; and the recession at the end of the twenty-first century's first decade plunged waterfront developers into financial crisis. Yet there are still hopes that one day a new tram line, connecting Leith and Princes Street, will further enhance the old port's prosperity.

Its dock area now boasts several waterfront attractions, the most celebrated of which is the British monarch's former royal yacht, *Britannia,* berthed beside the Ocean Terminal mall as a paying visitor attraction. Built on Clydeside in 1953, the *Britannia* sailed more than a million miles before being decommissioned in 1997. In this floating palace Queen Elizabeth II, on her overseas state visits, was supported by a staff of three hundred people as she entertained guests ranging from Churchill and Gandhi to Nelson Mandela and Bill and Hilary Clinton. Still on board is Her Majesty's Phantom V Rolls Royce, whose bumpers had to be removed each time it was hoisted on deck, so that it could be inserted neatly into the ship's garage. To set the table for dinner in the State Dining Room took three hours, and that grand saloon's pale interior contains everything from an Easter Island statuette to a narwhal's tusk. "A Yacht is a necessity and not a luxury for the Head of our Great British Commonwealth," Her Majesty once pronounced. Her subjects came to disagree, and *Britannia* has not been replaced. In contemporary Leith, this most singular and anachronistic phenomenon lures fascinated tourists. Preserved on board are attractions such as Princess Diana's honeymoon suite, the Queen's monogrammed frilly pillows, and the officers' mess, where senior members of the crew used a soft toy to play energetic games of "wombat tennis."

Back on terra firma, Leith's more than twenty church buildings include

25. An early nineteenth-century ferry arrives in Leith around the time that the young Charles Darwin visited the port and sailed on the Firth of Forth. William Daniell's coloured engraving, published in 1829, shows fashionably dressed ladies and gentlemen strolling and sitting on the waterfront not far from the docks where the Royal Yacht *Britannia* is berthed today.

those of the Scandinavian Lutheran Church (now the Leith School of Art), the Ukrainian Catholic Church of St. Andrew, and St. Thomas's Church, which was converted in the late twentieth century into a Sikh temple. Leith, because of its port status, was a popular place for immigrant communities over the centuries. When surveys of "aliens" were conducted during the period of the French Revolution and the Napoleonic Wars, Leith's resident foreigners (as recorded in the surviving manuscript records of Edinburgh City Archives) came from Prussia, Berlin, Saxony, Switzerland, Lithuania, France, Italy, America, Finland, Denmark, Holland, and plain "Abroad," but the largest number were Italians. Successive generations of immigrants made Leith relatively cosmopolitan, and an Italian presence remained notable. It was in the Catholic church of St. Mary Star of the Sea, in Constitution Street, on March 20, 1924, that twenty-two-year-old Carmela Maria (daughter of Pietro Rossi, a shopkeeper in Leith Walk) and twenty-three-year-old Alfonso Rudolfo Armando Antonio Paolozzi presented their only son, Eduardo Luigi, for baptism. The following year, Rudolfo, who loved machinery and built his own car from a kit, rented a confectionary shop at 10 Albert Street, just off Leith Walk. At home, the family spoke Italian dialect; around them the accents were those of working-class Scots.

Clean, neat, and beautifully arranged when photographed in the 1930s, the shop whose window bore the letters "A. PAOLOZZI" was absolutely the opposite of the dirty shopwindow eyed by the young William Chambers. The black-and-white photograph shows polished glass collaged with several rows of lettering advertising various brands of cigarettes; behind the lettered glass are serried rows of cakes, lines of bottles, and boxes ascending neatly from floor to ceiling. Standing proudly in its doorway, the confectioner, with his sleeves rolled up, looks proud of this sculpted order; his son, who would devote his career to collages, sculptures, and arrangements of objects, remembered how carefully the shopwindow had been "dressed" by a visiting confectionary representative.

Arrangement and order were part of life for the young Eduardo, who helped to run the shop. Before progressing to the "very grim" Holy Cross Academy in Leith, he was photographed at the age of eight with his forty-six classmates at Leith Walk Primary School. In that picture, the children have been arranged absolutely symmetrically in terms of gender: the front row is all boys; the second all girls; the third row has a boy at each end with girls in the middle; the fourth row has three boys at each end with girls in the middle; the back row, with Eduardo in it, is all boys. Muriel Spark, a middle-class Edinburgh girl born a few years earlier, hints at similar kinds of regimentation. The first paragraph of her classic novella of 1930s Edinburgh life, *The Prime of Miss Jean Brodie,* begins with the words "The boys," and the second with "The girls." In a society so enamoured of regimenting its young people, there was also, as *The Prime of Miss Jean Brodie* shows with penetrating wit, a darker side. Spark's closest schoolfriend, Frances Niven, recalled that their teacher, Miss Kay, had, like the fictional Miss Brodie, a strong admiration for Mussolini. In the back room of his Leith Walk shop, Rudolfo Paolozzi kept a picture of the Italian dictator, and the young Eduardo, photographed in Fascist youth-movement uniform beside his mother in 1934, was sent each summer to a Fascist summer camp on the Adriatic, where he did gymnastics, watched subtitled American films, admired the modernist design of the camp buildings, and took part in processions with "military priests" and Fascist insignia.

When Mussolini declared war on the Allies in June 1940, shortly after the British retreat from Dunkirk, children were already being evacuated from the Scottish capital for fear of aerial bombardment. Angry mobs roamed Edinburgh, Glasgow, and other cities. On June 11, 1940, the *Scotsman* carried an article titled "Rioting during Night of Big Round-Up." There had been violence in the streets the previous evening:

> While the Edinburgh police were busy rounding up Italians, anti-Italian feeling found vent in an orgy of window-breaking and looting in different parts of the city. . . . Crowds attacked ice-cream and fish and chip shops in Edinburgh, and large reinforcements of regular and special police were called out to deal with the demonstrators. . . . In Leith Street and Union Place, there were riotous scenes after ten o'clock. A crowd of over a thousand gathered, the great majority of them in the role of spectators. The trouble was due largely to irresponsible youths, who started stone-throwing. There are numerous shops in the vicinity occupied by Italians, and before the police were able to get control of the mischief-makers, many plate-glass windows were shattered. . . . The police made a number of baton charges.

Though he had tried to destroy or hide his fascist materials, Rudolfo Paolozzi found his shopfront reduced to splintered wood and broken glass. Not long afterwards, rather apologetic policemen took the confectioner away. Imprisoned briefly in Edinburgh's Saughton Prison as a sixteen-year-old, Eduardo later recalled his cell's beeswaxed floor, pottery chamber pot and pink china mug. Though he was soon released, and served in the British Pioneer Corps, he never saw his father again; along with many other Italian and German prisoners, the older man had been taken on board the SS *Arandora Star* to be interned in Canada. On July 4, 1940, the *Scotsman* reported that at six in the morning, while many on board were asleep, the vessel had been torpedoed by a U-boat. As the crowded ship's lighting system failed, panic ensued and about eight hundred of those on board, including Italian traders from Leith, lost their lives. Among them were Paolozzi's father and grandfather. Their bodies were never recovered.

The Paolozzi family's ancestral home, an Italian village near Monte

Cassino, was virtually destroyed in the carnage of World War II. All this provides the context for what is surely Edinburgh's most moving modern public sculpture. In July 1991, just over half a century after the death of his father and grandfather, Paolozzi's major bronze, *Manuscript of Monte Cassino*, cast in Germany and alluding to Italian history, was installed in Picardy Place outside St. Mary's Metropolitan Cathedral, where the Paolozzi family had gone to Mass in the 1930s. The sculpture is in three huge pieces—severed body parts in the shape of an ankle, a foot, and a hand. The huge foot seems almost a small, fortified hill; the hand holds in its fingers a toy ball, and on its palm (where rainwater collects in wet weather) are two mating bronze grasshoppers. The sculptor who had carried pasta up Leith Walk to his grandfather as a child and who remembered his mother and grandmother cooking recipes brought from Italy, liked the idea that local children could play on his great bronzes, which recall "ancient memories and shared childhood experiences." An excerpt from a medieval Latin poem is inscribed on the bronze, along with the date 1991 and Paolozzi's own name. In his writings, he quotes the poem as translated by Helen Waddell:

MS. OF MONTE CASSINO
Written to Paul the Deacon at Monte Cassino

Across the hills and in the valley's shade,
Alone the small script goes,
Seeking for Benedict's beloved roof,
Where waits its sure repose.
They come and find, the tired travellers,
Green herbs and ample bread,
Quiet and brothers' love and humbleness,
Christ's peace on every head.

FIVE

Medicine, Museums, Blood

Though twenty-first-century Edinburgh has promoted itself as a financial centre, using the phrase "Inspiring Capital," the city's most enduring capital is cultural and intellectual, much of it dating from the Enlightenment and the nineteenth century. Important to this fifth chapter, which invites readers to explore Chambers Street and its environs, are nineteenth-century developments in collecting and anatomizing which confirmed the city as a scientific hub, but also as a sentimental Victorian tourist destination: both of these legacies persist to this day, energizing a central university quarter that is, as well, an area of great museums. Not far off, overlooking the Meadows, the twenty-first-century high-rise apartment blocks of the Quartermile development, designed in part by Richard Rogers, stand alongside the old wards and operating theatres of a pioneering maternity hospital now converted into luxury flats. Opportunistically, the city recycles itself, its monuments of older intellectual and physical labour recast as thriving postmodern landmarks; but the most important institutions in this part of town confirm that it is still a place of ambitious brainwork and eclectic imagination.

Edinburgh is a city of four substantial universities—Edinburgh, Heriot Watt, Edinburgh Napier, and Queen Margaret—the oldest and greatest of which is Edinburgh. Today Edinburgh University regards itself as Scotland's pre-eminent international academic institution, though its intellectually distinguished, smaller, and more beautiful cosmopolitan rival, St. Andrews (standing spectacularly by the sea an hour's drive north), likes to point out that Edinburgh is a relative newcomer. Unlike the ancient medieval universities of Scotland—St. Andrews (the English-speaking world's third-oldest university, founded 1411–1413), Glasgow (fourth-oldest, founded in 1451), and Aberdeen (fifth, founded in 1495)—Edinburgh is a later, post-Reformation establishment. Its alumni include the twenty-first-century

British prime minister Gordon Brown, as well as David Hume and Sir Walter Scott, both of whom studied law.

Three St. Andrews graduates were vital to the founding of Edinburgh University. In the mid-sixteenth century, Robert Reid sought to set up colleges in the city: one for "bairnis" (children), one for law, and one "for thame that leirnis poetre and oratore." Though Reid's plans stalled, he left a posthumous bequest of money, and when the childless Clement Little died in 1580 he gave his substantial library to "his native town of Edinburgh and to the kirk of God thairin." In 1583 the eloquent, red-haired Robert Rollock from St. Andrews was appointed to be principal of the new college, later renamed the University of Edinburgh. When Rollock died in 1598, the city mourned him. Thirty poems in Latin and one in Greek were published in his memory. His *Select Works* of Calvinist-influenced theology were re-edited for publication in Edinburgh as recently as 1849, but remain among the world's least-read books.

Very different are the writings of Edinburgh University's most celebrated student, Charles Darwin. The young Englishman followed in the footsteps of his grandfather and his older brother, both Edinburgh medical alumni who were passionate about natural history. The university buildings that fifteen-year-old Darwin knew were not the original ones. Erected in 1616, those had become "extremely mean and inconvenient" by the late eighteenth century, when they were replaced by the new, far grander structure substantially designed by Robert Adam. Darwin's alma mater was entered through Adam's imposing triple archway—which still stands, looking a bit scuffed, where today's South Bridge becomes Nicolson Street. The university is built on a bombsite, specifically the site of the explosion that blew up Mary Queen of Scots's second husband, Darnley; but its teachers and students seem unperturbed. Completing the main building's great courtyard (partly to Adam's design, but more to the design of William Playfair, nephew of an Edinburgh professor) took several decades. The quadrangle was almost finished when Darwin arrived in 1825, but he would not have studied in the magnificent Playfair-designed library, now one of the university's glories. That did not open until 1827. Instead, when Darwin was a student, the crumbling seventeenth-century library, joined to what looked like a little cottage, still stood in the middle of the soaring new quadrangle which had been built around it. There were large cracks in the old library's walls; it was

26. The grand Old College quadrangle of Edinburgh University was almost complete when Charles Darwin arrived as a medical student in 1825. Designed by Robert Adam and William Playfair, the quadrangle's courtyard was excavated in 2011 by archæologists who unearthed remains of earlier buildings (including the one where Henry Darnley, the husband of Mary Queen of Scots, was murdered). Today such horrors are gracefully grassed over.

shored up with wood; and an improvised wooden corridor allowed books to be transferred from its upper storey to its grand, neoclassical neighbour. Enrolled in the natural-history class in his second year, Darwin, who had been borrowing books on entomology and zoology from the library in his first year, was granted free admission to the university's museum, which had just moved into its new, magnificent, Playfair-designed home.

Darwin grew friendly with the museum's scruffy but learned assistant keeper, the traveler and naturalist William Macgillivray, who was then beginning to establish himself as Scotland's leading nineteenth-century ornithologist and would soon produce his *Lives of Eminent Zoologists*. Though the splendid museum space can still be seen, its contents today are very different from those described in John Stark's proud account published the year Darwin arrived in Scotland's capital city:

> The *lower great room* is appropriated to the quadrupeds and other large animals. . . . The *upper great room* is lighted from the roof by three large lanterns, and from the side by three great windows. An elegant gallery runs round the whole apartment. The walls of the room are every where covered with splendid cases, covered with plate glass, for containing objects of natural history. The cases in the gallery are appropriated for the classical and magnificent collection of birds purchased by the college from M. Dufresne of Paris; the cases under the gallery for the valuable collection of birds already in the college. It is said the entire collection of birds amounts to about 3000 specimens; the most extensive in Great Britain, and not exceeded by many on the Continent. In the middle of the room, the floor of which is of iron and painted, are magnificent tables, covered with plate glass, and containing very fine collections of shells, insects, and corals. The *lower external gallery*, a very beautiful apartment, 50 feet in length, contains the great collection of insects, and a cabinet of minerals for the use of the students of mineralogy. The *upper external gallery* is 90 feet long, divided into three apartments of great beauty, and lighted from the roof by elegant lanterns. The smaller apartments contain preparations in comparative anatomy, the middle and larger room is appropriated for minerals. Another large room is to contain a collection of all the rocks and minerals of the British Empire, arranged in a geographical order.

Darwin found the ideas about mineralogy held by the official curator, his professor Robert Jameson, utterly devoid of interest. Yet this newly constructed museum—later home to the (live) university puma—surely helped to shape the mind of the Edinburgh student who kept detailed notes on bird-watching and who studied marine creatures, flowers, and other aspects of natural history instead of attending anatomy lectures. Darwin's earliest surviving notebook on field observations is a copy of *The Edinburgh Ladies and Gentlemens Pocket Souvenir for 1826*, its title page a composite picture of Edinburgh with a motto from Robert Burns: "Edina, Scotia's darling seat! All hail thy Palaces and Towers." In this diary Darwin recorded buying a ptarmigan, seeing a large flock of wheatears on Arthur's Seat, and catching a sea mouse. However, training at the university to be a doctor, he was often bored and discontented. He found most classes "intolerably dull"; "Dr. Duncan's lectures on Materia Medica at 8 o'clock on a winter's morning" were "something fearful to remember."

Yet Darwin did recall how the zoologist Robert Grant, "one day, when we were walking together[,] burst forth in high admiration of Lamarck and his views on evolution. . . . It is probable that the hearing rather early in life such views maintained and praised may have favoured my upholding them under a different form in my *Origin of Species*." While an Edinburgh student, Darwin read several of Grant's publications, along with other works of natural history, and later pointed out in *The Origin of Species:* "In 1826 Professor Grant, in the concluding paragraph in his well known paper (*Edinburgh Philosophical Journal*, vol. xiv, p. 238) on the Spongilla, clearly declares his view that species are descended from other species, and that they become improved in the course of modification."

Like Grant (and sometimes with him), the student Darwin collected marine creatures on the black rocks at Leith. He made friends with some of the Newhaven fishermen whose crews would be photographed less than two decades later by Hill and Adamson, and went sailing with them to trawl for oysters. Guided by Grant's theories and practice of natural history, and by microscopic observations he had made, Darwin read his first ever scientific paper to an Edinburgh University club for which Grant, who praised "my zealous young friend Mr. Charles Darwin," served as secretary. Darwin's earliest experiences of participating in scientific meetings were gained in

Edinburgh; he looked "with awe and reverence" at Walter Scott presiding over a meeting of the city's Royal Society, and listened with close attention to a lecture by the visiting naturalist John J. Audubon around the time that the first ten plates of Audubon's *Birds of America* were being engraved by the local firm of Lizars. Preserving and understanding specimens would be crucial to Darwin's career. He "had much natural-history talk" with William Macgillivray, who was "very kind" to him, giving him rare shells; and he recalled with gratitude the freed slave John Edmonston, "a negro [who] lived in Edinburgh, who ... gained his livelihood by stuffing birds, which he did excellently; he gave me lessons for payment, and I used often to sit with him, for he was a very pleasant and intelligent man."

At the age of seventeen Darwin gave up medicine, returned south after two years at Edinburgh, and went on to become a Cambridge University graduate. Yet in important ways it was Edinburgh University, Grant's inspiration, and the Scottish capital's scientific life which formed him. This student from England was part of a great procession of trainee physicians who flocked to the city in the eighteenth and nineteenth centuries, when its university boasted the most distinguished medical school in the English-speaking world. At the start of the 1700s, principal William Carstares had encouraged Edinburgh professors to specialize rather than to go on teaching across the curriculum. Throughout the following century, a remarkable professorial dynasty of Alexander Monro *primus,* Alexander Monro *secundus,* and Alexander Monro *tertius* (grandfather, father, and son) led the anatomy teaching. Edinburgh's most energetic Lord Provost, George Drummond, backed the setting-up of what is now called Edinburgh Royal Infirmary in 1729, and famous Edinburgh doctors of the nineteenth century included the developer of antiseptic medicine Joseph Lister, as well as the pioneer of chloroform James Young Simpson, whose experiments on himself may underlie *The Strange Case of Dr. Jekyll and Mr. Hyde,* written by his son's close friend R. L. Stevenson. Another Edinburgh University student, Arthur Conan Doyle, based the character of Sherlock Holmes on his medical professor, Joseph Bell, after whom the present-day university's Joseph Bell Centre for Forensic Statistics and Legal Reasoning is so resonantly named. The legacy of Edinburgh medicine belongs to fiction and criminology, as well as to history, and explains why the forensic pathologist

Dr. "Duckie" Mallard in the popular twenty-first-century American television series *NCIS* is presented as an Edinburgh graduate.

Edinburgh University likes to make much of its contribution to the Scottish Enlightenment, but Glaswegians point out relentlessly that Adam Smith was a professor at Glasgow, not at Edinburgh. Moreover, the Glasgow University–educated William Cullen, a friend of Adam Smith and David Hume, taught medicine and chemistry at Glasgow before he moved to his chair at Edinburgh and introduced the word "neurosis" into medical terminology; working with Cullen in Glasgow, some years before transferring to the capital, his former student Joseph Black, discoverer of carbon dioxide, also went on to discover latent heat. Such fine Glaswegian distinctions are usually glossed over in Edinburgh. David Hume, who later failed in his application for Adam Smith's former professorship at Glasgow, certainly studied at Edinburgh, but he was never a professor there; the same is true of the east-coast city's distinguished resident James Hutton, whose *Theory of the Earth* (1795) invented modern geology. Its centre freshly landscaped in 2011 and graced with a broad lawn, the spacious main quadrangle of Edinburgh University is a good place to ponder Edinburgh's eighteenth-century intellectual giants, even though it postdates them. The names of the university's Enlightenment professoriate tend to be less familiar now, though several were internationally celebrated in their day, and a few are still famous in ours.

Where once eighteenth-century Scottish rhetoricians such as Professor Hugh Blair pioneered the university teaching of English literature, and Enlightenment historians such as the small, deaf Principal William Robertson (chronicler of Scotland and America, his sister a landlady in the Canongate) delighted in "conjectural history," today the university may be more distinguished for "informatics" and conjectural science. The Scottish capital's most famous piece of postmodern conjecture is the elusive Higgs boson, that "scalar elementary particle" whose existence was posited by Edinburgh University professor of theoretical physics Peter Higgs. Scientists at CERN operating Europe's Large Hadron Collider, the world's biggest piece of scientific equipment, quested after the Higgs boson (nicknamed by some "the God particle") for decades, and eventually caught up with it in 2012, much to the delight of eighty-three-year-old New Town resident Professor Higgs, who had posited its existence some forty-eight years earlier and commented laconically, "It's very nice to be right sometimes. It has certainly been a long wait." Rather different, but almost as famous, is Dolly the Sheep (1996–2003), the first mammal cloned from an adult body cell. She is said to have been named after country-and-western singer Dolly Parton. Now stuffed by a taxidermist at Edinburgh's National Museum of Scotland, the ovine star was brought into being at the Roslin Institute by a team of Edinburgh University researchers—an appropriate achievement, perhaps, for Darwin's alma mater.

Intellectual and medical prowess in Edinburgh has never been confined to the city's oldest university. An emerging "bioquarter" is but one of the signs that scientific and cultural life is distributed throughout the Scottish capital. Yet historically there has been an undeniable concentration of brain-power in the area around the Old College quadrangle—from the National Library of Scotland on George IV Bridge to the Royal College of Surgeons of Edinburgh, now headquartered in the complex of buildings on Nicolson Street that includes Surgeons' Hall, designed by W. H. Playfair and built in the years 1829–1832. The Royal College is one of the world's oldest surgical associations. Today it has about 17,000 Fellows and Members, who qualify through demanding examinations and are based around the globe. This in-stitution was founded in 1505, when Edinburgh's Town Council granted privileges to the local barber-surgeons, incorporating them as a craft guild of the city and enjoining them to make sure their members "know Anatomy and the nature and complexion of every member of the human body." Bar-bers, the earliest surgeons, were used to wielding razors and other poten-tially lethal implements to cut hair and shave beards; it was important that they not make incisions elsewhere without the appropriate knowledge. In 1567, Mary Queen of Scots issued a royal charter which for the first time clearly set out the noncombatant role of military doctors. Surgeons played a lively part in Edinburgh's civic life, sometimes drawing on their alertness to human anatomy in surprising ways. "What a hideous thing it is for a Christian Protestant woman for her breasts to be strutting out thus," one randy Presbyterian tells a young woman in *The Assembly,* a late seventeenth-century satire on the kirk authored by Edinburgh surgeon and Latin poet Archibald Pitcairne.

During Pitcairne's time, a Surgeons' Hall was built in the High School Yards near the university. Through the auspices of the Town Council, cadavers were supplied for public dissection there from 1703. The founding of a Faculty of Medicine at the university in 1726 and the appointment of the Monro dynasty of professors helped to make Edinburgh world-renowned for anatomical teaching. Nonetheless, it was not until 1803 that the university established its Chair of Clinical Surgery. There was continuing rivalry, as well as some overlap, between the teaching of this subject by tenured academic staff and by surgeons beyond the university. The expertise of the latter lured students away from formal university courses to attend classes in Surgeons' Square and, later, at the Edinburgh Dental Dispensary. This dispensary was established in 1860 by Dr. John Smith (afterwards president of the College of Surgeons) at nearby 1 Drummond Street. Throughout that gruesome era, dentistry in Scotland was still completely unregulated.

Containing among other things a world-class collection relating to dental history, the Museum of the Royal College of Surgeons ranks as one of the most memorable collections accessible to any visitor to Edinburgh—but is not for the fainthearted. Its bottled lungs and fœtuses take visitors back to a milieu in which Darwin, conducted round the wards of the infirmary as a student, was traumatized by the screams and oaths of a young street urchin being cut open in the days before chloroform. From its inception, this place has been at once a gallery of healing and a chamber of horrors, its history bound up with one of the most notorious aspects of Edinburgh's past: the murders carried out in 1827–1828 by William Burke and William Hare.

The museum was established in 1824. Its founder, Dr. Robert Knox, was also the anatomist who, as part of his teaching at 10 Surgeons' Square, dissected the bodies of Burke and Hare's victims. Severely disfigured and left blind in one eye as a result of childhood smallpox, Knox had been a distinguished student who progressed from Edinburgh High School to the university's Medical Faculty. In 1815, along with Charles Bell, he helped to care for the wounded at the Battle of Waterloo. Like the student Darwin and Dr. Robert Grant in the mid-1820s, Knox read papers to Edinburgh's Wernerian Society, and was also involved with the Royal Society of Edinburgh. Darwin's professor Robert Jameson lectured on "Origin of the Species of Animals," while Knox's intellectual interests around 1827 (when Darwin left Edinburgh) related to speculations about vestigial anatomical structures common to many organisms. All this thinking about species' origins and development was part of Darwin's Edinburgh milieu. It was, as well, bound up

27. Dr. Robert Knox taught Edinburgh students how to dissect bodies. A charismatic orator, he was notorious for his association with the murderers Burke and Hare, who supplied him with very fresh corpses. This 1840s photograph of Knox, taken by Robert Adamson and David Octavius Hill, captures something of his fastidious dress sense.

with Knox's determination to establish for the Royal College of Surgeons a museum of comparative anatomy and pathology that would be comparable to Jameson's museum of natural history at the nearby university. Having become a Fellow of the College of Surgeons in 1825, the year Darwin came to the Scottish capital, Knox was appointed conservator of the pathological section of the new museum that same year. In 1826 the impressive collection of Charles Bell, a fellow Edinburgh surgeon, was moved to the museum, and Knox oversaw the transfer.

Throughout his professional life, Knox, later the author of a textbook entitled *The Edinburgh Dissector,* was a charismatic orator. In a previously unpublished letter (now in the National Library of Scotland) he informs Robert Chambers in quick, confident handwriting: "I am a fluent and ready speaker with vast memory and power to call up everything bearing on the point I then discuss." He dressed "in the highest style of fashion, with spotless linen, frill, and lace." Pointing out anatomical structures to students, Knox would gesture with "raised arm and pointed forefinger, upon which," his assistant Henry Lonsdale later recalled, "he wore an exquisite diamond ring." An 1840s photograph of Knox by Hill and Adamson shows this self-consciously stylish doctor finely dressed yet menacing, his large hands prominent, his darkened face partly obscured by a gleaming high-winged collar. By then, he was Britain's most notorious surgeon. What had made him so was his association with Burke and Hare.

At William Burke's Edinburgh trial in 1828, the judge, Lord Meadowbank, was reported as stating "that in the whole history of the country—I may say in the history of civilized society—nothing has ever been exhibited that is in any respect parallel to this case." The Burke and Hare murders were the first serial killings to attract major media attention. They added a new word to the language: the verb "burke" is defined by the *Oxford English Dictionary* as "to kill secretly by suffocation or strangulation, or for the purpose of selling the victim's body for dissection." Finding their sixteen victims among the destitute of the Old Town, the Irish immigrants Burke and Hare got them drunk and then "burked" them by kneeling on or otherwise compressing their chests while holding closed their mouths and noses. The bodies were quickly sold to Dr. Knox's assistant, David Paterson, for dissection. Knox, that swanky Fellow of the College of Surgeons who chose not to inquire where such an apparently endless supply of fresh flesh was coming from, cut them up for the instruction of his students.

Nineteenth-century Edinburgh anatomists were always eager for "subjects," as they called the cadavers. At the university, the professor of anatomy was guaranteed a supply of newly hanged felons to dissect, but the surgeons across the road had to make their own arrangements. Often they dealt on a no-questions-asked basis with "body snatchers" or "resurrection men," who exhumed recently buried corpses from graves. Eager medical students were sometimes shot at while engaged in this business. Body snatchers would smash through a coffin lid, fasten a rope round the neck of the corpse, and haul it up, often disfiguring the face to prevent recognition. The rigid body was then beaten into shape so that it would fit into a box for delivery to the dissector's premises. In some older Scottish churchyards, you can still see large, hull-shaped iron protectors that were placed over newly dug graves to frustrate such "resurrectionists."

Servicing this lucrative economy, Burke and Hare cut out the middle-man. Not for them midnight excavations in increasingly well-guarded grave-yards. Instead, they made a bee-line for living victims, selecting murderees among the "wretched dens of the old town." Many of their victims were never missed, or at least never effectively searched for. Secure in his fine sub-urban home at 4 Newington Place (today renumbered as 17), Knox did not deal with Burke and Hare directly, though he made sure his assistant, Pater-son, was able to pay them a customary fee of £10 per body—far, far more than the two shillings a day Burke had earned as a navvy helping to dig the nearby Union Canal. Not until Saturday, November 1, 1828, when neigh-bours began to ask questions about the disappearance of Mrs. Margaret Campbell, did investigators start to uncover the truth. After Hare cut a deal and revealed the crimes, Burke and his wife, Helen McDougal, were ar-rested. Held in the Calton Jail, they were put on trial.

The stories of several of their victims have become part of Edinburgh's mythology. One person they killed, Mary Paterson (unrelated to Knox's as-sistant), a young woman who had shown no signs of prior illness, was pre-served by Knox in whisky for three months before being dissected. In her 2010 study, *The Anatomy Murders,* Lisa Rosner quotes Burke confessing that the anatomist Knox "brought in a painter to look at [Mary Paterson], she was so handsome a figure, and well shaped in body and limbs"; Knox's assistant also recalled that her body was sketched by students—he said he kept one of the works produced. A later writer claimed that a drawing by "J. Oliphant" was based on such earlier artwork. This titillating, necrophil-iac picture shows a beautiful young woman's reclining body viewed from the rear, and recalls Velázquez's Rokeby Venus. As early as December 1828, be-fore Burke's execution, Walter Scott had heard that one of the victims was "a prostitute of uncommon personal beauty." Oliphant's image is of a piece with later, embellished accounts which claimed that the good-looking Mary had been recognized on the dissecting table by a medical student who had slept with her shortly before.

Recent research by Rosner suggests that Paterson was an eighteen-year-old "girl of the town" who had spent time in the Magdalene Asylum for "fallen women" in the Canongate, which she had left only a day before her murder. However elaborated, the story of the lovely young woman sordidly murdered, then relished and dissected by the respectable, unscrupulous Dr. Knox, contains the mixed voyeuristic elements of gentility and horror that often characterize aspects of Edinburgh's story. Mary Paterson comes to be endowed with the tragic loveliness of her fascinating namesake Mary Queen of Scots; Paterson's murderers are as brutally violent as those of Rizzio and Darnley; her eventual enemy, the dissectionist doctor, came from a family that claimed as an ancestor Mary Queen of Scots's old Reformation adversary John Knox.

The more the Burke and Hare murders were scrutinized, the more Robert Knox, who was never tried, seemed implicated. Why, when Knox dissected the lad, had he not recognized the familiar Old Town figure of the handicapped "Daft Jamie," immortalized in a drawing by local artist Walter Geikie. Others had thought it was Jamie, but Knox, who cut off the youth's distinctively deformed feet, had assured his students this could not be the corpse of anyone they knew. A punchy couplet in a popular rhyme summed up most people's perception: "Burke's the butcher, Hare's the thief,/And Knox the boy who buys the beef." Half-rhyming with the verb "buys," the noun "boy" seems scornfully familiar. The *Scotsman* implied that Knox must have realized what was happening; the doctor himself kept silent. He was burked and hanged, in effigy, by youths outside his house, which had all of its windows smashed.

After a twenty-four-hour trial on Christmas Eve 1828, Burke was hanged on January 28 the following year; Hare went free, eventually vanishing without trace. The criminal participation of Burke's wife, Helen, was judged "not proven." At the trial, evidence came from Robert Christison, the university's "professor of medical jurisprudence and medical police"—a forensic pathologist who later produced a standard work entitled *The Medico-Legal Examination of Dead Bodies*. One of Christison's colleagues, Professor James Syme, had as his assistant Joseph Bell, that other initiate of the Royal

College of Surgeons, who was famed for his brilliant deductions about patients' biographies and circumstances. Given to wearing a deerstalker hat when he went bird-watching, Bell chose as his assistant Edinburgh medical student Arthur Conan Doyle. "It is most certainly to you that I owe Sherlock Holmes," Doyle later wrote to him.

So narratives associated with the College of Surgeons passed into crime fiction. Indeed, Burke and Hare's activities and fate can seem almost conditioned by earlier Edinburgh imaginings. In the early nineteenth century, courtroom proceedings were routinely turned into books: trials are essential to Scott's Edinburgh novel *The Heart of Midlothian* (1818), while the digging-up of a corpse is part of the mystery of James Hogg's *Private Memoirs and Confessions of a Justified Sinner* (1824). The sins of Burke and Hare were novelized (crudely and anonymously) as early as 1829 in *Murderers of the Close*, and books setting out the factual minutiæ of the case appeared just days after Burke's hanging in the High Street, near St. Giles. Yet it would be hard to come up with a fictional plot better than the reality of the events: Burke's body was handed over for dissection to Knox's old rival, Edinburgh University anatomy professor Alexander Monro. His colleague Professor Christison struggled as students rioted, clamouring to be among the 30,000 people who viewed the killer's corpse.

Today the College of Surgeons museum has a display devoted to its founder, Robert Knox. He stands, dandily dressed, with one eye closed as if forever winking at posterity. Eventually, frozen out of the city's society, Knox did something no one from Edinburgh ever does lightly: he moved to Glasgow. Burke's death mask can also be seen in the museum. So can a pocket notebook, complete with pencil, reputedly made out of the murderer's skin. Edinburgh University has kept Burke's skeleton, now an anatomical model. Even more grotesquely, you can ask to see in the university library a document on which the killer's dissector, Alexander Monro (whom Darwin thought "so dirty in person & actions"), inscribed with a quill pen, "This is written with the blood of William Burke . . . taken from his head on the 1st of Feb. 1829"—surely Edinburgh's goriest manuscript.

After such horrors, some respite is called for. A short walk from where Monro dissected Burke's body lies a green, tranquil site, secreted from the city's cars and buses, though hardly free of insistent thoughts of mortality. Greyfriars Kirkyard affords striking vistas, as well as that sense of richly tex-

tured history which makes Edinburgh such an addictive city. In this churchyard are buried many of the Scottish capital's great and good, from Renaissance poet George Buchanan to chemist Joseph Black and architect James
Craig. Yet the graveyard is most famous in modern times for its association
with a terrier. This dog's indigent owner was an Edinburgh policeman, John
Gray, who died of tuberculosis in 1858 and was buried in Greyfriars Kirkyard. Many poor people fell sick in the days when the Old Town contained
more than 1,500 one-room apartments, each sleeping between six and fifteen folk. Often, canines fared better. For a decade after Gray's death, the
dog Bobby lingered by his master's grave; he was said to exit the churchyard
when the one-o'-clock gun was fired at the Castle, and to go for a lunch provided at the nearby Coffee House which his master had favoured in life.

So familiar and celebrated did this animal become that by 1867 a lady
from Leamington in England was quoted in the *Scotsman* as offering "to
subscribe for a kennel, to be placed over the grave so faithfully watched by
the poor dog, to protect him from cold and rain." Internationally, dog stories were popular, not least in Victorian Edinburgh, where physician John
Brown published *Our Dogs* in 1862, three years after his popular canine narratives in *Rab and His Friends*. In 1867, when a bylaw required Edinburgh's
dogs to be licenced, the Lord Provost, the famous publisher William Chambers, paid for Bobby's licence and had him presented with the brass collar
now in the Museum of Edinburgh inscribed "Greyfriars Bobby from the
Lord Provost 1867 licensed." By February 1868, the aging Bobby had his
portrait painted by Gourlay Steell, recently appointed Queen Victoria's animal painter for Scotland; Steell's picture of "that now famous and most esti-
mable of terriers," lying "with his head between his paws by his old master's
grave" was exhibited and admired at the Royal Scottish Academy. Sadly, on
January 17, 1872, the *Scotsman* published a notice of Bobby's death: "Every
kind attention was paid to him in his last days by his guardian, Mr. Traill,
who has had him buried in a flower-pot near Greyfriars' church."

The dog's afterlife was even more remarkable. In 1873, a fabulously
wealthy London banking heiress and animal rights campaigner, Angela
Georgina Burdett-Coutts (who also complained that year about the mis-
treatment of the horses which pulled Edinburgh's recently installed trams)
commissioned a memorial fountain to Greyfriars Bobby. Sited at the inner
edge of the pavement at the corner of George IV Bridge and Candlemaker

28. Affording pleasant glimpses of George Heriot's School behind its trees, Greyfriars Kirkyard is an inner-city haven of peace. Here are memorials to the great and good of Edinburgh—from Renaissance poet George Buchanan to James Craig, planner of the New Town. Perhaps the kirkyard's best-known resident is Greyfriars Bobby, buried by his guardian in a flower pot.

Row, the monument has an octagonal granite base that was intended as a drinking place for dogs. Above, on top of a column, the bronze statue of the sitting Bobby can still be seen, sculpted by William Brodie. Apparently unrelated to his famous namesake, Deacon Brodie, this other Brodie also made sculptures for the Scott Monument. He produced statues of worthies such as Lord Cockburn and (in Princes Street Gardens) Sir J. Y. Simpson—but it is his bronze of Greyfriars Bobby which is Edinburgh's best-loved piece of public sculpture.

The canine hero's story had local appeal, but was also researched from afar. Most famously, Chicago investigative journalist Eleanor Atkinson drew on it for her 1912 book *Greyfriars Bobby*. Atkinson had never visited Scotland's capital city. She had, though, grown up listening to the work of Burns and Scott, her mother's favourite poets, and had read about Edinburgh from her childhood. Clearly she admired Walter Scott's dog-loving propensities, as well as the widely republished 1809 speech on cruelty to animals by

Edinburgh-born radical lawyer Lord Erskine, but her favourite animal character seems to have been "Dr. Brown's immortal Rab." Atkinson's book
presents Bobby's story as "quite the most complete and remarkable ever
recorded in dog annals." Her Skye terrier ventures across the city, even clambering (and eventually rolling) down the Castle Rock. Influenced by Scotland's once-popular sentimental "kailyard" (cabbage-patch) fiction, Atkinson's story was comfortingly sentimental; its original dust jacket advertised a
"refutation of the Darwinian theory of universal conflict for a survival of the
fittest." *Greyfriars Bobby* was the reverse of Tennyson's "Nature, red in tooth
and claw." Reviewed in such American magazines as the *Atlantic Educational Journal* and *The Smart Set: A Magazine of Cleverness,* it became an
approved nursery favourite for younger readers, even if the *Scotsman*'s re-
viewer thought that "its American origin is discernable," and complained
that some of its supposedly Scots locutions "rather grate on Scottish readers." Almost half a century after its first publication, Walt Disney filmed the
narrative. Since then, it has been further diffused through television, radio,
and the Web. There is a replica of Bobby's statue in San Diego, but only
in Edinburgh can you trot across the street from the small, shaggy bronze
sculpture and, following the terrier's 1860s route, proceed into Greyfriars
Kirkyard.

This burial site affords splendid views of the Castle to the north, and of
the elaborate Renaissance architecture of George Heriot's School to the
southwest. A bequest from "Jinglin Geordie"—James VI's royal goldsmith,
George Heriot—led to the building of the original school, a "hospital" (char-
ity school), in the mid-seventeenth century. Its architecture is based partly
on a design for an Italian palace by Sebastiano Serlio, and partly on the Lowland Scottish royal abode at Linlithgow. Turreted, cupolaed, and breathtak-
ingly ornate with its 220 carved windows, the Jacobean school was built to
provide for the "fatherless bairns" of guildsmen—skilled artisans—who had
died before they could see their children educated. This school, which educated the orphaned painter Henry Raeburn, still offers free places to children of widows and assisted places to children of families below a certain
income threshold, but is now one of many expensive educational establishments in a city where far more people are privately educated than anywhere
else in Scotland. The building's inner quadrangle is richly adorned with
carvings, including representations of the four continents; Australasia had

not been discovered by Europeans when this school was built. Paving slabs in the inner quadrangle bear incised numerals from 1 to 180. On these, the original male pupils had to line up each morning, in all weathers, to be counted. Still visible, the regimented numbers are close together. Perhaps the boys were small. Maybe they were simply being encouraged to keep warm.

If one of the best glimpses of Heriot's is from the western corner of Greyfriars Kirkyard, the viewer should not miss the small memorials there to Walter Geikie and William McGonagall. Geikie (1795–1837) is the artist who, in the 1820s and 1830s, did most to depict working-class people in nineteenth-century Edinburgh. A posthumously published volume of his work, entitled *Etchings, Illustrative of Scottish Character and Scenery* (1841), contains pictures such as "Apples, 5 a Ha'penny," in which a hatted street vendor urges children to buy fruit from his barrow, and an illustration of fishwives with donkeys bearing panniers full of herring; in this image, one of the women is being asked by a man who holds out a coin, "Are you sure it's gude, Mistress?" Fishwives selling fish from wicker creels were still being photographed on Edinburgh streets in the 1940s, but Geikie depicted them in their heyday. He also portrayed an elderly shawled woman and her labourer husband, who is spooning his breakfast from a tin dish, eyed by their dog.

This artist seems to have been everywhere in working-class Edinburgh. He recorded the Newhaven fishing community which Charles Darwin had known, shortly before the calotypists Hill and Adamson photographed it. On the cobbled roadway near St. Giles, Geikie drew the hanging of William Burke "on the spot," with one man clambering on another's shoulders for a better view. He also made a superb drawing from life of that dumb boy known as "Daft Jamie," later one of Burke and Hare's victims, who was said to have walked through the Old Town "with one of his arms contracted upon his breast"; in the image, barefoot Jamie hunches in old patched trousers with ragged cuffs. Other drawings, such as "May Rennie Peeling Potatoes" (in the collection of the National Gallery of Scotland), have been admired for their dignity. By turns a humorous caricaturist, a shrewd observer, and an architectural recorder, the well-liked Geikie often sketched in the roadway. It is said that just six days before his death he was painting a scene in the High Street with one of his young nephews on his knee.

Deaf and dumb from the age of two, Geikie seems to have used sign language at home and was a founder of the world's first church for the deaf. It still meets in Edinburgh. Special education for deaf people had been available in the Scottish capital since the eighteenth century, when Samuel Johnson, visiting in 1773, thought Thomas Braidwood's "college of the deaf and dumb" an institution such as "no other city has to show." Later, seven years before Geikie's death, publisher James Donaldson left money to build and endow Donaldson's School, a grandly Gothic building set back behind a large lawn in the city's West Coates. Designed by William Playfair and completed in 1851, it came to specialize in educating deaf children and, before its teachers and pupils moved to another site outside Edinburgh in the early twenty-first century, they contributed to the installation of the memorial plaque to Geikie now set into one of the walls of Greyfriars Kirkyard. It quotes two lines from a much longer poem written in the artist's memory— a work that imitates, fittingly if a little awkwardly, the verse of Robert Fergusson:

> Come join wi' me, sons o' Auld Reekie,
> To weave a wreath for glorious Geikie,
> Wha lighted scenes, auld, black, an' smeeky,   *smoky*
>   Wi' glamourie;   *enchantment*
> While humour braid, wi' wit right sleeky,   *broad*
>   Dwalt in his ee.   *eye*

Very close to Geikie's memorial tablet is a plaque in memory of another son of Edinburgh, the "poet and tragedian" William McGonagall, whose verse is often thought to be the world's worst. McGonagall, who spent a good deal of his life in Dundee, was buried in a pauper's grave in Greyfriars Kirkyard in 1902. And so, in close conjunction for the rest of time, are a poet famed for declaiming histrionically his execrable rhymes and a fine artist who was profoundly deaf.

In Robert Louis Stevenson's day, the cemetery was overrun with cats. So much for its most famous dog. Stevenson remembered a gravedigger pointing out to him a soon-to-be demolished house beside the churchyard where "Burke, the resurrection man, infamous for so many murders at five shillings a head, used to sit . . . , with pipe and nightcap, to watch burials going forward on the green." In and around the combined Old and New Greyfriars churches, the National Covenant, pledging Scotland's loyalty to Presbyterian worship, had been signed by Covenanters in 1638, just a few years before Edinburgh lost maybe a third of its population to one of several outbreaks of plague. The National Covenant document is now displayed in the pleasant calm of the Museum of Edinburgh, but Covenanting times were vicious. Persecuted by Royalist judge George "Bluidy" Mackenzie, many Covenanters froze or starved to death when part of Greyfriars Kirkyard was turned into a concentration camp in 1679. The Martyrs' Monument of 1706 recalls how "They did endure the wrath of enemies, / Reproaches, torments, deaths and injuries"; their persecutor, one-time novelist Lord Advocate Mackenzie, has his own grand mausoleum not far off. In Stevenson's boyhood, "It was thought a high piece of prowess to knock at the Lord Advocate's mausoleum and challenge him to appear. 'Bluidy Mackenzie, come oot if ye daur!'"

The graveyard's rich collection of seventeenth-century tombstones was photographed by Hill and Adamson in the 1840s. In one picture of Mackenzie's mausoleum, a figure looks a little as if he is playing the game Stevenson mentioned; but other calotypes record the tombs' melancholy grandeur. Photographer Thomas Keith came here later, as did his American admirer Alvin Langdon Coburn in 1905, when he photographed a single leafless tree against the tombs. The site, set aside as a graveyard in 1562 and occupying the ground of a medieval monastery, is haunting and said to be haunted. Yet it is also life giving, in good weather at any rate—a calm, recuperative space near busy roads and tourist-thronged museums.

Running from the north side of the university to a junction opposite the statue of Greyfriars Bobby and the entrance to Greyfriars Kirkyard, Chambers Street is named after William Chambers (1800–1883), the Lord Provost of Edinburgh who was most prominent among the city's many dog lovers. His oddest publication, *Fiddy: An Autobiography of a Dog* (1851), may help to explain why he was so moved by the fidelity of Greyfriars Bobby that he presented that famous canine with an engraved collar. With his younger brother Robert, whose anonymously published *Vestiges of the Natural History of Creation* caused a Victorian scandal and influenced Darwin, William established the once world-famous firm of W. and R. Chambers, publishers of reference books, dictionaries, and, from 1832, the popular paper *Chambers's Edinburgh Journal*. The Chambers brothers were both philanthropic, though very different in character. Robert was wonderfully scholarly. Among his unpublished papers in the National Library, you can still find such nuggets as his transcription (in Deposit 341/58) of an August 1787 certificate releasing Robert Burns from a writ issued against him by May Cameron, a Highland servant who had become pregnant after sleeping with Burns in Edinburgh; on the back of it, Chambers identified a fragment of a song in Burns's hand (a fragment missed by subsequent editors):

The piper went to Falkland fair,
    She was Patie Burnie's mither
Mony a bony lass was there
    Who twit their father and their mither.

    Chorus
Twa and twa they made the bed
    Twa and twa they lay thegither
When they had na room enough
The tane lap on aboon the tither.

Tune[:] the Ruffian's Rant.

His scribbling this on the back of a legal document about May Cameron rather sums up Burns's attitude towards Edinburgh servant lasses; but if Robert Chambers delighted in collecting such old lore, his brother, William, was more of a hardheaded businessman. Children of a bankrupt, the Chambers brothers learned their business selling books in Leith Walk, and always published for "the people." Edinburgh had been a centre of printing since 1509, and in the nineteenth century publishers such as Constable, Ballantyne (whose printing press is imaginatively displayed in the Writers' Museum), Blackwood, Nelson, and the cartographers Bartholomew helped to make it a capital of print, employing many typesetters, bookbinders, journalists, and authors.

In 1843 *Chambers's Edinburgh Journal* printed an account of "Messrs Chambers's Soirée," held annually for the workers at their Edinburgh plant. William praised their premises—which had a library, boys' school, boys' and girls' Sunday school, and savings bank—as a recognized "model for factory management." By that time, "about 7,000,000" issues of the periodically published *Chambers's Information for the People* had been "disposed of—scattered all over the United Kingdom and the Colonies." After enjoying "fruit, cake, and lemonade" at the soirée, the Chambers workers and management listened to "songs, glees, and the performance of an instrumental band." Then Robert Chambers, speaking at a time when Chartist radicals were agitating for votes and the economy was depressed, assured "the working man" that "the amount of the wages of each man depends, again, on fixed laws of our mundane economy, as fixed, apparently, as those which regulate the movements of the planets."

The Chambers brothers, like other Edinburgh employers, were staunch Victorian capitalists, but comparatively enlightened ones. Later centred round dictionaries and encyclopædias, their business lasted in Edinburgh until 2009. In the middle of Chambers Street, Lord Provost William's statue stands on a base designed by Hyppolyte Blanc, who helped to remodel the Castle. Round that base, relief panels representing Literature, Liberality, and Perseverance communicate the old publisher's declared ideals. The roadway's northeast corner is dominated by a wall of Edinburgh University's main building; farther along, at the western end, the magnificently restored former Royal Scottish Museum is now amalgamated with its mighty post-modern neighbour, the National Museum of Scotland. The Museum— free, capacious, and skilfully curated—ensures that Chambers Street remains rich in "information for the people." The Museum of Scotland also affords wonderful, windy views from its rooftop terrace.

While *Chambers's Edinburgh Journal* was in its heyday, the Royal Scottish Museum, originally the Museum of Science and Art, was designed in 1861 by the melancholy Irish architect and engineer Francis Fowke, who later drew up plans for London's Royal Albert Hall. Though Fowke's Albert Hall designs were modified, in Edinburgh his museum was built as he intended. Restored in 2011 to its original splendour, it stands as his masterpiece, the airy interior of its Great Hall aptly described as "a huge elegant bird-cage of glass and iron." Though this museum's collections range from Egyptology to costume and natural history, at its heart is a narrative which celebrates ways in which amateur as well as professional scientists from Scotland investigated civilizations, explored the globe, and made intellectual breakthroughs. Glories of the past are celebrated through exhibits such as the Nobel Prize awarded to Alexander Fleming for his discovery of penicillin; but the museum also seeks to interact with a continuing tradition of Scottish scientific endeavour. Edinburgh's pioneering annual Science Festi-

29. Suitably monumental, the National Museum of Scotland dominates the southwest corner of Chambers Street with its late twentieth-century round tower. Farther along Chambers Street, the museum is joined to Francis Fowke's superbly airy building of 1861, originally designed as the Museum of Science and Art.

val, first held in 1980, has run projects on topics from robotics to the interface between poetry and science. In its imaginatively constructed core narrative, the Museum of Scotland, mindful of its original title as the Museum of Science and Art, seeks to reveal similar connections between scientific achievement and other areas of culture. In so doing, like the Royal Society of Edinburgh, it articulates Scottish traditions of intellectual generalism and the interplay between science and quite different forms of creativity, rather than becoming trapped in the "two cultures" model which, sadly, dominated many twentieth-century debates about the arts and sciences.

Emphasizing artistic engagement with science, the former Royal Museum is joined physically to its modern sibling, purpose-built as the National Museum of Scotland. A handsome late twentieth-century building, the National Museum displays artistic treasures as well as some large pieces of industrial machinery, including one of the world's oldest surviving steam engines. Built in 1786, the year Robert Burns first published his *Poems* and visited Edinburgh, this steam engine uses technology modified to great effect by James Watt in Glasgow, where in 1769 Watt had invented his separate condenser (also displayed in the museum). Engines like this one, manufactured by the English firm of Boulton and Watt, were exported across Europe in the eighteenth and nineteenth centuries. Their early adoption helped to make Scotland one of the most intensely industrialized nations on earth; but it was Glasgow and the west, rather than Edinburgh, that used them most. The museum's big Boulton and Watt engine is run regularly, while its even larger, more starkly dramatic cousin, a Newcomen engine which once pumped water from Kilmarnock coal mines, is also in daily operation.

Though the National Museum presents narratives of Scotland as a whole, deploying artefacts ranging from geological specimens through prehistoric tools to modern vehicles, some of its exhibits do relate particularly to Edinburgh—and not only to the Scottish capital's glories. Here visitors can see the Maiden, a beheading machine rather like a guillotine, which, from 1564 until 1710, was used for public executions on Castlehill, in the Grassmarket, and at the old Edinburgh Cross on the High Street. This portable oak-and-metal killing device could be disassembled and packed flat for ease of transportation. It offered convicted criminals a death quicker than hanging, and its own deviser was beheaded by it in 1581. Edinburgh was the nation's principal place of judicial slaughter, but did not always keep that business to itself. When the Marquis of Montrose was executed for rebellion against King Charles I on May 21, 1650, an eyewitness wrote: "His sentence was, to be hanged upon a gallows thirty feet high, three hours, at Edinburgh Cross; to have his head stricken off, and hanged upon Edinburgh Tolbooth, and his arms and legs to be hanged up in other public towns in the kingdom, as Glasgow, &c." That revealingly offhand phrase "Glasgow, &c." indicates nicely that the Scottish capital's attitude towards its western counterpart has a long, dismissive history. Edinburgh would display Montrose's head; Glasgow would get one of his off-cuts. Montrose's remarkable poem "On Himself, upon Hearing What Was His Sentence" records eloquently in its measured lines a determined commitment in the face of execution (the Scots word "airth" means "part"):

Let them bestow on ev'ry Airth a Limb;
Open all my Veins, that I may swim
To Thee my Saviour, in that Crimson Lake;

Then place my purboil'd Head upon a Stake;
Scatter my Ashes, throw them in the Air:
Lord (since Thou know'st where all these Atoms are)
I'm hopeful, once Thou'lt recollect my Dust,
And confident Thou'lt raise me with the Just.

As well as nobility, a stubborn sense of righteousness has run throughout much Scottish piety. The National Museum of Scotland holds the mysterious Monymusk Reliquary, an ornamental box beautifully designed to preserve holy relics in medieval Catholic Scotland; yet that museum also stands in a city which, even as the Enlightenment approached, could seem unflinchingly harsh in religious matters. In 1697, Sir John Clerk of Penicuik, an enlightened art patron, watched with approval as an impoverished twenty-year-old orphan and Edinburgh student, Thomas Aikenhead, became the last person in Britain to be executed for blasphemy. John Locke later acquired a copy of the statement Aikenhead wrote on the last day of his life, in which he defended "reason" and "a pure love to truth."

In eighteenth-century Edinburgh, the Enlightenment was powered both by the atheistic David Hume and by those several Church of Scotland ministers who were to the fore at Edinburgh University. Such very different parties could meet socially, and get along, albeit uneasily, sometimes clashing in print. Their co-existence emblematizes Edinburgh as a city of intellectual light; but it remained, as well, a place of stygian darkness. Seventeen tiny decorated pinewood coffins, each about four inches long and containing a small clothed human effigy, were found on the northeastern slope of Arthur's Seat in June 1836. Now among the National Museum's oddest exhibits, their meaning has never been fully explained. Some think they may have been made by a carpenter determined to commemorate the known victims of Burke and Hare. Looking like ghoulish children's toys, they caught the attention of the city's most celebrated modern crime novelist, Ian Rankin, who worked them into his 2001 novel *The Falls* as emblems of "Edinburgh's blood-soaked past." Arthur's Seat, where they were found along with "a variety of witch's accoutrements," is also the setting for a possible encounter with the devil in what may be the greatest of all novels to use the Scottish capital as a location: James Hogg's eerie *Private Memoirs and Confessions of a Justified Sinner* (1824). Set in the period just after Aikenhead's execution and published anonymously a couple of years before Burke and Hare began their killing spree, that disturbing novel was written by a man well used to mixing with Edinburgh's literati. Deviously, mischievously, and with a certain Auld-Reikieish glee, he did his best to imply that the true author of this chronicle of wickedness and bloody deeds was in fact a Glaswegian.

⤙ Glasgow ⤚

‎ SIX ‎

City Hearts

Rightly regarded as a bighearted city, Glasgow has several urban hearts. This chapter moves amongst them, traversing three inner-city miles and uncovering some of the often obscured historical and ideological foundations of the present-day municipality. Glasgow's oldest heart, faithful and still beating, is the medieval Cathedral, about a mile east of the present-day town centre. Renaissance Glasgow had its heart farther south, in the area surrounding Glasgow Cross, between the Cathedral and the River Clyde; nearby lies Glasgow Green, open ground given to the city in the fifteenth century and a traditional heartland of political radicalism. From the late 1700s, however, a more modern municipal heart—George Square—began to develop. Once a "hollow filled with green-water, and a favourite resort for drowning puppies," today the Square is Glasgow's undoubted centrepiece. Long decked out with bronze memorials (which modernizers want relocated), it deserves to be the starting point for anyone sizing up the city.

George Square is a sustained volley of British Empire Victoriana. Though conceived in the Georgian 1780s, it was almost entirely redeveloped in the nineteenth century. Its monuments and monumentality confirm Glasgow as an ornate city of imperialism, and are themselves no strangers to strife. The first statue was erected before Queen Victoria's accession to the throne—and was soon vandalized by local residents. In 1819, a fine statue designed by John Flaxman was erected (as the inscription around the base puts it) "to commemorate the military services of Lieutenant General Sir John Moore," a heroic "Native of Glasgow" whom "his fellow citizens" wished to honour. Born in the city's Trongate to a literary doctor and a professor's daughter, Moore was schooled in Glasgow but made his name on imperial battlefields. Soldiering through America, Canada, the Caribbean, Ireland, Egypt, and across Europe from Corsica to Sweden—slashed to the skull, felled by fever, shot through the head—he seemed unkillable. Eventually, this

30. Dominated by the City Chambers building, George Square is the heart of present-day Glasgow. Its imposing public monuments pay tribute to Glaswegians who died in many a war. Yet its tallest column was erected to carry a statue of an Edinburgh man, Sir Walter Scott. Glaswegians are broad-minded, as well as big-hearted.

battling Scotsman was cut down by French cannon shot at the Battle of Corunna (in northwestern Spain) in 1809, having said, reportedly, "I hope the people of England will be satisfied." No one in today's Glasgow could say that without sarcasm.

Yet, in his day, Moore exemplified Glaswegian service for a British Empire led by England but with Scotland contributing administrative *nous* and expendable fighting force. Soon to George Square was added a statue of a Glasgow carpenter's son named Colin Campbell, whose first battlefield service was with Moore in Spain. Campbell eventually fought all across the Empire in territories ranging from Barbados to Hong Kong, growing rich in combat against Sikhs in India during the 1840s, then against Russians in the Crimean War, where his bright-uniformed Scottish Highland troops were nicknamed "the thin red line." Later, Campbell led the suppression of the 1858 Indian Mutiny and so saved Britain's dominion over that subcontinent. Victorian Glasgow, presenting him with a sword of honour, loved such sons, and Campbell, though he spent little time in his native city, took the name of its river when Queen Victoria, Empress of India, conferred a knighthood on him: he chose the title "Lord Clyde." From one angle, Moore and Campbell can be seen as "men's men," even, in a city with a reputation for generous toughness, as examples of Glaswegian "hardman" machismo. Their world was at heart homosocial. Unmarried, leaving no known descendants, they might have felt at ease in a George Square where almost all of the statues depicted males; the sole woman was their celebrated monarch, haughtily confident on her pacing horse and holding what looked like a spear but was actually her regal sceptre. Her military commanders were, par excellence, fighters for empire, and many Glaswegians sailed abroad as their cannon fodder.

Though George Square, so much grander than its Edinburgh namesake, is, like many of the surrounding streets, quintessentially Victorian, Queen Victoria hardly saw it. She and Prince Albert (who pronounced Glasgow Cathedral "a magnificent building") visited in 1849, when the Square appeared "like a neglected churchyard." Not many months earlier, gun-toting rioters had scared the city's establishment during Europe's radical revolutions of 1848. The queen stayed away for almost forty years. Nothing, however, is more redolent of imperial Glasgow than the excitement which greeted her return in August 1888 to open the splendid new Municipal Buildings in George Square. By that date, the Square was described by a London newspaper as "one of the finest civic enclosures in the whole kingdom," even if Glaswegian wags nicknamed it "our local Valhalla." Its memorial statues ranged from one of Glaswegian chemist Thomas Graham, inventor of dialysis, to Robert Peel, pioneer of Victorian policing, sculpted in bronze by popular local artist John Mossman.

George Square remains solemnly impressive. Its statues have been rearranged over the decades, but it is still dominated by the 1888 Municipal Buildings, today termed the City Chambers. Designed by William Young from the nearby industrial town of Paisley, this grand Victorian fantasy of authoritarianism, headquarters of Glasgow City Council, was built while the city had some of Europe's worst slums; yet it strives hard to evoke the regnant architecture of Rome and Venice. When Queen Victoria stopped by in 1888, it was still a building site. The *Glasgow Herald* explained that she would perform the opening ceremony "without . . . alighting from her carriage." Glaswegians grew ecstatic about this rare royal visitor. To let her

sense their city's grandeur, the city's artisans made a "Glasgow Gold Cas-
ket," its front bearing "a view of the new Municipal Buildings from George
Square, with [a] small sketch on each side representing Railway and Shipping Commerce." Preparing to welcome Her Majesty, the city's magistrates
ordered themselves new robes made of black corded silk, lined with white
satin, and trimmed with ermine. Decorated masts and banners were erected,
in the hope they would make George Square and other parts of the city look
unassailably Venetian.

Yet the queen, more used to Edinburgh than Glasgow, represented the
remoteness, almost the untouchability of authority. Just as the high plinths
in George Square raised its statues far above common passersby, so on Victoria's visit to this most architecturally Victorian of cities, a ruthless apart-
heid separated hoi polloi from civic dignitaries. Nearly 1,200 policemen
manned barricades designed to keep common folk far from their monarch.
But as soon as her train arrived at the vast (now demolished) St. Enoch's
Station, people began to topple off the boxes and barrels they had piled up
in an effort to glimpse her. Some boys who had climbed onto the roof of
a public urinal fell through it when the glass panes shattered. Except for
those granted spaces in specially erected stands round its perimeter, the
crowds were cleared from central George Square by constables; "a little
ragged urchin escaped" their "vigilance," and onlookers cheered with typically Glaswegian gusto as he dodged among the officers. Addressing its
largely prosperous middle-class audience, the *Glasgow Herald* noted this
with wry amusement; but less than three decades later, when the boys who
fell through the urinal roof and the jinking urchin were mature men, it was
just such working-class people who would turn against Glasgow's authority
figures, whom they saw as oppressively controlling their lives and excluding
them forever from the city's structures of power.

After the queen's brief visit in 1888, the new City Chambers was finished
to a standard of sumptuous imperial opulence. Inside, where few of the poor
from the slums ever went, visitors could ascend by "an elevator, fitted up by
the American Elevator Company with a luxuriantly appointed car," or could
stroll up the magnificent pillared marble staircase past alabaster panels to
the Banqueting Hall. The French monarch Louis XVI and the Doge of Venice are among those whose architecture is invoked in these interiors.

Locals and tourists alike still marvel at the Faience Corridor and the now silk-wallpapered Lord Provost's Room, to which Victoria in 1888 presented a splendid Lord Provost's chair. Yet, however exotic, this municipal extravaganza has a confident Glasgow accent. Its Banqueting Hall is in part decorated with murals painted in 1899–1902 by some of those artists nicknamed the "Glasgow Boys." John Lavery has depicted nineteenth-century industrial scenes, contrasting somewhat with the darker portrayal of a medieval Glasgow Fair by E. A. Walton. In time, on the exterior of the building's frontage, a pediment was added to celebrate Queen Victoria's jubilee. It shows the monarch receiving homage from her imperial subjects; a little way off are depicted the trades and industries of Glasgow.

If Victorian empire and heady opulence are part of the story of George Square, so is rebellion against such things. The splendour of the City Chambers also explains the counterbalancing tradition of socialist radicalism which sprang from the city's poor. Just three decades after Glaswegians and the queen rejoiced in the opening of their civic palace, guns were mounted on it and trained on a rebel underclass no longer content to be treated as battlefront sacrifices. Machine guns on turrets threatened George Square rioters during the "Red Clydeside" era around the end of World War I. The suffragette movement and struggles over tenants' rights had helped to radicalize Glaswegian women, such as Gorbals-born hunger striker Helen Crawfurd, imprisoned in Glasgow's Duke Street Prison in 1913 after attacking police officers who were attempting to disrupt a suffragette meeting. Immediately after her release, Crawfurd smashed the windows of an army recruiting office. Later she bombed Glasgow's Botanic Gardens. Militant women as well as men were involved in World War I rent strikes, as socialist parties in Glasgow and elsewhere made inroads into the ruling Liberal government at Westminster. Local schoolteacher John Maclean—another hunger striker, who was hostile to what he saw as an imperialist-capitalist war—was repeatedly arrested as he tried to campaign for an independent Scottish republic governed by "Celtic communism." George Square may seem to be all po-faced Victoriana, but in the minds of many Glaswegians it is associated with a history far more disruptive and radical.

Appointed Consul for Soviet Affairs in Great Britain in the wake of the 1917 Russian Revolution, John Maclean opened a consulate at 12 Portland

31. Glasgow schoolteacher John Maclean, appointed consul for Soviet Affairs in Great Britain after the 1917 Russian Revolution, became an icon of "Red Clydeside." An anti-war campaigner, Maclean denounced World War I as "capitalism dripping with blood from head to foot," and urged workers to undertake revolutionary activities. This photograph was taken after his release from prison in December 1918, when the authorities had attempted to certify him insane.

Street, Glasgow. Yet he soon fell out with the Soviet authorities because of his desire for Scottish independence. One winter's day, in the volatile political climate of early 1919, around 60,000 men and women campaigning for a forty-hour working week were addressed by their leaders in George Square, while a few representatives of the protesters were allowed into the City Chambers. When the protesters' spokesmen emerged, one of them

32. David Kirkwood is batoned by police after trying to calm angry demonstrators in George Square in 1919. An engineer, Kirkwood had been deported to Edinburgh from Glasgow because of his socialist agitation. Following the "Bloody Friday" riots of January 31, 1919, in George Square, he was charged with sedition. This press photograph helped to secure his acquittal.

was clubbed by a policeman. The George Square crowds were then baton-charged by police. The date, January 31, 1919, is known as "Bloody Friday."

Fearing Russian-style revolution and worried that Scottish soldiers might join it, the London government sent in 10,000 armed English troops and brought tanks onto Glasgow's streets. No uprising happened, but history was turning against the sort of triumphalist imperialism that had given rise to the architecture of the City Chambers. Before long, several of those George Square protesters arrested in 1919 had been elected as members of the British Parliament at Westminster, where socialist parties were gaining power. By 1922, the Independent Labour Party had won ten out of fifteen of Glasgow's parliamentary constituencies; a Communist named Walton Newbold was elected to represent the nearby industrial town of Motherwell.

This was the electoral high point of the so-called Red Clydeside movement. Broken after hunger strikes and terms of imprisonment, John Maclean died in 1923; more than 10,000 mourners attended his funeral. The following year, the more moderate Scottish Labour politician Ramsay MacDonald was able to form the first Labour government at Westminster, but the events of George Square in 1919—Glasgow's last full-blown political riot—remain etched in Scotland's political consciousness. Maclean is celebrated in poetry by Edwin Morgan for believing the poor should have access to life's riches and for having let the authorities "know that Scotland was not Britain." The Gaelic poet Sorley MacLean called his namesake simply "Iain mòr MacGill-Eain": "great John Maclean." Today most Glaswegians know something of the era of Red Clydeside and John Maclean, but not one of the radicals of that era is represented among the statues in George Square. Glasgow's most iconic civic site, the Square remains a place of heartfelt ideological conflict, a monument to Victorian imperial values—yet it is also haunted by those values' opponents. Men and women uncommemorated in bronze live on in the hearts of Glasgow's people, who have continued to crowd the Square for protest rallies. A 1992 photograph shows about 40,000 men and women massed there at a peaceable political gathering. The single banner reads: "Free Scotland."

The external grandeur and internal opulence of the City Chambers teeters on the edge of decadence. Rumours of administrative corruption have long been part and parcel of life in a city famed, like Chicago, for grid-plan streets and enterprising gangsters. Every so often, whispers give way to spectacular revelations and further rumours of scandal. Most recently, in 2010, the Socialist Leader of Glasgow City Council resigned suddenly, confessing to cocaine use. More sober and restrained than the City Chambers are George Square's other monumental Victorian edifices. The imposing former General Post Office may look just a little like the Post Office in Dublin which was headquarters to the leaders of Ireland's 1916 Easter Rising, but the Glasgow building has never witnessed a revolution. The one-time George Square branch of the Bank of Scotland, built in 1869 at the corner of St. Vincent Place, lost its sobriety when its long, polished dark-wood counter was transformed into the bar of a late twentieth-century theme pub; where once dark-suited, gentlemanly bank tellers checked ledgers under the ornate plasterwork and high, glass-domed ceiling, now thirsty punters sink their pints. Indoors and out, Glaswegians take Victorian grandeur for granted, and nowhere more so than when they walk through George Square. Among its statues are those of Liberal prime minister William Gladstone, as well as poet Robert Burns and engineer James Watt; but it says something about Glasgow's broad-mindedness that on a high, fluted Doric column, pride of place has been given to the likeness of an Edinburgh man—Walter Scott. Erected in 1837, the western city's monument to Scott predates the capital's by several years—a fact seldom mentioned in Edinburgh.

Even as George Square was developing into modern Glasgow's civic centerpiece, its Enlightenment citizens persisted in hanging out their washing to dry over its grass. Glaswegians have long treasured greenness. Gardeners are celebrated with biblical rhetoric inside the dome of the historic Trades Hall in Glassford Street, and a (sometimes ironic) local nickname for this city remains "the dear green place"—derived from the ancient Celtic *glas cau,* meaning "green hollow." Once nestling in its own grassy landscape, the city's original ecclesiastical focal point and still one of its most recognizable landmarks—the Cathedral—lies today about a mile east of George Square, at the other end of Cathedral Street.

Glasgow Cathedral is the finest building in Scotland which survives substantially intact from the twelfth and thirteenth centuries. Though thoroughly decentred by later building projects, it marks the earliest city centre, and is as essential as George Square to a proper understanding of Glasgow. Consecrated in 1197, the present building replaced an earlier church sacred to the memory of the sixth-century St. Kentigern, also fondly termed St. Mungo—from the Gaelic for "dear friend." Glasgow's patron saint, Mungo seems to have died around the year 612 beside the altar of his cathedral. Very little is known about him, but tradition has it that his mother was St. Thenew, known also as St. Enoch, her name now preserved incongruously in that of Glasgow's large, postmodern St. Enoch Centre shopping mall.

Some late-medieval sources say Mungo came from Fife, and the emblems of Glasgow's coat of arms (granted officially in 1866, but using much earlier motifs) relate to some of his miracles: finding an unfaithful queen's wedding ring inside a salmon; resurrecting the tame robin of his mentor St. Serf; acquiring (perhaps from the pope) a handbell; and restarting a monastery's fire by causing branches from a hazel tree to ignite through the power of prayer. Mungo's emblems—fish, bird, bell, tree—are still recalled in a Glasgow rhyme about the city's coat of arms:

Here's the Tree that never grew,
Here's the Bird that never flew;
Here's the Bell that never rang,
Here's the Fish that never swam.

The legends of Mungo are all about activity and a wonderful interaction with nature. This riddling rhyme is, oddly, about negativity. Tree, bird, bell, and fish remain frozen in heraldic stillness on the city's coat of arms.

Awe, sometimes in short supply in Glasgow, is easy to feel when you stand in the dark crypt close to St. Mungo's tomb. Here the most ancient heart of Glasgow is hidden now below ground level, in a magnificent grove of stone underneath the Cathedral's floor. Close by is a twelfth-century wall bench and a vaulting shaft carved with plant-like decorations; the rest of the medieval crypt dates from the thirteenth century. Around the tomb rise four great carved columns, branching into arches that rhyme, in turn, with further arches beyond. The effect is like being in the midst of a hushed, lamplit forest, a prayer-space of grace but also of enormous solidity: one remains conscious, though not fearful, of the many tons of masonry supported by the elegantly branching, stylized organic forms. This is Glasgow's sacred grove.

Upstairs, at the level of the cathedral's main entrance, the thirteenth-century building manages to be at once plain in its massive, slightly asymmetric cruciform design, yet also soaringly elaborate. The cathedral is 285 feet long, its nave more than a hundred feet high, but—modified in the fifteenth century, then subjected to later attacks and restorations—the structure feels bigger. Separating choir from nave is a choir screen, or "pulpitum" —the only one of its kind left in a pre-Reformation nonmonastic church in Scotland. Though sixteenth-century Protestant Reformation iconoclasts got rid of altars attached to pillars in the nave and dedicated to such saints as St. Christopher, St. Kentigern, and St. Serf, nineteenth-century architects did more damage. They tore down two towers at the Cathedral's western end, and awkwardly altered the western façade. Today, its exterior blackened by centuries of industrial pollution and its fifteenth-century spire retopped after an eighteenth-century lightning strike, Glasgow Cathedral is a resolute

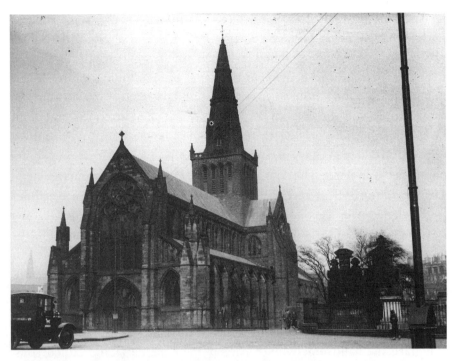

33. A 1935 view of Glasgow Cathedral, looking toward the Necropolis beyond. The present cathedral building was consecrated in 1197, replacing an earlier church sacred to the memory of Glasgow's patron saint, St. Kentigern, also called St. Mungo.

survivor. Usually approached from the west, past busy roads, it seems cut off by traffic from the present-day city centre. Nearby, the red-sandstone Barony Kirk asserts the city's insistent Victorianism. Yet, set against the hillside beyond, which was once surmounted by the medieval bishop's palace but is now given over to the remarkable Glasgow Necropolis, the Cathedral's situation makes the most of the natural landscape. This building is the most obvious architectural statement of the city's proud antiquity, as well as the great emblem of its spiritual life. Other grand edifices have come and gone nearby —Robert Adam's huge, domed 1792 infirmary lasted little more than a century before Glaswegians demolished it—but the Cathedral sustains and is sustained by its city.

Townhead, close to Glasgow Cathedral, has long been a poor area. Working in a studio above a corner shop, the artist Joan Eardley sketched and painted its gregarious children in the 1950s. Her pictures mix graffiti, tenement stone, washing hanging out to dry, and kids at play. One family of twelve, the Sampsons, became her regular models, and several of the Sampson children were photographed, their hair combed but awkwardly cut and their faces mischievously alert, in the midst of her studio's clutter. Their mother disliked the Eardley pictures her children brought home as gifts; she tore them up and threw them on the fire. Much later, when she found out how collectible Eardley's work had become, she realized, "We'd burned millions." Today the blackened tenements Eardley painted are largely stone-cleaned or demolished, but the poor are not gone; down-and-outs are often seen round the back of the Cathedral or over in the grounds of the Necropolis. Burdened with legacies of ill-health and substandard housing, Glasgow has long struggled to look after its socially disadvantaged, as monuments in the Cathedral graveyard hint. One memorial beside the Cathedral's east door commemorates George and Thomas Hutcheson, two seventeenth-century brothers who were successful Glasgow businessmen and left money to build a "hospital for entertainment of the poor, aged, decrepit men," as well as a school for orphans. The brothers' statues were sculpted in 1655 and still grace the handsome white façade of their rebuilt (1805) Hutchesons' Hospital, which stands with its fine clock tower in Ingram Street, not far from George Square; their school for orphans, like so many of Edinburgh's charitable schools, has metamorphosed into a fee-paying co-educational establishment in a city suburb, though its traditional school song still hints at a stern attitude towards the original pupils:

> In 1640 the school began
> With twelve boys on the roll.
> They bent their will to the grim book drill
> For the good of body and soul.

Singers of the song then chant "Hutchesons! Hutchesons!" in rowdy celebration.

The bodies, if not the souls, of many Victorian Glaswegians lie under the remarkable monuments of the Necropolis just east of the Cathedral. In the late 1700s, the area was called Fir Park; tellingly in the early nineteenth century, it became Merchants' Park. At its summit, the well-off men of Glasgow's Merchants' House erected an almost 200-foot-high memorial to John Knox, which still surmounts the hill and proclaims that the famous Protestant Reformer's legacy has led to "Honour, Prosperity, and Happiness." In 1831, at the age of thirty-six, John Strang, a side-whiskered, well-traveled Glaswegian man of letters, published his *Necropolis Glasguensis, with Osbervations* [*sic*] *on Ancient and Modern Tombs and Sepulture.* This pamphlet argued that "a nation's cemetery, and monumental decoration afford the most convincing token of a nation's progress in civilization and the arts." Contending that "a garden cemetery and monumental decoration, are not only beneficial to public morals . . . but are likewise calculated to extend virtuous and generous feelings," Strang invoked the Catacombs of Rome, the Père Lachaise Cemetery in Paris, and other necropolitan glories. He was not alone in wanting what he called an "eyesweet" landscape of tombs for Glasgow, and in 1832 a local Jewish jeweller, Joseph Levi, became the first person to be interred there.

From the start, the Necropolis was interdenominational and international. Its dead range from an exiled Polish freedom fighter, a German locomotive builder, and a Parisian professor of fencing (his memorial in the shape of a raised blade) to many of Victorian Glasgow's doughty merchants and industrialists. Even though some monuments are in a dangerous condition, they form an astonishing array. An impressive Celtic cross memorializing a policeman is one of the earliest surviving works of Glasgow architect Charles Rennie Mackintosh, who once lived nearby, while the city's most eclectically minded architect, Alexander "Greek" Thomson, designed the commanding 1867 monument to his Presbyterian supporter the Reverend Alexander Ogilvie Beattie, who died after commissioning from Thomson a great city church in St. Vincent Street. Much stranger than either of these memorials, the large Douglas Mausoleum—part Christian sepulchre, part Hindu temple—confirms the Necropolis as an architectural wonderland. Some original cemetery paths are grassed over, but the ground is well maintained. If a significant number of the dead are men from Glasgow's imperialist past, such as East India Company officers, most made their money closer to home.

The most fascinating monuments are the least predictable: the twice-life-size bust of David Prince Miller memorializes an actor in Glasgow's nineteenth-century "penny geggie" (cheap theatre) shows; a stumpy stone structure carved with a laurel wreath and lyre commemorates wood-turner William Miller (1810–1872), who dwelt close by in Dennistoun. Known throughout Britain and beyond as the "Laureate of the Nursery," in his early thirties he wrote "Willie Winkie," whose opening lines children can still recite. First published in 1841, the poem was soon anglicized, but was re-printed in its original Scots in Miller's 1863 *Scottish Nursery Songs and Other Poems,* dedicated "To Scottish Mothers," where it begins:

> Wee Willie Winkie
> Rins through the toun, *runs*
> Up stairs and doun stairs
> In his nicht-gown,
> Tirling at the window, *twirling*
> Crying at the lock,
> "Are the weans in their bed, *children*
> For it's now ten o'clock?"

Some of the other poems in Miller's book seem less suitable to nursery use. An example is the solemn English-language "The Poet's Last Song," whose speaker says, "Bring me my lyre" as "the cup of misery soon shall fill."

The Necropolis has many reminders that childhood and childbirth in nineteenth-century Glasgow were often linked to death. Wealthy merchant and shipowner Allan Gilmour, author of *Remarks and Observations by Allan Gilmour on a Tour of America in 1829,* was widowed when his wife, Agnes, died at the age of thirty-three. Decades later, and still a single parent, he was buried alongside her near a sandstone obelisk on which a relief carving shows two very young boys in petticoats, heads bowed, clasping a sister, also young, on whose knee sits a skilfully rendered baby. The inscription reads simply, "Beloved Mother." Mortality rates in nineteenth-century Glasgow were markedly high. Even living in a well-kept, newly constructed 1870s tenement in Fir Park, the young Charles Rennie Mackintosh lost four siblings in infancy. The Necropolis chronicles many such bereavements. One memorial, to "CORLINDA LEE, QUEEN OF THE GIPSIES," states that she died at 42 New City Road, Glasgow, in 1900. "Her love for her children was great, and she was charitable to the poor. Wherever she pitched her tent she was loved and respected by all." Mrs. Lee's bronze relief portrait has been stolen from her monument, but the sandstone structure still records her young grandchild, "Baby May," and the dates when she was "given" and "taken."

Entry from the Cathedral precincts to the Necropolis is through a grand

34. Provand's Lordship, now the oldest house in Glasgow, was built in 1471 and enlarged two hundred years later. Its floorplan is medieval. Today a small museum, it stands close to Glasgow Cathedral and within sight of some very different high-rise architecture.

1838 gateway whose striking black-and-gold iron gates were cast at a city-centre foundry in Queen Street. At the centre of each gate is the gilded sailing-ship emblem of Glasgow's Merchants' House—"the clipper on top of the world"—and the Merchants' House Latin motto, *Toties redeuntis eodem* ("So often returning to the same place"). The way into the Necropolis was originally over the "Bridge of Sighs," which lies beyond these gates and was built in 1833–1834 to span the Molendinar Burn. That ancient stream, associated with St. Mungo, became increasingly polluted; it was culverted over in 1877. If visitors can no longer glimpse this long-treasured Glaswegian watercourse, they can at least see a single medieval house, Provand's Lordship, which was built in 1471 and still stands at 3 Castle Street, on the other side of the Cathedral precincts. Its masonry is largely of the late Middle Ages, as are its oak floor beams. The house was extended in 1671, its windows altered then or later. Inside, the floor plan is medieval: three equal-size rooms on each storey. Furnished with sixteenth- and seventeenth-

193

35. Cast at a city-centre foundry in Queen Street, the grand, black-and-gold painted Victorian gates to the Necropolis feature the emblem of the Glasgow Merchants' House—"the clipper on top of the world"—and that institution's Latin motto, which means "So often returning to the same place."

century items, Provand's Lordship, like the Cathedral, speaks of Glasgow's venerability. Glaswegians have the additional satisfaction of knowing that no small house of comparable antiquity survives in Edinburgh.

Until the nineteenth century, similarly ancient properties stood nearby, but the rest of the area has been extensively remodeled. Not far off, the modern St. Mungo Museum of Religious Life and Art now stands on the site of the perimeter wall of the medieval Castle of the Bishops of Glasgow, and contains a mélange of exhibits relating to many faiths—from a New Caledonian ceremonial axe to a nineteenth-century Chinese dragon robe that was worn in Bernardo Bertolucci's film *The Last Emperor*. From the top floor of the museum, visitors loath to venture among the tombs of the Necropolis can get a fine view of its monuments, looking past the gates to the Bridge of Sighs and the dominant hilltop statue of John Knox, with the Cathedral itself on the left. Inside the museum, on the same floor, artefacts from Glasgow's many faiths, including Hinduism, Islam, and Christianity, are juxtaposed in a somewhat higgledy-piggledy fashion. Some exhibits allude to the city's Protestant-Catholic tensions—not only through modern Protestant insignia, but also through a portrait of that most famous of all Scottish Catholic Renaissance monarchs, Mary Queen of Scots, who fled the battlefield when her forces were defeated for the last time in 1568, at Langside—now a Glasgow suburb proud of its verdant Queen's Park.

So much building and rebuilding has gone on since Mary's time that to perceive Renaissance Glasgow requires a purposeful act of imagination, as one stands amongst the city's formidable Victorian and more recent buildings. Yet Renaissance Glasgow does persist, and is best represented by two steeples, each a survivor stubbornly present in the twenty-first-century city. Together, these make visible at least a hint of the "Glasgua" which seventeenth-century Scottish Latin poet Arthur Johnston saw as having its "Head held high among sister cities." Praising churches which towered over house roofs, Johnston was writing of the area around Glasgow Cross. In the century that followed the Reformation, this became the heart of the town— close enough to the Cathedral and its associated college to retain links with ecclesiastical and academic life, yet sufficiently far from these structures to encourage new building and commercial expansion along the Clyde.

Erected in the first half of the fifteenth century, the original Tolbooth (the main municipal building of a traditional Scottish burgh) was removed in the seventeenth century and rebuilt as "a very fair and high-built house" with a new tower. It stood where its steeple still stands—at Glasgow Cross, a four-way intersection. Here the east-west streets of the Trongate and Gallowgate met, joined at right angles by the north-south axis of the High Street (running away from the river towards the Cathedral) and the Saltmarket, which heads southwards towards Glasgow Green and the Clyde. This basic street plan still exists, but the thin and square seven-storey Tolbooth Steeple of 1625–1627, erected around the time Arthur Johnston was praising Glasgow in Latin, is all that remains of one of the principal late-Renaissance buildings. Locked up and lonely among surrounding tenements and more recent structures, it is now a dignified traffic island, head held high above an intersection of busy inner-city roads.

To visualize these streets as they were at the end of the Renaissance and in the Enlightenment does require effort, but the nearby 1592 tower of the Tron Theatre (in former days the Tron Church) on the Trongate and the more distant 1665 Briggait steeple of the former Merchants' House on the Bridgegate (now site of a splendidly restored Victorian fishmarket) may help. These were among the spires drawn by Dutch artist John Slezer in his 1670s view of Glasgow, showing a small city surrounded by woodland and hills. The Tron tower, built on the site of the 1484 pre-Reformation Catholic church of St. Mary and St. Anne, had its spire added in the 1630s. It is all that survives of the Renaissance kirk, destroyed by fire in the late eighteenth century. Solidly constructed, with its own built-in bootscraper for the merchants' boots, the Merchants' Steeple at the Briggait was part of a seventeenth-century institution which looked after the welfare of entrepreneurs' families who had suffered bereavement or financial crisis.

Since the sixteenth century, Glasgow had been a base for incorporated crafts guilds which brought together workers such as tailors, weavers, and metalworkers ("hammermen"). There were 361 craftsmen in the city just after King James VI of Scotland succeeded Queen Elizabeth as monarch of England in 1603, and two years later the Trades House (which now occupies a handsome Adam building, the Trades Hall, in Glassford Street) was founded to regulate Glaswegian business. At that time, well over two hundred Glasgow merchants were exporting such commodities as cattle, fish, wool, dairy products, and hides. They imported corn and (not least from France) wines. The area around Glasgow Cross became these merchants' hub—"a spacious quadrant, in the centre whereof their market-place is fixed," noted the mid-seventeenth-century English visitor Richard Frank. He added that the Tolbooth was a "prodigy, infinitely excelling the model and usual build of town-halls." It was also a place for the public exhibition of civic justice. When a Glasgow tradesman killed a rival's dog in 1612, he was put in the stocks at the Cross, with the stinking carcase of the animal shoved right under his nose.

Glasgow's principal "four streets handsomely built in form of a cross" impressed Thomas Tucker in 1656, when he surveyed the nearby inhabitants. Tucker concluded that, with the exception of students from the university (which then stood in the High Street), they were all "traders and dealers." At that date, many of the properties around the Cross were thatched two-storey dwellings, some faced with stone, but many with wood. These burned easily. Inner-city thatched houses, even thatched tenements, persisted through the eighteenth century, but the seventeenth- and eighteenth-century Glasgow Cross repeatedly impressed visitors. In 1662, John Ray admired a city "well built, cross-wise"; with its college buildings, it was "somewhat like unto Oxford, the streets very broad and pleasant." Later seventeenth-century City Council legislation against the throwing of "excrement, dirt, or urine" from windows meant that the old civic centre escaped some of the more notorious dangers of Edinburgh street life. For Daniel Defoe in the 1720s, Glasgow was very much "a city of business," exhibiting "the face of trade." The mercantile-minded Defoe walked to Glasgow Cross and found it good:

> Where the streets meet, the crossing makes a spacious market-place by the nature of the thing, because the streets are so large of themselves. As you come down the hill, from the north gate to the said cross, the Tolbooth, with the Stadhouse, or Guild-Hall, make the north east angle, or, in English, the right-hand corner of the street, the building very noble and very strong, ascending by large stone steps, with an iron balustrade. Here the town council sit, and the magistrates try causes, such as come within their cognizance, and do all their publick business.

Eager to defend the advantages of political union with Scotland's southern neighbour, the Englishman Defoe stresses the commercial advantages offered by the right to trade with England's former colonies. Some Glasgow merchants had extended their dealings as far as Barbados in the mid-seventeenth century, but it was in the eighteenth that increasing trade with places like Virginia and the Caribbean helped to bring in money that transformed the area—not least that part now designated the Merchant City. Wealth enriched merchants around Glasgow Cross, but the Cross was also a point of intersection between commerce and academia. Students and merchants mixed. More than that, the students were sometimes merchants' children who themselves became traders, going on to benefit both their municipality and their alma mater.

One story among many illustrates this. After a failed Scottish scheme to establish a colony at Darien (Panama) in Central America, John Campbell from the West of Scotland settled in Jamaica, sending his son Colin to matriculate at Glasgow University in 1720. Five years later, Colin's brother William matriculated too. Having returned to the Caribbean with a taste for science, Colin Campbell later set up an observatory there, then passed his scientific instruments to another Glasgow alumnus, Alexander Macfarlane, who owned a Jamaican sugar plantation and established his own observatory on the roof of his house in Kingston. Elected a Fellow of London's Royal Society, Macfarlane was an "ingenious and learned mathematician." Like the rest of the Scots in Jamaica, he was also thoroughly involved with the slave trade. He had an annual contract for the transportation of Ibo slaves, and in 1747 alone, around the time he was subscribing to the publication of Colin MacLaurin's 1748 *Account of Sir Isaac Newton's Philosophical Discoveries,* he bought 121 slaves. When this thriving, Glasgow-connected merchant and astronomer died in 1755, he bequeathed to Glasgow University his fine hoard of scientific instruments. Shipped to Scotland, this collection was slightly damaged in transit, so the university employed a young man who lived nearby to clean and repair the artefacts. Earlier, this youth had tried to establish himself as an engineer near Glasgow Cross, but had been prevented from doing so by the guild of hammermen, jealous of their own privileges.

The young man's name was James Watt. In the nearby Clyde port of Greenock, his father had been involved in the construction of the first crane in that town, used to unload produce from the slave plantations of Virginia. In August 1757—after Watt had repaired the instruments from Jamaica, which included a fine Gregorian telescope—Glasgow University erected a

36. The Tolbooth Steeple, now islanded at Glasgow Cross, is a splendid survivor of Renaissance Glasgow. Near this tower, which was once part of a larger building, eighteenth-century "tobacco lords" paraded in their red gowns. Thanks to these traders and others, this part of Glasgow acquired the soubriquet "the Merchant City."

new building, the Macfarlane Observatory, on a hill just a short walk from Glasgow Cross. Special medals were struck to celebrate the observatory's founding, and Watt (whose statue later graced George Square) moved on from his restoration of scientific instruments to taking part in other aspects of the university's endeavours. He assisted the chemistry professor Joseph Black, participating in discussions about how to improve steam engines to power vehicles and manufacturing processes. Out of such work emerged Watt's design for a "separate condenser," which allowed steam engines to run far more efficiently, and so encouraged the development of steam-powered industrial factories. Such establishments made Glasgow richer and more powerful, but the smoke from their chimneys close to Glasgow Cross would so pollute the air that within decades the Macfarlane Observatory would be rendered almost useless.

This story, with its tangled interactions between academia, commerce, slavery, science, industrialization, and pollution, is emblematic of Glasgow as an intellectual, trading, and manufacturing crossroads in the eighteenth century. Except for the street layout, the Tolbooth Steeple, and a very few other vestiges, Glasgow Cross has changed out of all recognition. Imitating older originals and topped by a unicorn, the present-day Mercat Cross was designed by Edith Burnet Hughes in 1930; up the High Street, a twenty-first-century housing development called Collegelands confronts downmarket shops and tenements. The Macfarlane Observatory, the city-centre university, and most of the merchants' premises are all long gone, though the Old College Bar (claiming that it was established in 1515) seems to have outlasted centuries of scholarly drinkers.

One of the telescopes from Jamaica which James Watt cleaned remains in the collection of Glasgow University's Hunterian Museum, now on Gilmorehill in the city's west end. The era when local merchants imbibed "Glasgow punch," which mixed Jamaican rum with lemon juice, sugar, and lime, is memorialized—along with darker aspects of the city's relationship with the Caribbean—in the name of Jamaica Street, which runs down to the Clyde. If you walk east along the Trongate, on the side of the street farthest from the river, towards Glasgow Cross, then about a hundred yards before the Tolbooth Steeple you come to the site where eighteenth-century merchants known as "tobacco lords" liked to congregate and promenade in red gowns, dominating the pavement next to a vast 1735 equestrian statue of

King William III—"King Billy"—with his sword drawn. Presented to the city by a Glaswegian imperialist who became governor of Madras in India, this statue of the Protestant crusher of Catholics at the 1690 Irish Battle of the Boyne was moved long ago, and now stands, railed off, among trees just west of Cathedral Square. There was a certain irony in the fact that those red-gowned merchants, rich from the slave labour on sugar and tobacco plantations, were strutting their stuff near Glasgow Cross beside a statue whose long Latin inscription includes a phrase about Europe's being saved from "SERVITUTIS IUGUM," "the yoke of slavery."

In eighteenth- and nineteenth-century Glasgow, however, some thought the lot of slaves no worse than that of the local poor. This attitude was mis-guided, but working conditions in many of the city's mills and factories were undeniably grim. A rapidly growing urban underclass was subjected to eco-nomic abuse and even, on occasion, to physical assault. Some violence was judicially sanctioned, a form of official retaliation designed to keep the poor in their place. One sunny Wednesday in August 1820, two years after the publication of Jane Austen's *Persuasion* and the year Walter Scott published *Ivanhoe,* a Glaswegian called Thomas walked towards Glasgow Green to chop a man's head off. Around the middle of the afternoon, he carried out the act he had been thinking about all day. It took him about a minute, and he used an axe. James Wilson, Thomas's victim, who knew him by name, was a tinsmith in his early sixties who trained pointer dogs. He lived in the Lanarkshire village of Strathaven, a little south of Glasgow. Wilson was witty, and sometimes made up satirical verses. An occasional churchgoer, he had a taste for Tom Paine's *Age of Reason.* Several of his friends were weavers, and for some years he had entertained democratic ideals. That was what got him killed.

James Wilson was one of a considerable number of people in the Glas-gow area who were involved in the Radical uprising of 1820. The mad Brit-ish monarch, King George III, had died shortly before, and in London there had been an attempt by radicals to assassinate government ministers. Very few people in the Glasgow area had the right to vote, and the powers-that-be wanted to keep things that way. Born above his father's shop in Glasgow High Street, the most notorious Scottish democratic radical of the eigh-teenth century had been the middle-class lawyer and Latin poet Thomas Muir, tried in Edinburgh and then transported to Australia in 1794. Memories were long and fear of democracy was strong, so when a poster campaigning for "Equality of Rights" and dated "Glasgow, 1st April, 1820," was distributed around the city, the authorities soon summoned the military. Issued on behalf of "those who intend to regenerate their country," the poster urged its readers, if they supported equal rights, to "show to the world that We are not the Lawless, Sanguinary Rabble, which our Oppressors could persuade the higher circles we are—but a BRAVE AND GENEROUS PEOPLE, determined to be FREE[;] LIBERTY or DEATH is our *Motto,* and We have sworn to return home in *triumph*—or return *no more!*"

In April 1820, fired up by this rhetoric, and often armed, in April 1820 "many hundreds drilled during the day time in the Green of Glasgow" and elsewhere around the city. Determined to arrest those who had been enthused by the ideals of the "most *wicked, revolutionary* and *treasonable*" poster, government troops fought radical weavers in the streets close to Glasgow Green. When things went wrong, James Wilson was among about twenty-five men from Strathaven who were marching into the city with a banner bearing the words "Scotland Free—Or a Desert!" Wilson was arrested, and later that summer sentenced to death. A mythology soon grew up around the radicals who were imprisoned and tried at several locations in Scotland in 1820, but we know some sustained themselves by singing Robert Burns's famous song, "Scots, wha hae wi' WALLACE bled," inspired not just by the freedom fighter William Wallace but also by the democratic ideals of the American and French Revolutions:

> Lay the proud usurpers low!
> Tyrants fall in every foe!
> LIBERTY's in every blow!
>   Let us DO, OR DIE!

On August 30, 1820, his arms pinioned, and dressed in white clothing edged with black, James Wilson was taken to die at the edge of Glasgow Green. He walked towards his execution, the Tory newspaper the *Glasgow Herald* recorded, "with a pretty firm step." Thomas, the headsman, dressed in a loose black cloak, his face concealed with a crepe mask, was carrying both knife and axe. When Wilson saw the multitude who had streamed over Glasgow Green to see him killed, he turned and said "carelessly" to his executioner, "Did you ever see sic a crowd, Tammas?" He then ascended the scaffold to be hooded. People in the crowd cried "Murder!" but a heavy presence of riflemen, dragoons, and other soldiers kept order with a show of force.

About five minutes after the body was suspended, convulsive motions agitated the whole frame, and some blood appeared through the cap, opposite the ears, but upon the whole he appeared to die very easily. At half past three, after hanging half an hour, his body was lowered upon three short spokes laid across the mouth of the coffin, his head laid on the block with his face downwards, and the cap taken off, when there was again a repetition of the disapprobation of the crowd. The person in the mask, who had retired into the Hall when Wilson ascended the scaffold, was now called; he advanced to the body, which was placed at the front of the scaffold, amidst the execrations of the people, and after calmly feeling the neck for a moment, he lifted the axe, and at one blow severed the head from the body, which he held up, and pronounced, "This is the head of a traitor."

Though there is no monument to Wilson on Glasgow Green, the place has long been associated with popular radical struggles for democratic rights. Originally given to the people of the city as common grazing land by a fifteenth-century bishop, the grassy space itself, rather than any statuary, asserts freedom. For more than two centuries developers have sought to erect houses on, mine coal under, or drive roads through what is now a public park used by some of Glasgow's poorest citizens. The developers have been fought off, usually with success; part of the park, the "drying green," was used for centuries—until 1977—for hanging up household washing, latterly on lines suspended between "clothes poles." Around the time of the 1832 Reform Bill, which extended (somewhat) the democratic franchise, 70,000 people gathered on Glasgow Green in support of the reforms. On April 13, 1872, the Green hosted a large open-air women's suffrage meeting, where an audience of around a thousand was addressed by Scots-Italian campaigner Jessie Craigen. Most of her attentive listeners, according to the *Women's Suffrage Journal*, were "working men of the most intelligent type."

Associated with political activism, trade unionism, female emancipation, and the European temperance movement, and still a place of radical ideas as well as of down-and-outs, the Green was once, too, a site for popular theatre.

Incongruously, it also displays military-imperial paraphernalia that range from Britain's first monument to Admiral Nelson, victor at the 1805 Battle of Trafalgar, to one of the world's most remarkable terracotta fountains, donated by a nineteenth-century manufacturer of pottery and toilets, Sir Henry Doulton, during the 1888 Glasgow International Exhibition. Restored in 2005 and looking thoroughly grand, this three-storey fountain is surmounted by yet another local image of Queen Victoria, who towers regally over figures representing her Scottish, English, and Welsh soldiery, her navy, and her subject peoples of Australia, South Africa, India, and Canada. So fine is the sculpted detailing that even the raised lettering on the buttons of uniformed imperial fighters can be made out. In case not everyone got the message, Sir Henry gave a speech about the fountain in 1890:

> It symbolizes the Empire. I don't think Englishmen, at least most Englishmen, rightly appreciate—I hope you do in Glasgow—the greatness and glory of our empire. The Queen rules over something like one-fifth of the inhabitants of the globe, and our material supremacy will stand or fall together. . . . May I dare to hope of the people of Glasgow that, inasmuch as this fountain has some lessons to teach, they will draw some of these lessons: that they will see how our empire was won by the enterprise of our discoverers and by the self-abnegation of our missionaries, and how it has been maintained by the valour of our soldiers.

Many nineteenth-century Glaswegians would have loved this oratory. Four years later, the terracotta statue of Queen Victoria was completely destroyed by a lightning strike; but despite the best efforts of modern West of Scotland vandals, it has now been restored to its triumphalist imperial grandeur.

The true monument to the spirit of Glasgow Green—to James Wilson, the supporters of women's suffrage, and others—is hardly the Doulton Fountain. Instead, it is to be found inside the building which stands behind that fountain and is known as the People's Palace. This large red-sandstone museum contains displays about Glaswegian popular culture and political life, not least the sometimes radical political activities associated with the working-class communities around the Green. High inside, under the central dome, are striking 1987 murals commissioned from artist Ken Currie by the Palace's far-sighted former curator Dr. Elspeth King. These paintings commemorate the 200th anniversary of the day on which dragoons shot

37. The elaborate, three-storey Doulton Fountain of 1888 is surmounted by Queen Victoria. Behind it on Glasgow Green is the domed, red-sandstone People's Palace, a museum of Glaswegian popular history.

three protesting weavers who were part of a strike for better conditions in what was then the nearby village of Calton. Other paintings in Currie's series commemorate the 1820 rising in which James Wilson was executed; the agitation of the Great Reform Bill period; Red Clydeside; the Hunger Marchers of the 1930s, and those Glaswegians and others who fought against fascism in the Spanish Civil War; the Upper Clyde Shipbuilders' "work-in" of 1971–1972; and the Miners' Strike of the 1980s. Wishing to show "the ebb and flow of an emergent mass movement, where the real heroines and heroes were the many unknown working-class Scots who fought so selflessly for their rights," Currie, who painted these images when he was twenty-seven, has gone on to become one of Scotland's best-known figurative artists. Idealistic and strikingly iconographic, his murals, like the artefacts in the museum below them, tell a story very different from that of the Doulton Fountain.

The People's Palace offers a treasure trove of special everyday things— from the handsome green shopfront of a re-created dairy, its spherical lamp reading "BUTTERCUP" above the door, to radical handbills, portraits of old Glasgow characters, and the "big banana boots" designed by artist John Byrne to be worn by Glaswegian comedian Billy Connolly in the 1972 *Great Northern Welly Boot Show,* a satire based around the Upper Clyde Ship-builders' work-in. Free, like all the city's museums, the Palace was originally proposed by Liberal Unionist councillor Robert Crawford and was championed around its inception by nineteenth-century Glasgow bailie William Bilsland, a baker who spoke out in favour of free libraries, museums, galleries, and parks. Long proud of its community spirit, Glasgow was one of the first cities in the world to offer a network of municipally coordinated public services: from swimming pools and hospitals to refuse collection, libraries, and museums.

Displaying a proud exposition about Glaswegian struggles for democratic freedom, the People's Palace foregrounds telling local minutiæ. At its back, the spectacular "Winter Gardens," a vast Victorian glasshouse larger than the museum itself, makes a convincingly tropical Scottish tea-room. When the museum first opened in 1898 as a cultural centre for residents of Glasgow's east end, the original plan had been for it to receive visitors only once a week, for three hours on Sundays. Controversy over this generated additional publicity, and within the first six months more than half a million people flocked to see it. At that stage, exhibits about local history were confined to a single floor, and there were displays of history paintings as well as arts and crafts. The surprised and surely middle-class curator recorded how a crowd of riveters stood for half an hour discussing the "niceness" of lacemaking and embroidery, though he felt it necessary to post bills warning against "the spitting habit." Right up to the 1970s in Glasgow (and even in Edinburgh), bus interiors had a painted notice: "NO SPITTING."

Respiratory diseases, relatively low life expectancy, poor high-school attainment, and urban deprivation were and are serious problems in Scotland's great western city. In its Victorian way, the People's Palace was a well-received attempt to improve the quality of life in the Glasgow Green area. The Green is famous, too, for its part in the Industrial Revolution. In the summer of 1765, while taking a breath of air and walking across the Green, local resident James Watt, who had been engrossed in discussing how to improve steam engine workings, came up with his notion of the separate condenser. Though Watt's accounts of his 1765 invention tend to be dryly technical, an 1817 manuscript gives a most engaging version of the story, recording that his great idea struck him while he was "in the Green of Glasgow ... about half way between the Herd's House and Arn's Well." These pastoral landmarks are long gone, and the Green is much changed since Watt's day, but later reminders of the Industrial Revolution are still to be found hereabouts. The most spectacular is the Templeton Business Centre, formerly the Templeton carpet factory, its elaborate crimson brick, red terracotta, and red sandstone frontage of 1888 designed to evoke the bright colours of the carpets then woven inside. The Templeton factory was built (like parts of the City Chambers) to invoke the Doge's Palace in Venice, but conceals a former mill where weavers from the surrounding Calton once toiled. Behind the façade of this factory, whose origins go back to 1823, grand carpets were created for homes and halls in places ranging from Glasgow to New Zealand.

Today almost all the mills and large factories of this part of the city have disappeared, replaced by shops, offices, and modern social housing sited right beside remainders of former times. In Calton's Abercromby Street Burial Ground, visitors can see an obelisk that marks the grave of the Glaswegian Reverend James Smith (1798–1871), a minister for forty years in America, where in Springfield, Illinois, he became pastor and friend to Abraham Lincoln. President Lincoln later appointed Smith as U.S. consul in Scotland. For all its pockets of social deprivation, the redeveloped Calton boasts a few handsome eighteenth-century buildings; nearby is the city's second-oldest church, the beautiful St. Andrews-in-the-Square, which in 1745 sheltered Bonnie Prince Charlie's army. In 1776 this kirk—today a concert hall marketed as "Glasgow's Centre for Scottish Culture"—was the venue for the marriage of the abusive Glasgow lawyer James McLehose and his young bride, Agnes Craig, later famous for her passionate affair with Robert Burns. The poet sent Agnes (or "Clarinda," as he called her) one of his most famous love songs, just before she sailed to Jamaica:

> Ae fond kiss and then we sever;
> Ae farewell and then forever!
> Deep in heart-wrung tears I'll pledge thee,
> Warring sighs and groans I'll wage thee.

When Burns wrote those passionate lines, the eighteenth-century Calton was already fast industrializing, its rainy daytime skies coming to look at times oddly and grimly benighted. Early twentieth-century photographs show the skyline beyond the Templeton factory filled with tall, discoloured chimneys, which kept the atmosphere densely polluted. The Calton is much cleaner now, and Glasgow Green greener. People can stroll beside the postindustrial River Clyde, pondering the rich, conflicted legacies of the radical weavers, Victoriana, the fondly kissed Agnes McLehose, and the commercially canny James Watt.

✣ SEVEN ✣

Poverty and Wealth

Where the Clyde flows past Glasgow Green, on the opposite bank stands the area known as the Gorbals. No one knows why it is called that. Some onomastic enthusiasts say the name derives from a Scots legal term for tithes; others, that it is a corruption of two old words, *gar* and *baile,* denoting "the town's land." More lyrically minded etymologists have tried to connect the name with a Scots word for an unfledged bird—harking back, perhaps, to a time when the Gorbals was open fields. Certainly as late as 1784 a writer in the *Glasgow Magazine* admired "the *verdant lawns and flowery meads* with which the village of Gorbals is encircled," though a couple of years earlier the river had burst its banks and people had been sailing boats through Gorbals streets.

This flooding continued in the following decade, putting one contemporary surveyor "in mind of the serio-comic lucubrations of Ovid, in his poetical details of the deluge." In the 1790s, to travel from Glasgow Cross to the Gorbals by sedan chair cost a penny. So long as there was no torrential rain, the journey was pleasant. Each day, in Gorbals main street, people strolled past the castle-like home built by the Elphinstone family, to whom the surrounding land had been feued in 1579; old folk recalled that the early eighteenth-century village consisted of a few ale-brewers' thatched houses on each side of the road southwards from the old bridge across the Clyde. In the language of the Enlightenment and Romantic eras, the Gorbals was picturesque, quaint.

An independent barony in the seventeenth century, the "villages and lands of Gorbals" had resisted coming under the aegis of Glasgow; but throughout the 1700s, Glasgow's control over the place grew. Weavers began to arrive in considerable numbers, building properties between the old houses around 1730; after a 1748 fire, much of the Gorbals had been rebuilt, sometimes with three-storey blocks of tenement housing. In 1771, there were

209

around 3,000 inhabitants; twenty years later, by which time Glasgow had assumed full authority over the Gorbals, that number had almost doubled.
The weavers had well over 500 looms; there was "a small neat steam engine"
at a growing coal-pit; and locals, perhaps with Edinburgh's New Town in
mind, expected that before long "a new Glasgow will probably be raised on
the south side of the Clyde." Still, for all the Gorbals parish minister's com-
plaint that the presence of sixty pubs "hurt the morals of the people not a
little," the area remained "remarkable for good fruit," according to the 1791
Statistical Account of Scotland which also mentioned a "Leper's House . . .
founded and endued by a lady, of the name of Campbell, about the year
1350," and a nearby *"Leper's Churchyard."* The medieval village of Gorbals
was still remembered.

Yet in the nineteenth and twentieth centuries, the image of the place
changed dramatically. An early indication of this comes from broadsides
now in the National Library of Scotland reporting the "horrific murder" of
Mary Jamieson, a Gorbals resident who dealt in fish and had her throat
slashed with a razor on Apri 6, 1824. She had earlier borrowed the razor to
shave her husband. Two of her children screamed when they discovered
their mother's corpse "on their return from the Cotton Mill, to dinner, about
two o'clock. . . . The unfortunate woman's wind-pipe was completely severed, and the floor of the house presented a shocking scene of blood." Soon
afterwards, her husband, William Divan, was arrested, found guilty, and executed, "and his body given for dissection." Mary was described as "very
industrious"; her husband, an immigrant Irish weaver, had been constantly
"endeavouring to get possession of her earnings, for the purpose of en-
abling him to join in company with his acquaintance, which was the cause
of all the quarrels in the family." By the 1820s, the Gorbals was a place with
social problems and tensions around immigrants. Just a few months after Mary Jamieson met her end, a Bengali hawker in his thirties who had
been brought to Britain as a house servant "was found suffocated in his
own House, in Crown Street, Gorbals of Glasgow, on Thursday the 11th
Nov. 1824." A broadside "Elegy" on his death notes that he seemed to have
been choked "by sulphurous coal," which he had put on the fire on a cold
winter night before going to sleep in his confined, poorly ventilated home,
"a box, which was drawn by wheels."

Though the Gorbals welcomed immigrants—not least Irish and Italian Catholics, as well as Jews—conditions were tough. A serious cholera outbreak occurred in 1832. A few years later, Sidney Smith, one of the founders of the *Edinburgh Review,* delivered a course of lectures in Gorbals' Baronial Hall; the series was titled, "National & Legislative Morality, and the Physical and Mental Education of the People." While members of the local bourgeoisie were ready to pay a shilling for his four improving talks, the surrounding streets had a reputation for unrest. Chartists in the area pressed for an extension of the democratic franchise beyond the middle classes, and on March 24, 1845, the *Glasgow Herald* reported a "Socialist disturbance in Gorbals" involving a Mrs. Martin, "who has gained some notoriety as a Socialist lecturer" and was criticizing the preaching of the minister in the 1,100-seat John Knox Free Church. As members of the congregation cried, "Turn her out!" and even "Burn her!" captain of police James Richardson intervened. Though the *Herald* thought people like Mrs. Martin and her colleagues, "a Socialist missionary, and his wife," should be kept in "their own dens," the police captain (an admirer of the egalitarian-minded Robert Burns, whose writing desk he had inherited) seems to have acted as much to protect the agitators as to arrest them.

It may have been hard for the policeman James Richardson not to sympathize with socialist ideals in a Gorbals now dominated by the chimneys of grim cotton mills and other industrial structures such as the loud, acrid Govan Bar Iron Works, which manufactured "Patent Improved Steam Hammers." Local mill workers, many of them women, participated in the Bread Riots of 1848, demanding food for the unemployed; special constables shot and killed six protesters. Sketches made by artist William Simpson from that decade onwards reveal crumbling buildings and the upper premises of the Old Baronial Halls converted into a taproom; photographs taken around 1870 show the Halls being demolished, a poster for cheap ale in a window, new tenements being erected in their place.

It is the Gorbals of these tenements that became famous in the twentieth century—not just through photography, drama, and film, but also through popular literature. Yet if you visit the Gorbals today, almost no nineteenth-century tenements remain. Even the high-rise housing which replaced them is being demolished, though Glasgow as a whole still contains more than half of the tower blocks in Britain above twenty storeys. Nevertheless, the image of the Gorbals as a tenement community came for decades to define the entire city, in the minds of many in the wider world.

One of the earliest, most influential writers to mythologize the area was the Glasgow-educated imperialist and novelist John Buchan. Eventually becoming governor general of Canada, Buchan had attended the by-then substantially middle-class Hutchesons' Grammar School (in his day situated in the Hutchesontown area of the Gorbals) from 1888 onwards. His father was minister of John Knox Free Church. Now demolished, Buchan's school building was already smoke-blackened by the 1890s, when the young Buchan taught in the Knox Free Church's Sunday School. In *Huntingtower* (1922) and other novels, Buchan introduced a gang of wee working-class laddies, the Gorbals Die-Hards: under-age "shock-troops" who support the hero, a Glasgow grocer. Without entirely understanding the meaning of the words, the Gorbals Die-Hards sing songs that owe more to the socialist Sunday schools of the early twentieth century than to the teachings of John Knox Free Kirk:

Proley Tarians, arise!	
Wave the Red Flag to the skies,	
Heed nae mair the Fat Man's lees,	*no more; lies*
Stap them doun his throat!	*Stuff*

Despite their aggressively militant chanting, the Gorbals Die-Hards are sentimentalized street urchins. They may hymn the "Proley Tarians," but they help to defeat Bolshevik schemes and other plots in Buchan's highly readable, politically conservative thrillers. Male fighting children of the slums, his Die-Hards epitomize camaraderie, their gang warfare seen as a force for good.

More sensationally atrocious Gorbals gang warfare enlivens the best-selling 1935 novel *No Mean City: A Story of the Glasgow Slums,* co-authored by Alexander McArthur (presented as "writing from an address in the Gorbals") and H. Kingsley Long, a journalist who had described mobsters in Chicago. Saturated in domestic violence and street fighting, though surprisingly alert at times to issues of gender, *No Mean City* is set in the early 1920s. It focuses on the rise and fall of "Johnnie Stark, 'Razor King' of the Gorbals," who slashes his enemies with cut-throat blades. In this sensationalized

Gorbals, politics and religion are far less important than gang battles: "Communism, of a sort, was preached at many a street corner, but the Gorbals jeered at the politicians.... Some of the slum-dwellers were 'Prodisants' and the others 'Catholics,' but not one in ten thought of his religion as anything but a label or a banner to fight under." The Razor King is eventually killed in Crown Street, where John Buchan had gone to school. *No Mean City* is an awkward mixture of sometimes patronizing sociological comment and melodramatic fiction. Presented as a novel, it was accompanied by a journalistic appendix designed to show that the authors "have not drawn an exaggerated picture," and quoting newspaper items:

> "RAZOR SLASHING." Sir, It is depressing nowadays to take up one's paper and read the daily catalogue of assaults and murders with knives, razor and other lethal weapons. Indeed, razor slashing and stabbing are becoming so common that they appear to be accepted as part of our modern youth's recreation, etc., etc.
> —Letter to Editor, *Glasgow Evening Times*, 14/3/30

None of the quotations from newspapers included by McArthur and Long specifically mentions the Gorbals, but *No Mean City* views that area as emblematic of the close-knit nature of a working-class slum community in what the book more than once terms, with irony, "the Empire's second city."

Sentimentalized or not, the perceived relationship between camaraderie and gang violence continues to ignite later Gorbals narratives, such as Robert McLeish's play *The Gorbals Story* (filmed in 1949) and Ralph Glasser's vivid memoirs of early twentieth-century life, *Growing Up in the Gorbals* (1986). Glasser belonged to what was once a substantial Yiddish-speaking immigrant community in the Gorbals (there were at least 185 Jewish families by the time of the 1891 Census). In sharply detailed prose, he recalls how his early twentieth-century family lived

> in a mid-Victorian tenement of blackened sandstone in Warwick Street, near the Clyde, in the heart of the Gorbals, a bustling district of small workshops and factories, a great many pawnshops and pubs and little shops, grocers, bakers, fish-sellers and butchers and drysalters, tiny "granny shops"—where at almost any hour of the day or night you could buy two ounces of tea, a needle, *Peg's Paper* and *Answers*, a cake of pipe-

clay, a hank of mending wool—public baths and a wash-house, many churches and several synagogues. The streets were slippery with refuse and often with drunken vomit. It was a place of grime and poverty, or rather various levels of poverty and, in retrospect, an incongruous clinging to gentility, Dickensian social attitudes and prejudices.

Notorious, yet also a nursery of many who made their mark, the Gorbals had been birthplace to Allan Pinkerton in 1819. Son of a local weaver and a millworker, he became an ardent Chartist, campaigned against slavery, was married in Glasgow Cathedral, emigrated to America, and there founded the Pinkerton's detective agency. Other famous sons of the Gorbals range from the millionaire grocer Sir Thomas Lipton (born in Crown Street in 1850, and later the founder of Lipton's Tea, as well as a celebrated yachtsman in the America's Cup) to Benny Lynch (1913–1946), who became Scotland's first world boxing champion in 1935 and successfully defended his flyweight title over the next three years. The area produced artists and scientists, such as the internationally renowned stained-glass artisan Oscar Patterson (born in the Gorbals in 1863) and David Carlaw, who crafted a superb display for the 1888 Glasgow International Exhibition: a working model of the marine steam engine from the ship *Buenos Aires*—"the most beautiful engine model ever produced." Yet it was the sense of the place as a violent slum, albeit one with a fierce community spirit, which drove urban planners of the 1950s and 1960s to demolish its tenements and replace them with bleak, windswept, high-rise social housing.

Gone were many of the scenes of children (usually boys) photographed for *Picture Post* in 1948, playing in tenement backyard puddles. Instead, architect Basil Spence designed twenty-storey slab-like blocks of "streets in the air," where residents would enjoy their own balconies high above landscaped grounds. In practice, the elevators broke down, the wind howled through the open spaces around the flats, and the multi-storey dwellings were regarded by many of the inhabitants as "deserts wi' windaes [windows]," to use a phrase of the Glasgow comedian Billy Connolly. Since 1993 these tower blocks have been demolished, and another Gorbals has arisen on a more human scale. Some of its buildings, such as a three-storey block topped with a postmodern flat-cap roof, have a distinctive visual signature. Others suggest that the Gorbals has continued to host immigrant communi-

38. A man walks through a puddle in a Gorbals back lane in 1948, when the periodical *Picture Post* commissioned photographer Bert Hardy to take a series of evocative pictures of the area.

ties. There is now no sign of the Club for Indian and Pakistani Seamen, which was a feature of 1960s Gorbals; but on Gorbals Street itself, the outline of the 1984 brick-walled Glasgow Central Mosque is unmistakable, its golden dome adding uncompromising contemporary richness to what was long the city's most famous, even notorious area. Recently, the mosque has been the site of arguments over whether or not women should be allowed to become voting members of this major place of worship. The Gorbals remains a locus of social struggle.

Near the mosque, a little farther south along Gorbals Street, is the unpromising 1989 pale brick frontage of the Glasgow Citizens Theatre. Behind that façade is a splendidly preserved working playhouse first opened in 1878. The structure has retained its statues of Burns, Shakespeare, and the classical muses. With encouragement from James Bridie and other Glasgow dramatists, the Victorian building became the Citizens Theatre in 1945. It continues to stage classic plays—from Shakespeare to Goldoni—in the heart of the Gorbals. During modern times, its most famous years were probably in the 1970s and 1980s, when director Giles Havergal, designer Philip Prowse, and dramaturge Robert David MacDonald staged productions that ranged from a *Hamlet* whose protagonist wore nothing but a loincloth to MacDonald's 1980 dramatization of Marcel Proust's *A la Recherche du Temps Perdu;* a theatrical stroke of genius using frames within opulent frames, this play was cheekily entitled *A Waste of Time.* The same, Thatcherite decade saw Gorbals old-age pensioners in rain hats shopping frugally in the Unemployed Workers' Food Co-Operative. From eighteenth-century meadows to die-hard violence and Marcel Proust, this part of Glasgow has long been a place of reinvention.

If the Gorbals became a byword for poverty and deprivation, not far to the northwest, across the Clyde, lies an area with a substantially different history, whose very name—the Merchant City—establishes clear connections with prosperity. Just south of George Square, the district now boasts designer shops and downtown apartments, but is steeped in Glasgow's imperial past. Roads such as Cochrane Street, Glassford Street, Ingram Street, and, a little to the west, Buchanan Street bear the surnames of those eighteenth-century Glaswegian traders known collectively as "tobacco lords." Other thoroughfares, such as Virginia Street (where almost obliterated painted names of long-dead merchants can still be discerned around

39. Located in the heart of the Gorbals, the Citizens Theatre has a modern brick façade which masks a stylish Victorian auditorium. A famous and resilient Glasgow institution, it continues to stage classic drama ranging from Shakespeare and Goldoni to Beckett.

some doorways) and, to the west and towards the river, Jamaica Street, indicate the slave-owning territories they dealt with. As the eighteenth century and the British Empire developed, tobacco and sugar from transatlantic plantations made Glasgow commandingly rich.

Before Scotland's 1707 political union with her southern rival, while the Scots were still forbidden by the English to trade with England's overseas colonies, James Gibson, a merchant involved with the failed Scottish attempt to colonize Darien in Central America, drowned at sea in a hurricane. His brother Walter, however, married into Glasgow's merchant class, became the city's Lord Provost, and defied the English by trading successfully in sugar with England's transatlantic territories. Daniel Defoe was surprised to find that Glasgow had "no statue, no grateful inscription, to preserve the memory of Walter Gibson."

Certainly, after 1707, other Glaswegians followed Gibson's example. At first, they used borrowed trading vessels; then, beginning in 1718, when the *Glasgow* crossed the Atlantic, they relied on West of Scotland ships. These merchants sought tobacco at least as much as sugar. As local student James Arbuckle put it in his verse pæan to powdered tobacco, *Snuff,* published in Glasgow in 1717:

> Far from the *British* Isles the Land is seen,
> (A vast Expanse of Ocean spread between)
> Where grows the *Plant,* whose leaf calcin'd and bruis'd
> In such Abundance is by *Britons* us'd.
> Thither the Sailor led by Hopes of Gain,
> Directs his Journey through the pathless Main.

Early eighteenth-century Glasgow dealers did their best to encourage such voyages in "Hopes of Gain." Yet "a rigid frugality governed the merchants of Glasgow at this time," wrote municipal historian John Gibson, a trader in the Gallowgate, as he looked back from 1777.

In the early eighteenth century, families like the Buchanans, whose ancestors included Renaissance Scottish Latin poet George Buchanan, established themselves as tobacco-dealing dynasties. Eventually, they gave their name to Buchanan Street and built several mansions, including one (long since demolished) on nearby Virginia Street. By 1735, there were at least sixty-seven trading "ships, brigantines, and sloops" that berthed on the Clyde. Some had plain names: the *America,* the *Glasgow,* the *Virginia Merchant.* Others rejoiced in more colourful appellations: the *Buttercup,* the *Little Page.* These vessels' destinations included Virginia, Jamaica, St. Kitts, and Boston. For a long spell after 1750, Glasgow's trade with America (and elsewhere) increased year after year. In 1771, from Virginia alone, lists of imports included 73,000 feet of mahogany, 480 gallons of rum, and nearly 34 million pounds of tobacco. Reciprocating, Glaswegians sent the Virginians everything from brimstone and frying pans to more than 400,000 pounds of woollens and "2,971 and nine-twelfth dozens of hats." Americans liked clothes from Glasgow. The University of Chicago possesses a letter dated September 20, 1759, in which George Washington writes from Mount Vernon in Virginia asking for "Plaid Hose ... to be sent from Glasgow in the usual manner and number."

When Washington ordered his Glaswegian apparel, the city's Lord Provost was Andrew Cochrane, one of the leading "Virginia merchants." It was Cochrane who had earlier admitted Adam Smith as a "Burgess and Gild

Brother," and who in 1743 had founded Glasgow's Political Economy Club. At its meetings, Smith soon presented ideas about free trade which he would develop in *The Wealth of Nations*. Cochrane and his brother were principals in one of Scotland's biggest commercial firms, tobacco traders William Cunninghame and Company; but their further mercantile interests ranged from a local sugarhouse to the Greenland Fishing Company and the Glasgow Ship Bank. Another business partner of William Cunninghame diversified from trading Virginian tobacco into supplying iron to Glasgow manufacturers, as industrialization began to advance. The Industrial Revolution was fuelled locally by money from commerce that often depended on American and Caribbean slaves.

On the Town Council, Andrew Cochrane worked with Archibald Ingram, whose concerns extended from the tobacco and linen trades to book collecting and an academy of the fine arts. When Ingram was Lord Provost, he encouraged the opening of a concert hall to replace Glasgow's first playhouse, denounced in 1764 by kirkmen as a "temple of Satan" and burned down in a riot on its opening night. Ingram married Rebecca, sister of the tobacco magnate John Glassford, whose numerous business ventures ran to brewing, tanneries, banking, dyeing, and investing in the Forth and Clyde Canal Company. As a young man, Glassford had collaborated with other Glasgow merchants to act as publishers of a theological work about the "Beginning of a Godly Life"; in his late sixties, celebrated for his "great genius and abilities for trade," he helped to found the Glasgow Chamber of Commerce. Glasgow-educated novelist Tobias Smollett has one of the characters in his 1771 novel *Humphry Clinker* describe how he "conversed with Mr. G—ssf—d, who I take to be one of the greatest merchants in Europe. In the last war, he is said to have had at one time five and twenty ships, with their cargoes, his own property, and to have traded for above half a million sterling a year."

Repeated as fact in James Denholm's 1797 *Description of the City of Glasgow*, these numbers indicate Glassford's commercial power. Unsurprisingly, given his business interests, he opposed the war with the American colonies, which wrecked the Glasgow tobacco trade from the mid-1770s, bankrupting some and leaving Glassford to die in 1783 owing more than £50,000. George Washington, freedom fighter and slave owner, may have had a soft spot for Glassford's business empire. In 1777, Washington wrote to an American commander on behalf of an agent for John Glassford and Company, suggesting the man might be given safe passage if he "leaves the Country on Account of his business and not as an Enemy to us."

Tobacco helped to make Glasgow great and prosperous. Famously clad in their ankle-length red gowns and tricornered black hats, the tobacco lords patrolled the streets of the Merchant City, brandishing their canes. Most erected fine mansions with great lawns in Glasgow's Whitehill and Govan districts; long ago built over, these rich homes survived long enough to be photographed by Thomas Annan in the later nineteenth century. One of the earliest, Shawfield House, was on the site of what is now Glassford Street. While leading his rebellion against the London-based Protestant Hanoverian monarchy, Bonnie Prince Charlie, the Catholic Stuart claimant to the British throne, lodged there in 1745 and fell in love with Glasgow merchant's daughter Clementina Walkinshaw. She bore the prince his only child. Few architectural remnants of this era of the Merchant City remain; but the still-extant courtyard of the Tobacco Exchange and the Virginia Chambers in Virginia Street were tobacco lords' meeting places, while the mansion of William Cunninghame of Lainshaw, the only major tobacco lord to survive the economic upheavals of the American War of Independence, survives as part of what is now Glasgow's Gallery of Modern Art.

Erected in the years 1778–1780 on what had been farmland, the Cunninghame mansion was regarded by some as Scotland's finest urban residence. Over the centuries, it has done duty as a bank, as the city's first telephone exchange, and as a very grand public library. In addition to its æsthetic properties, its central location, fronting on Queen Street from the handsome early nineteenth-century Royal Exchange Square, makes it a fitting, though hardly vast, Gallery of Modern Art. The present-day building houses changing international exhibitions and a collection that emphasizes links between overseas artists and work produced in Glasgow itself. Its external Corinthian columns and front portico are later additions, as is the superb early nineteenth-century extension to the rear—now the main part of the art museum. To get some sense of the tobacco lord's mansion, you need to examine the intervening part of the structure. Entering it, visitors should pause in the central saloon with its oval domed light-well. This was the style in which tobacco lords lived, an elegance founded on the cruelest imperial suffering.

In the background of a painting of John Glassford and his family (now in

40. Substantially altered in later eras, Glasgow's present-day Gallery of Modern Art, in Queen Street incorporates a former tobacco lord's residence, the Cunninghame mansion. Erected in 1778–1780, the mansion was regarded by some as Scotland's finest urban residence. Placing a traffic cone on the head of the equestrian statue outside the Gallery of Modern Art is now a Glaswegian tradition.

the People's Palace museum) there once stood a black servant. Painted in 1760s Glasgow, the picture's nine white figures look confident and happy, holding flowers, a lute, and one another's hands. Their feet are on a richly patterned carpet, and a bowl of fruit in the centre suggests cornucopia in a city where some merchants grew their own peaches and grapes. When the picture was painted, the presence of the black servant was another indication of the Glassfords' wealth, but also a hint at those riches' provenance. Distant slavery was generally accepted by the Glaswegian merchant classes: its labour helped to make possible their burgeoning industries, their new concert hall, their expanding artistic and intellectual life. Yet some grew increasingly worried about it. In the first, 1776 edition of *An Inquiry into the Nature and Causes of the Wealth of Nations,* Adam Smith, whose title page pronounced him "Formerly Professor of Moral Philosophy in the University of Glasgow," pointed out that Edinburgh was "in trade and industry . . . much inferior to Glasgow" and that Glasgow was a place "where there has lately been a considerable rise in the demand for labour." He also stated that across the Atlantic "the blacks, indeed, who make the greater part of the inhabitants both of the southern colonies upon the continent and of the West Indian islands, as they are in a state of slavery, are, no doubt, in a worse condition than the poorest people in Scotland or Ireland."

Sometimes, though not always, Smith seems to see slaves principally as an economic commodity. His Glasgow University colleague John Millar, who later supported both American independence and the egalitarian ideals of republican France, wrote a pioneering sociological study entitled *Observations Concerning the Distinction of Ranks in Society* (1771). In the book, he mentions "the terror in which" a slave "is held," but, like Smith, appears to view slaves mainly in terms of financial transactions. Towards the conclusion of the work, however, Millar does describe slavery as "pernicious," stating, "It is a matter of regret that any species of slavery should still remain in the dominions of Great Britain."

Throughout the decades that followed, opposition to slavery increased in Glasgow and elsewhere. Probably it was in the nineteenth century that someone painted over the black servant in the Glassford family portrait. It was easier to deal with issues about slavery and "the negro" if they were distant rather than pressing concerns. Only gradually did Glaswegians, happy to have inherited civic wealth built on empire, tobacco, and sugar, come to

41. The lower part of Buchanan Street is home to some of Glasgow's most elegant shops. Now pedestrianized, the long-fashionable street boasts many fine nineteenth-century buildings. According to the *Glasgow Herald* in 1896, it was "the principal street of the city."

accept the antislavery cause. "The attendance of Ladies will be highly acceptable," announced a notice about a meeting of the Glasgow Anti-Slavery Society in November 1830, though a piece of counter-propaganda contradicted Adam Smith by implying that the condition of the urban poor in nineteenth-century Scotland was worse than that of "the Poor NEGROES in the WEST INDIES, who Work Eight Hours per Day, and *NEVER DIE BY THE DYKE SIDE for WANT of FOOD or MEDICAL ATTENDANCE.*" Glasgow found it hard, and perhaps still finds it hard, to come to terms with having grown into a hub of wealth as a result of complicity with slavery.

It has always been easier to focus on the architecture, dazzle, and hard work of this leading "city of the Empire" than to focus on the vicious downside of Glaswegian imperialism. Yet to emphasize exclusively that downside would be misguided. Capitalist prosperity brought Glasgow confidence and style, nowhere more evidently than in some of its grandest thoroughfares.

Though the name of Sauchiehall Street may be better known, by 1896 the *Glasgow Herald* was describing Buchanan Street, which takes its name from the tobacco-trading family, as "the principal street of the city." A spacious upscale shopping area, now pedestrianized, Buchanan Street retains that status today; all visitors to the city should stroll along it. Thronged, elegant, and architecturally rich, it runs gently down a slope from the Glasgow Royal Concert Hall and the Buchanan Galleries mall to the little turreted red-sandstone former Underground station (now a café) at its foot. Gazing down this vista from a high pedestal outside the concert hall is a statue of Donald Dewar (1937–2000), founding father of Edinburgh's modern Scottish Parliament and the first person to hold the title First Minister of Scotland. Round the statue's base, highlighted in gold, the words THERE SHALL BE A SCOTTISH PARLIAMENT are repeated on each side—just so they can't be missed. In life, Dewar was a respected Labour MP for the Glasgow Anniesland constituency; in his afterlife, his statue has been repeatedly vandalized (assailants liked to tear off its spectacles) and so has been raised, like the statues in George Square, to a lofty eminence. On that perch, hands behind his back, the lanky and bookish architect of political devolution in Scotland stands in a bronze suit, staring, a little blearily perhaps, down his native city's most opulent Victorian shopping street. On a winter's day, the far end of the roadway almost vanishes in mist. Mr. Dewar needs those spectacles.

Buchanan Street is no ancient thoroughfare like the High Street. It is named specifically after Andrew Buchanan, the tobacco lord who, before being bankrupted by the American War of Independence, bought land in this area, which was then so rural that words like "Croft" and "Meadowflat" were applied to it. Buchanan Street's first, late eighteenth-century houses were substantial dwellings, their gardens separated by high walls; city officials specified that the roadway should be kept at least seventy feet wide. Unusually, we can view the development of this street through the attentive eyes of a child. Born around 1814, Daniel Frazer lived and worked for much of his life there. In 1885 he published *The Story of the Making of Buchanan Street*, which includes his personal reminiscences. His parents were used to strolling through green fields where Donald Dewar's statue now stands.

An old man once recalled that in his youth—the era of Daniel Frazer's own childhood—he had shot a covey of partridges between what became

Gordon Street and the head of Buchanan Street. Haystacks had stood not long before on the west side of Glassford Street, where plum trees overhung a nearby brick wall. Living in Argyle Street, close to the southern end of Buchanan Street, around the age of seven Daniel Frazer enjoyed peering each day at "the antics of a bear in the back cellar of a hairdresser, who afterwards killed it on the premises for the manufacture of 'genuine bear's grease.'" Looking at a new tenement where a fashionable silk shop was setting up next to a glass-and-china merchant, the boy also "watched with astonishment the putting in of huge plate-glass windows, four of the panes of which were rounded ones, in a shop a few doors east of Buchanan Street, on the north side of Argyle Street. These were the earliest plate-glass windows seen in Glasgow."

This part of town was coming to be associated with fine goods, not least merchandise designed to appeal to ladies. In 1827, the year Daniel and his widowed mother moved into 107 Buchanan Street, the Argyle Arcade was being constructed as a glass-roofed lane of shops running off Buchanan Street and, after a ninety-degree turn, exiting into another retail thoroughfare, Argyle Street, close to where those new plate-glass windows had been installed. A chic touch of Paris in Glasgow, the light-filled arcade is still there, the oldest covered mall in Scotland. Couples amble through it hand in hand, choosing wedding rings from its profusion of jewellers' shops. Red geraniums grow from window boxes under a white-painted, cast-iron-reinforced trelliswork of roof beams. A 2009–2011 restoration, which involved investigating fifteen earlier repaintings, has brought back the Argyle Arcade's original green-and-white colour scheme, and preserved details such as its cast-iron "fish-scale" panels and globular hanging lights, which were once illumined by gas. In 1838 a cavalry officer armed with lance, sabre, and carbine was fined for galloping on his charger through this most exclusive of Glaswegian alleyways. By mid-Victorian times, its shopkeepers included perfumers, milliners, hosiers, glovers, music sellers, lace and muslin printers, and bootmakers.

During 1827, along the road from the recently completed arcade, new houses were being finished at Number 107. Daniel Frazer's neighbours were merchants, a fashionable music teacher, lawyers, and "an elderly lady, a miser, who, for economy of candle light, went to bed with daylight, even during the depths of winter, and compelled her servant to do the same." This was

42. Constructed in the 1820s, the Argyle Arcade is Scotland's oldest covered mall. In 1838 a cavalry officer was fined for galloping through it on his charger. Today it is filled with jewellers' shops.

solidly bourgeois territory. Yet handily nearby were the shops of a greengro-
cer, a cabinetmaker, a piano maker, and a chemist. In those days, most of the
buildings in Buchanan Street were self-contained houses, but a few—such
as a nearby baker's, where Daniel watched shelves being loaded with fresh
"fine bread" each morning—combined shops and private homes. Today the
block at 101–111 Buchanan Street, where Daniel grew up, is the only 1820s
Buchanan Street housing left, though close to Gordon Street at 95–97 is an
1820s frontage with an 1880s attic added; and the small classical frontage at
87–89 is thought to date from around 1830.

Evading his elocution lessons, Daniel Frazer participated in weekly
stone-throwing fights in Mitchell Street; and in 1832, when the mansion of
tobacco lord William Cunninghame was converted into the Royal Exchange
(now the Gallery of Modern Art), Daniel enjoyed watching, from a place of
safety, "a battle on the streets . . . carried on with great fury between the
Scotch and Irish workmen employed on the buildings." Fires provided further excitement. Dense acrid smoke filled lanes beside Buchanan Street on
January 10, 1829, when Daniel rushed round with his pals to St. Vincent
Place to see the Queen Street Theatre burning down. Excitingly, the heat
made his mother's front windows so hot they hurt his fingers. A couple of
years later, fire ravaged the back premises of the boy's house; the family had
to be evacuated, wrapped in blankets. In the course of the nineteenth century, blazes destroyed premises in and around Buchanan Street. Several of
the grand Victorian buildings still prominent there were erected to replace
blackened shells.

In his mid-teens, Daniel began to help out at the Buchanan Street drug-
gist's shop owned by his older brother. Sometimes he would be left in sole
charge, dispensing poisons such as laudanum to customers, or offering advice about how to cure a hangover by imbibing soda water. He recalled that
"excessive drinking" was a common problem. When Daniel Frazer grew up,
he remained largely abstemious, a nonsmoking, unsporty, literature-loving
Free Presbyterian who conducted family worship, went with his wife and
children to church twice each Sunday, and stocked his bookshelves with
complete editions of Walter Scott and John Calvin. A solid representative of
Victorian Glasgow's Protestant bourgeoisie in what was then a predominantly Liberal city, the prosperous Frazer voted for the British Liberal prime
minister William Gladstone. He also joined a Glasgow Volunteer corps of

part-time soldiers, parading on one occasion in front of Queen Victoria—or so his son James, the anthropologist and author of *The Golden Bough,* recalled.

By 1892, retired from active work as the leading partner of Frazer and Green, Chemists and Druggists, Daniel had seen Buchanan Street change almost out of all recognition. As late as the 1850s, premises between Gordon Street and the bottom of the road had been flooded periodically by human effluent from the St. Enoch's Burn, the stream over which part of Buchanan Street was built. Workmen improving sewers remembered unearthing bodies thought to be from the cemetery of the ancient chapel of St. Enoch, mother of St. Mungo, but the Victorian glories of Buchanan Street were not to be held back by such grisly discoveries. After several fires, the famous furnishings emporium of Wylie and Lochhead, near the foot of the road, erected a version of its earlier premises at Number 45, beside the pilastered front of the Stewart's and Macdonald's warehouse. These buildings survive, incorporated into one large-scale department store—Frasers—with its striking galleried four-storey interior covered in pale-green and cream terracotta. In the age of Burberry and Giorgio Armani, Frasers remains architecturally splendid; staff clean with care the gilded tops of its internal columns, under an ornate arched roof of glass. Ascending from the entrance level, the broad, wooden-banistered staircase leads to galleries whose cream-coloured pillars are decorated with portrait medallions. The place reeks of expense. Nearby is the old *Glasgow Herald* building, constructed in 1870 and saved from fire six years later. At attic level its lofty frontage is still graced by Glaswegian sculptor John Mossman's original statues of Johannes Gutenberg and William Caxton. Its striking rear elevation, in Mitchell Street, was redesigned by Charles Rennie Mackintosh in the 1890s.

When Nathaniel Hawthorne was American consul in Liverpool during the mid-1850s, he described Glasgow as "very magnificent," with the shops of Buchanan Street "excelling those of London." Today's Buchanan Street is a Victorian and Edwardian cornucopia, albeit a slightly rearranged one. The Art Nouveau Mackintosh interiors of the former Cranston's Tea Rooms at Number 91 were re-created, in the 1990s, as the Willow Tea Rooms, upstairs at Number 97. On the floor above these, the low-backed black chairs and crisp white tablecloths of another Mackintosh tearoom (this one Chinese) are unexpectedly counterpointed by an interior of turquoise-painted square gridwork and golden, pagoda-shaped lamps—a reconstruction of a tearoom originally in Ingram Street. Below, on the floor above street level, the Willow Tea Rooms have the architect's signature high-backed black chairs, lantern-like lighting, and some small grey-upholstered window seats at the front, overlooking Buchanan Street. Here shoppers can order standard fare or—if they want something more special—a champagne afternoon tea from smart, black-and-white-uniformed waitresses. Buchanan Street still epitomizes upscale Glaswegian style.

In the second half of the nineteenth century and just before World War I, Buchanan Street and its long-running rival, Sauchiehall Street, vied with each other to attract discerning customers to their premises for everything from "Swiss embroidered net curtains" and reproduction antique furniture to finely crafted deckchairs and hammocks. In the summer holidays of 1914, Wylie and Lochhead at 45 Buchanan Street touted, for the benefit of cautious "families leaving town," the secure facilities of their "fireproof strong room . . . where silver and other valuables may be stored." The way in which Buchanan Street catered to Glaswegian aspirational opulence—as it still does—is captured in an early twentieth-century advertisement in which "Wylie & Lochhead, Limited, Artistic House Furnishers," trading "by appointment to King Edward VII," advertise to customers their "French tapestries in the style of Louis XVI," whose "subdued tones" make them "ideal" for covering "drawingroom furniture."

Though not all sold such swanky goods, a number of Buchanan Street's traditional nineteenth-century local businesses continued to trade until the late twentieth century; many were gradually replaced by national and multi-national stores. Near the entrance to the Argyle Arcade, Wylie Hill and Company, known in the 1890s as "importers of American goods and other specialities," still boasted one of the city's best toy departments in the 1960s. Even longer-lived was the Clyde Model Dockyard, its name redolent of Glasgow's past. Founded in 1789, originally to make ship models for the Admiralty, in a later incarnation the dockyard occupied retail premises in the Argyle Arcade, its 1960s windows crammed with Meccano sets, Bayko building kits (for making miniature houses out of metal rods and prefabricated parts), model railway engines by Hornby and other makers, and innumerable specialist models. It was expensive—its customers consisted primarily of men, rather than boys. After it closed, a replica of its frontage was preserved in

Glasgow's former Transport Museum, along with an armada of model ships. These have since been moved to the spectacular Riverside Museum.

In terms of architecture, the two more modern shopping malls that are entered from Buchanan Street—the Princes Square complex, with its post-modern metal-and-glass roof and elaborate ironwork in front, and the more stolid Buchanan Galleries—seem less special than the pre-Victorian Argyle Arcade, for all that they offer a far wider range of goods. The Buchanan Galleries opened in 1998, eight years after the Stalinist-looking Glasgow Royal Concert Hall was built as part of the celebrations marking Glasgow's year as "European City of Culture." Its outside wall adorned with a large City of Glasgow coat of arms and the motto "Let Glasgow Flourish," the concert hall has an impressively august interior. Reinvigorating the top of the street, these buildings complete the effect of a thronged and vibrant civic space. For retail outlets and promenading, Buchanan Street, with its splendid heritage of Victorian and Edwardian architecture and modern shopfronts, remains Glasgow's formidable counterweight to Edinburgh's Princes Street. It cannot match the latter's view towards Edinburgh Castle, but Glaswegians, local patriots one and all, maintain that it has better shops.

῀᾿ EIGHT ᾿῾

Street Life, Masterpieces,
Tenements, Books

Sauchiehall Street is a Glasgow shibboleth. Since at least 1859, people have inquired about the meaning of its name. "Sauchie" refers to "sauchs," the Scots word for willow trees; "hall" is probably an anglicized corruption of "haugh"—Scots for a piece of level ground. The modern road runs westwards for more than three miles from the top of Buchanan Street; way beyond the tangled interruption of motorways at Charing Cross, it joins another long shopping and residential artery, Argyle Street. In the 1870s, "what is now Sauchiehall Street" was still remembered as a place that at the close of the eighteenth century had been "a common country road, of the worst type." Regarded by some in Victorian times as the city's most fashionable retail thoroughfare, it conducted shoppers towards the developing, upmarket West End. Increasingly, tenements displaced villas and gardens as it extended away from the city centre. Today Sauchiehall Street's finest hours have passed, but its eastern section still brims with life and architectural treasures. These include Alexander "Greek" Thomson's 1865 Grecian Buildings; Charles Rennie Mackintosh's 1903–1904 reconstructed Sauchiehall Street Willow Tea Rooms; the lofty, red-sandstone Charing Cross Mansions, designed around 1890 by Glasgow School of Art graduate Sir John James Burnet; and, on the way to those mansions, the splendidly Art Deco Beresford Building (now apartments), constructed in 1938 at a cost of £200,000 and described, when it opened, as "Scotland's first 'skyscraper' hotel."

Present-day visitors readily perceive Sauchiehall Street's past glories, which are evident in the appearance of its Victorian buildings. Surveying these, this chapter, like the one that follows it, discusses several of the later nineteenth and early twentieth-century buildings whose style and contents helped to make Glasgow such an impressive civic beacon of the arts. In some ways a continuation of Buchanan Street, Sauchiehall Street was central to the artistic as well as to the mercantile culture of later nineteenth-century

Glasgow. In the mid-1850s, on a city block at Numbers 254–290, a man named Archibald McLellan—a Tory coachbuilder and bibliophile, collector of old masters, and former president of the Glasgow Dilettanti Society—masterminded the construction of a grand art gallery to house his extensive hoard. Designed by prosperous Glaswegian architect James Smith and completed after McLellan's death, the façade of this once-domed building still stands, despite a 1980s fire. The city bought the McLellan Galleries and their holdings in 1856, creating Britain's first civic-funded art gallery.

As early as 1857, the Sauchiehall Street premises were hosting displays of new art from the local area, as well as exhibiting historic treasures. McLellan's collection is now incorporated into the Glasgow City Art Gallery at Kelvingrove—but in sometimes unexpected ways, the often-refurbished McLellan Galleries in Sauchiehall Street have played a part in Glaswegian life. When delegates from the National Association for the Promotion of Social Science visited them in 1860, among participants in the association's fourth annual conference was Dr. Edward William Pritchard. The doctor had moved that year from Edinburgh. Soon he was practising medicine from 131 Sauchiehall Street, and he is best remembered as the last person to be publicly hanged in Glasgow. After poisoning his mother-in-law and his wife, the dandyish womanizer Pritchard maintained in his confession that he had acted "in an evil moment (being besides somewhat excited by whiskey)." At his execution in July 186,5 he wore one black kid glove on the gallows and was watched by a huge, sometimes boisterous crowd on Glasgow Green. The spectators included summer day-trippers on an excursion from Scotland's capital: "several members of the Edinburgh Phrenological Society, who were understood to have come with special permission from the Crown for the purpose of taking a cast of the criminal's head."

Not all criminals with links to Sauchiehall Street were murderers. As the city grew busier in the 1870s, when the newly installed horse-drawn trams used this long thoroughfare as one of their principal routes, the packed street saw some stylish and downright odd misdemeanours. Engagingly, a man named Duncan Smith was caught stealing thirteen bottles of champagne and a gallon of brandy from a spirit shop there in 1872. Three years later, in one of the oddest of all Glasgow trials, Margaret Pirie, saleswoman in a tobacconist's at Number 43, was accused along with other Glaswegians of selling highly "indecent match-boxes." These small pasteboard containers were adorned with what the prosecution saw as "profane, indecent, and obscene printed photographs, drawings, paintings, or representations;" their defenders maintained that the images were "simply 'statuary,' and that there was much worse in the Kibble Palace"—the recently built glasshouse in Glasgow's Botanic Gardens which featured Apollo and his nude classical companions. A secondary defence was that similar matchboxes had been seen "in one of the principal tobacconist's in Edinburgh." In Glasgow, this cut little ice. The bailie who presided at the trial found the accused parties guilty and pointed out that it was his duty as a West of Scotland magistrate "to prevent anything of the kind being sold in shops which tended to demoralize the citizens."

Safe and undemoralized, Glasgow's most prosperous bourgeoisie paid three guineas each to hire upper-floor window seats on the Sauchiehall Street frontage of the Grand Hotel, Charing Cross, so that they could peer down at the royal procession when the diminutive Queen Victoria rode past in her carriage during the 1888 Glasgow International Exhibition. Sauchiehall Street's shops were lavishly decorated for this gala event. The warehouse of Messrs. Copland and Lye at 165 and 167 (famous for "velveteens in all the art shades") had a maroon-and-yellow ornamental banner hanging in an upper window. Decorative spears flanked this; the building's wrought-iron fencing was lined with crimson, and its other ironwork was ornamented with extravagant flourishes of feathers. Brand-new in 1888, the great domed Panoramic Building in Sauchiehall Street, proud of its European-style Continental Restaurant and Ladies' Café, was lavishly decked out with evergreens (today it is a much-modified music venue). Inside it, that year and next, Philipp Fleischer, an artist from Munich, painted his panorama of the Scots defeating English invaders at the 1314 Battle of Bannockburn—all axe-wielding, red-bearded warriors. Parts of it can still be seen at Peebles Hydro in the Scottish Borders.

From at least the 1860s, Sauchiehall Street cultivated a taste for the fashionably exotic. Indeed, it was the sort of Glasgow street where people from Edinburgh could feel almost at home. Several shops were occupied by businesses which also traded in the capital's Princes Street. One was H. Salomon & Co., offering Glaswegians "gentlemen's French boots," as well as "self-acting India-rubber clogs just come to hand." A dash of genteel frenchification appealed to upscale West of Scotland shoppers, who have long had a fondness for pizazz. When electric lighting came to Glasgow in 1893, Sauchiehall Street was one of the first areas to benefit; as if to match the illumination, the shops intensified the dazzle of their marketeering rhetoric. Walter Wilson & Co. (based, too, in Princes Street, Edinburgh) pronounced themselves "The Largest Silk Mercers and Drapers in the Kingdom"; among their tea cosies, "'Bluebell' patterns" were "quite the novelty of the season." Down the road at Number 290, the French-accented "Treron et Cie." proclaimed that they were nothing less than "the Leading Modistes in Europe."

Most Glasgow businesses were run by men, but Treron's Sauchiehall Street branch was then managed by a Miss E. H. Robertson, who was proud of "the most *recherché* stock of artistic millinery out of London." When twenty-first-century Glasgow promotes itself as "Scotland with style," it is alluding not just to its present-day designer-clothing stores, but also to a heritage of fashion sense developed when the city was at the blaze of its imperial high noon. During a tour of Glasgow in 1895, His Highness the Shahzada Nasrulla Khan, son of the ameer of Afghanistan, visited what Edinburgh's *Scotsman* newspaper termed "the erstwhile aristocratic West End district"; but his hosts made sure, too, that he was driven past the shops of Sauchiehall Street.

With its "Fine Art Galleries," this street was ideal for the "stall-holders and assistants in fancy costume" who graced the 1895 "Art Exhibition and Grand Fancy Fair" of the "Lady Artists' Club"; the celebrated "Glasgow Boys" were then painting, but so were women such as Bessie MacNicol and Annie French, now sometimes termed "Glasgow Girls." For those intent on other things in Sauchiehall Street, at Number 251 a half-crown (a coin worth one-eighth of a pound sterling) would buy a single false tooth from Mr. Goodman, "Surgeon Dentist," who advertised "Painless Gas Extractions" for a further five shillings. Novel 1890s pleasures included a Sauchiehall Street Skating Palace. This drew large crowds, many (in an era when Glasgow's links with Japan prospered) applauding the visiting Royal Yokohama Troupe of Jugglers. In 1896, countless people yielded to the powerful attraction of a "cinematographe," famed not so much for screening exotica as for showing Glaswegians moving pictures of familiar local attractions: the Gordon Highlanders marching down Buchanan Street, or a Clyde steamship docking at a pier.

Sauchiehall Street was already a centre for photography, hosting exhibi-

43. Sauchiehall Street remains one of Glasgow's busiest shopping streets. Parts of its eastern end are now reserved for pedestrians.

tions in several galleries, including the studios of T. and R. Annan in the handsome, Dutch-style former townhouse which still survives as a military museum at Number 518. Here, in 1907, Glasgow School of Art graduate Jessie M. King held her first solo exhibition. Steeped in Art Nouveau, King worked as a book illustrator, ceramicist, and jewellery and textile designer. She was central to the evolving Glasgow Style, which was substantially established by women designers such as the Raeburn and Macdonald sisters. After Impressionism, the Glasgow Style was arguably the first artistic movement in the world in which women played a major role. King would have been familiar with the splendid black front door that Charles Rennie Mackintosh (Margaret Macdonald's husband and collaborator) designed in 1882 for the Glasgow Society of Lady Artists at 5 Blythswood Square; that door still exists *in situ,* with its numeral 5 inside an oval medallion and its stylish, ankle-level letterbox. Later, in Paris, King mixed with Henri Matisse, S. J. Peploe, and other painters. She went on to set the visual tone for the finest of all Glaswegian illustrated books: *Glasgow, the City of the West,* published in 1911.

The best place in Sauchiehall Street to get some sense of the Art Nouveau world which meant so much to King is in the re-created Willow Tea Rooms. This restaurant was designed inside and out by C. R. Mackintosh for the Glasgow entrepreneur Catherine Cranston, whose brother, Stuart, claimed for Glasgow the "invention" of the tearoom. Stuart and Kate came from a family whose business interests included (at 172 Sauchiehall Street, in Edinburgh's Princes Street, and elsewhere) Cranston's Waverley Temperance Hotels—"Recommended," the advertisements read, "by the celebrated J. B. Gough as 'the only home he has found since leaving his own in America.'" In Sauchiehall Street, Buchanan Street, and other fashionable shopping areas, Miss Cranston established tearooms with a markedly artistic ambience and what was perceived as avant-garde feminine décor. Her distinctive premises offered more food and far more exciting surroundings than those of her brother's establishments. Determined and uncompromising, she and her eateries became Glasgow institutions—there is even a book of reminiscences called *Tea at Miss Cranston's.* Described by English architect Edwin Lutyens as "a dark, fat, wee body with black sparky luminous eyes," Catherine Cranston (in private life Mrs. Kate Cochrane) was one of Mackintosh's greatest architectural patrons. In a small, chic building at 217 Sauchiehall Street, you can still take tea in one of her restaurants, though it is said to be troubled with damp.

Despite the fact that some of the Willow's fitments have gone—the fireplace from the Salon de Luxe, with its distinctive wrought iron and tiles, is now in London's Victoria and Albert Museum—many of the original decorative details of the tearooms remain in place. The ground floor is now a jeweller's shop, but the white exterior is much as it was when Mackintosh designed it in 1903, and the pale, almost abstract plaster relief panels and stained-glass windows with willow motifs (appropriate to this street of "sauchs") all survive. Diners sit around a balcony on cream-painted reproduction Mackintosh chairs, which are fashioned with the designer's distinctive very high backs. Even if aspects of the twenty-first-century dining experience may seem slightly inauthentic, it remains a uniquely Glaswegian pleasure. Miss Cranston's first, Edwardian customers would have been able to look out on Sauchiehall Street's new electric trams and observe an alarming increase in motor vehicles. Heading into the east end of the street was "an almost continuous procession of [tram] cars" throughout the day, as surviving film footage confirms. Accidents increased as trams, horse-drawn carriages, carts, and motorized transport all menaced shopping pedestrians. Sauchiehall Street would not get its first automated traffic signals until 1929, and Glasgow's first pedestrian crossing, at the junction of Sauchiehall Street and Buchanan Street, was installed as late as 1936. The city remains famous for jaywalkers.

The late Victorian and Edwardian eras were Sauchiehall Street's Indian summer. In 1904, the Treron department store took over the entire block that had been built originally as the McLellan Galleries. Announcing themselves as "Paris in Glasgow," and calling their grand new setup "Les Magasins des Tuileries," in vision and rhetoric they epitomized some, but not all, of the aspirations of Glasgow's ambitious women. Soon, in the years leading up to World War I, a "well dressed lady . . . producing a hammer from her muff" would cause consternation on Sauchiehall Street by smashing six windows at nearby Copland and Lye's drapery store in a suffragette protest; male university students plotting "having a go at the suffragists" would attack and wreck the shop occupied by the Women's Social and Political Union, at Charing Cross; and suffragette incendiary Frances Gordon of 502 Sauchiehall Street would yell out, "Trust in God and keep on fighting!" when sentenced to a year's imprisonment by a Glasgow judge. But the Edwardian advertising of Treron et Cie., whose "palatial and artistic environments" afforded "luxurious appointments, delightful surroundings, charming music, absolute freedom, endless comforts and conveniences" aimed at "ladies of discrimination," envisaged a calmer splendour:

THE TUILERIES WAREHOUSES ARE NOT IN RIVALRY WITH EXISTING DRAPERY WAREHOUSES IN SCOTLAND, BUT HAVE BEEN DESIGNEDLY ESTABLISHED TO OUT-DISTANCE OR AT LEAST KEEP PACE WITH THE GREAT DRAPERY STORES OF PARIS AND LONDON . . .

FORTY-EIGHT BEAUTIFUL SHOW WINDOWS FILLED FROM END TO END WITH THE NEWEST AND BEST PRODUCTIONS FOR MAY 1906, ADMITTEDLY THE FINEST WINDOW DISPLAY OF THE NEW GOODS FOR SUMMER EVER SEEN IN SCOTLAND. GREAT WINDOW DISPLAYS OF PARIS MODEL GOWNS, PARIS MODEL COSTUMES, PARIS MODEL COATS, EXQUISITE NEW BLOUSES, NEW TEA-GOWNS, AND NOVELTIES OF EVERY KIND FOR LADIES' WEAR, SELECTED FROM THE BEST SOURCES IN LONDON, VIENNA, BERLIN, AND PARIS.

Situated "on the plateau, 254 to 290 Sauchiehall Street," and mentioning Paris as often as possible, Treron's was one of Glasgow's great feminine public spaces. It was certainly more clearly gendered than the street's new picture houses, such as that of British-American Theatres Ltd. farther west at Number 535; but both were signs of a burgeoning consumer culture. As it had been in the nineteenth century, when it hosted Albert Hengler's Grand Cirque—more music hall than circus—Sauchiehall Street was at the heart of early twentieth-century entertainment. Glaswegians went to the cinema more frequently than anyone else in Britain. From 1912, this street boasted two of the most luxurious cinemas outside London: La Scala (which let courting couples watch the movie from a shaded tearoom) and the Picture House opposite (with its colonnaded Palm Court foyer, chandeliers, and tapestry panels). In July 1914, when King George V and Queen Mary toured Scotland's capital of "the business West," they passed, but did not enter, these palaces of silent-movie pleasure.

Not long afterwards, during World War I, the same street gave its name to a trench-warfare line at distant Gallipoli, and served in Glasgow as a base for the British Red Cross Society. At Number 138, the society's secretary appealed to the public to donate billiard tables for the use of "nervous and insane soldiers" who had been traumatized on the Western Front. In that era of the disease known as trench-foot, outside in the street men with sandwich-boards advertised a patented under-sock invented by local entrepreneur John Logie Baird, who would later come up with another invention: television. In 1916, "trench concerts"—supposedly performed "under the identical conditions in which improvised concerts are held in the fighting line"—were staged in the refurbished McLellan Galleries; concertgoers could also see exhibitions of a Zeppelin engine, along with replicas of trenches and dugouts. Times had changed decisively. Soon the McLellan Galleries hosted a public lecture entitled "How To Combat Venereal Disease"; women queued outside the Sauchiehall Street Employment Exchange to volunteer for war work; and the manageress of Miss Cranston's Tea Rooms down the road was fined for overcharging. The social history of this single street sums up many aspects of Glasgow—from the chilling and petty to the resolutely warmhearted.

In the 1920s, when the city had more dance halls than anywhere else in Britain and when Sauchiehall Street alone boasted several, the shops on Sauchiehall Street offered well-off Glaswegians a vast array of goods—everything from Japanese embroidered kimonos and Havana cigars to false teeth and foreign newspapers; but the street's cosmopolitan flavour was not for everyone. In 1928 the Reverend John MacNeilage, a Free Church minister, complained that at "the east end of Sauchiehall Street, one saw at night that there had been a decided progress in the Parisian direction—the direction of Sodom and Gomorrah." Others who walked the street had different priorities. On August 25, 1923, a pageant and procession in support of Scottish Home Rule passed by, en route to Glasgow Green, but in the following decade the same route was marched by crowds of the unemployed. Women carrying babies sang the socialist anthem "The Red Flag." In 1930, as store takings fell, the *Scotsman* asked, "Is Sauchiehall Street, the shopping centre of Glasgow, beginning to lose its attraction?"

During the Great Depression, the old gradually gave way to the newfangled: vaudeville continued to flourish at the Glasgow Empire Theatre (a notoriously unforgiving Sauchiehall Street venue), but the 1933 opening of the Meteor Film Producing Society at Number 234 heralded "a new industry for the city." Although that fledgling Glasgow industry did not take off, films accompanied the city's liveliness, in sometimes unexpected ways. In the course of the 1934 Glasgow University rectorial elections, a kilted Scottish Nationalist committeeman entering a Sauchiehall Street cinema with his girlfriend was kidnapped by Liberal university students, who mocked his wish for an independent Scotland, removed his kilt, and made him walk back embarrassedly through the city centre. Nationalists complained that the BBC, headquartered in London, treated Scotland as "provincial" and didn't even know how to pronounce "Sauchiehall Street," whose first syllable rhymes with the Scots word "loch" but never with the English word "lock." The thoroughfare itself managed to combine being both Scottish and cosmopolitan. In 1938, during Palestine Week, it welcomed the Zionist Federation to a meeting in support of a Jewish national homeland and against persecution in "the dictatorship countries," just as it had earlier welcomed a visit from the sultan of Zanzibar. The sultan had been assured by the principal of Glasgow University that for more than two hundred years his colleagues had encouraged the study of the classical language and literature of Islam; but Sauchiehall Street's most architecturally stunning small cinema, the 1913 Salon Theatre at Number 90, whose brightly tiled Moorish exterior was occasionally mistaken for that of a mosque, had already closed for good.

Newer signs of cosmopolitanism came in early 1939, when an association to champion and enliven Scottish culture, the Saltire Society (founded at Glasgow University three years earlier), supported a McLellan Galleries exhibition of "banned pictures" from Germany, including Expressionist works such as Franz Marc's *Blue Horses* and paintings by Max Beckmann and Oskar Kokoschka. That same spring, the 850-seat Cosmo Cinema (today the Glasgow Film Theatre, or GFT) was launched. Behind its brick European-modernist façade on Rose Street, just off Sauchiehall Street, it showed mainly foreign-language films and was the only purpose-built arthouse cinema outside London. In 1928, its champion, Charles Oakley, helped to found the Glasgow Film Society—the world's first film association. Pioneering Scottish documentary filmmaker John Grierson spoke at the Cosmo's opening. He said he believed it would contribute not just to cultural vigour, but also to the city's democratic and social life, presenting cinema as an instrument of observation and enlightenment as well as a form of art and entertainment. Grierson was right; this cinema has remained a treasured local institution. Today, Glasgow's rather different Renfrew Street Cineworld is the world's tallest multistorey picture house.

Soon after the Cosmo opened its doors in 1939, Glaswegians were shocked to find swastikas scratched onto Sauchiehall Street shopwindows, along with the words "We don't want Jews." The street's cosmopolitanism won out, however, and during World War II an office at Number 38, the base for the Women's Auxiliary Air Force, appealed for "Balloon Fabric Workers," while at Number 450 the recently formed Women's Display and Information Centre exhibited such North African combat-zone fabrics as the "finest cotton sandfly netting." Though Sauchiehall Street was still significantly feminine in its emporia, concepts of the feminine were changing, and the street had come a long way since its Victorian "velveteens." Throughout the Second World War, when housewives were exhorted to recycle paper, the great stores stayed open despite air-raid blackouts and shortages, regaining some energy after the conflict ended. Yet they began to fade slowly in the 1960s, more rapidly in the 1970s. Some of the finest old shops were destroyed by fire; others, simply by fashion. Major department stores such as Watt Brothers (its buildings dating from the early twentieth century) and Marks and Spencer (in Sauchiehall Street since the mid-1930s) remain, but today Glasgow's upscale shoppers are more likely to be found in Buchanan Street or the Merchant City, if not at home on the Web.

Nowadays, in order to sense something of Sauchiehall Street's remarkableness, visitors can stand on its south side, looking uphill at the junction with Scott Street. Immediately in front are the Grecian Chambers, designed in pale sandstone by Alexander Thomson in 1865 and adorned with his characteristic motifs; up the hill on the right is the soaring rear elevation of the Glasgow School of Art, designed by Charles Rennie Mackintosh. This is the only place in Glasgow where you can take in the work of the city's two greatest architects in a single glance. The Grecian Chambers, their interior radically reconfigured in 1998, now house the Centre for Contemporary Arts, welcoming the international avant-garde to an art gallery, performance area, cinema, café, and other facilities in a space previously known as the Third-Eye Centre; farther up the hill, Mackintosh's building remains very much a thriving school of art, architecture, and design. The vibrancy and location of these structures testify to the past grandeur and the continuing liveliness of the now partially pedestrianized Sauchiehall Street—a road that remains, a little against the odds, the best-known thoroughfare in Glasgow.

Running parallel to the eastern part of this great street, but at a slightly higher elevation, is a road most famous for a single building. Erected on a challenging hillside site (its central and eastern sections were built in 1897–1899), the Glasgow School of Art at 167 Renfrew Street is the city's greatest architectural masterpiece, and arguably the world's most stylishly appropriate educational building. Mackintosh had studied at the school while it was still based in Sauchiehall Street. Born in 1868, the son of a Glasgow policeman, Mackintosh grew up near the Necropolis, where he made early drawings; his first large-scale watercolour was of Glasgow Cathedral. Yet he was internationally minded. The School of Art building, which he designed when he was in his late twenties, draws on Japanese and English as well as older Scottish influences. Most of all, perhaps, he was influenced by the ethos of the school itself.

When a really detailed biography of Mackintosh comes to be written, it will need to draw substantially on the ideology of Glasgow's late nineteenth-century School of Art. Founded in 1840, the school had succeeded the short-lived eighteenth-century Academy of the Fine Arts, established by the Foulis brothers at Glasgow University. The new art school began in Ingram Street, then moved to Sauchiehall Street's Corporation Buildings (the McLellan Galleries) in 1869, when it was called Haldane's Academy. At that time it had 1,164 students, who attended classes from 7 o'clock to 9 o'clock each morning. After 1888, when this bracing schedule was discontinued, the students were allowed to sleep late.

Their teachers, however, grew admirably challenging. On November 2, 1889, the *Scotsman* reported that the school's inspirational thirty-four-year-old English director, Francis Newbery, had given a speech arguing that "any school of art . . . should meet the needs of the community in which it was placed." Newbery maintained that conventional art schools "stamped out every vital growth of the artistic power" in painters, producing "a class of workmen and designers whose sole merit consisted in the fact that their knowledge and skill were of use to nobody." Yet Newbery was no crude utilitarian. He saw art schools as "not commercial but artistic institutions." He emphasized that "good art and public taste were not usually synonymous terms."

Led by a director unafraid of controversy, eager to communicate high standards, and committed to the education of artists who respected what were called "handicrafts," the Glasgow School of Art had a clear vision of excellence and was regarded as one of Britain's finest art colleges. In the 1892 National Competition Prizes, the "Gold Medal [was] . . . taken by Chas. R. McIntosh [*sic*] for Architecture." Newbery spoke at the ceremony where Mackintosh's achievement was praised. According to the press, he said "it spoke badly for the industrial arts of the nineteenth century" that the question of a separation between technical education and fine-art training should have arisen. "In the heyday of art the artist was the craftsman and the craftsman was the artist. Glasgow was handicapped by the fact that what was called art in London did not pass muster as good art in Glasgow, and *vice versa*. He [Newbery] desired a distinctive school of art for Glasgow. . . . What was wanted in Glasgow was an improvement in art industries so that there might be no need to apply to foreign labour and production." Greeted by applause, these sentiments, with their hint of cultural nationalism and civic pride, may have appealed to Glaswegians' industrial-commercial *nous,* and even to a spirit of economic protectionism. Yet they also had an idealistic aspect, to which Mackintosh responded in his own work.

Two years later, as reported in the *Glasgow Herald,* one of the School of Art's grandees, Sir Francis Powell, summed up the institution's ethos with a statement on the function and aims of fine art and design:

> Both branches of study should be pursued together. . . . To be able to produce good ornament was one of the highest gifts, one of which any artist might be proud. . . . It was a very noble employment to make the commonest things of everyday life beautiful—[applause]—for they were seen by the poor as well as the rich, and appealed to all. Were they not shown by the Creator's wondrous care in the most insignificant prod-ucts that nothing should be too lowly on which to exert their best efforts, and that to add beauty to make lovely our world's goods was a very high calling.

Stressing that "the care and time expended on a loved subject was always delightful to see," and that "it always imparted a strange, undefinable charm, touching some harmonic chord in our souls," Powell's words can sound platitudinous. Yet, however crudely, they articulate ideals which spurred the more imaginative Mackintosh not just to plan the new Art School's iconic exterior and interior, with their eye-catching angles and superbly functional spaces, but also led him to design its clocks, door panels, furniture, and fittings—from the janitor's box and air-conditioning machinery-housing to the superlatively modeled lampshades in its library. Whereas Powell spoke of "the leaves of the trees" and "the flowers of the field," Mackintosh contended: "Art is the flower. Life is the green leaf."

Mackintosh had a preternaturally astute sense of structure and volume. He was also an adorer of poetry. While training at the School of Art, he belonged to a small, mainly female group of literature-loving art students who called themselves "the Immortals." In April 1896 he drew and painted his future wife, fellow "Immortal" Margaret Macdonald, in a stylized Art Nouveau manner, with red roses and other organic forms. Mackintosh's title, *Part Seen, Imagined Part,* alludes to the last verse of Wordsworth's poem "To May," where the poet articulates a vision of perfection:

> Season of fancy and of hope,
> Permit not for one hour,
> A blossom from thy crown to drop,
> Nor add to it a flower!
> Keep, lovely May, as if by touch
> Of self restraining art,
> This modest charm of not too much,
> Part seen, imagined part!

Mackintosh had himself photographed in 1893 wearing a soft shirt and a vast, floppy cravat tied in an elaborate rose-like bow, as if he were trying hard to look like the Irish Celtic Twilight poet W. B. Yeats. Yet for all his bohemian extravagances, he had a keen and subtle sense of "self restraining art."

You can see that in his buildings. Viewed from the front, the Glasgow School of Art exhibits strikingly configured masses dominated by huge rectangular windows that provide excellent light to paint by. The frontage is quite plain but also incorporates decorative aspects, such as flower-shaped stanchions and wrought-iron window brackets, which grow like roses in front of the great studio windows. Shortly before winning the competition to design the School of Art in 1896, Mackintosh had been reading with enthusiasm *Architecture, Mysticism and Myth,* the first book by W. R. Lethaby.

This English architect valued a holistic approach to building design, arguing that "if we trace the artistic forms of things, made by man, to their origin, we find a direct imitation of nature." Mackintosh's buildings, furniture, and two-dimensional artworks constantly refer to natural forms, particularly to flowers; he is said to have wanted fresh roses brought daily to the students' studios at the School of Art. Yet his love of the organic goes hand in hand with a delight in angular, constructed geometries that may make American onlookers think of Frank Lloyd Wright. Mackintosh fused his poetic imagination with the constructional skills so prevalent in his native city of shipbuilders, locomotive engineers, and manufacturers.

The front door of the Glasgow School of Art is a fine example of this mixture. Approached up a narrowing flight of fifteen stone steps which focus the eye on its tall, rectangular aspect, the doorway extends above twin black doors, all rectangles and squares. In the centre, over the heads of all who come and go, is a square panel, decorated with squares within squares. Its distinctive lettering (a signature touch, also designed by Mackintosh) reads: THE GLASGOW SCHOOL OF ART. Yet above this rectilinear geometry, and surrounding it, is carved stonework with curving stylized figures and flower motifs. At the foot of the steps, a gently curvilinear wrought-iron arch supports a rectilinear iron box—the lamp that lights the entry.

Constantly balancing curvy, flowing Art Nouveau forms with what look like more stark, straight-lined modernist or constructivist geometries, Mackintosh's style is effortlessly eclectic, while also attuned to functionality. The Glasgow School of Art draws, in its design, on sources as different as Scottish tower houses and Japanese heraldic symbols. Its architect's sense of verticality is nowhere more evident than on the Scott Street exterior whose windows ascend without interruption through three storeys. Still, no one can appreciate this building as one of the world's most memorable without going inside. Though it is a working educational institution, not a museum, regular tours (usually conducted by well-informed art students) are available, and visitors to Glasgow should do their best to take one. Built in more than one section because of a delay caused by financial overruns and economic problems, the School of Art is not huge; it just has a unique personality. High above, at the rear, the "hen run" once frequented by female students (working-class Glaswegians traditionally address a woman as "hen") affords expansive views over the city from a strikingly geometric lightweight

44. The sweeping front steps of Charles Rennie Mackintosh's Glasgow School of Art, at 167 Renfrew Street, draw the eye toward its elegant twin black doors.

wood-and-glass walkway, which contrasts pleasingly with the heavier curvaceous loggia beyond. The building's very corridors and stone stairways are glorious, and throughout you can see Mackintosh's remarkable furniture *in situ* and even in use. The library, a dark-wood, balconied forest with tiny touches of primary colours and hanging lamps that look a little like miniature tower blocks is the most haunting of all the interior spaces. Mackintosh designed it to invoke trees and other natural forms, yet it is stylized to such an extent that it does so subliminally.

I spent my teens going to Saturday-morning art classes in this building, and learned early that, filled with uniquely imaginative angles, it is a wonderful place in which to work, walk about, and ponder. Mackintosh designed other exceptionally resonant exteriors and interiors for Glasgow's citizens. His tearooms for Miss Cranston were the height of advanced taste, while some of his best furniture (including examples of those signature, very-high-backed chairs) can still be seen in Glasgow University's Hunterian Art Gallery. Just south of the Clyde, Scotland Street School, its front and rear elevations arrestingly different, is another of this charismatic architect's finest public buildings. To see his domestic masterpiece, you must travel along the north bank of the Clyde to Helensburgh, where Mackintosh designed the Hill House for the family of Glasgow publisher Walter Blackie. The architect spent a considerable time with this family, observing how they lived, before he designed their new home. The Blackies and their children delighted in its luminous interiors, and so do tourists from all round the world, now that it is owned by the National Trust for Scotland.

Almost all of Mackintosh's buildings are in Glasgow and the surrounding area, but it took Glaswegians a long time to come to terms fully with his imagination; moreover, for all that his designs were acclaimed by contemporary avant-garde journals in Vienna and other continental European cities, he could find little work outside Glasgow. With his artist wife, Margaret Macdonald Mackintosh, with whom he often collaborated, he moved eventually to the south of England, then, as architectural work dried up, to Port Vendres in the south of France. Living there in cheap hotels, Mackintosh, artist to the last, painted fine watercolours of local places. Several are now in the Hunterian Art Gallery. Suffering from cancer of the tongue, the designer of the Glasgow School of Art died almost forgotten in a London nursing home in 1928. A few years later, he began to be hailed as a pioneer of modern architecture—but in Scotland many ignored his legacy, or misunderstood it. At a sale in the 1930s, part of one of his revolving bookcases was mistaken for a radio ærial. In 1973, his admirers founded the Charles Rennie Mackintosh Society, now headquartered in Glasgow's Mackintosh-designed Queen's Cross Church. The society has saved several of his buildings from demolition. Today lauded internationally, this architect's work is regarded in Glasgow with appropriate love and pride, for all that the city sometimes struggles to maintain it. These structures belong neither to the nineteenth nor to the twentieth century. Instead, they fuse the best of both with a panache at once unique and democratically approachable.

Like so many of his Glaswegian contemporaries, Mackintosh grew up living in a Victorian tenement. The Tenement House at 145 Buccleuch Street—a short walk northwest of the School of Art, though some distance from Mackintosh's childhood home—is the best place in the city for tourists to sample this quintessentially Glaswegian way of life. The first individual Glasgow tenement to be recorded stood in the Trongate and incorporated a stone bearing the date 1591. It seems to have been four floors high, taller than other sixteenth-century tenements, which rose only to two stories and an attic. The word "tenement" comes from the Latin *tenementum,* "a land-holding." Many of Glasgow's tenements were and are handsome dwellings. Some, though, were notorious for slumminess.

In the seventeenth century, two fires destroyed city-centre areas around the Saltmarket. The first was in 1652; the second in 1677, when "a malicious boy, a smith's apprentice, . . . being threttned, or beat & smitten by his master, in revenge whereof sets his workhouse on fyre in the night tyme." Raging for eighteen hours, the first fire alone destroyed the homes of about a thousand families; the second was also "a great conflagration." Prisoners had to be rescued from the Tolbooth (then in use as a jail), and that building's great clock was incinerated. Glasgow was so shaken that it even sent a deputation to Edinburgh to investigate the capital's "ingyne for casting water on land that is in fyre"—Scotland's first fire-engine. After such blazes, there was considerable rebuilding; and as the eighteenth-century advanced, tenements grew ever more popular, not least because they allowed substantial numbers of people to live in the city centre. Defoe admired these tenement "houses . . . all built of stone, and generally uniform in height, as well as in front. The lower stories, for the most part, stand on vast square Doric columns, with arches, which open into the shops, adding to the strength, as well as beauty of the building." The best later eighteenth-century "lands," or tenements, retained this beauty. Built in 1784, Spreull's Land which once stood at 182 Trongate, was decorated with columns along its front, while inside was a splendid elliptical "hanging stair," its broad, unsupported stone steps built into the wall of the stairwell, curving round like a meticulously whorled shell.

Not all tenements were so grand. As the Industrial Revolution advanced, more and more workers flocked to Glasgow to labour in cotton mills and other factories. Congregating in the city centre, especially during the recessions of the early nineteenth century, these folk sought cheap lodgings. Areas of the urban heartland grew dense with hastily erected tenements. From 1801 to 1861, the city's population grew five-fold, from just under 80,000 to almost 400,000. Slums proliferated, especially around the Saltmarket. The neighbouring Goosedubbs area, recalled in George Mills's nineteenth-century novel *The Beggar's Benison,* "used always to be estimated as one of the lowest, dirtiest and vilest of purlieus to be found anywhere." In 1839, a year after the publication of *Oliver Twist,* London's Jelinger C. Symons wrote that "disease, crime, population and commerce culminate in Glasgow." Viewing this Scottish industrial city of around a quarter of a million souls, Symons maintained that its population had increased fifteen-fold in the preceding century, which meant that it was growing "with greater rapidity than any other city in Europe." Accompanying a policeman to apprehend a housebreaker, he headed through the area around the Saltmarket and High Street to the wynds (narrow streets) near the Trongate.

This quarter consists of a labyrinth of lanes, varying from 7 to 14 feet in width, out of which numberless entrances open into small square courts, appropriately designated "closes" with houses, many of them in a dilapidated state, of two stories high, and a common dunghill reeking with filth in the centre. Most of these habitations are let out in flats by a fellow called the Laird, who is usually a pawnbroker or a whisky dealer in the ground floor. The flats are again divided into one or two rooms; the better ones being let to families who can afford to pay for them, but a great proportion being lodging rooms, tenanted by an old crone who lets nights' lodging at from a penny to threepence per head, according to the accommodation afforded. We entered at least a score of these dens. The lower class predominates, and revolting as was the outward appearance of these places, I confess I was little prepared for the filth and destitution within. In some of these lodging rooms we found a whole lair of human beings littered along the floor, sometimes 15 and 20 in number, some clothed, and some naked, men, women and children all huddled promiscuously together. Their bed consisted of a layer of musty straw, intermixed with ambiguous looking rags, of which it was difficult to discover any other feature than their intense dirtiness. There was, generally speaking, little or no furniture in these places; not even in the rooms let to families, beyond a few stools and one or two grimy platters and dilapidated pans.

Symons, who had examined London's Dickensian slums as well as social conditions across Europe, had never seen "anything one-half so bad." He cites statistics showing that Glasgow's mortality rate had worsened from one in forty-four in 1822 to one in twenty-four by 1837; England averaged one in fifty-one.

It was an especially grim place for the poorest children. In their anthology *Glasgow Observed* (1987), Simon Berry and Hamish Whyte quote from Victorian courtroom records an eyewitness's transcribed declaration about the death of an abused six-year-old "climbing boy," or chimney-sweep's assistant, cleaning his thirty-seventh chimney vent on a chill, rainy day:

> About three in the afternoon the little Boy came down the Chimney of an apartment where Declarant was at work, and the Boy was complaining bitterly of cold and seemed to be very much exhausted & "far through." That his Clothes were in a wettish state, and the Boy on leaving said apartment went to the one immediately above, & as the flooring was not laid the Declarant could see between the Joists. That Hughes the Prisoner was there and he was swearing at the Boy and threatening him. That after the Boy had got so far up said Chimney Hughes took a stick and put it up the Chimney and Kept thrusting away there, but whether he hit the Boy or not the Declarant cannot say.

By 1858, Glasgow's tenements had grown higher, its unsanitary slums worse. "Shadow," the author of *Midnight Scenes and Social Photographs, Being Sketches of Life in the Streets, Wynds and Dens of the City* (1858), takes readers at night along the High Street to "the Bush and Tontine Closes, almost entirely inhabited by the lowest thieves and prostitutes. . . . These closes, or lanes, are scarcely more than four or five feet wide. Overhead are lofty old houses approached by dirty dilapidated stairs. . . . In Bush close, . . . we proceed to the cellar below . . . by a damp, earthy-smelling old stair, dark as the grave, and celebrated, we are informed in professional language, for 'many a

45. In 1868 Thomas Annan photographed women and children in a lane at 80 High Street. The image is part of his study *Old Closes and Streets of Glasgow*, the first comprehensive series of photographs to document an urban slum.

good skin,' or robbery." This was the townscape photographed around 1870 by the Sauchiehall Street–based photographer Thomas Annan for his *Old Closes and Streets of Glasgow*, the first comprehensive series of photographs in the world to document an urban slum. Near open sewers, children sit on the flagstones of narrow alleys; washing hangs from poles sticking out from windows above. Often five or six stories high, the tenements let little light into the thin lanes between them. For a century or more after these photographs were taken, Glasgow wrestled with slum-clearance programmes.

In the Victorian and Edwardian eras, the usual solution to tenement slums was better tenements. Commissioned by the Glasgow City Improvements Trust, Annan finished his most famous slum photography in 1871. In the ensuing five years, well over 20,000 new tenement houses were built throughout districts such as Govanhill, Springburn, and Maryhill. The long views down many new, tenemented Glasgow streets were not slum vistas; the best tenements were designed with panache. At the same time that "Shadow" was investigating midnight urban "dens," the now-demolished tenements of Queen's Park Terrace at 355–429 Eglinton Street were being built to designs by Alexander "Greek" Thomson. Regular yet robustly imaginative, their frontages ran towards a corner based on the Roman temple of Venus at Baalbek. Internal plasterwork celebrated classical motifs.

By no means every Glasgow tenements exhibited such exuberance, but Thomson's sweeping 1869 Great Western Terrace is to this day monumental and superb, while across that same road Kirklee Terrace—with its high sash-windows, window boxes, and basement fruit trees—is still a stately example of Glaswegian grandeur. Such designs were likewise influential. If the tenement is associated with Glasgow's heritage of slums, it also emblematizes the city's Victorian and Edwardian brio. Tenements were built of white sandstone, and then, when that ran out, red sandstone. Industrial grime coated them in black, but antipollution laws from the 1960s onwards led to some being sandblasted clean. Interrupted by a banking crash of 1878 and its lengthy aftermath, tenement building continued until just before World War I. In the mid- and later twentieth century, many tenements were cleared to make way for tower blocks. Now some of those seem so like slums that they, too, have been razed.

To equate the tenement with destitution in Glasgow is misguided. Even the once-notorious Gorbals at one time boasted some fine tenements. In the late 1860s, Gorbals Main Street was a thoroughfare through a rundown village. The coming of new tenements transformed the area. A photograph of nearby Crown Street in 1900 shows a wide roadway with tram lines at its centre and a prosperous-looking population, the men wearing bowler hats, ties, and watch fobs; the girls, too, in hats; the women well dressed. Lasses caught on camera playing in a Gorbals playground in 1910 wear soft hats and neat pinafores; a lad on a swing is clad in a smart sailor suit. All have carefully polished shoes. What turned the Gorbals into a slum was partly the migration of the better-off to garden suburbs, leaving behind the proto-types of the Gorbals Die-Hards. Tenements per se were not to blame. In-deed, with their common stairs and weel-kent (well-known) neighbours, some even came to be romanticized for promoting community spirit.

All this should be borne in mind by visitors to the upstairs Tenement House in Buccleuch Street, not far from the Glasgow School of Art. Now owned by the National Trust for Scotland, this property was built in 1892. Just one year earlier, a writer in the *Glasgow Herald* had described "the new class of tenement" whose "in-the-fashion" interiors "must be fitted with kitchen ranges, hot and cold water, grates, tiled hearths, and bath-rooms, with elaborately constructed baths and wash-hand basins." In the shared ar-eas of such buildings (which tenants took turns cleaning) "entrances and stairs are constructed of ornamental tiles" and "the elongated windows are filled with 'cathedral' glass." Though not as fancy as some contemporary tenements in the West End or in Pollokshields, the Tenement House boasts several such refinements. Importantly, in terms of its amenities, it was con-structed in the year the Burgh Police Act (of Scotland) required tenements to have internal sanitation, rather than make do with the back-court outside privies that were common then and for decades afterwards in poorer areas.

The Tenement House, as today's visitors see it, looks much as it did in the time of its long-term resident, Agnes Toward (1886–1975). Miss Toward moved there with her widowed dressmaker mother in 1911, worked for forty-five years as a shorthand typist, and kept her apartment like a time capsule. In the 1970s the flat was saved by Anna Davidson, niece of Miss Toward's church elder. It was opened to the public by the National Trust in 1983. Downstairs on the entry level, a similar flat contains an exhibition on the his-tory of tenements, as well as items from Miss Toward's personal archive. Nineteenth-century coloured pictures for a girlhood scrapbook give way to instructional leaflets from the Ministry of Food in an era of rationing: "Once upon a time cooks used to think a good soup needed 3 or 4 hours cooking, and that to be nourishing it must be made from meat and bones. Today we know better." This display provides a good insight into the life of a tenement dweller in the twentieth century. So does Miss Toward's flat upstairs.

The apartment at 145 Buccleuch Street is a museum where intimacy is paramount. A square hallway opens onto a parlour, a bedroom, a kitchen, and a bathroom. That's all. Yet from the toilet, with its black wrought-iron cistern whose raised lettering spells "St. Mungo," to Miss Toward's World War II gas mask in its cloth-covered box or her mother's well-used 1860s American Wheeler and Wilson sewing machine, these domestic rooms are captivating. The kitchen, its iron "range" used for heating, for cooking, and for keeping flatirons warm, also contains a coal bunker and a pot of Miss Toward's uneaten jam: "Plum 1929." Agnes Toward was not rich. She had to live prudently, paying her rent quarterly and keeping careful track of the days each month which were set apart "for the use of the Wash-house and Back Court," so she could wash her clothes and hang them out to dry. She would never have expected that among all the tenements from Victorian and Edwardian Glasgow, her home would be selected to be passed down to posterity, as reverently treasured as a diamond.

Round the corner from the Tenement House, the long gentle arch of a late twentieth-century pedestrian footbridge lets walkers cross the busy Charing Cross interchange and the cavernous, thronged M8 motorway beneath. This stroll marks a shift from the hillside tenements of Buccleuch Street to the Woodside area, with its calm terraces, mosque, distant church spires, and Victorian streets leading to the green space of Kelvingrove Park. Nothing, however, could be less green than the tangle of roads by the M8. They scythe through what were once tenement communities. Glasgow's town planners of the 1960s and 1970s sought to deliver an efficient motorway system capable of speeding thousands of cars right to the heart of the city. Cleaving vast roads through Charing Cross and nearby St. George's Cross was the planners' way of achieving this.

Dramatic in its traffic roar and its lesion-like cut through an older townscape, the motorway and its attendant slip-roads are particularly striking at night; then, as the poet Edwin Morgan puts it, "the flyovers breed loops of light." But the road system has also produced weird disjunctions. One of these takes the form of a modern office block eventually erected on top of an aborted flyover (overpass) which for years had constituted a "bridge to nowhere"—part of a through-road that was never completed. Another mismatch is that between the concrete chasm of the motorway and the elaborate domed, red-sandstone Victorian building which sits almost above it on North Street. The copper-clad dome over this structure's rotunda is topped with a jaunty, early twentieth-century sculpture—a windblown woman striding forth, holding a scroll. This female figure represents Literature, and beneath her is the Mitchell Library—the city's greatest public book-hoard. As if ignoring the advice of her more stolid sister, Wisdom, who sits above what was once the library's main entrance, Literature now races heedlessly towards the traffic pit of the motorway below.

Among Europe's largest municipal reference libraries, the Mitchell Library is at the heart of Glasgow's democratic book culture. Like other local institutions, it owes its magnificence in part to the wealth derived from slavery. It takes its name from Stephen Mitchell (1789–1874), whose money came from his family's tobacco firm, founded in Glasgow in 1825 and ending up in the ownership of Imperial Tobacco. Mitchell, whose marble portrait bust still sits in the building named after him, never married. He left Glasgow nearly £70,000 to establish a free library from which "no books should be excluded on the ground that they contravene present opinions on politics or religion." Popular from its inception, the collection was originally housed in two large flats in Ingram Street. In addition to general holdings, it included, from the start, three special collections: a "Poets' Corner" which contained all Scottish verse, with a special emphasis on Robert Burns; a hoard of books and other materials about Glasgow; and a gathering of works printed in the city from 1638 onwards. These specialities were given architectural distinction when the library moved to its grand, even grandiose new premises in North Street. The building's memorial stone was laid by Andrew Carnegie in 1907, and the Mitchell was opened in 1911 by Lord Rosebery, who annoyed his hearers by joking that it was "a cemetery of books."

Today some of the library's older spaces, such as its Burns Room, do feel mausoleum-like. Yet—hosting a literature festival and a digital library, as well as a very intensively used rare- books and public-records department—the library has not only grown but successfully reinvented itself in recent decades. Back in 1884, one Glaswegian argued:

It is not possible in the case of a public library to accurately measure the advantage which its visitors derive from it: but when it is seen that year after year numbers of all classes and all ages obtain an acquaintance with the great works of our literature; that students come again and again for the study of the textbooks of their special subjects; that artisans obtain the technical works relating to their several trades; and that in number-less instances time that would otherwise be spent idly or worse, is occupied with instruction or entertainment, it cannot be doubted that a great power is exerted for the good both of individuals and the community.

Probably these words were written by John Oswald Mitchell—no relation of Stephen, but another mercantile citizen committed to Glasgow's public library system, to local history, and to Burns. Author of short biographies of famous Glaswegians, J. O. Mitchell advocated the study of Scots vernacular culture and regretted (according to the *Glasgow Herald* on Burns Night 1888) that "Burns is grown almost a dead language to the [people of] quality, and even the common folk, thanks to School Boards and other modern influences, are fast losing their good Scotch." While opposed to socialism, J. O. Mitchell wanted a return to the Scots vernacular as a way of "drawing us together," though his idealism did not extend to the Gaelic language, whose popular influence he saw as *"nil."* This Mitchell's views can be seen as part of late nineteenth-century arguments about Scottish cultural identity that to some extent continue to this day. The great public library Stephen Mitchell endowed now possesses a superb collection about the history of Glasgow. It functions at its best as an educational resource which stands independent of (though in no way hostile to) institutions of mainstream education.

Over the decades, the Mitchell Library's collections have been enriched by some remarkable bequests. One of these came in the 1920s through the family of Henry Dyer. Son of an Irish immigrant, Dyer had died in 1918 at the age of seventy. In the 1860s, he had gone to evening classes at what was then called Anderson's College (now Strathclyde University, northeast of George Square). Other evening-class students at Anderson's included Yozo Yamao from Japan, who was then working in a Clyde shipyard. After Dyer had served as an apprentice to a Glasgow engineering company, and had graduated with a B.Sc. from Glasgow University, he was recommended by an influential Glaswegian professor as a suitable person to become principal of Japan's Imperial College of Engineering. In Tokyo, with help from Yozo

A·TENEMENT·OF·OLD·HOUSES·

46. A classic item among the Mitchell Library's collection of Glaswegiana is Jessie M. King's small volume *The City of the West*, published in 1911. The book includes this illustration, entitled "A Tenement of Old Houses," depicting historic taverns near Glasgow Cross on the High Street.

Yamao, Dyer designed a fresh course structure. Its success helped to spur a new, practically minded generation of Japanese engineers who went on to play a major role in transforming their country. Appointed to the Japanese order of the Rising Sun, Dyer returned to Glasgow after a decade. Now he mentored Japanese students who came to study engineering in the city. He also wrote books on industrial history and on Japanese culture, viewing Japan as "the Britain of the East." His 6,000-item bequest to the Mitchell Library covers a range of topics in Japanese life, as well as including beautiful scrolls and albums of the *Ukiyo-e* (Pictures of the Floating World) school, illustrating Kabuki actors, flowers, warlords, and birds.

It is indicative of the range covered by the Mitchell Library that its collections should range from Japanese art to what is now regarded as the world's first regular comic-book magazine, John Watson's *Glasgow Looking Glass* (1825–1826), which is credited with pioneering the use of the phrase "To be continued," as well as the "word balloons" or "speech bubbles" in narrative cartoon series. Better-known are the Burns manuscripts which the library holds, among them one of "Auld Lang Syne" and, in prose, Burns's only surviving letter written in the Scots tongue—usually the poet wrote his letters in decorous formal English. The strengths of the Burns material extend well beyond original manuscripts, and include secondary sources—editions, translations, critical books, and pamphlets written in more than thirty languages. A catalogue of many of the printed materials, published in 1996, ranges from speculations about the bard's medical history to orations given at the unveiling of Burns statues around the globe. For anyone with an interest in the work of Scotland's most famous poet, the Mitchell holds one of the most important hoards on the planet.

It is also a centre for contemporary writing; its collections encompass the personal library of the poet Edwin Morgan, and manuscripts by Glaswegian Booker Prize–winner James Kelman, and by Alasdair Gray, the Glasgow novelist whose *Lanark* (1981) is a milestone in modern Scottish fiction. Local authors who have used the Mitchell's collections most imaginatively include Frank Kuppner, whose poetry in *A Bad Day for the Sung Dynasty* was stimulated by looking at some of the library's Chinese holdings. Kuppner's 1989 "novel of sorts," *A Very Quiet Street*, features the Mitchell Library, where the book was researched. It centres around the 1908 murder of Marion Gilchrist, an elderly woman who lived nearby in West Princes Street. Her case became notorious because it resulted in one of the most famous Scottish miscarriages of justice: a Silesian Jewish immigrant, Oscar Slater, who lived for a time at 435 Sauchiehall Street, was wrongly convicted of killing her. Several attempts were made to have Slater (who returned voluntarily from New York to face trial) set free; Arthur Conan Doyle was among his supporters. Glasgow detective John Thompson Trench worked heroically to establish that Slater had been framed, but those efforts destroyed Trench's career, and he died long before Slater was eventually freed, in 1928, after nearly twenty years' incarceration. Though Kuppner's book suggests that the real murderer was an academic related to Marion Gilchrist, the killer has never been identified with absolute certainty—and probably never will be.

As if disgusted by the nearby roar of the motorway, the great Mitchell Library has turned its back on Charing Cross. Whereas earlier visitors entered the building through a portal on North Street, beneath the figures of Literature and Wisdom, today the main entrance is situated to the west, on Granville Street. It leads towards a modern foyer which includes a welcoming cafeteria and theatre complex. Originally this side of the Mitchell was occupied by the St. Andrew's Halls, a Victorian glory where on December 21, 1884, Oscar Wilde delivered to a full house a lecture entitled "Artistic v. Modern Dress" (he objected to that masculine "glossy silk cylinder," the top hat); but when fire gutted the Halls in 1962, the library expanded, developing a substantial lecture room as well as a theatre. In the 1980s, when local novelists such as Gray and Kelman were attracting international attention to Glasgow as a place of the literary imagination, the Mitchell represented an unignorable aspect of a city where books have long been seen to matter. In the 1990s its most literary librarian, Hamish Whyte, editor of the classic Glasgow poetry anthology *Noise and Smoky Breath,* published bibliographies of the work of Edwin Morgan and the Glasgow-domiciled poet and dramatist Liz Lochhead, who in 2010 became Scotland's "Makar," or National Poet. Currently, the Mitchell Library, like public libraries elsewhere, seems to be in transition. Some of its grander spaces can feel a little empty. Its more scholarly aspect is less in evidence, and planned exhibitions on the history of Glasgow in writing have yet to come fully into flower. Yet, with its recent activities ranging from providing support for the Glasgow Women's

Library (once housed near the Tron Theatre in a distinctively feminine space generously enhanced by donated sofas) to caring for the extensive photographic collection of Thomas Annan's former Sauchiehall Street studio, the Mitchell remains a Glasgow ark, however awkwardly beached on the edge of a motorway's loud and interminable blur.

Art, Learning, Arsenic, and Architecture

For all it can seem a grid of endless traffic, Glasgow is determinedly a place of art. Signs of this throng the city centre—from the thick-haired portrait bust of Beethoven at the back of a former piano factory on Renfrew Street to the sculpted lineup of Homer, Shakespeare, Dante, Michelangelo, Leonardo, Raphael, and others that now forms part of the Mitchell Library. Yet the evidence for Glasgow as a hub of culture lies even more in its present-day people. It is they who provide the staff, the base, and the infrastructure for the Royal Scottish National Orchestra, the Scottish Chamber Orchestra, the BBC Scottish Symphony Orchestra, and Scottish Opera, as well as for the National Theatre of Scotland. All of these, please note, are headquartered in Glasgow rather than in the Scottish capital. Proud of their democratic book culture, Glaswegians have been glimpsed more than once sitting in buses or trains while hunched over Kafka. They make more pilgrimages to art galleries than to football matches, and one of the most consistently popular visitor attractions in Scotland is the Glasgow Art Gallery and Museum, in the parklands at Kelvingrove.

As with so many other Glaswegian institutions, the origins of Kelvingrove's spectacular museum are bound up with the city's Victorian past. Those origins also owe something to rivalry with Edinburgh. Kelvingrove Park, beside the River Kelvin in the city's west end, was the site of vast exhibitions in 1888, 1901, and 1911. The first of these, attended by six million people (more than the entire Scottish population), was the Glasgow International Exhibition. Well aware that Edinburgh had held its own International Exhibition two years earlier, Glaswegians succeeded in outdoing it. Their chosen site, Kelvingrove Park, had been laid out in 1853 in fields previously occupied by thatched cottages. Intending a show-stopping, profitable spectacle sufficient to fund a new art gallery, local architect James Sellar erected in 1888 "Baghdad by Kelvinside"—a hybrid architectural array of temporary exhibition buildings drawing on Byzantine as well as North African and Indian styles.

In Britain's imperial heyday, this was empire as spectacle. One crowd-pulling exhibit was Robert Gibb's painting *The Thin Red Line,* showing Glaswegian Colin Campbell's Scottish Highland troops defending the Empire at the Battle of Balaclava. Other exhibits spoke to Glasgow's place in imperial trade. "Tobacco girls" each produced up to 2,000 handmade cigarettes a day. About three dozen Clyde shipyards displayed the largest collection of model vessels ever seen: these included miniature versions of a steam yacht built on the Clyde for the Russian czar, and the world's largest merchant steamship, *City of New York*—again Clyde-built. On a site overlooked by a replica of the bishop's castle that had once stood near Glasgow Cathedral, distant imperial territories from India and Ceylon to Australia and Jamaica displayed their goods, produce, and even their people. On a visit to the exhibition, Queen Victoria, Empress of India and sovereign of all the Empire, met the Glaswegian organizing committee, whose members included the distinguished local physicist later ennobled as Lord Kelvin. At Kelvingrove, Her Majesty sat on a royal dais. Specially constructed and arranged on four descending levels, this structure measured thirty by twenty feet. Enthroned on it, the British monarch was herself Glasgow's rarest imperial exhibit. The city never saw her again.

Profits from the municipal extravaganza of 1888 bankrolled the splendidly adorned red-sandstone art museum. The centre of the building's north façade is somewhat improbably modeled on the Spanish Baroque cathedral of Santiago di Compostela; the composition is ornamented with statues of St. Mungo and of spirited figures representing everything from Painting and Sculpture to the Industries of Glasgow at the court of the Roman god Mercury. Inside, a soaring, marble-floored main hall is wonderfully over the top. It features a giant, carved Glasgow coat of arms, and has the names of the city's trades blazoned on an arcade of piers. Proud of its Glaswegian workers, the great central hall is also decorated with the names of thirty-six international composers and boasts an elevated Victorian organ. This vast instrument was restored in 1988; it has 2,889 working pipes, but those visible on its elaborate walnut front are purely decorative. First played in 1901, the organ is still the star of regular free concerts which, like the surrounding building, feature a typically Glaswegian mixture of high culture and

47. Opened in 1901, the Glasgow Art Gallery and Museum, at Kelvingrove, is modelled in part on the Spanish Baroque cathedral of Santiago de Compostela. While admiring works by Titian, Rembrandt, Van Gogh, and Matisse, visitors can enjoy free concerts played on the gallery's elevated Victorian organ, which boasts 2,889 working pipes.

inclusive populism. Squealing children and rapt old ladies gaze at television monitors to see close-ups of the organist's footwork.

The Glasgow Art Galleries, arguably the city's best-loved public space, were fully renovated in 2009, their display areas extended, and their exhibits rearranged in a dazzling postmodern baroque. A Spitfire aircraft hangs suspended from wires in midair between the balconies of the western hall, flying low over taxidermied animals and a dizzying array of other exhibits. To those who blanche at such hybrid clutter, it can be pointed out that this challenging mixture is entirely in keeping with the spirit of the huge International Exhibition in Kelvingrove Park in 1901, the year of Queen Victoria's death, when the building was first opened. At that time the galleries, which some thought vulgar and "far too much a casino," were marketed robustly as containing "the greatest art Collection ever gathered under one roof."

Crowds flocked to see not just paintings, but exhibits of bookbinding, machine guns, sugar-processing technology (in those days, Glasgow made 80 percent of the world's sugar-refining equipment), full-size locomotives from the city's three main manufacturers (who amalgamated in 1903 to form the largest locomotive builders in Britain), and fresh eggs from the St. Mungo Poultry Company. There was, as well, a global jumble of wonders: not just highlights from the British Empire, but also a Japanese garden, a Russian village designed by an admirer of Charles Rennie Mackintosh (who also exhibited), and, from the United States, the vibrantly percussive band of John Philip Sousa. Visitors ranged from British royalty and His Majesty the Crown Prince of Siam to more publicity-shy locals, such as courting couples who carefully sought places in the shrubbery where they would not be illuminated by the festive searchlights that played regularly across the park.

It is easy to smile at these showy International Exhibitions that attended the construction of the Kelvingrove Art Galleries, but they were supremely successful. The 1901 displays attracted well over eleven million people. A decade later, when the new buildings played their part in the park's Scottish Exhibition of National History, Art, and Industry, more than nine million flocked to see everything from Flora Macdonald's slippers to a full-size working "ærial railway," which took giddy visitors "flying across the Kelvin" in a dirigible with a large, basket-like compartment adventurously suspended below it. The buildings of the 1911 exposition were a pre-Disney Disneyland of big temporary castles, closely modeled on Scottish originals, and even a pastiche Auld Toon, or Olde Toun, complete with an enticing "Olde Toffee Shoppe." After all of the above had been deflated, unbolted, disassembled, and cleared away, the Art Galleries stayed on and prospered.

This imposing sandstone structure had a narrow escape from Nazi bombing in 1941, when a shell landed nearby, badly damaging a group of statues on a bridge over the Kelvin. That same night, as firewatchers kept a lookout from the roof-space above Glasgow University's Bute Hall, 260 bombers blitzed the Clydeside shipyard towns of Greenock and Clydebank, destroying entire housing estates. A famous photograph shows a mangled tram car still standing amidst the rubble of devastated tenements where hundreds of people had perished. Incendiary bombs set whole streets of Clydebank alight, and survivors of the Clydebank Blitz recall being strafed in the roadway as sparks fell between the girders of half-built, roofless brick shelters. Isa Mackenzie, who was twelve at the time, recalled, "It was like being in a horror film." Yet only a couple of years after this Clydeside atrocity, there occurred a far more welcome wartime incident which transformed the great cultural holdings of Glasgow, confirming it as a world-class city of art.

That moment came in 1943, when Sir William Burrell, a former local councillor and Clyde shipping magnate, decided with his wife that their superlative art collection should be bequeathed to Glasgow. The Burrell gift—which will be described in detail later in this chapter—was part of the larger-scale development of the modern west-coast city as an artistic centre. The man to whom Burrell communicated his decision was Tom Honeyman, the now-legendary director of Glasgow's Art Galleries. Trained as a doctor at Glasgow University, Honeyman had taken evening classes at the Glasgow School of Art. After a decade in medicine, he joined a local art dealership run by McNeill Reid, J. M. Whistler's godson and a man whose art-dealer father had been painted by Vincent Van Gogh. One of Van Gogh's portraits of his friend Alexander Reid now hangs at Kelvingrove; someone who knew both artist and sitter said they looked like twins: "They even dressed somewhat similarly, though I doubt if Vincent ever possessed anything like the Harris tweeds Reid usually wore."

Honeyman loved Van Gogh's vivid portrait of Reid, and later coined the term "Scottish Colourists"—now used to refer to the group of fine early twentieth-century Scottish painters who moved between Scotland and France, developing bright post-Impressionist palettes. Increasingly expert in contemporary painting, Honeyman worked hard to convert a sometimes skeptical Glasgow public. When an exhibition of modern Polish art was staged in Sauchiehall Street's Annan Galleries in 1940, he warned "visitors unfamiliar with modern art" that they should not be "upset because they were seeing something different, something bizarre."

Appointed director of Glasgow's Art Galleries the previous year, this impressive arts administrator was well connected. To mark his appointment, local collector William McInnes presented the Art Galleries with Matisse's *Head of a Young Girl*, for which McNeill Reid had paid £60 at auction. Five years later, encouraged by Honeyman, McInnes bequeathed his entire collection to Glasgow. It included works by Bonnard, Braque, Cézanne, Picasso, Renoir, and Seurat. Some of McInnes's paintings, such as Matisse's luminous *Pink Tablecloth* and Van Gogh's *Blute-Fin Windmill, Montmartre*, are still among the jewels of the Kelvingrove collection. Beyond these treasures, Honeyman added works which had been acquired by Glasgow industrialists with a taste for such painters as Corot and Courbet. He also bought paintings using the Art Galleries' very modest purchasing fund: £150 for a fine Derain, £450 for an Utrillo.

If Honeyman's talents and reputation led to Glasgow's receiving the gift of the Burrell Collection, that might be seen as his greatest achievement. Yet he in no sense rested on his laurels. The culmination of his tenure as a museum director came in 1952, when he persuaded Glasgow Corporation to spend £8,200 buying Salvador Dalí's *Christ of St. John of the Cross.* In this remarkable work, based on the Spanish mystic's vision of seeing the crucified Christ hanging in midair, Christ is viewed from above as he hangs gazing down at the world. Specifically, he sees a boat by the Lake of Galilee. Though the "mad price" paid for this painting drew criticism, the picture has since become one of Glasgow's most famous, worthy of discussion alongside its Rembrandts and its 500-year-old vision of *The Adulteress Brought before Christ*—once attributed to Giorgione but now regarded as painted by Titian. At Kelvingrove and in its other art museums, which include the Burrell Gallery and the Gallery of Modern Art, Glasgow possesses the finest municipally owned art collection in Britain. If one exempts the galleries of capital cities, its picture hoard is among the best in the world.

In his 1971 autobiography, *Art and Audacity,* the enthusiastic Glaswegian patriot Honeyman asks his readers, "Did you know we are the best equipped city in the Commonwealth in the matter of public parks and open spaces?" and answers, "I know, nobody told you!" Visitors often assume that Glasgow, with its industrial past and postindustrial present, will lack greenery, but the opposite is true of the "dear green place." In Bellahouston Park, in 1938, King George VI and Queen Mary opened an exhibition "to illustrate the progress of the British Empire at home and overseas"; it attracted more than twelve million people. Nowadays, many decades after it closed, what remains is the expansive verdant space, on part of which, in 1996, a version of Charles Rennie Mackintosh's elegant, white-walled "House for an Art Lover" was built from the architect's unrealized plans. Parks and art go together in Glasgow. In the city's west end, Kelvingrove Park is only one of the large green urban havens, but surely among the best. Walking past its statuary, one can glance up towards the fine Victorian terrace of Park Circus, which looks more than a little Parisian if the sun shines; beyond lie the shining towers of the 1856 Free Church College, now cleansed of their industrial grime and converted into apartments.

To stroll through Kelvingrove Park is to sense impressive landmarks all around, but it is also to glimpse, through the trees, sculptures of the great and good once connected with the city. Up on the hill near Park Circus, astride a restless horse, is the helmeted, Indian-born imperialist Field Marshal Earl Roberts of Kandahar, Pretoria, and Waterford. Below this bronze equestrian statue, an inscription on the elaborate granite pedestal quotes from Roberts's speech in Glasgow on May 6, 1913: "I seem to see the gleam in the near distance of the weapons and accoutrements of this Army of the future, this Citizen Army, the warder of these islands, and the pledge of the peace and of the continued greatness of this Empire." World War I broke out sixteen months later, and Roberts died in 1914 on a visit to British troops in France. On one side of the base of his statue is a relief carving depicting kilted troops marching in pith helmets.

Across the park, the Scottish Victorian sage Thomas Carlyle, modelled in roughly hewn grey granite and more than ten feet tall, looks as if he is adjusting a malfunctioning hearing aid. On plinths just the other side of the tree-lined avenue called the Kelvin Way, Lord Kelvin and his academic colleague Lord Lister (who pioneered antiseptic surgery while Lecturer in Surgery at Glasgow University around 1860) sit in long robes, their bronze backs turned to the grassy slopes of Gilmorehill. Lister gazes out confidently, but Kelvin holds a pencil, his eyes intent on his notepad; in wet or foggy weather, a drip often hangs from his nose. With its walkways beside the river, and its paths between lawns extending towards Charing Cross, Kelvingrove Park is a memorial to Glasgow's intellectual and artistic greatness. It is also a fine place to wander on a sunny day. Close to the statues of Kelvin and Lister is a more modern, semi-abstract bronze sculpture, *The Psalmist,* by Estonian-born Jewish sculptor Benno Schotz, the Glaswegian who had earlier repaired the Nazi-bombed statuary on the Kelvin Way. *The Psalmist* stands in a small memorial garden commemorating Tom Honeyman and his wife; this tranquil space was created by, among others, the Glasgow Art Gallery and Museum Association and the Glasgow Tree Lovers Society.

Many of those who amble through Kelvingrove Park and along the Kelvin Way towards the Kelvin Hall sports arena are students at the city's oldest academic institution, the University of Glasgow. Now situated in the west end on Gilmorehill, the university stood for most of its first four centuries on its city-centre site on the High Street which linked the Mercat Cross to the Cathedral. Founded in 1451 by papal decree, it is Scotland's second-oldest academic institution (after St. Andrews). It first held classes in the Cathedral, then shifted to Rottenrow (Rat Row), until in 1460 James, Lord Hamilton, granted to the university its substantial High Street premises. Originally, it was a centre for theological training and served a town of perhaps 2,000 people. As late as the 1600s, with their 100–150 students, the academic buildings resembled in size and appearance a small Oxford or Cambridge college. A high tower presided over two quadrangles and several small internal gardens; the nearby Blackfriars Church lay across a garden wall. After the sixteenth-century Protestant Reformation, Andrew Melville had taken charge of Glasgow's university and encouraged its lecturers, or "regents," to specialize more. Melville's nephew wrote, with a certain local rhetorical flourish, that there was "na place in Europe comparable to Glasgow for guid letters, during these years, for a plentifull and guid chepe mercat of all kind of langages, artes and sciences."

That sense of the university as a "mercat" (market) hints at something which became clearer a century or so later: the developing relationship between academia and Glasgow's merchants. In 1730, when Francis Hutcheson was appointed professor of moral philosophy, he was one of the first of a new breed of professors who lectured in English, rather than in the traditional Latin. Hutcheson discoursed on beauty, virtue, the passions, and the moral sense, but was aware, too, of finance: "How powerfully might the Example of a wisely generous Father, at once teach his Offspring the true *Value* of Wealth or Power, and prevent their *Neglect* of them, or foolish *throwing* them away, and yet inspire them with a *generous Temper,* capable of the just *Use* of them!"

Hutcheson's student Adam Smith came to the University of Glasgow as a fourteen-year-old in 1737, returning as a professor in 1751, when his first specialist classes were on rhetoric and belles lettres. This made Smith the first university instructor in the English-speaking world to teach English literary texts: he pioneered the subject we now call "English lit." Yet, like his mentor Hutcheson, who heralded the Scottish Enlightenment, Smith was alert to financial wealth. Even his literary lectures show economic awareness, arguing, "'Tis the Introduction of Commerce or at least of opulence which is commonly the attendent of Commerce which first brings on the improvement of Prose." Teaching in a city where tobacco lords and other merchants helped to support printing, Smith in his early university literature classes theorized: "Where the Inhabitants of a city are rich and opulent, where they enjoy the necessaries and conveniences of life in ease and Security, there the arts will be cultivated and refinement of manners a neverfailing attendent." In Smith's day, the university printers, brothers Robert and Andrew Foulis, produced Latin, Greek, and English editions that were regarded as models of their kind. Now these volumes are eagerly collected.

Smith's economic theory developed from his early literary and philosophical lectures. So did his emphasis on the importance of a society bound together by mutual sympathy. In *The Theory of Moral Sentiments*—published in 1759, while he was teaching at Glasgow—he championed the kinds of social cohesion and mutual sympathetic awareness that counterbalanced the alienating effects of an increasingly industrial society. If some of his thoughts in that book were attuned to the world of Glasgow merchants with whom he mixed, and several of whom he had taught, Smith also spoke out against "sordid" slave masters and that system of which the tobacco lords were well aware: "Fortune never exerted more cruelly her empire over mankind, than when she subjected those [African] nations of heroes to the refuse of the jails of Europe, to wretches who possess the virtues neither of the countries which they came from, nor of those which they go to, and whose levity, brutality, and baseness, so justly expose them to the contempt of the vanquished." Smith's economic attitude towards slavery in *The Wealth of Nations* (1776) can seem less outspoken; but unlike his Edinburgh philosopher friend David Hume, he was prepared to denounce this stain on contemporary "Commerce."

Selective quotation has tended to reduce Glasgow's most famous professor to the narrow modern category of "economist." Yet the subjects on which he lectured and wrote, ranging from classical and modern literature to philosophy and the "invisible hand" of competition in economic activity, show that he was interested generally in systems of circulation—linguistic, ideological, and commercial—rather than in any one specific modern discipline. For all that this theorist of the distribution of labour was born in Kirkcaldy on Scotland's east coast and spent a good deal of time in Edinburgh, it was at Glasgow that Smith was student, teacher, and, eventually, university rector. At Glasgow, the most famous student he taught was James Boswell, the future biographer of Samuel Johnson. Boswell studied rhetoric and belles lettres with Smith, and was proud to have done so. But whereas Edinburgh boasts Alexander Stoddart's imposing twenty-first-century bronze of Smith at the heart of the Royal Mile, Glasgow's only statue of Smith (carved in marble in the 1860s by Germany's Hans Gasser) is tucked away indoors where few people see it, at the university on Gilmorehill. This academic location may be fitting, but it also suggests that the west-coast city, with its impressive mercantile heritage, has not recognized fully the stellar importance of its best-known public intellectual.

By the nineteenth century, the area around the old University of Glasgow in the High Street was growing increasingly disreputable. Erasmus Darwin visited while he was an Edinburgh student, and wrote from Glasgow to his more famous brother Charles on March 9, 1826, that "the Students here actually play at foot ball within the precincts of the college: you never did see such a set since you was born & please God never again." He did, though, find the Hunterian Museum (endowed in 1783 by Glasgow alumnus William Hunter, a great London surgeon) "well worth going to"; its collections, which have grown considerably, remain at the heart of the oldest of today's three Glaswegian universities. While Strathclyde University and its more recent neighbor Glasgow Caledonian University remain city-centre establishments, the University of Glasgow is now the most important institution in the city's west end.

The move to Gilmorehill in 1870 separated the academics from the Cathedral, which had nurtured them, but it provided a superb new location. The modern University of Glasgow has turned its back on the street called University Avenue, and faces instead the River Kelvin beyond. Originally designed by Sir George Gilbert Scott, the English architect of London's St. Pancras Hotel, the magnificent Victorian Gothic main building took decades to complete. One of the city's noblest landmarks, its lofty, spire-topped tower on its hilltop setting makes this structure all the more imposing when viewed from the riverbank and parklands below. While it looks splendid from the front, most students entering the old buildings do so from University Avenue, and have to climb stairs less salubriously positioned (beside the old toilets) before they ascend to the fine, broad lawns of the East and West Quadrangles.

48. The Victorian Gothic main building of Glasgow University, on Gilmorehill, towers above Kelvingrove Park. Arguably the city's most splendid landmark, it was designed by George Gilbert Scott.

Not completed until the 1920s, the West Quad is where Edwin Morgan (1920–2010), Glasgow's best-loved modern poet, had his first-floor office in what used to be the Department of English Literature. Morgan's nimble, ambitious poems celebrate metamorphic energies, not least those of his city; his best book is titled *From Glasgow to Saturn,* and his memorial service— a national event—was held in the university's Bute Hall, where Morgan's friend and collaborator the saxophonist Tommy Smith enriched the obse- quies with a long, heartfelt wolf-howl. In the 1970s, Morgan was joined for a time on Gilmorehill by the much more bohemian artist and novelist Alas- dair Gray (born in 1934), who lives nearby and who was employed then as the university's writer-in-residence. Morgan's office was calm, ordered, meticulously tidy; Gray's the reverse. A distinguished alumnus remembers that, as a young man, he entered Gray's West Quadrangle room to find the artist attentively depicting a mature female model who sat naked in front of his desk.

Even in the liberated 1960s and 1970s, Scotland's universities did little to encourage nudity; but they have long championed a tolerant sense of humanity. Also in the West Quad is the dark-paneled Humanity Classroom (Latin was called "Humanity" at the oldest Scottish universities), which has been preserved as a traditional lecture hall. In this room, until at least the 1980s, classics students would be asked oral examination questions about the ancient world while they perched on the hefty, historic, and high-backed Blackstone chair, with sand sifting through an hourglass above their heads as they racked their brains for answers. When the Humanity Classroom is unlocked, visitors can still sit on its hard, semicircular wooden bench-seats which accommodated generations of Glasgow students, who sometimes sang to or jeered at their professors, but more often solemnly took notes.

Outside, between the East and West Quadrangles, are the splendid, neo-Gothic cloisters that lead to the university's imposing graduation halls up-stairs. Like the City Chambers in George Square, but more nobly, the Gilmorehill building speaks of Glasgow's imperial past. In New Zealand's South Island, it has been imitated by the designers of Otago University, while a stone tablet in the Glasgow cloisters pays tribute to "James McGill, 1744–1813, Student in Arts of the University of Glasgow, Trader, Soldier and Statesman in Canada and Founder of McGill University, Montreal."

Visitors to Gilmorehill are likely to enjoy the Hunterian Museum, en-tered by a sweeping staircase above the cloisters. This museum's rich and varied holdings include a collection of scientific instruments invented by or belonging to the university's most famous nineteenth-century scientist, Glasgow Irishman William Thomson. Better known as Lord Kelvin, this re-searcher—after whom the "kelvin," a unit for measuring heat, is named—grew up in the old college on the High Street where his father was mathe-matics professor. William matriculated as a student there in 1834, at the age of ten. The following year he and his brother made an "electrical machine" which, their sister Anna recorded, "gives strong shocks." After studies at Glasgow and Cambridge (where a street is now named after him and where his work on electricity inspired the great Scottish scientist James Clerk Max-well), Thomson was appointed to the Glasgow Chair of Natural Philosophy, as physics was then called, in 1846. He was twenty-two. Investigating heat and electricity, he continued to make machines, turning down the offer of a chair in Cambridge because, as he put it, "the convenience of Glasgow for getting mechanical work done" allowed "means of action which I could not have in any other place."

Thomson thrived in one of the great capitals of Victorian industry. In 1851, he was the first person to enunciate what became the second law of thermodynamics: "It is impossible, by means of inanimate material agency, to derive mechanical effect from any portion of matter by cooling it below the temperature of the coldest of the surrounding objects." His emphasis on the inevitable "dissipation of mechanical energy" has a Calvinistic accent, but he also believed in energy's "transformation," and became a leader in a group of Scottish physicists who developed the far-reaching "science of energy." In Glasgow's old college, Thomson set up Britain's first university physical laboratory. At Gilmorehill he had a new, purpose-built lab. Knighted for his work on submarine telegraphy, which used his instruments, he experimented with all kinds of science, from acoustics to hydroelectric power, and is credited with seventy patents.

A professor who lived in some style (he owned a large yacht, for sailing on the Clyde), Kelvin was an entertaining teacher. Known to fire a rifle for demonstration purposes during his Gilmorehill lectures on acoustics, he also played to students on a French horn, a cornet, and an African thumb piano. His "elephant gun" and several musical instruments survive in the Glasgow University collections, as do many of his laboratory instruments and strikingly sculpted scientific models in wood, wire, and other materials. Kelvin is said to have glued and wired these together during vacations; as he told a lecture audience at Johns Hopkins University, Baltimore, in 1884, "I can never satisfy myself until I can make a mechanical model of a thing." From a wooden model of quartz crystals to beads glued in the form of a three-dimensional soap bubble, Kelvin's Glasgow improvisations were appropriate to a city obsessed with mechanical construction. His house, Number 11 in the elegant Professors' Square on Gilmorehill, can still be seen; thanks to him, it was the world's first home to be lit entirely by carbon filament lamps. He had wired it, he told his friend Prime Minister Gladstone, "from attic to cellar." His electrical wires, also used in his laboratory, are among Glasgow University's quirkier museum pieces.

Kelvin would still recognize his house, but no professors now live in Professors' Square. A few still resided there in the 1970s, their Victorian homes splendidly cluttered, odd shoes jammed among books in the bookcases. Today, much of the Gilbert Scott main building of the university is given over to a swarm of administrators. A plethora of other structures fills the campus.

Built in the later twentieth century, the pale, soaring University Library is the largest of its kind in Scotland, its treasures running from a ninth-century medical text, the earliest substantial Western manuscript in the nation, to the scrapbooks of Edwin Morgan. Next to it, the Hunterian Art Gallery includes re-created Charles Rennie Mackintosh domestic interiors and a painting collection with fine Chardins and Scottish Colourists. Perhaps more surprisingly, the Hunterian also displays one of the world's best exhibitions of the works of the Scottish-descended American artist James McNeill Whistler, godfather to Glasgow art dealer McNeill Reid.

If you walk westwards down University Avenue, in the opposite direction from the Kelvin Way, you pass the glass-fronted twenty-first-century Wolfson Medical Building and come to the intersection with Byres Road, once an area of cattle farming and today a breezy centre of west end life. A stalwart presence since the 1840s, when people played curling on a nearby pond, the historic Curlers Tavern (now called Curlers Rest), with its two-storey frontage adorned with carriage lamps, is but one of many Byres Road pubs and restaurants frequented by local residents and students alike. Since a high percentage of Glasgow's university students originate from the city and areas nearby, it is not unusual to be both a local resident *and* a student. Byres Road is arty, a little bohemian—an attractive mélange of traditional tenements and busy shops. In Ashton Lane, which leads off it, Alasdair Gray, whose novel *Lanark* is set partly in Glasgow and partly in a strangely imagined terrain, painted murals in a wittily named upscale restaurant, the Ubiquitous Chip, which is celebrated for, among other things, its vegetarian haggis. Founded in nearby Ruthven Street in 1971 by Ronnie Clydesdale, "the Chip" moved to Ashton Lane eight years later; its diners have ranged from Glasgow writers and anti-apartheid campaigners to Mick Jagger, Princess Margaret, and Kylie Minogue—though not all at the same table. More of Alasdair Gray's distinctive wall paintings can be seen on the walls, stairways, floors, and high ceilings of the former church at the northeast corner of Byres Road, where that street intersects with Great Western Road. Now styled Oran Mor (Gaelic for "the Great Music"), this ex-kirk is a popular arts venue, its restaurant and bar noisily crowded at night.

Considerably more tranquil, entered from the corner of Great Western Road diagonally opposite Oran Mor, Glasgow's Botanic Gardens are a favourite of parents with toddlers, as well as a haunt of magpies, pigeons, and grey squirrels. Running parallel to part of Great Western Road and confronting handsome terraces of housing built for the Victorian bourgeoisie, the Botanic Gardens today extend across twenty hectares bordering the River Kelvin. They have occupied some of this site since the 1840s, but their origins lie in a different, much smaller location: the old, city-centre University Physic Garden, which once lay behind the High Street. James Sutherland, who looked after the Edinburgh equivalent, assisted in its creation in 1706 "for the ornament of the College and for the students improvement in the skill of Bottany." Throughout their history, the gardens have been a sensitive guide to Glasgow's air quality. Their modern historian, Eric W. Curtis, quotes Professor William Cullen and a colleague pointing out in 1754 that the plants are "very much exposed to the smoke and soot of the Town"; the establishment of a type foundry next door did not help, since it defiled the atmosphere through its use of lead, antimony, tin, and copper. By the early nineteenth century, the city-centre Physic Garden's ground was "very barren." In 1813, when Thomas Hopkirk, Fellow of the Linnean Society, published his pioneering *Flora Glottiana: A Catalogue of Indigenous Plants on the Banks of the River Clyde, and in the Neighbourhood of the City of Glasgow* with local bookseller John Smith & Son, he drew his examples from what were then neighbouring rural places such as Tollcross and wooded Cambuslang, not from the city itself, with its struggling, polluted Physic Garden.

A plaque on a back wall at the east end of Fitzroy Place, on Sauchiehall Street, marks the spot where Glasgow's second Botanic Garden was instituted by Hopkirk and others at "Sandyford" in 1817. Christian Glassford, daughter of the tobacco lord John Glassford, was Hopkirk's mother. His uncle, Henry Glassford, was a founder of the new Botanic Gardens. This kinship network is further indication of the close-knit nature of Glasgow's historic merchant elite, linking local commerce and intellectual life. Through the broad gates of the gardens at Sandyford, merchants brought plants imported from America and the Caribbean. As well as advocating a new "Merchants' Park" (later the Necropolis), Hopkirk published an illustration of his "Royal Botanic Garden" in the 1825 *Glasgow Looking Glass*. Depicting well-dressed men, women, and children promenading in front of substantial glasshouses, the picture is captioned, "This fashionable place of resort has this season been more numerously attended than ever. We observe that additional grass walks have been added to the Promenade ground, and the

excellent Trumpet Band of the 5th Dragoons, we believe, will be in attendance on Saturday next. The splendid Cactus Seciosissimus which has been
in flower for some time past has given increased interest to the Houses.—
Vide et crede."

That Latin flourish ("See and believe") hints at the *bon ton* Hopkirk
wished to establish, but his gardens were also scientifically important. In the
early 1820s, young David Douglas (after whom the Douglas fir is named)
worked there as a gardener, attending lectures by the University of Glasgow's professor of botany, William Jackson Hooker. The professor took
Douglas on several plant-collecting field trips to the Highlands, recognizing
his great potential as a field naturalist. In 1823, Douglas set out on travels
that would take him as far as Vancouver, California, and even Hawaii, where
he was gored to death by a wild bull in 1833.

During his short life, Douglas sent back numerous specimens of plants
to Britain's botanic gardens, including those of Glasgow. Yet in 1838, two
years before Hooker moved to become head of the great Royal Botanic Gardens at Kew, a Glaswegian committee was again concerned about the effects of pollution, which "renders the air less pure for many plants." At first,
many kinds of pine trees had been grown at Sandyford. "Now throughout
the Garden there is not a single healthy pine of any species." When the garden had been laid out, there had been hardly any houses west of Buchanan
Street; thirty years later "almost a third of the city [was] west of that line,"
sending up smoke from a vast array of chimneys. A revealing barometer of
Glasgow's air quality, the gardens fled farther west.

In 1840, when they moved to their current site, the city was planning a
long new thoroughfare, still one of its most impressive streets. Great Western Road—where, opposite the Botanic Gardens, passersby can admire the
monumental Grosvenor Terrace (designed by John Thomas Rochead in
1855) and the spectacular tenements of Great Western Terrace (designed by
Alexander "Greek" Thomson in 1869)—might channel elegant promenad-
ers to the lawns and glasshouses. City planners also hoped that the greenery of the Kelvin would provide a sustaining habitat. Laid out by Thomas
Hopkirk's own household gardener, Stewart Murray, on part of a drumlin
(a gently sloping mound of materials left behind in prehistory by a melting
glacier), the new Royal Botanic Garden was to be "a powerful instrument"
for the "moral improvement" of "well informed but poorer . . . artisans."

Though there was normally a charge for admission (which funded the Garden and kept out riffraff), one week each summer the site was opened gratis. As many as 34,000 people visited in a single day, eager to see such curious exotica as the banana—"resembling a short cucumber." Plant donors soon included David Livingstone, the famous missionary and African explorer, who was born in nearby Blantyre in Lanarkshire and who had studied at Anderson's College on George Square. There he had met his close friend "Paraffin Young," inventor of the important industrial process of distilling oil from shale. As the Empire and the Victorian flower gardens grew, so did the industries which polluted them.

Glasshouses offered some protection. In 1871 the finest of these, the Kibble Crystal Art Palace, was erected thanks to the entrepreneurship of wealthy John Kibble, who had this palatial structure transported from the garden of his West of Scotland seaside mansion. Inside his vast glass pleasure dome, among palms and orchids, Victorian Glasgow certainly flourished. Gladstone, while he was rector of the University of Glasgow, once orated at the Kibble Palace for ninety nonstop minutes; on another occasion, massed singers performed "Rule, Britannia" (as well as "Rhine Wine" and the Scots song "Tullochgorum") when Gladstone's political rival Benjamin Disraeli was installed as rector.

Then, as now, the glasshouse was a treasured public space festooned not just with plants, but also with white marble statues. Quick, tactful thinking ensured that "the naked graces of Apollo" were clothed in "a decorous covering of calico" when American evangelists Dwight Moody and Ira Sankey preached there in 1874. Today its walkways are graced by several biblical sculptures—Cain, Eve, the Sisters of Bethany—often bewitchingly nude. Nothing is stranger in a Glasgow winter than to step into the glasshouse, among dripping soursop trees from Central America; under the high glazed dome of the Kibble Palace soar Natal wild banana trees from South Africa's Eastern Cape. Above your head a Southeast Australian Golden Mimosa blossoms bright yellow in the Scottish January, and damp ferns brush your hair close to the marble Victorian erotica of a turbaned, yet curiously European-looking bare-breasted Nubian slave girl.

When the Kibble Palace was restored—magnificently—in 2006, investigators discovered that it had been designed to contain, beneath its large, well-stocked fish pond, a substantial chamber in which cunningly concealed

49. Erected in 1871 thanks to the generosity of John Kibble, the Kibble Palace is the architectural centrepiece of Glasgow's Botanic Gardens. Inside, the palace's nude statues were clothed in "a decorous covering of calico" when American evangelists Dwight Moody and Ira Sankey preached there in 1874.

musicians might perform. Today, as attendants pass with trolleys of silver teapots for conference delegates, or as a jazz concert wafts its improvisations through the palms, visitors can enjoy a fine display of plants in this structure, whose gorgeousnesses, including its central dome 146 feet in diameter, demonstrate why the *Gardeners' Chronicle* in 1889 described Glasgow as "about the most pushing and prosperous community in the kingdom." Though the city expanded to envelop nearby green spaces and though it continued to fight a running battle with pollution, neither the old "blow-hole" of a subterranean railway at the now-demolished Botanic Gardens Station, nor even a freakish 1968 hurricane, has prevented this oasis, today free and owned by the city, from remaining a steamy glory of Glasgow.

Curbing the use of coal fires, the 1956 Clean Air Act brought new and renewed possibilities. Twenty-first-century visitors can see, in a separate area beyond Kirklee Road, the outdoor David Douglas Collection of plants (such as the ponderosa pine and the poached-egg plant, *Limnanthes doug-*

lasii) introduced to Europe by Glasgow's most famous gardener. In summer you can sit outdoors in the Gardens' green, cultured calm. Over in the Rose Garden a recently installed black, Mackintosh-style bench memorializes Neil Reid Baird, "Musician and Violin Maker," while another seat near the glasshouse invites passersby to "sit awhile and consider life's simple pleasures."

Few, though, associate this relaxed space with the city's most notorious Victorian murder. The Curator's House in the Botanic Gardens, an Italianate structure designed in 1840 by Charles Wilson before he became architect of such grand Glasgow terraces as Park Circus, was for a time the lodging of Jersey-born Pierre Emile L'Angelier. In 1855, when he was in his early thirties, L'Angelier—a lover of botany—presented a flower to the nineteen-year-old eldest daughter of the wealthy James Smith, a Glasgow architect whose designs for the McLellan Galleries were then being translated into stone in Sauchiehall Street. L'Angelier's inamorata, Madeleine, had long dark hair, large dark eyes, and a "clear, sweet treble" voice. She wrote to him saying that his flower was fading, and added: "I wish I understood botany, for your sake, as I might send you some specimens of moss. But, alas! I know nothing of that study." No botanist, but generally well educated, this imaginative young woman quoted a verse from *Solitary Hours,* by the spirited, melancholy poet Caroline Bowles:

I never cast a flower away,
The gift of one who cared for me,
A little flower, a faded flower,
But it was done reluctantly.

Madeleine Smith's father disapproved of his daughter's friendship with the Bothwell Street office clerk Emile. More than once, their exchange of letters was broken off. In his Botanic Garden lodgings, Emile discussed the relationship with Mrs. Sharp, the curator's wife, who was aware that her lodger enjoyed a clandestine correspondence with a girl called Madeleine, or "Mimi," whom he was "in the way of meeting." Mrs. Sharp thought that Emile, a regular churchgoer, was "very steady and temperate." She kept in touch with him when he moved into other lodgings farther down Great Western Road.

Madeleine had known Emile since she was sixteen. They never married, but by late 1855 she was addressing him as "My dear darling husband." In one letter, she rejoiced in "being fondled by you" and signed herself "Mimi L'Angelier." Writing of "an hour of bliss" and of how "if we did wrong last night, it was in the excitement of our love," Madeleine delighted in their covert liaison. Interrogating her about her menstrual cycle, Emile worried that she might not have been a virgin when they first slept together. In July 1856, she wrote to him from a country house where he continued to visit her secretly: "I did laugh at your pinning my little flower to your shirt. I always put your flowers into books, in the drawing-room, there I can go and look at them at any time. Do not weep, darling, fond husband, it makes me sad to think you weep. Do not do it, darling; a fond embrace and dear kiss to you, sweet and much beloved Emile. Our intimacy has not been criminal, as I am your wife before God—so it has been no sin our loving each other. No; darling, fond Emile, I am your wife."

The affair of Madeleine and Emile belongs to the era of Tennyson's poem "The Princess," with all its heady botanic eroticism,

> Now folds the lily all her sweetness up,
> And slips into the bosom of the lake:
> So fold thyself, my dearest, thou, and slip
> Into my bosom and be lost in me.

With references to "the gardens," to Buchanan Street, and to Sauchiehall Street, this couple's letters are revealing of Glaswegian middle-class life. The well-off Smith family had their country home at Rhu, near Helensburgh, farther down the Clyde; in the city, they lived for a time on a corner of Blythswood Square, at Number 7, whose handsome elevated front door still beckons between stone pillars at the top of a flight of eight steps. Madeleine and her sister shared a basement bedroom fronting on Blythswood Street. The lovers' correspondence is intensely passionate, its overemphatic endearments hinting at uncertainty and frustrated longing. "My night dress was on when you saw me," writes Madeleine to Emile, who has glimpsed her when he slipped notes in white envelopes through her window; "would to God you had been in the same attire." Yet only a month later, in February 1857, one of Madeleine's letters is returned to her, and she maintains, "My love for you has ceased." She begs her lover, "For God's sake do not bring your once loved Mimi to an open shame ... Emile, do not drive me to death

50. The Smith family home on the corner at 7 Blythswood Square remains a handsome Glasgow building. Madeleine Smith and her sister are said to have slept in a basement bedroom.

. . . Emile, for god's sake do not send my letters to papa; it will be an open rupture. I will leave the house. I will die. . . . I am mad. I am ill. . . . [Papa] will hate me as a guilty wretch. . . . I put on paper what I should not . . . Do not inform on me—do not make me a public shame. . . . I shall be ruined."

A few months later, Emile was found dead. Medical examinations (including one conducted by Edinburgh forensic surgeon Robert Christison) revealed that he had been poisoned with arsenic. Now engaged to another man, Madeleine had several times purchased that toxin. Arrested, she confessed that she had bought the poison; popular papers such as *Chambers' Edinburgh Journal* had advised that if she diluted it and applied it to her skin, it would improve her complexion. Sent for trial to Edinburgh, the twenty-two-year-old was led from the cells, emerging through a trapdoor into the Scottish capital's High Court. She stood in the dock impassively, hearing her love letters, "written . . . in the most licentious terms," read aloud to a crowded courtroom. There she was accused of a "criminal intimacy" and of living in the "depth of degradation." She was also charged with murder. After a nine-day trial, the all-male jury found her not guilty of one charge of poisoning with intent to kill, and, resorting to a useful Scottish verdict, declared two other similar charges "not proven." The *Scotsman* reported that when the verdicts were announced, "cheering came from the audience, especially from the galleries." Madeleine's "head slightly fell, and her face broke into a bright but somewhat agitated smile."

This courtroom drama was a media sensation. Putting a young Glaswegian on trial in Edinburgh, it brought together sex, poison, and betrayal. Soon booksellers had sold 10,000 copies of the best-selling *Trial of Miss Madeleine H. Smith, before the High Court of Justiciary, Edinburgh, June 30th to July 9th, 1857, for the Alleged Poisoning of M. Pierre Emile L'Angelier, at Glasgow.* The book reprinted the love letters from court transcripts, along with the brilliant rhetoric of John Inglis, who (though in private he may have considered her guilty) quoted Shakespeare in his courtroom defence of Madeleine, suggesting that her volatile lover might have committed suicide. Edinburgh papers relished the spectacle of this Glasgow crime. Whereas the *Scotsman* described the accused simply as "lady-like" and commented on her expression of "extraordinary nerve," to the *Glasgow Herald* she was "very pretty." The *Herald*'s reporter detailed fully her "white straw bonnet, black silk mantle, grey cloak, brown silk gown, lavender gloves, and . . . silver-mounted smelling-bottle in her hand."

To some, Madeleine was a femme fatale. Her "not proven" case was pored over by Victorian Britain because it was a puzzle in which the truth, as the *Times* of London put it, "is for ever destined to be hidden." Yet it also fascinated because of the erotic passion revealed. Jane Welsh Carlyle thought Smith "a little incarnate devil"; more coldly subtle, George Eliot damned her as "one of the least fascinating of murderesses"; Nathaniel Hawthorne, touring the Scottish Highlands, observed newspaper reports being read aloud in hotels to groups of excited travellers. Twenty-first-century readers may be struck by the patriarchal rhetoric surrounding the case; also by what it reveals about male repression of and curiosity about female sexual pleasure. Summing up at Smith's trial in Edinburgh, the judge said to the jury's "gentlemen" with regard to Madeleine's supposed aim of poisoning her lover, "I don't think you will consider it so unlikely as was supposed that this girl, after writing such letters, may have been capable of cherishing such a purpose." The trial was not just about murder; it was also about the politics of gender. This was sensed by Dorothy L. Sayers, who drew on it for her classic 1930 crime novel *Strong Poison;* and by David Lean in his stylish 1949 movie, *Madeleine.* More recently, and transposed to the later nineteenth-century era of the Glasgow Boys, aspects of Madeleine Smith's case underpin Jane Harris's engrossing 2011 novel *Gillespie and I.*

When the trial was ended, the *Scotsman* recorded, a body double left the court in a cab, staging a faint in front of "the eager gaze of the mob." The real "Miss Smith," meanwhile, in "straw bonnet, dark ribbons, and green veil," travelled home "to her father's house." Four years afterwards, in the south of England, she married an artist named Wardle who worked for William Morris and was friendly with Pre-Raphaelite painters. As Lena Wardle, she had two children and acted as treasurer and librarian to the Bloomsbury branch of the Socialist League. Later, after separating from her husband, Lena went to America and found a new partner, an Irish New Yorker named William Sheehy. Madeleine Smith had reinvented herself, but the mystery she had been part of did not go away. Henry James, who had read about her when he was fourteen, later wrote with darkly ironic insight, "She precisely *didn't* squalidly suffer, but lived on to admire with the rest of us, for so many years, the rare work of art with which she had been the means of enriching humanity." Far from Glasgow's Blythswood Square and Botanic Gardens, she and her American lover lived for a time on Eighth Avenue in Manhattan. When Lena Wardle Sheehy died in the Bronx in 1928, she was buried, like Frederick Douglass and several of the children of Buffalo Bill, among the beautiful flowerbeds and blossoming trees of Mount Hope Cemetery, in New York.

The Madeleine Smith trial took place as Glasgow was approaching its architectural zenith. Two of Madeleine's male relations, architects both, had designed some of the buildings in Royal Exchange Square off Buchanan Street. Her father was the architect behind the asymmetrical Græco-Roman front of the old Victoria Baths at 106–108 West Nile Street, in the city's burgeoning commercial district. All through Madeleine's lifetime, the ancient empires of Greece and Rome were being plundered as architectural models for the rapidly expanding imperial city of Glasgow. Yet whereas in Edinburgh's New Town planning, chaste classicism ruled, in a Glasgow made rich through shipbuilding, locomotive construction, iron- and steelmaking, and heavy industry, there was delight in adventurously polymorphous variety. Architecture in the second city of the Empire at its most spectacular looked to other empires, too—those of the pharaohs' Egypt, Hindu India, even ancient Assyria. As an architectural style, classicism could certainly be followed, but also remixed, riffed on asymmetrically, hybridized, and reinvented for ambitious West of Scotland capitalists awash with old and new cash.

Still, there were convincing attempts at "standard" classicism. Blythswood Square, where Madeleine was alleged to have poisoned Emile by handing him cups of arsenic-laced cocoa from her basement bedroom window, was part of the larger Blythswood New Town development laid out in the 1820s half a mile or so west of George Square. Emile's office in Bothwell Street was also housed in this grid-planned expansion, seemingly North American in its regularity of urban blocks, even if much disrupted by later building. While Madeleine and Emile were lovers, construction was under way at the iron-framed Gardner's Warehouse in Jamaica Street; appearing almost entirely made up of windows, this structure drew on the style of Renaissance Venice. During the year of Madeleine's trial, the original bank building at 8 Gordon Street, said to be modeled on Rome's Farnese Palace, was completed. On its exterior are panels and pediments ostentatiously depicting children printing money, Commerce supported by Navigation and Locomotion, Glasgow linked to Trade and Manufacture, and—broadmindedly, if last and least—Edinburgh linked with Science and Art. This was the work of an Edinburgh architect.

Gordon Street is a good place to get a sense of Victorian commercial Glasgow. On its south side stand the cast-iron columns of the palazzo-like Ca' d'Oro Building, designed in 1872 as a furniture warehouse and substantially restored after a 1987 fire. Rail travellers emerge from the hearty concourse of Central Station, with its steely silver World War I shell just inside the front portals, to see opposite, on the north side of Gordon Street, an imposing, high, column-fronted stone building capped with twin domes. The domes and top storeys are Edwardian additions; the first four storeys are the work of Glasgow's most stunningly eclectic mid-Victorian architect, Alexander Thomson. For visitors, there can be no more appropriate welcome to this lapsed imperial *polis*.

Most people, including many modern Glaswegians, are not sure what to make of Alexander Thomson. Perhaps one way to comprehend him is to re-call Thomas De Quincey's 1846 description of Glasgow:

> So vast a city, having more than three hundred thousand inhabitants . . .
> nearly all children of toil; and a city, too, which, from the necessities of
> its circumstances, draws so deeply upon that fountain of misery and
> guilt which some ordinance, as ancient as "our father Jacob," with his
> patriarchal well for Samaria, has bequeathed to manufacturing towns,—
> to Ninevehs, to Babylons, to Tyres. How tarnished with eternal canopies
> of smoke, and of sorrow; how dark with agitations of many orders, is the
> mighty town.

Thomson was attracted to De Quincey's words. At the end of his life, he used a quotation from the same essay to enhance the culmination of his 1874 lecture on Egyptian architecture: De Quincey's description of an ancient Egyptian head of Memnon as exemplifying "sublimity" and provoking "the breathlessness which belongs to a saintly trance." Thomson knew Glasgow thoroughly, and, like De Quincey, saw it biblically. In his writings on archi-tecture, Thomson quotes Burns and Tennyson, Ruskin and De Quincey; but most of all he borrows the words of the Bible. An elder of the United Presbyterian Kirk (and probably a freemason), he loved the passage from the Book of Revelation where "John saw 'the Holy City, new Jerusalem, coming down from God out of Heaven.'" In Glasgow, drawing particularly on Egyp-tian and Greek elements, and planning churches based on the Temple of Solomon, Alexander Thomson sought to build such a city.

An autodidact who had nineteen siblings and was orphaned at the age of thirteen, Thomson is the most ambitious architect Glasgow has ever pro-duced. In 1868 he proposed replacing his city's slums with a vast new, tenemental townscape whose streets would be roofed over with glass. He thought the "universe but a diagram of the mind of God"; the architect, with his own plans and diagrams, was co-creator: "A design is a Creation of the Imagination," he stated, maintaining that the "Architect" operated "within the sphere of Poesy." Having scrutinized Glasgow's structures, admiring both long-lasting tenements and handsome Greek revival buildings, Thom-son knew he dwelt in a remarkable time and place: "We live in a great city —our merchants are princes"; but he wished to fuse in new ways the ar-chitect's æsthetic sense with available engineering and commercial hardheadedness. "The last thirty years have seen immense sums expended on engineering works, which must necessarily exist for generations to come. But, with very few exceptions, little artistic skill has been bestowed on them."

In Glasgow, Thomson knew that new technologies could further artistic grandeur: "With our Derrick cranes and our steam-engines we could lift and set stones on our walls of three or four tons weight." He knew, too, that imperial technologies of travel, printing, photography, and research afforded access to an international and transhistorical stylistic vocabulary. Architects now possessed

> aids and facilities in the practice of their art which, in no former age, was ever dreamt of. They are built about with books, containing examples of every known style. If an architect wants an idea, he does not require to fly away into the region of imagination to fetch it—it is ready at hand on the adjoining shelf, and needs only to be reached down. Treatises upon everything connected with building are multiplied and piled up to an extent that defies perusal. Our builders, besides having access to all these mountains of knowledge, have mechanical aids unknown in the days of our fathers. For building materials, besides iron and brick, our neighbourhood abounds in stone, which for quality, variety, and abundance, is unequalled in the kingdom, and what have we made of it all?

Published in the *Glasgow Herald* on February 23, 1859, this call to arms, delivered at the Glasgow Architectural Society in the Thomson-designed Scottish Exhibition Rooms in Bath Street, has something of a manifesto quality. The buildings Thomson planned lived up to it, bringing to Glasgow's streets a remarkable hybrid of biblical antiquity and ambitious modernity. At 84–100 Union Street, his monumental "Egyptian Halls"—with their Assyrian scroll capitals topping slim piers—exemplify his contention that "our modern engineers use girders to span spaces where formerly arches would have been resorted to, and that with an economy of means and stability of structure that puts the arch to shame."

The Presbyterian Thomson hated arches. He associated them with the "Romish" (that is, Roman Catholic) architecture of the Victorian Gothicism championed by England's great Catholic architect Augustus Pugin. Gilbert Scott's commission to build the new University of Glasgow disgusted

Thomson and made him jealous. What he loved were grand streetscapes that fused Greece, Egypt, and modern building technology into a tenemental sublime: "Our street ranges must ever continue to be built on horizontal principles, the Gothic must be regarded as a discordant feature in our vistas." Gothic architecture showed a despicable "inveterate perpendicularity." Horizontality, for Thomson, had a religious allure. Invoking the art of Turner and of the Edinburgh-born David Roberts, who painted architectural scenes from ancient Egypt, he hymned "the mysterious power of the horizontal element in carrying the mind away into space, and into speculations upon infinity." Such rhetoric suggests that Thomson's Moray Place (where the architect lived, at Number 1) or his lengthy and imposing Great Western Terrace—along with other extended tenement perspectives on Great Western Road—are not there just to provide housing for the well-off; they are there to inspire religious experience.

Thomson had a solemn view of his calling. If architecture was art, he maintained, "religion has been seen as the soul of art from the beginning." Yet he kept, too, a sense of humour. In a lecture entitled "The Spirit of the Egyptian Style," he quoted from poet Horace Smith's "Address to the Mummy at Belzoni's Exhibition," published in Smith's *Gaieties and Gravities:* the poem hails a being who has frequented Egypt's "temples, palaces and piles stupendous,/ Of which the very ruins are tremendous." Thomson sought to bring the stupendous and tremendous glories of Thebes and Karnak not only to middle-class Glaswegians, but also to warehousemen and passersby. Whereas the opium addict De Quincey, who spent some time in the city trying to evade his Edinburgh creditors, saw Glasgow as biblically troubled, Alexander Thomson, familiar with the apocalyptic extravaganzas of Romantic painters like John Martin, sought to give it more than a dash of Old Testament epic splendour.

Thomson's nickname was "Greek," and he did love Greek architecture— but he prized Egypt just as much. Never leaving the British Isles, he voyaged far in the pages of books. He adored Glasgow, but, after the Victorian era, Glasgow did not always return his adoration. As twentieth-century planners turned against the tenement, preferring the verticality of tower blocks, several of his best buildings were lost. World War II bombs destroyed his Queen's Park Church; fire ravaged his Caledonia Road Kirk. You can walk round the exterior of Thomson's remarkable, daringly asymmetrical

St. Vincent Street Free Church (built 1857–1859), a Solomonic temple-cum-acropolis topped with a surprising piece of verticality, part spire, part phallus, part minaret; and you can marvel at this building's marvellously eclectic ornamentation, where Greek and Assyrian, Hindu and Egyptian consort together in a Glaswegian imperial sublime. Yet if you wish to inhabit fully Greek Thomson's architectural imagination, the best place to go is his suburban villa at Holmwood in the suburb of Netherlee, a short walk from Muirend rail station.

With its long, slitted wall joining the citadel-like villa to a coach house, and its almost Assyrian gates, Holmwood (now owned by the National Trust for Scotland) is both alluring and forbidding. Set above a lawn in wooded grounds, the house looks like an asymmetrical assembly of small Greek temples. Pictured from the front in Thomson's 1868 volume *Villa and Cottage Architecture,* it appears stern and military. One of the modern designers whose work seems to have influenced Thomson was the Prussian royal family's unflinching architect, Karl Friedrich Schinkel. Whether or not you like Holmwood, it is utterly remarkable, its horizontality fully built into the landscape, its gently pitched roofs (a Thomson signature) bearing at their

51. Holmwood House, designed by the great Victorian architect Alexander Thomson in the late 1850s, is one of the most striking examples of Glaswegian domestic architecture. Set in parklands, the building looks every inch a plutocrat's palace.

eaves unusual, antenna-like adornments. At the top of the roof, and above the house's main stair, is a cupola whose inside is supported by sculpted chimeræ and whose curved glass is etched with stars.

At Holmwood, Thomson also designed the interiors and furniture. The dining room has a twenty-one-panel frieze showing scenes from Homer's *Iliad*, a black marble fireplace decorated in gold, and magnificent high, carved doors of varnished American yellow pine ornamented with mahogany. Built for a local businessman, Holmwood is a plutocrat's palace. Its parlour boasts almost floor-to-ceiling glass in a stunning bay window. Its upstairs drawing room has large, facing mirrors and a star-spangled ceiling, offering a mixture of illumination bordered by dark grandeur. Thomson disliked external gutters and drainpipes; at times, modern workmen have found it difficult to repair Holmwood's leaking roof. Yet, now lovingly restored, this lavish villa houses some of the very few surviving examples of Thomson's monument-like furniture. No house in Glasgow gives such a good impression of the city's imperial sublimity. That splendour, like the well-heeled elegance of Edinburgh New Town, co-existed with horrific slums: this is an architecture of inequality. But Glaswegians were in thrall to their dreams of empire, and Alexander Thomson expressed those ambitions in stone.

If Thomson's imaginings were enterprisingly hybrid, the aspirations of other prosperous Glaswegians were frequently more stolidly conventional. On Saturday, January 18, 1902, a Glasgow councillor who lived in Great Western Road sat among 270 diners in the now-defunct Windsor Hotel. They were gathered at a commemorative dinner for James Watt, hosted by the Institution of Engineers and Shipbuilders in Scotland. After toasting the British monarchy and "the Imperial Forces," the assembled company heard speeches praising the greatness of Scottish shipbuilding and the engineering genius of Watt. In Edinburgh, the *Scotsman*'s reporting of some of the speeches, and of the diners' perhaps tipsily enthusiastic responses, gives a good flavour of Edwardian Glasgow's self-image:

> Sir Digby Murray, in submitting the toast of 'The City of Glasgow,' said
> . . . Glasgow had often been spoken of as the third city of rank in the
> United Kingdom (Cries of 'The Second')—it had been long spoken of as
> the third—(laughter)—but, even supposing that were the case so far as
> many respects were concerned, in other respects, for instance, in her

shipbuilding and engineering, she stood first, not only in the United Kingdom but also in the world. (Applause.)

Lord Provost Chisholm, in responding, said there remained now, and had remained for the last decade not the shadow of a doubt as to the position which Glasgow occupied in the enumeration of the cities of this country. (Laughter and applause.) . . . In the population of the city of Glasgow they stood second, distanced by London alone. (Applause) . . . Amongst the cities of the world there were few, if any, which stood out more clearly as 'man-made' than the city of Glasgow. (Laughter and applause). . . . Whether they referred to those great and gigantic works which the deepening and straightening and widening of the Clyde had rendered possible, those vast shipbuilding yards that lined the Clyde right down to the old Port-Glasgow; or whether they thought of the railway systems which had their termini in Glasgow, or that extraordinary series of local intercommunication by underground railways or subways, or the remarkable electric installation, the electric tramway system, or whether they thought of numerous other adaptations of engineering skill and science, they saw how much Glasgow owed, how wholly it had been built up by the labour and skill and genius of men. How largely also were the inhabitants of the city indebted to these large works, not merely for the means of subsistence, but for the training which was given to intelligent workmen. (Applause.)

Laughing and clapping his hands, the councillor from Great Western Road very much belonged to a city which had triumphed through industry and engineering. He knew, too, the terrible problems of Glasgow's poor, some of whose substandard housing he was attempting to have cleared. Yet for all his keen sense of the lives of the disadvantaged, this man relished the pleasures of the rich. His own family were shipowners and shipbuilders. The following year, as a Glasgow bailie, he dined with the king and queen in the City Chambers. Not long afterwards, among palm trees, elaborate drapes, and floral displays, he listened while the Unionist prime minister A. J. Balfour orated in Glasgow's St. Andrew's Halls about the reorganization of the navy, the need to further develop the British Empire, the importance of the Union between Scotland and England, and the strength of "the Imperial Forces."

The name of this Glaswegian councillor was William Burrell. Whereas in an earlier century tobacco lords had been at the heart of the city's wealth, intermarrying and forming shifting alliances, now it was the turn of shipping magnates and captains of industry. Burrell's dark-haired sister Mary married James Mitchell, who belonged to the Mitchells of the shipping firm Edminston and Mitchell. Photographed in 1895 wearing a long white dress and clasping a dark, hanging ribbon, Mary was being painted by "Glasgow Boy" John Lavery to celebrate her twenty-first birthday. Like several others in the city, the Burrells were a family whose money came from engineering and trade, but who were attracted increasingly by art. Won by capitalist cunning and labouring muscle, the industrial spoils of nineteenth-century Glasgow were often purged of their associations with slum life and industrial pollution by being laundered into high culture. The collection of industrious Glasgow coachbuilder Archibald McLellan had formed the original core of the city's art museum. T. G. Arthur and Arthur Kay were partners in a Glasgow warehousing firm, but also Victorian and Edwardian purchasers of paintings by Courbet, Rembrandt, Van Dyck, Goya, Manet, Degas, and Whistler. Burrell wished to join this collecting elite. He started buying pictures in his teens.

From his youth, he was a very shrewd speculator in shipping. In January 1902, around the time he sat as a moustachioed thirty-nine-year-old with short, slightly receding hair, listening with fellow shipbuilders and others to speakers toasting Glasgow and Empire, Burrell the businessman was described by a friend in a letter:

> He sells his fleet when there is the periodical boom and then puts his money into 3 per c[ent] stock and lies back until things are absolutely in the gutter—soup kitchen times—everyone starving for a job. He then goes like a roaring lion. Orders a dozen large steamers in a week, gets them built at rock bottom prices, less than ½ what they'd have cost him last year. Then by the time they're delivered to him things have begun to improve a little bit and there he is ready with a tip top fleet of brand new steamers and owing to the cheap rate he's had them built at, ready to carry cheaper than anybody. Sounds like a game anyone could play at but none of them have the pluck to do it. They simply sit and look at him "making money like slate stones" as he expresses it.

By the middle of World War I, Burrell the speculator had sold his fleet. He began to devote himself almost wholly to amassing artworks. As a collector he had been encouraged not least by Van Gogh's Glasgow dealer friend Alexander Reid, whom Burrell recalled as someone who "did more than any other man has ever done to introduce fine pictures to Scotland and to create a love of art." Reid steered Burrell towards the Glasgow Boys and Whistler. Yet Burrell's eclectic tastes ranged from drawings by *Punch* cartoonist Phil May to classic Chinese ceramics. He bought pieces from every historical period and from many civilizations—but only if he was sure he was getting a bargain.

By 1901, Burrell was the biggest individual lender of works to the Glasgow International Exhibition, on whose general organizing committee he also sat. The dining room in his home at 8 Great Western Terrace had all its walls covered floor-to-ceiling in medieval and Renaissance tapestries. Burrell liked to buy tapestries; he felt you got more for your money. His astuteness in choosing both artworks and the dealers to advise him meant that his collection grew almost unrivalled. To house it, he bought a castle in the Scottish Borders. Eventually moving there, he did not forget Glasgow. Having loaned work from his hoard to both Edinburgh's National Gallery (on whose board he sat) and to the National Gallery in London, he donated about eighty paintings and drawings to Kelvingrove in 1925. It was a characteristically canny move. Two years later, he was knighted.

Several public galleries courted Burrell. From the early 1930s onwards, he began to suggest that he might seek a permanent home for his collection; but he was a hard man to deal with. As he aged, he grew increasingly parsimonious. In his castle, he carried a key to unlock the boxes that encased the light switches. This prevented others from squandering his electricity. Family members had to apply for the key. The master switch for the whole castle's supply was installed in his bedroom, and he habitually turned it off at 10:00 P.M. When burglars were suspected of being near the castle, Sir William discharged both barrels of a shotgun from his bedroom window. A staunch Unionist and Imperialist, he complained that the British were "evidently intent on throwing away India as we have done Southern Ireland and Egypt." When instructions came from Edinburgh that all the iron railings around his castle were to be confiscated without compensation and melted down as part of the war effort, he was furious. Now Edinburgh would never get his collection.

So imagine the glee in the West of Scotland the following year, when, after Sir William had sent a telegram to summon from Kelvingrove his friend Tom Honeyman in December 1943, it was announced that the Burrell Collection would be presented to the city of Glasgow. "In all history," as the English art historian John Julius Norwich has put it, "no municipality has ever received from one of its native sons a gift of such munificence." The Burrell Collection is not only vast (it contains around 8,000 items), but also of superlative quality. In Burrell's famous assembly of French pictures (Boudin, Cézanne, Chardin, Courbet, Delacroix—and on through a whole alphabet of *jouissance*), among more than twenty works by Degas are the superb oil painting *The Rehearsal* and the beautifully toned pastel *Jockeys in the Rain.* In each of these, the artist makes daring pictorial use of apparently empty space and compositional diagonals. Burrell's tapestry collection is among the best in the world. The vagaries of the sale room meant that he had to divide the Beaufort Tapestries with the Metropolitan Museum in New York and the Rijksmuscum in Amsterdam; but his portion, with its storks, lions, and unicorns, is energetically superb. Other tapestries he treasured feature fifteenth-century Burgundian peasants hunting rabbits with ferrets and nets; Dutch handlers trying to keep order among a procession of sixteenth-century camels; and Hercules on horseback, in shining armour and wearing a soft hat bearing his name, initiating the Olympic Games.

About a quarter of the Burrell treasure trove is made up of pieces from China, a favourite being the large, green-robed ceramic figure of a cross-legged Buddhist disciple—a *lohan*—which Sir William bought for £350. It was made in the autumn of 1484 by a craftsman called Liuzhen for a "believer Wang Jin-ao, his wife Miaojin, and his son Wang Qin and the priest Daoji." So says the inscription on its side, and today that *lohan* features on a fine poster for the collection. Burrell was so concerned that his valuable artefacts should not be damaged by atmospheric pollution that it took Glasgow a long time to be able to meet the conditions of his bequest. In 1983, however, Queen Elizabeth II shook hands with Sir William's smiling eighty-six-year-old daughter at the opening of the purpose-built Burrell Collection gallery on the south side of Glasgow in the 361-acre Pollok Park.

No museum on such a scale had been built in twentieth-century Britain. Designed by Barry Gasson and colleagues, it is designed to interact with the landscape. A great glass wall lets many of the exhibits be seen against nearby woodland, "making," as Gasson put it, "the grass, the trees, the woodland plants, the bluebells and bracken, a context for the display of the Collection." Well-loved by Glaswegians and tourists alike, the building re-creates rooms from Burrell's castle, incorporates his hoard of medieval architecture and stained glass (some of it bought from the collection of William Randolph Hearst), and is a late twentieth-century visual triumph. Yet its success in no way outshines the beautiful parkland surrounding it—all highland cows, rhododendrons, and daffodils. Nor should it eclipse the nearby 1740s mansion, Pollok House, another Glasgow favourite, famous not least for its subtle and haunting El Greco portrait of a lady wearing a grey fur wrap. If Burrell's wealth came from shipbuilding, shipowning and commerce, his name survives in the twenty-first century wholly translated into art.

Water

For shipping magnate Sir William Burrell, as for so many others, water was Glasgow's defining element. The River Clyde shaped the city's development in ways that seem strange in the early twenty-first century. Today that long, historic watercourse is principally for looking at, rather than for sailing on. In Victorian times and for much of the past hundred years, to voyage "doon the watter"—downriver from Glasgow—was a quintessential West of Scotland pleasure. You can still do it, but only in season and if you pick your time very carefully. Not so long ago, steamships—Clyde steamers—took thousands of people from city-centre quays on excursions to the islands of the Firth and beyond. Schoolchildren marvelled at engine rooms' gleaming rods and churning paddles, or waved from the rails of their chosen vessel to friends waiting on a pier. "The Clyde made Glasgow, Glasgow made the Clyde," runs a traditional saying. Throughout the Industrial Revolution and after, it seemed self-evident the river's story was one of commerce, prosperity, and shipbuilding; but that was only one way to regard the city's principal waterway. Though for several centuries the Clyde appeared to belong to Glasgow, it does not. Yet, however vestigially, Glasgow still likes to feel that it belongs to the Clyde.

Nowadays, when the shipyards no longer play a dominant role, the city is trying to recast its relationship with the river in terms of amenity, environmentalism, and leisure. In some ways, this marks a return to pre-industrial narratives which viewed the watercourse not in terms of pollution and imperial trade, but as an abundant natural habitat. When seventeenth-century poet Arthur Johnston hymned Glasgow, he praised the Clyde (in Latin, "Glotta") for the purity of its water flowing through a landscape of apple orchards and roses. From source to firth, the river is more than a hundred miles long. Inland from Glasgow, its stream still winds through fruit-growing areas of the upper Clyde Valley. On steep, wooded riverbanks at New

Lanark, the 1786 cotton mills of David Dale, developed into a model community with its own welfare programmes by utopian socialist Robert Owen and others in the early nineteenth century, are now a World Heritage Site. Healthy, thriving, and proud of having Britain's first infant school (founded in 1816), the New Lanark social experiment attracted international attention, encouraging such ideal communities as New Harmony in Indiana, whose Owenite newspaper was edited by the adventurous Scotswoman Fanny Wright. Beside the Clyde, New Lanark's remarkable complex of buildings now includes a museum, holiday flats, and a hotel.

Yet for all that the welcoming banks of the Clyde were a cradle of the Industrial Revolution, and beyond New Lanark the men, women, and children of nearby coal-mining communities endured gulag-like conditions, the riverbanks were also a place of romantic beauty. In 1802, between New Lanark and Glasgow, J. M. W. Turner painted watercolours of the torrential Falls of Clyde; none of these paintings now hangs in Glasgow, but one is in Edinburgh's National Gallery. In some of them, invoking Mark Akenside's "Hymn to the Naiads," Turner includes a group of naked women on the rocks below. The English artist, like the Scottish Latin poet Johnston before him, could see the Clyde as a locus of classical beauty. Though Turner did not paint Glasgow itself, the city and its river could be viewed through a similar lens by local poets—at least before the smokestacks arose. Printed and sold in the Saltmarket, the long poem *Glotta,* written in 1721 by the student James Arbuckle, hymns the fertile riverbanks' natural habitat and presents as naiads the Glaswegian washerwomen who, as *"Sol"* (the sun) sets over Glasgow Green, hitch up their plaid skirts to stamp on sheets and garments the way winemakers might tread grapes:

Thro' flow'ry Vallies, and enamel'd Meads,
The hastening Flood at length to *Glasgow* speeds.
Its *Northern* Bank a lovely Green displays,
Whose e'ery Prospect fresh Delights conveys.
Alternate Shades of blowing Flow'rs we view
Of various Tincture, wash'd in fragrant Dew.
Here the shrill Larks their mattin Songs repeat,
The yielding Air the tender Strains dilate,
As o'er the Surface of the Stream they glide;

And sweetly languish on the Silver Tide.
Here, when declining *Sol* extends the Shades,
Resort victorious Throngs of charming Maids.
Not fabled *Paphos,* or th' *Arcadian* Plain,
Could ever boast a brighter Virgin Train;
More gentle Looks, or Eyes more sparkling show,
Or Cheeks that with a livelier Crimson glow.
What envious Pow'r then first contriv'd, or made
That Foe to Beauty, and to Love, a Plaid?
Destruction seize the guilty Garb, that holds
Conceal'd such Charms in its malicious Folds.
Of this, *O Thyrsis,* could thy Strains unshrine,
Thy *Sacharissa,* how the Fair would shine!
Her bright Example would the Law impose,
And all the Green a Gallaxy disclose.

Classicized, feminized, its nearby "verdant Turf" and "Mead" (meadow) sugared with more than a hint of voyeurism, this Clyde is very different from the river of heavyweight Victorian shipyards. It is, though, the selfsame watercourse Daniel Defoe admired a few years after Arbuckle's poem appeared. The author of *Robinson Crusoe* thought "the country between Pasely and Glasgow, on the bank of the Clyde," outstanding for "fertility" and "healthiness."

In Glasgow, however, the river was then unpredictable. One June in the mid-1720s, Defoe "went over dry-footed without the bridge . . . the water was scarce over the horses' hooves," while "children and boys playing about, went every where, as if there was no river, only some little spreading brook." Yet on another occasion he saw the stream so broad that it had "fill'd up all the [eight] arches of the bridge" and inundated the city streets. Householders were panicking "for fear of their houses being driven away by the violence of the water." As the decades passed, in order to enable larger international trading ships to berth in Glasgow itself, rather than farther west at Newark (later renamed Port Glasgow), proposals were advanced to make the river's upper reaches more navigable. English engineer John Golborne, who surveyed the Clyde in 1768, put forward successful plans to use jetties downstream, as well as intensive dredging to narrow and deepen the channel. James Watt, too, was involved in these operations. They turned Glasgow into a deepwater port. Almost simultaneously, Watt's improvements to the steam engine played their part in the industrialization that increasingly dirtied the Clyde's waters. By the time Dorothy Wordsworth spoke to washerwomen on the "bleaching ground" of Glasgow Green, "bordering on the Clyde," in 1802, there was a large indoor wash-house; and although "the women were very civil," she found "a want of cleanliness" among the poorer people in the streets and thought Glasgow had no particular "natural advantages." Urban pollution was blighting the place.

A decade later, botanist Thomas Hopkirk noted in his *Flora Glottiana* that there was "shining pond-weed . . . in the Clyde frequently," and could identify "bird cherry" trees on the riverbanks, as well as close to the Kelvin. Yet by 1820, when artist John Knox painted a view looking north over the old Glasgow Bridge, though there was still greenery on the hillside behind, dark smoke trailed from several tall chimneys, most obviously from the huge conical kiln of an old Bottle Works near the city-centre quayside called the Broomielaw. Today, fronting Knox's glassy river and shining pale in the sunlight, neoclassical buildings bookend the Roman Catholic chapel erected in the years 1814–1817. Renovated by P. P. and C. W. Pugin when it became a cathedral in 1889, that church still stands opposite the Gorbals, on the Clyde's north bank; after being blackened by industrial grime, it has recently been splendidly restored.

In Sam Bough's watercolours of the Clyde, painted around 1860, smoke from steam vessels and chimneys obscures some of the buildings; the old Glasgow Bridge has been replaced by the 1847 Victoria Bridge, and tenements flank the Catholic chapel. Sailing ships, steamboats, and smaller vessels throng the busy river. Not many years later, in 1881, more than nightfall has darkened the waterfront buildings grimy with pollution in the inner-city oil painting *Shipping on the Clyde*, by John Atkinson Grimshaw. His Clyde is very much the river which Alexander Smith had imaged as stygian in his mid-nineteenth-century poem "Glasgow":

> And through thy heart, as through a dream
> Flows on that black disdainful stream;
>   All scornfully it flows,
> Between the huddled gloom of masts,

Silent as pines unvexed by blasts—
    'Tween lamps in streaming rows.
O wondrous sight! O stream of dread!
O long dark river of the dead!

The urban "noise and smoky breath" in Smith's poem are telling. The breath was not just exhaled tobacco smoke, but also inhaled industrial fug. If people in earlier ages had caught salmon in Glasgow's principal river, by 1910 another local poet, Charles J. Kirk, began his "Ode to the Clyde" by hailing the "great black-bosomed mother of our city, / Whose odoriferous breath offends the earth"; dryly he went on to point out that "No salmon hast thou in thy jet-black waters, / Save what is adhering to the tins." It would be the late twentieth century before efforts at purification allowed the river to welcome back some of its long-lost fish stocks.

52. The River Clyde in 1955. Though shipbuilding on the Clyde had passed its heyday, the mid-twentieth-century river was still busy with vessels.

Today the Clyde is a place to ponder not just Glasgow's industrial past and largely postindustrial present, but also aspects of the city's culture which are much less widely known. Though an image of Father Clyde—along with sculptures of classical deities, James Watt, and other mortals—can be seen on the façade of the former Clyde Navigation Trust headquarters on the Broomielaw, more striking is the stark, elevated fibreglass statue of a woman with upraised arms which stands on the Clyde Walkway at Custom House Quay, just east of Glasgow Bridge. An inscription under the statue reads, "Better to die on your feet than live forever on your knees." Erected in 1979, the year Margaret Thatcher became Britain's prime minister, this nine-foot-high statue depicts the Spanish Communist Dolores Ibárruri. A celebrated orator, Ibárruri is believed to have been the inspiration for the character of Pilar in Hemingway's *For Whom the Bell Tolls.* Entitled *La Passionaria,* the sculpture of her by Arthur Dooley memorializes the men and women who went to fight Fascism at the time of the Spanish Civil War. More than 10 percent of British casualties on the anti-Fascist side in Spain were Glaswegians. Denounced in 1979 by right-wing politicians, who vowed to have it removed, this monument is one of the few public tributes to the city's great heritage of political radicalism, and a reminder that such a tradition involved women as well as men.

Among those who went to Spain from Glasgow was Jenny Patrick. Her father owned an upmarket dress shop on Sauchiehall Street. When Jenny's mother died and her father remarried, his new wife dressed Jenny in cast-offs, saving the finery for her own daughter; Jenny, however, was an independent spirit. After training as a typesetter, in 1914 she joined the Glasgow Anarchist Group, which in 1920 became the Glasgow Communist Group. Chair of the editorial committee of its short-lived 1921 Glaswegian magazine *Red Commune,* she was arrested in its offices while making a cup of tea. Imprisonment for sedition followed. Having served her sentence, Patrick continued to work for communist and anarchist causes, operating with her partner, anarchist Guy Aldred, from Bakunin House at 13 Burnbank Terrace, off Great Western Road. Impoverished but determined, from 1933 they lived in a one-room flat in a decaying tenement at 5 Balliol Street, near Charing Cross. In 1936 Jenny Patrick went to Spain, along with her Glaswegian friend Ethel MacDonald. Jenny sent back to Glasgow reports from Barcelona, where she and Ethel became broadcasters. Surviving the Civil War,

Jenny returned to Glasgow and worked twelve-hour shifts producing radical literature. "Bright, intelligent, and disdainful of weakness," she continued to campaign into her eighties and died, housebound, in 1971. In the National Museum of Scotland, a 1918 photograph signed "your loving chum, Jenny," shows her standing proud and alert. The statue of *La Passionaria* by the Clyde memorializes the idealism of many campaigners like her.

Though the river is predominantly thought of in terms of male and industrial images, its history is bound up with Glasgow's women and with greenery as well as grime. The Clyde's present identity—whether represented by the soaring Clyde Arc (opened in 2006 and immediately nicknamed "the Squinty Bridge"), which links Finnieston with the old Plantation area and the new "International Financial Services District" opposite, or by the 2011 Riverside Museum designed by Zaha Hadid, farther west on the north bank—suggests a wish to pay tribute to engineering and shipbuilding glories of the past, but by no means to be confined by them. In the Govan "Media Village" and elsewhere, probably more women than men now work by the riverbanks. Radio producers, online journalists, and television professionals have taken the place not only of most of the shipbuilders, but also of the naiads and washerwomen.

If some areas of Clydeside have been subtly regendered, others speak clearly of the days when docks and quaysides were regarded as almost exclusively a man's world, a zone of testosterone, riveting, and steel. Such is the Clydeside iconically imaged in the memorable Second World War paintings of shipbuilders by war artist Stanley Spencer, or in Scottish filmmaker John Grierson's Oscar-winning 1960 documentary *Seaward the Great Ships,* made for Films of Scotland and the Clyde Shipbuilders Association. One magnificent heavyweight memorial of those days is the 165-foot giant cantilever Finnieston Crane, which stands on the north bank of the Clyde not far from the Scottish Exhibition and Conference Centre, and which has passed now from engineering into elegy. This huge crane testifies to the time when Glasgow was an international leader in shipbuilding. The world's largest crane was erected nearby in 1911 by the local Arrol Company on the opposite bank at Govan, but was demolished in 2007. Other great cranes stood (and some still stand, unused) not far off.

While there remains some large-scale (particularly military) shipbuilding on the river, it is nothing compared to what it once was. Paddle-driven steamships were pioneered in late eighteenth-century Scotland. Henry Bell launched his *Comet* on the Clyde in 1812, and by the decade of the 1830s (when Glasgow's population grew by 37 percent) the locality was famous for producing powerful steam engines used in the era's "dark satanic mills." Shipbuilding, too, was on the rise, increasingly making use of readily available local iron and steel. James Watt had designed the pumping technology used in Scotland's first drydock, opened in Port Glasgow in 1762, when sailing ships were still built of timber and Glasgow's transatlantic tobacco trade was thriving. Later, evolved from the ideas of Watt's technology, the "Scotch boilers" and triple expansion engines of the Clyde powered much Victorian shipping. Numerous vessels were built farther downriver at Dumbarton, Greenock, and elsewhere, but Glasgow itself was a major naval construction centre. From 1898 to 1913, for example, the Govan-based Fairfield Company alone launched almost a hundred ships, including twenty-two large passenger liners and many destroyers for the Royal Navy. By 1913 the William Denny yard (headquartered downriver at Dumbarton) had built more than a thousand vessels. In that year, less than two decades before the Finnieston Crane was erected, Glasgow and the surrounding region were constructing nearly a fifth of global maritime tonnage.

Early twentieth-century Glasgow was one of the world's heavy-engineering hubs, a European Detroit. The city and its Lowland Scottish environs had pioneered hot-blast processes for the iron industry (developed by the manager of the Glasgow Gasworks); entrepreneurs with a base at Glasgow's Lancefield Quay linked, for the first time in one commercial concern, engineering and shipbuilding; and in 1903 Glasgow developed Europe's biggest locomotive maker, the North British Locomotive Works at Springburn. This "Titan of its trade" could build 800 locomotives in a single year, exporting about half of them to the British Empire and shipping many others beyond. The Clyde Navigation Trustees' Crane Number 7, now known as the Finnieston Crane, was built to manœuvre boilers and engines into newly fabricated ships. It also lifted railway engines weighing as much as 175 tons.

Looking up at this monumental structure calls to mind the early twentieth-century "rhapsody" with which Clydeside writer George Blake opened his book *Clyde Waters*. A family is travelling on a steam train, with its "sulphurous smoke," from Glasgow's now-demolished St. Enoch's Station

53. The Finnieston Crane (Clyde Navigation Trustees' Crane Number 7) still towers above the redeveloped inner-city River Clyde. Erected in 1931, the crane could lift railway engines weighing as much as 175 tons.

past "a water's edge studded with the uprights and gantries of shipyards," heading to the Firth of Clyde town of Greenock. There, at Princes Pier, with its cream-and-lime-green "Bavarian style" clock-towered brick buildings, "a fleet of steamers lay against the pier. Your first sight was a forest of gleaming, varnished masts and red-and-black funnels, with coloured pennants and flags fluttering against the northern sky." Remembered in the year 1952, Blake's version of middle-class Glaswegians setting off on their 1908 holidays was not inaccurate, but had a picture-postcard quality. As long ago as 1872, *Tweed's Guide to Glasgow* had stated of the Clyde: "Its colour is inky, its composition muddy and its effluvia at times, when the steamers are churning up its hidden ugliness, beastly." Two years later, a "Report on the Pollution of the River Clyde" cited an estimate that "the whole discharge into the River daily," excluding rainfall, was 400 million gallons. Sewage purification schemes helped, but the growth of heavy industry—shipyards, locomotive works, engineering plants—did not. Glasgow's prosperity was a dirty business.

Glaswegians were intensely proud of it, though. Many delighted in the sometimes bitterly cold yards, where "almost every man . . . was an artist in one of the arts that go to the building of a ship." Exploited by their clique of imperialist, capitalist bosses, nineteenth-century shipyard workers could take comfort from being among the world's best. As the socialist politics of "Red Clydeside" intensified around the time of World War I, both capitalism and imperialism were fiercely interrogated; workers' expectations increased, international competition expanded, and labour relations grew hostile. Class warfare and anti-Catholic attitudes blighted many yards. Yet the industrial landscape remained spectacular. In his 1935 novel, *The Shipbuilders,* George Blake wrote: "Up and down the River the bows of vessels unlaunched towered over the tenement buildings of the workers and people passing could hardly hear themselves speak for the clangour of metal upon metal that filled the valley from Old Kilpatrick up to Govan."

Visually stunning—with their staircases zigzagging ten flights or more up the hulls of partially built ships, their vast swinging crane arms, their piles of beams and piping, huts, platforms, and gantries—the shipyards were, throughout the nineteenth and twentieth centuries, a generally tough, almost homosocial environment. A 1934 photograph of the liner *Queen Mary* under construction at Clydebank shows a yard populated with flat-capped working-class male workers crossing ærial walkways, descending staircases, striding across rails, walking away from the ship at what looks like the end of a shift. A relatively small number of women toiled in the yards, some tracing designs, others doing French polishing—but in this photograph, there is not a woman to be seen. Though women did labour in mills and factories, the heavy engineering so important to Glasgow's image helped to produce a civic identity that was resolutely masculinist. "There is no gentle / place for a woman here," wrote poet Joan Ure in 1968.

Throughout the twentieth century, as shipbuilding and heavy industry slowly but inexorably declined, Glasgow continued to be thought of as a hard, stereotypically masculine place. By 1971, when five major shipyards which had amalgamated as Upper Clyde Shipbuilders (UCS) ran out of money and the Conservative Westminster government refused them a loan, the engineer, labour activist, and Communist Party of Great Britain member Jimmy Reid became the best-known among those who led a well-disciplined, almost all-male "UCS work-in": the opposite of a strike. Its supporters ranged from Billy Connolly, himself a former shipyard worker, to John Lennon, who sent a donation. The work-in succeeded in slowing the shipyards' decline, but photographs of the protestors were among many icons reinforcing the image of Glasgow as well-nigh utterly masculine. Telling his 8,500 men that there was to be "no hooliganism, no vandalism and no bevvying [drinking]," Reid became a folk hero. Elected rector of Glasgow University, he had his powerful oratory reported at length in the *New York Times*. Yet Glasgow has often lacked heroines. The most widely celebrated feminine-gendered Clydesiders were almost exclusively ships.

Metallically stalwart, industrially heroic, the Finnieston Crane may be an appropriate monument to the mythologized masculinity of shipbuilding and Glaswegian heavy industry. No longer working, it has become an artwork. Glaswegians view it with pride, nostalgia, and a sense of the need to move on. The last railway engine it hoisted—in 1988 during the Glasgow Garden Festival, held opposite at the former Prince's Dock—was made entirely of straw. Created by local sculptor George Wyllie, this "straw locomotive" was eventually set on fire in what seemed a public funeral rite for the heavy-engineering tradition. On another occasion, Wyllie (who donated some of his sculptures to help raise money for the new Riverside Museum in 2010) floated down the Clyde a giant paper boat, which went on across the Atlantic. Part political protest, part *jeu d'esprit,* his origami vessel and straw locomotive, so evidently transient, wittily and lovingly called to mind a tradition of grandly engineered, Clydebuilt originals that looked as if they might last forever, but did not.

Few of today's major buildings in the area around the Finnieston Crane would have been recognized by Glasgow's workforce during the heyday of shipbuilding. Yet the complexly engineered postmodern structures of large contemporary landmarks—such as the Scottish Exhibition and Conference Centre complex (the shape of whose Clyde Auditorium, designed by Norman Foster in 1995, has earned the local nickname "the Armadillo") and the 2001 curved, titanium-clad Glasgow Science Centre (looking rather like the inverted hull of a beached ship at Prince's Dock across the river)—conjure up, deliberately or not, the ideals and triumphs of earlier eras. So, in its way, does the Glasgow Tower beside the south-bank Science Centre. Opened in 2001 and said to be the tallest tower in the world whose entire structure can rotate 360 degrees, this 110-yard-tall mast with its high viewing gallery has had its problems. Difficulties with the thrust bearing on which it rotates soon led to a two-year closure. Occasionally the lifts have failed. If you have to get down in a hurry without them, there are 523 stairs.

Hit by early twenty-first-century economic recession but spurred on by the arrival of the 2014 Commonwealth Games, vast building and renewal projects continue to transform parts of the city, not least those close to the water. Sometimes history is simply hidden. Areas around Plantation Quay, a name redolent of Glasgow's tobacco-era links with the slave trade, were not so long ago renamed Pacific Quay. Presumably this sly airbrushing of their past made these zones a more acceptable-sounding location for the Science Centre and the nearby twenty-first-century Digital Media Village. Some of the latter's un-village-like buildings, orphaned by bleak, often rain-swept carparks, house the headquarters of BBC Scotland, designed by David Chipperfield, and other broadcasting operations. Much of their car-parking is on the site of the 1988 Glasgow Garden Festival. Under the patronage of Prince Charles and Diana Princess of Wales, that extravaganza brought together an uneasy, Thatcher-era co-habitation of displays—from a "Railway Heritage Garden" to a "Coca-Cola Roller."

The Garden Festival's greening of the docklands has gone. Asphalt is back. Yet the festive, sponsorship-savvy gardeners marked a determination on the part of Glasgow to move into the postindustrial era—something the area and the city as a whole managed to do with aplomb. Many were surprised, and some outraged, when in 1990 Glasgow won its title "European City of Culture." A part of the place's cultural inheritance, yet oddly islanded in what seems destined to be a twenty-first-century "creative industries" quarter on both banks of the river, the Finnieston Crane is a resolute survivor. Like the ornate Govan Town Hall, built just across the Clyde in the glory days of shipbuilding, it is a presence from another age. Yet, always dynamic, Glasgow has deftly reinvented its shipbuilding heritage as a postmodern visitor attraction.

Emblematizing this more than anything else is the Riverside Museum. Designed by Zaha Hadid and opened in 2011, when it attracted more than half a million visitors within its first two months, it is Hadid's first major British public building, and combines manifest architectural ambition with deceptive structural simplicity. Fronting on a quayside where the three-masted, late-nineteenth-century, Clyde-built sailing ship the *Glenlee* (known

54. Designed by Zaha Hadid and opened in 2011, the Riverside Museum is a treasure trove of transportation, filled with models of Clyde-built ships, and actual vehicles ranging from a gleaming Glasgow tram to the world's oldest bicycle. Reflected in the dark, floor-to-ceiling glass is an 1896 sailing ship, the *Glenlee*, now permanently anchored on the Clyde outside the museum and known to Glaswegians as "the Tall Ship."

to Glaswegians as "the Tall Ship") is berthed, the waterfront elevation of the sleek Riverside Museum has the most singular outline of any building in Glasgow. To many viewers its roofline invokes ships' prows; at the same time, it looks like a fever chart—as if it graphed the fortunes of Clyde shipbuilding or the vertiginous spikes and plunges of the Western economy during the years of its construction. Yet viewed from the water by people crossing the river on the centuries-old route of the Govan Ferry, or seen from the air by passengers arriving at the nearby Glasgow City Heliport, the building is also dashingly calligraphic. Its end-on roofline casts a pale, rippling glyph over the dark, glassy depths below; and its silvery roof, when seen from the air, constitutes a fluid geometric swoosh, a bend in a new, high-tech river between the River Clyde and the River Kelvin.

Standing at the confluence of these two Glasgow rivers, the modern Riverside Museum occupies the site of the former Pointhouse shipyard of A. and J. Inglis, and looks across the Kelvin to the former offices of another former shipyard, that of D. and W. Henderson, where, at low tide, you can see what is left of decaying wooden slipways once used to launch proud ships. Among the many other vessels built at the Inglis yard, one deserves special mention: the *Waverley*—today the world's last surviving seagoing paddle steamer—was launched in 1946 and still, in season, carries passengers "doon the watter," its thrashing paddles eloquently articulating the Clyde. Commemorating yet also in some ways transcending such a glorious local heritage, the Riverside Museum has been described by its architect as "a third metallic river" at this point of confluence. More mundanely, yet utterly appropriately, it looks from some angles like a fabrication shed, a great industrial works in the form of a new monument which pays tribute to the Clyde's heritage of gleaming engineering.

Zaha Hadid has something of a reputation for producing designs that look exciting as computer graphics but are hugely challenging to engineer. Designed so that its sweeping, pistachio-green interior has absolutely no pillars, yet supporting a 2,500-ton roof and clad in 24,000 zinc panels, the Riverside Museum was thought by some to be unbuildable. The Baghdad-born, London-based Hadid, who first visited Glasgow in the 1980s to go clubbing, likes what she has called the city's "toughness" and "open-mindedness." Though she has spent little time in this Scottish city, it is undeniable that the interior of her building, and not least the highlighted zooming curves of its ceilings, are attuned to the imagination of its greatest poet, the Edwin Morgan who so treasured the "loops of light" he perceived in the flyovers of Glasgow's motorway system. This is a museum not of art but of industry, and most specifically of transport: from the world's oldest bicycle to modern electric vehicles. Appropriately, it transports its visitors, most of whom enter through a main door at the end of the building farthest from the river, not just towards that once great watery gateway to the world, the Clyde, but also into an imaginative fantasy which involves tiered rows of cars climbing its walls, bicycles suspended in an upside-down velodrome from its roof, ship models gliding past on delicate moving belts, and vast locomotives inviting children to step freely aboard.

Here is a ludic presentation of so much that Glasgow once made, and still recalls with love and affection. Largely stilled and sanitized, this, smoke-free, is the Industrial Revolution. The dynamism of the flowing building gives to its 3,000 exhibits a speed that they no longer possess in themselves.

High above eye level as well as closer to the ground, "motors," as Glaswegians like to call them—bubble cars, MGs, Minis—queue to go nowhere, other than into the viewer's imagination. The Clydeside area that once built automobiles (the Argyle at Dumbarton, the Hillman Imp at Linwood), great ocean liners (the *Queen Mary,* the *Queen Elizabeth,* the *Queen Elizabeth II*), locomotives, trams, and other vehicles now has this building to stand as its fullest memory bank, allowing Glasgow to make subtle synaptic connections with its past, and at the same time reinvent elements of that past as part of its twenty-first-century identity.

So the Riverside Museum is a place where children can see what welding produced on the Clyde, and where, through interactive displays, they can learn how to use a welding torch and mask. If today's museumology insists on the digital, there is no denying the staunch physicality of some of the Riverside Museum's star exhibits, such as the local double-decker Springburn tram or the more exotic 150-tonne South African vintage locomotive—which turns out, after all, to have been designed and manufactured in Glasgow. Entire re-created streets allow people to wander over the cobbles and walk into an Edwardian photography studio, or hear the warm, guttural accents at the bar of the Mitre Pub, or visit a re-creation of Giovanni Tognieri's Duke Street Glaswegian Italian Café from the 1930s, or "Mr. Drysdale Shoe and Bootmakers," or a 1960s garage. Populist and avant-garde, the Riverside Museum is the apotheosis of the shed, its combination of art and science, sophistication and vox pop quintessentially Glaswegian.

Outside, the landscape around still seems patchy, even incoherent. The arresting modern buildings are spectacular one-offs; the environment in which they sit still speaks of dereliction or of vacancy and blight. Yet, with the 2014 Commonwealth Games as their centrepiece, Glasgow's planners have continued to think big, with the Hydro Arena, a 12,000-seat circular indoor venue designed to open in 2013 between the armadillo-shaped Scottish Exhibition and Conference Centre and the Finnieston Crane. Planned to host music events as well as the gymnastics competitions of the Commonwealth Games, the Hydro promises to be another modern Clyde landmark, a new focus of Glaswegian internationalism and energy.

An emblem of the Clyde's internationalism and its vigour is certainly the 1896 sailing ship the *Glenlee,* now anchored outside the Riverside Museum after sailing four times around the world, laden with everything from wheat to guano. The antiquity of this waterway as an ancient sustainer of Glasgow is represented by the more modest Govan Ferry, which takes passengers from the Riverside Museum across to Water Row in Govan, where the Old Parish Church is home to thousand-year-old carved stones featuring ancient horsemen, snake-headed solar discs and house-shaped "hogback" designs. Setting the river in an even more ancient and philosophical light is the artwork designed by Ian Hamilton Finlay in 1990 to "dramatize" the site of the 1879 George IV Railway Bridge over the Clyde, removed in the 1960s. Passersby who look west from the present-day city-centre Jamaica Bridge can see, standing in the water, eight substantial pillars of Dalbeattie granite, remnants of the 1879 imperial structure. On these, under Finlay's direction, the words "ALL GREATNESS STANDS FIRM IN THE STORM" (which Finlay attributed to Plato) have been carved in English and in Greek.

From the nearby Broomielaw, hundreds of thousands of Glaswegians once sailed downriver; a little farther west, from Yorkhill Quay, the vessels of the Anchor Line took early twentieth-century families to New York and Boston; some miles farther west, on the Firth of Clyde at Helensburgh, John Logie Baird grew up and developed the scientific intelligence which, on May 27, 1927, led him to transmit from London to a fourth-floor room of Glasgow's Central Hotel some of the world's first long-distance television pictures. Today, as in its past, Glasgow continues to be associated with the unexpected and with the modern, as well as with the glories of past eras. If all greatness does stand firm in the storm, then at the heart of the city there remains constant what may be one of its greatest assets—an advantage all the more worth treasuring because forever liquid and denied to Edinburgh: its great, sinuous, busy, and resonantly impressive inner-city river.

Coda

The Falkirk Wheel

In central Scotland, on the railway line between Glasgow and Edinburgh, lies the town of Falkirk. Nearby, the world's first coast-to-coast ship canal opened in 1790. This Forth and Clyde Canal allowed barges and other vessels to pass below thirty-two swing bridges, to negotiate forty-five locks, and to glide over twenty-five aqueducts between Glasgow and the start of the Forth estuary, several miles west of Edinburgh. A few decades later, in 1822, the construction of the Falkirk locks let the otherwise lock-free Union Canal join with the Forth and Clyde Canal to permit boats to sail eastwards to a point just a little southwest of Edinburgh Castle, thereby accomplishing, thanks to skilled engineering and the work of canal-digging Irish navvies (including the murderer William Burke), a voyage between Glasgow and Edinburgh.

Used intensively to transport freight, by around 1830 this city-to-city route also carried an annual total of 200,000 passengers. Horse-drawn "swiftboats" crossed the country in a little over seven hours. A few years later, the journey time was more than halved when travellers sped through Falkirk Station on the new Edinburgh and Glasgow Railway, its engines puffing smokily from city centre to city centre. As John Wilcox put it, promoting his 1842 *Guide* to this new rail line, it was "an object of great moment to facilitate the means of communication between the two cities by every means suggested by the intelligence of the age." Earlier ages, too, had sought to link western to eastern Scotland, even before Glasgow and Edinburgh existed. Since at least the second century A.D., when the Romans oversaw the construction of the Antonine Wall—a great earthen rampart and ditch running across "Caledonia" between a point on the Clyde northwest of modern Glasgow and what is now Bo'ness on the Forth, about ten miles west of Edinburgh—commentators have noted that the distance across the slim waistline of the nation at this point is small: west and east are separated, as Tacitus put it in his *Agricola,* only "angusto terrarum spatio"—"by a narrow strip of land." More than 1,700 years after the death of that Roman historian, and while the Industrial Revolution gathered formidable steam, it seemed reasonable to connect Scotland's greatest east- and west-coast cities in order to enhance what Wilcox called their "rapidly increasing intercourse."

Yet relations between Glasgow and Edinburgh seldom did run smooth. Competing canal plans led to more strife than accord. Though some Enlightenment intellectuals such as Adam Smith might savour the best of both cities, others in Edinburgh had little appetite for the eastwards expansion of Glaswegian industrial grime. Riding west from Scotland's capital in 1787, Ayrshire farmer Robert Burns crossed the still-incomplete "grand canal" and noted, near Falkirk, the vast Carron Iron Works which had opened twenty-eight years earlier, in the year of his birth. He detested the place:

We cam na here to view your warks,	*came not; works*
In hopes to be mair wise,	*more*
But only, lest we gang to hell	*go*
It may be nae surprise . . .	

Not all travellers in the era of the Industrial Revolution thought they were going to hell as they headed from Edinburgh towards Glasgow, encountering the outgrowths of mining and heavy engineering which proliferated across central Scotland—but many people must have gawped and grimaced when they saw Carron's infernal furnaces. Not far off, the Romans had long before erected at this remote limit of their ancient empire a temple to the god Terminus. Now gone, it stood for many centuries, as if proclaiming, "Thus far and no farther."

With the waning of the Industrial Revolution, the enormous ironworks near Falkirk fell into disuse—for all that today's huge petrochemical plant at nearby Grangemouth might seem its sprawling postmodern reincarnation. Severed by new roads, infilled with earth or rubbish, and overhung by low, fixed bridges, the canal network between Glasgow and Edinburgh rotted away as the twentieth century aged. Falkirk's impressive staircase of eleven locks which had joined the Forth and Clyde to the Union Canal, lowering boats from the one to the other while descending, lock after lock, more than a hundred feet over a distance of a mile, ceased to operate in 1933. In the 1960s, both canals were closed. Though people could travel by land from

Glasgow to Edinburgh in the late twentieth century, just as in the eighteenth and nineteenth centuries, no longer could anyone sail across from the west to Auld Reikie. It was as if, after the passing of Scotland's industrial dominance and the loss of the riches of the British Empire, these two famous cities were moving resolutely farther apart.

Then, at the start of the twenty-first century, something remarkable happened. Outside Falkirk, there arose one of modern Europe's cleverest structures—the world's first ever rotating boat lift. This visually arresting fusion of sculpturesque architecture and satisfyingly elegant heavy engineering was constructed to make possible again, after almost three-quarters of a century, a fully navigable waterway between Glasgow and Edinburgh. Opened by Queen Elizabeth II in 2002, the Falkirk Wheel entrances all visitors, especially those who come aboard it. From a distance, onlookers see what appear like giant, stylized heads of big-eyed birds made out of steel. On closer inspection, these turn out to be the beaked top sections of huge rotating beams that stand as high as a nine-storey building. Threaded inside the lofty eye-sockets of the bird-heads is a caisson—a large, watertight chamber. Into this sails a boat from the upper-level Union Canal. Then, gradually, one bird-head dips as if to drink; as it does so, another, counterbalancing bird-head (the bottom of the same huge beam) begins to rise from a large pool, a basin on the Forth and Clyde Canal about a hundred feet below. This rising bird-head also contains a boat-filled caisson of water. Slowly, and greatly to the glee of passengers aboard pleasure craft within the two caissons, each draws level with the other until the two pass each other in mid-air. Visitors on the vessels inside each caisson—usually barges with names such as *Archimedes*, which take tourists on short trips simply to experience the Wheel—smile with delight. Sedately, thanks to gravity and a series of eight hydraulic motors, the barge from the displaced top caisson slowly descends to the canal basin below, and the barge from the bottom caisson, raised aloft, ascends to the level of the canal above, ready to sail off along a long, hoop-topped aqueduct and through a tunnel which penetrates the almost two-thousand-year-old rampart of the Romans' Antonine Wall.

A triumph of art and monumental engineering, the Falkirk Wheel—strictly speaking, not a wheel but a rotating beam—turns on its motionless central hub. Designed by the firm of RMJM, who were also closely involved in building the Scottish Parliament, the Wheel appears, as described by its

55–59 (counterclockwise from below). This series of photographs shows the Falkirk Wheel in action, as it transports vessels between the Forth and Clyde Canal beneath, and the Union Canal above. Opened in 2002, the Falkirk Wheel is the world's first rotating boat lift.

architect, Tony Kettle (who worked out aspects of its construction using his children's Lego), "a beautiful, organic flowing thing, like the spine of a fish." Metallic, yet invoking shapes from the natural world, it reminds some spectators of a benign prehistoric creature, and appears to others like an echo of avian forms. This subtle but satisfyingly elemental wonder of the modern world is set in a vista that the 1842 railway enthusiast John Wilcox praised as "unsurpassed in the kingdom." Yet whether gazing up at the Wheel through the slanting glass roof of the visitor centre close to its foot, or looking at it from road, railway, or either canal, people nowadays are entranced less by the surrounding landscape than by this unique manmade structure. As it rotates first one way, then the other, it gives the impression that the two canals are somehow shaking hands—each extending its long, thin wrist of water as it engages in complexly greeting the other. What you see when you visit the Falkirk Wheel in twenty-first-century Lowland Scotland is something long regarded as almost impossible: a thoroughgoing, lasting, and utterly compelling handshake between Glasgow and Edinburgh.

Further Reading

List of Illustrations

Credits

Acknowledgments

Index

Further Reading

While I hope the absence of footnotes enhances the companionability of the style, I suspect some readers may wish a little guidance about sources and further reading. Where sources could be suggested elegantly within the main text, I have gestured towards them. Researching the book, I relied repeatedly on several databases, including the British Library's Nineteenth-Century British Newspapers collection (specifically for the digitally searchable *Glasgow Herald*); ECCO (Eighteenth Century Collections Online); the *Scotsman* Digital Archive; Scran; and the websites of the institutions detailed in the preceding chapters. Digital newspapers were supplemented by paper ones, especially the *Herald* and the *Scotsman*.

On the architecture of Edinburgh, I had frequent recourse to *The Buildings of Scotland: Edinburgh,* by John Gifford, Colin McWilliam, David Walker, and Christopher Wilson (Yale, 2003), as well as to such specialist studies as the second edition of A. J. Youngson's *The Making of Classical Edinburgh* (Edinburgh, 1988) and the publications of the Old Edinburgh Club, whose centenary conference was a boon to me; on the architecture of Glasgow, especially valuable were *The Buildings of Scotland: Glasgow,* by Elizabeth Williamson, Anne Riches, and Malcolm Higgs (Yale, 2005); Andor Gomme and David Walker's *Architecture of Glasgow* (revised edition, London, 1987); and Ray McKenzie's *Public Sculpture of Glasgow* (Liverpool, 2002). Also useful were the writings of James Macaulay, Robert Macleod, and Gavin Stamp.

On the social history of both cities within larger Scottish contexts, the works of T. M. Devine, Leah Leneman, and T. C. Smout were of great help. The best modern one-volume chronicles of each city are Michael Fry's *Edinburgh: A History of the City* (London, 2009) and Irene Maver's *Glasgow* (Edinburgh, 2000), though I have an indebtedness to and a soft spot for the work of the remarkable scholar David Daiches, one of very few people who have authored a book on Glasgow in addition to a book on Edinburgh. As I know to my gain, Hamish Whyte has edited or co-edited the best Glasgow anthologies, including *Noise and Smoky Breath* (Glasgow, 1983), *Mungo's*

Tongues (Edinburgh, 1993), and (with Simon Berry) *Glasgow Observed* (Edinburgh, 1987), though *A Glasgow Keek Show* (Glasgow, 1981), edited by the splendid Glaswegian social historian Frank Worsdall, is also very lively. Edinburgh has been less well served by modern anthologists (something I would like to remedy one day), so the best volume remains the very old *In Praise of Edinburgh,* edited by Rosaline Masson (London, 1912), followed by the largely topographic prose collected by David Daiches in *Edinburgh: A Travellers' Companion* (London, 1986), the slim selection of verse in Lizzie MacGregor's *Luckenbooth* (Edinburgh, 2007), and the all-too-short snippets in Ralph Lownie's *Auld Reekie* (Edinburgh, 2004). On the other hand, whereas Glasgow lacks book-length literary guides, Edinburgh boasts several: Trevor Royle's *Precipitous City* (Edinburgh, 1980) has been followed by the more recent A-to-Z guides by Allan Foster (2005) and Andrew Lownie (2005).

As mentioned in my main text, there are thousands of books about each of these two cities, many written by life-long devotees of one or the other, such as the nineteenth-century polymath Robert Chambers in Edinburgh and the twentieth-century journalist Jack House in Glasgow. Two that approach from unusual angles are Chiang Yee's 1948 account, *The Silent Traveller in Edinburgh,* and Carol Craig's provocative 2010 book *The Tears That Made the Clyde: Well-Being in Glasgow.* Classic accounts such as those by R. L. Stevenson and Daniel Defoe, or prose works such as novels by George Blake, Alasdair Gray, and James Kelman (Glasgow) or by Candia McWilliam, Walter Scott, and Muriel Spark (Edinburgh), have been mentioned in the preceding chapters. Rather than attempting to catalogue innumerable worthwhile volumes devoted to Glasgow or to Edinburgh, I shall conclude by mentioning just half a dozen books—three associated with Glasgow, three with Edinburgh—which I found particularly useful; readers in search of more specialist materials may find these volumes rewarding for insights into people from one city or the other. The books in question are the 1858 account of Glasgow, *Midnight Scenes and Social Photographs: Being Sketches of Life in the Streets, Wynds, and Dens of the City,* by "Shadow" (Alexander Brown), reprinted in Glasgow in 1976; T. J. Honeyman's autobiography *Art and Audacity* (London, 1971); and Eleanor Gordon and Gwyneth Nair's *Murder and Morality in Victorian Britain: The Story of Madeleine Smith* (Manchester, 2009). The three linked to Edinburgh are Michael F. Graham's academic study *The Blasphemies of Thomas Aikenhead: Boundaries of Belief on the Eve of the Enlightenment* (Edinburgh, 2008); *Eduardo Paolozzi: Writings and Interviews,* edited by Robin Spencer (Oxford, 2000); and Lisa Rosner's detailed account of the crimes of Burke and Hare, *The Anatomy Murders* (Philadelphia, 2010).

List of Illustrations

1. Glasgow viewed from the south, 1695 — 8
2. Edinburgh pictured from the north, 1695 — 11
3. Skyline of Edinburgh, seen from Princes Street — 18
4. The cupola of Glasgow's Holmwood House — 25
5. Edinburgh Castle, above Princes Street Gardens — 44
6. Mons Meg, one of the world's oldest large cannons — 47
7. The Camera Obscura seen from the north — 57
8. View of the Royal Mile looking eastward — 61
9. The interior of St. Giles, 1948 — 62
10. Old lodging houses in the Cowgate, 1912 — 67
11. The Museum of Edinburgh, with Huntly House — 77
12. Bronze statue of the poet Robert Fergusson — 83
13. The Scottish Poetry Library — 87
14. The Royal Palace of Holyroodhouse — 92
15. The Scottish Parliament at Holyrood — 95
16. The Scott Monument, in Princes Street Gardens — 103
17. Masons carving the Scott Monument, 1840s — 106
18. The National Gallery and the Royal Scottish Academy — 112
19. Foyer of the Scottish National Portrait Gallery — 116
20. Charlotte Square, with the Albert Memorial — 122
21. Sculpture of Isaac Newton, by Eduardo Paolozzi — 129
22. Landform by Charles Jencks and Scottish National Gallery of Modern Art — 131
23. Calton Hill, with National Monument — 134
24. The Royal Botanic Garden at Inverleith — 142
25. The port of Leith, 1829 — 147
26. Old College quadrangle, Edinburgh University — 153
27. Dr. Robert Knox, 1840s — 160
28. Greyfriars Kirkyard — 166
29. The National Museum of Scotland — 173
30. George Square, with the City Chambers — 180

31. John Maclean, icon of "Red Clydeside," 1918   184

32. David Kirkwood and police, George Square, 1919   185

33. Glasgow Cathedral, 1935   189

34. Provand's Lordship, the oldest house in Glasgow   193

35. The Victorian gates to the Necropolis   194

36. The Tolbooth Steeple, at Glasgow Cross   199

37. The Doulton Fountain and the People's Palace   205

38. A Gorbals back lane, 1948   215

39. The Citizens Theatre, in the heart of the Gorbals   217

40. The Gallery of Modern Art, Queen Street   221

41. The lower part of Buchanan Street   223

42. The Argyle Arcade, Scotland's oldest covered mall   226

43. Sauchiehall Street, Glasgow   235

44. Charles Rennie Mackintosh's Glasgow School of Art   246

45. Tenement photograph by Thomas Annan, 1868   251

46. Historic taverns, by Jessie M. King, 1911   257

47. The Glasgow Art Gallery and Museum   263

48. The main building of Glasgow University   271

49. The Kibble Palace, in Glasgow's Botanic Gardens   278

50. The Smith family home, Blythswood Square   281

51. Holmwood House, designed by Alexander Thomson   288

52. The River Clyde in 1955   299

53. The Finnieston Crane, on the River Clyde   303

54. The Riverside Museum, designed by Zaha Hadid   307

55–59. The Falkirk Wheel in action   314–315

Credits

1. Harvard College Library, Widener Library, Br 9118.74 PF.
2. Harvard College Library, Widener Library, Br 9118.74 PF.
3–4. Clifford Boehmer / Harvard University Press.
5. John Bethell / The Bridgeman Art Library.
6–8. Clifford Boehmer / Harvard University Press.
9. Time & Life Pictures / Getty Images.
10. From Robert Chambers, *Traditions of Edinburgh* (London: W. & R. Chambers, 1912), p. 240.
11–13. Clifford Boehmer / Harvard University Press.
14. Getty Images.
15–16. Clifford Boehmer / Harvard University Press.
17. With kind permission of the University of Edinburgh / The Bridgeman Art Library.
18–24. Clifford Boehmer / Harvard University Press.
25. Private Collection / The Stapleton Collection / The Bridgeman Art Library.
26. Clifford Boehmer / Harvard University Press.
27. With kind permission of the University of Edinburgh / The Bridgeman Art Library.
28–30. Clifford Boehmer / Harvard University Press.
31. Getty Images.
32. Harvard Depository P 229.10 F v. 1555 (1919).
33. Getty Images.
34–37. Clifford Boehmer / Harvard University Press.
38. Getty Images.
39–44. Clifford Boehmer / Harvard University Press.
45. Harvard Art Museums / Fogg Museum, Purchased through the generosity of Melvin R. Seiden, P1985.9.11. Photo: Imaging Department, copyright © President and Fellows of Harvard College.
46. From Jessie M. King, *The City of the West: A Book of Drawings* (Edinburgh: T. N. Foulis, 1911), xx.
47. Harvard Art Museums / Fogg Museum, Purchased through the generosity

of Melvin R. Seiden, P1982.363.7. Photo: Imaging Department, copyright ©
President and Fellows of Harvard College.

48–51. Clifford Boehmer/Harvard University Press.

52. Copyright © Culture and Sport Glasgow (Museums)/The Bridgeman Art
Library.

53–59. Clifford Boehmer/Harvard University Press.

Acknowledgments

Alice Crawford sustained me with love and shrewd advice throughout this project, as did our teenage children, Lewis and Blyth. This was true especially when I smashed up my right hand and arm during the last stages—an injury attributable neither to Glasgow nor to Edinburgh. The first section of this book and all the Edinburgh material benefited from being read and commented on by Sara Lodge, whose astute, shaping intelligence and incisive phrasing were gifts to the volume; as a principled Edinburgher, however, she would not be cajoled into reading the chapters on Glasgow. My trusted Glaswegian advisor, Kenneth Dunn, supplied deft advice, provided kind hospitality, and tramped across the city with me more than once as I checked inscriptions on statues; later, David Kinloch commented with characteristic humour and shrewdness on the Glasgow material, looking it over with his painterly poet's eye. Thanks also to the keen-eyed photographer Norman McBeath for several extended lunches, for a joint foray into the 2011 Edinburgh Art Festival, and for making sure I saw the broken nose of the goddess at the Temple of Hygeia. Over the generations, I owe particular debts to my parents, Nelson and Betty Crawford, who taught me about Glasgow with love and pride; and to Maimie Hamilton, with whom I spent wonderful childhood holidays in Edinburgh: nothing in that twenty-first-century city made quite the same impression on me as seeing, wholly tarnished but improbably still extant by the outer door of her ground-floor tenement flat in Comiston Gardens, the name "Hamilton" on my late Aunt Maimie's long disused brass bell.

I would like to acknowledge the staff of all the institutions mentioned in this book. I shall not list those again here, but wish to make special mention of some of the libraries whose resources—human, in the form of helpful librarians and archivists, as well as inanimate, in the form of books, film, manuscripts, and photographs—have contributed to my writing. These include the Beinecke Library, Yale University; the Bodleian Library, Oxford University; Birmingham Public Library; Edinburgh City Library; Edinburgh University Library; Glasgow University Library; Harvard University Library;

the Library of Congress; the Mitchell Library, Glasgow; the National Library of Scotland; St. Andrews University Library; and the Scottish Poetry Library.

Material from "Ms. of Monte Cassino, Written to Paul the Deacon at Monte Cassino," in the 1929 edition of *Mediæval Latin Lyrics,* translated by Helen Waddell, appears in Chapter 4 by kind permission of Louise Anson at Helen Waddell's Estate.

Thanks to Susan Wallace Boehmer at Harvard University Press, who first sounded me out about the idea which became this book; to Kathleen McDermott, who became my cordial editor at the Press; to the typescript's three anonymous peer-reviewers; to Maria Ascher, whose expertise helped me craft the copyedited typescript; to Cliff Boehmer for the specially taken photographs; to Isabelle Lewis, who drew the maps; to the resourceful picture researcher at Harvard, Andrew Kinney; and to my always energetic agent, David Godwin of David Godwin Associates, as well as to his colleague in London, Anna Watkins.

Index

Abbeyhill, 71, 74
Abbotsford, 58
Abercrombie Street Burial Ground, 207
Aberdeen University, 151
Academy of St. Luke, 110
Academy of the Fine Arts, 242
Acheson, Sir Archibald, 75
Adam, Robert, 51, 118, 120–122, 125, 140, 152, 189
Adam, Robert Moyes, 143
Adam, William, 94
Adamson, Robert, 105, 106, 117, 135–136, 155, 160, 161, 168
Advocates' Library, 59, 64–65
Aikenhead, Thomas, 175, 176
Akenside, Mark, 296
Alan, Alexander, 10, 17
Alasdair, Alasdair mac Mhaighstir, 91
Albert, Prince, 122, 181
Albert Memorial, 122, 123–124
Aldred, Guy, 300
Alesius. *See* Alan, Alexander
Alston, Charles, 140
America, 15, 19, 32, 65–66, 147, 179, 214, 217, 218, 219–220, 264, 275, 276
American Civil War, 80
American War of Independence, 4, 19, 219–220
Anderson, Robert Rowand, 115, 116
Anderson's College, 256, 277
Annan, Thomas, 136, 220, 236, 251, 252, 260, 265
Annand, David, 82, 83
Anniesland, 224
Ann Street, 125
Antelope, 14
Anthony, John, 143

Antonine Wall, 311, 313
Arandora Star, 149
Arbuckle, James, 218, 296–297
Argyle Arcade, 225–226, 229
Argyle car, 309
Argyle Square, 119
Argyle Street, 225, 231
Arnot, Hugo, 9, 20, 78
Arrol Company, 301
Arthur, T. G., 291
Arthur's Seat, 18, 88, 93, 94, 95, 155, 175
Ashton Lane, 274
Assembly Halls, 57–58, 97
Athens, 27–28, 113, 133, 134, 135
Atkinson, Eleanor, 166–167
Audubon, John J., 156
Auld Reikie (nickname), 17
Austen, Jane, 59, 201
Australia, 201, 204, 262
Aye Write Festival, 35

Baird, John Logie, 239, 279, 310
Bakunin House, 300
Balfour, A. J., 290
Balfour, James, 139, 140
Ballantyne (publishers), 171
Ballantyne, R. M., 125
Balliol Street, 300
Balmoral Hotel, 101, 109
Bank of Scotland, 5, 7, 39, 103, 186
Bannockburn, 233
Barbados, 198
Barker, Robert, 3
Barony Kirk, 189
Barrie, J. M., 117
Bartholomew (cartographers), 171
Bath Street, 286

BBC, 86, 239, 306

BBC Scottish Symphony Orchestra, 261

Beattie, Rev. Alexander Ogilvie, 191

Belford Road, 128

Belgrave Mews, 126

Bell, Charles, 159, 160

Bell, Henry, 302

Bell, Joseph, 156, 163–164

Bellahouston Park, 266

Bellany, John, 130

Beresford Building, 231

Bernstein, Marion, 25

Berry, Simon, 250

Bilsland, William, 206

Bissell, George E., 138

Black, Ian, 40

Black, Joseph, 85, 157, 165, 200

Blackfriars Church, 12, 268

Blackie, Walter, 247

Blackmore, Stephen, 143

Blackstone Chair, 272

Blackwood, William, 138, 171

Blackwood's Edinburgh Magazine, 6, 124, 138

Blair, Hugh, 60, 85, 110, 119, 157

Blair, Tony, 97

Blake, George, 302–303, 304

Blake, William, 128

Blanc, Jean Hippolyte, 45–46, 172

Blantyre, 277

"Bloody Friday," 185

Blythswood New Town, 284

Blythswood Square, 280, 281, 283, 284

Blythswood Street, 280

Borrow, George, 44

Boswell, James, 65, 270

Botanical Society of Edinburgh, 140

Botanic Gardens. *See* Royal Botanic Garden Edinburgh

Botanic Gardens (Glasgow), 183, 233, 274–279

Bothwell, Earl of, 11, 90

Bothwell Street, 279, 284

Bough, Sam, 298

Bowles, Caroline, 279

Braidwood, Thomas, 169

Brewster, Patrick, 138

Bridie, James, 216

Briggait Steeple, 196

Bright, Joseph, 80

Britannia, 146, 147

British Council, 34

British Library, 128

British Sociological Society, 55

Brodie, Jean (sister of the Deacon), 79

Brodie, Deacon William, 78–79, 166

Brodie, William (sculptor), 166

Broomielaw, 298, 300, 310

Broughton Street, 127

Brown, Gordon, 152

Brown, Jenny, 124

Brown, Dr. John, 165, 167

Brown Square, 119

Bruce, King Robert the, 45

Bruntsfield Place, 69

Buccleuch Street, 248, 253

Buchan, John, 212, 213

Buchanan, Andrew, 224

Buchanan, George, 60, 89, 90, 105, 165, 166, 217

Buchanan Galleries, 224

Buchanan Street, 218, 223–230, 231, 234, 236, 237, 241, 280, 283

Buckham, Alfred G., 114

Burdett-Coutts, Angela Georgina, 165

Burke, William, 85, 120, 159–164, 168, 169, 175, 176, 311

Burn, William, 129, 131

Burnbank Terrace, 300

Burnet, Sir John James, 231

Burns, Robert, 19, 28, 56, 59, 66, 70, 78, 79, 81–82, 84, 85, 96, 113, 116, 123, 134, 137, 155, 166, 171, 173, 187, 202, 207–208, 211, 255, 256, 258, 285, 312

Burrell, Mary, 291

Burrell, Sir William, 265, 289–294, 295

Burrell Collection, 265, 266, 291–294

Bute House, 121

Byres Road, 274
Byrne, John, 206
Byron, Lord, 59, 117

Cadell, Francis Campbell Boileau, 129
Ca' d'Oro Building, 284
Caledonian Railway Company, 29
Caledonia Road Kirk, 287
Calton (Glasgow), 205, 207, 208
Calton Hill, 3, 51–53, 94, 95, 97, 101, 106, 113, 118, 121, 131, 133–138, 144–145
Calton Jail, 162
Calvin, John, 14, 227
Cambuslang, 275
Camden, William, 12
Camera Obscura, 50–58
Cameron, May, 171
Campbell, Colin, 180–181, 262
Campbell, John, 198
Campbell, Margaret, 162
Campbell, Stephen, 130–131
Campbell, Thomas, 23
Canada, 75, 107, 179, 204, 212
Candlemaker Row, 165
Canmore, King Malcolm, 49
Canongate, 74–99, 157, 163
Canongate Kirk and Kirkyard, 80–83
Canongate Tolbooth, 75
Canonmills, 125
Cape Club, 84
Carfrae, James, 79
Carfrae, John, 79
Carfrae, Mrs., 79, 84
Caribbean, 14–15, 19, 20, 51, 139, 179, 198, 200, 219, 222, 275
Carlaw, David, 214
Carlyle, Alexander, 21
Carlyle, Jane Welsh, 282
Carlyle, Thomas, 117, 267
Carnegie, Andrew, 255
Carrick, Alexander, 45
Carron Iron Works, 312
Carstares, William, 156

Castle Esplanade, 44, 50
Castlehill, 44, 50, 53, 58, 74, 84, 174
Castlehill School, 68
Castle Rock, 43, 44, 49, 50, 102
Castle Street (Edinburgh), 119
Castle Street (Glasgow), 193
Cathedral Square, 201
Cathedral Street, 187
Cathkin Park, 29
Caxton, William, 228
Celtic Connections, 35
Celtic Football Club, 29–30
Central Hotel, 310
Centre for Contemporary Arts, 241
Chadwick, Edwin, 25
Chambers, Robert, 24, 67, 125, 161, 170–172
Chambers, William, 60, 82, 145, 148, 165, 170
Chambers's Edinburgh Journal, 6, 170, 171, 281
Chambers Street, 151, 172–175
Charing Cross, 231, 233, 237, 254, 259, 267, 300
Charing Cross Mansions, 231
Charles I, King, 59, 174
Charles II, King, 59
Charles, Prince (Charles Edward Stuart), 91–92, 115, 117, 207, 220
Charles, Prince (contemporary), 306
Charles Rennie Mackintosh Society, 247
Charlotte Square, 104, 120–125
Chartists, 211
Chinese culture, 39, 141, 142, 228, 292, 293
Chipperfield, David, 306
Chomet, Sylvain, 35
Chopin, Frédéric, 125
Christison, Robert, 163, 164, 281
Church of Scotland, 57–58, 72, 97
Cinemas, 234, 238, 239–241
Citizens Theatre, 216, 217
Clapperton, Thomas J., 45
Clerk, Sir John, 175
Clyde Arc, 301
Clyde Auditorium, 305

Clydebank Blitz, 264–265
Clyde, Firth and River, 15, 16, 19, 25, 37, 195, 196, 198, 209, 218, 262, 290, 295–310
Clyde Model Dockyard, 229
Clyde Navigation Trust, 300, 302, 303
Clydesdale, Ronnie, 274
Clyde Shipbuilders Association, 301
Clyde Valley, 295–296
Clyde Walkway, 300
Coburn, Alvin Langdon, 170
Cochrane, Andrew, 7, 218, 219
Cochrane Street, 216
Cockburn, Lord Henry, 51–52, 63, 122–123, 126, 133, 166
Colonies, the (Edinburgh), 125
Colvin, Calum, 117, 131
Comet, 302
Commonwealth Games, 39, 306, 309
Connolly, Billy, 206, 214, 305
Conroy, Stephen, 131
Conservative Party, 97
Constable (publishers), 171
Cooper, James Fenimore, 104
Copland and Lye, 233
Corstorphine Hill, 39
Cosmo Cinema, 240–241
Cotton, 22, 210
Covenanters, 64, 76, 169–170
Cowgate, 66, 67, 86
Craig, Agnes. *See* McLehose, Agnes
Craig, James, 51, 105, 118–120, 121, 135, 165, 166
Craigen, Jessie, 203
Cranston, Catherine, 236–237
Cranston's Tea Rooms, 228, 236–237, 239, 247
Crawford, Robert, 206
Crawfurd, Helen, 183
Creech, William, 66, 78
Crichton's Close, 86, 87
Crown Street, 210, 213, 252–253
Crozier, William, 113
Cullen, William, 157
Culloden, 92
Cunninghame, William, 219, 220, 221, 227

Currie, Ken, 131, 204–205
Cursiter, Stanley, 101
Curtis, Eric W., 275
Custom House Quay, 300

Daguerre, Louis, 94
Daiches, David, 4
Dale, David, 296
Dalí, Salvador, 266
Dalrymple, David (Lord Hailes), 17
Daniel Stewart's and Melville College, 126
Darien, 96, 217
Darnley, Henry Lord, 48, 89–90, 152, 153, 163
Darwin, Charles, 55, 59, 140–141, 143, 147, 152–156, 158, 159, 160, 164, 168, 170, 270
Darwin, Erasmus, 270
David I, King, 13, 88
Davidson, Anna, 253
Dean Bridge, 125–126
Dean Cemetery, 126
Dean Gallery, 111, 126–128
Dean Orphanage, 126
Dean Village, 126
Defoe, Daniel, 7, 197, 217, 248, 297
Degas, Edgar, 111, 291, 293
Deguy, Michel, 86
Denholm, James, 219
Dennistoun, 191
Denny shipyard, 302
De Quincey, Thomas, 285, 287
Derain, André, 130, 266
Detroit, 38, 302
Devolution, 97–99
Dewar, Donald, 98, 224
De Wet, Jacob, 93
Diana, Princess of Wales, 146, 306
Din Eidyn, 9, 43
Disraeli, Benjamin, 277
Disruption (1843), 135–136
Divan, William, 210
Dolly the Sheep, 128, 158
Donaldson, James, 169

Donaldson's School, 169

Dooley, Arthur, 300

Douglas, David, 276, 278–279

Douglas, Gavin, 49

Douglas, Sir William Fettes, 114

Doulton, Sir Henry, 204

Doulton Fountain, 204–205

Downie, David, 48–49

Doyle, Arthur Conan, 66, 156, 164, 259

Drummond, Flora, 80

Drummond, Provost George, 119–120, 156

Drummond Street, 159

Dublin, 16, 186

Duffy, Carol Ann, 124

Duke Street, 183, 309

Dumbarton, 302, 309

Dunbar, Gavin, 13

Dunbar's Close, 81

Dunn, Douglas, 97

Dyer, Henry, 256–258

Dynamic Earth, 74, 88

Eardley, Joan, 130, 189–190

Ebsworth, Joseph Woodfall, 105

Edinburgh Calotype Club, 136

Edinburgh Castle, 17, 27, 43–50, 112, 136, 311

Edinburgh City Art Centre, 105, 111, 114

Edinburgh City Chambers, 37, 74

Edinburgh College of Art, 28, 45, 127, 143

Edinburgh Cross, 174

Edinburgh Dungeon, 70

Edinburgh Festival Fringe, 34

Edinburgh High School, 159

Edinburgh International Book Festival, 122, 123–124

Edinburgh International Festival, 34, 63, 86

Edinburgh Military Tattoo, 44–45

Edinburgh Miscellany, 5–6

Edinburgh Napier University, 151

Edinburgh Park, 138

Edinburgh Review, 6, 63, 124, 126, 211

Edinburgh Royal Infirmary, 156

Edinburgh Town Council, 52, 158

Edinburgh University, 58, 78, 121, 127, 143, 151–158, 164, 172, 175

Edinburgh Zoo, 39

Edmonston, John, 156

Eglinton Street, 252

Egyptian Halls, 286

Eisenhower, Dwight, 108

Elgin, Lord, 133

El Greco, 111, 113, 294

Eliot, George, 124, 282

Eliot, T. S., 63

Elizabeth I, Queen, 5, 48, 90, 196

Elizabeth II, Queen, 92, 94, 97, 146, 293, 313

Elliot, Gilbert (Lord Minto), 15, 16, 17, 119

Emancipation Monument, 138

Encyclopaedia Britannica, 6, 12, 85

Enlightenment, 12, 85, 96, 134–135, 140, 157, 196, 268

Ewing, Dr. Winifred, 97

Fairfield shipyard, 302

Fair Intellectual Club, 5–6

Falkirk, 311, 312

Falkirk Wheel, 311–316

Ferguson, Adam, 85

Fergusson, John Duncan, 129

Fergusson, Robert, 18, 19, 46–47, 60, 81–84, 85, 86, 93, 124, 144, 169

Fettes College, 97

Fife, 100, 187

Findlay, John Ritchie, 114

Finlay, Ian Hamilton, 106–107, 310

Finnieston, 301

Finnieston Crane, 301, 302–303, 305, 306, 309

Fir Park, 190, 192

Fitzroy Place, 275

Flaxman, John, 179

Fleischer, Philipp, 233

Fleming, Alexander, 172

Fleming, Marjorie, 101

Flodden, 10, 88, 107

Flodden Wall, 10, 15

Floral Clock, 108, 109

Forrest, George, 141
Forsyth, Robert, 20, 21, 28
Forth, Firth and River, 10, 44, 61, 100, 124, 141, 143
Forth and Clyde Canal, 21, 219, 311, 312, 313, 314
Forth Bridges, 29, 127, 141
Foster, Sir Norman, 305
Foulis, Robert and Andrew, 242, 269
Fowke, Francis, 172, 173
France and French culture, 45, 54, 86, 88–89, 93, 147, 196, 247
Frank, Richard, 197
Franklin, Benjamin, 85, 140
Fraser, Malcolm, 86, 87
Frasers (department store), 228
Frazer, Daniel, 224–228
Frazer, Sir James George, 228
Free Church of Scotland, 58, 239, 267
French, Annie, 234
Fry, Michael, 37, 38
Fyffe, Will, 35

Gainsborough, Thomas, 113
Galloway, Janice, 36
Gallowgate, 196
Gardieloo, 17
Gardner's Warehouse, 284
Gasser, Hans, 270
Gasson, Barry, 293
Gear, William, 130
Geddes, Jenny, 59, 60
Geddes, Patrick, 53–56, 110
Geikie, Walter, 163, 168–169
George III, King, 201
George IV, King, 93
George IV Bridge (Edinburgh), 59, 66, 158, 165
George IV Railway Bridge (Glasgow), 310
George Heriot's School, 166, 167–168
George Square (Edinburgh), 38, 119
George Square (Glasgow), 179–187, 190, 200, 216, 256, 272, 277

George Street, 109
Georgian House, the, 123
Gibson, James, 217
Gibson, John, 15, 218
Gibson, Walter, 217
Gilchrist, Marion, 259
Gillies, Sir William, 111, 130
Gilmorehill, 267, 268, 271, 272, 273
Gilmour, Allan, 192
Gladstone, William Ewart, 187, 227, 273, 277
Glasgay Festival, 35
Glasgow Anarchist Group, 300
Glasgow Architectural Society, 286
"Glasgow Boys," 32–33, 292
Glasgow Bridge, 298, 300
Glasgow Caledonian University, 270
Glasgow Cathedral, 12, 13–14, 104, 181, 187–189, 192, 193, 195, 196, 214, 242, 262, 268
Glasgow Central Mosque, 216
Glasgow Central Station, 284
Glasgow Chamber of Commerce, 4, 219
Glasgow City Art Gallery. *See* Kelvingrove
Glasgow City Chambers, 33, 180, 181–186, 207, 272, 290
Glasgow City Council, 181
Glasgow City Heliport, 307
Glasgow City Improvements Trust, 252
Glasgow Communist Group, 300
Glasgow Cross, 195, 196, 197, 198, 199, 200, 201, 209, 257
Glasgow Empire Theatre, 239
Glasgow Film Society, 240
Glasgow Film Theatre, 240–241
Glasgow Gallery of Modern Art, 220–221, 227, 266
Glasgow Garden Festival, 305, 306
Glasgow Green, 196, 201, 202–207, 208, 209, 232, 239, 296–297, 298
Glasgow Herald. See Herald (Glasgow)
Glasgow International Exhibition (1888), 32, 233, 261–262
Glasgow International Exhibition (1901), 264
Glasgow Looking Glass, 258, 275–276

Glasgow Magazine, 209

Glasgow Merchants' House, 190, 193, 194, 196

Glasgow Necropolis, 189, 190–194, 242, 275

Glasgow Royal Concert Hall, 224, 230

Glasgow School of Art, 33, 130, 236, 241, 242–247, 253, 265

Glasgow Science Centre, 37, 305, 306

Glasgow Ship Bank, 219

Glasgow Society of Lady Artists, 234, 236

Glasgow Style, 236

Glasgow Tower, 305–306

Glasgow University, 12, 13, 151, 198–200, 222, 240, 242, 247, 256, 264, 267–274, 276, 286

Glasgow University Library, 274

Glasgow Women's Library, 259–260

Glasser, Ralph, 213

Glassford, Christian, 275

Glassford, Henry, 275

Glassford, John, 219–222, 275

Glassford, Rebecca, 219

Glassford Street, 187, 196, 216, 220, 225

Glenlee, 306–307, 309–310

Glover, William, 52

Gododdin, 43, 88

Golborne, John, 297

Goose Pie, the, 109

Gorbals, 183, 209–217, 252–253, 298

Gorbals Baronial Halls, 211

Gorbals Die-Hards, 212, 253

Gorbals Street, 216, 252

Gordon, Douglas, 131

Gordon, Frances, 237

Gordon Street, 225, 227, 284

Gormley, Anthony, 132

Govan, 220, 301, 302, 304, 310

Govan Bar Iron Works, 211

Govan Ferry, 307, 310

Govanhill, 252

Govan Old Parish Church, 310

Govan Town Hall, 306

Graham, Robert, 140–141

Graham, Thomas, 181

Grant, Elizabeth, 122

Grant, Robert, 155, 159

Granville Street, 259

Grassmarket, 78, 174

Gray, Alasdair, 36, 37, 258, 259, 271, 274

Gray, John, 165

Gray, John Miller, 115

Great Western Road, 274, 276, 279, 287, 300

Great Western Terrace, 252, 276, 287, 290, 293

Grecian Chambers, 241

Greenock, 15, 198, 264, 302, 303

Greville, Robert, 141

Greyfriars Bobby, 165–167

Greyfriars Kirkyard, 10, 136, 140, 164–170

Grierson, John, 240–241, 301

Grigor, Murray, 109

Grimshaw, John Atkinson, 298

Grosvenor Terrace, 276

Gutenberg, Johannes, 228

Hadid, Zaha, 301, 306, 307

Haig, Field Marshal Douglas, 123

Haldane's Academy, 242

Hamilton, James Lord, 268

Hamilton, Margaret, 75

Hamilton, Thomas, 126, 133, 134

Hampden Park, 30

Hardie, Gwen, 131

Hardy, Bert, 215

Hare, William, 85, 120, 159–164, 168, 175, 176

Harris, Jane, 283

Harriston, William, 22

Hart, W. D., 53

Havergal, Giles, 216

Hawthorne, Nathaniel, 228, 282

Hearst, William Randolph, 294

Heart of Midlothian Football Club, 30

Helensburgh, 247, 280, 310

Hemingway, Ernest, 300

Henderson, D. and W., 308

Henderson, Robert, 53

Hengler's Grand Cirque, 238

Henley, W. E., 79

Henry VIII, King, 88

Henry, George, 33

Herald (Glasgow), 4, 33, 181, 182, 202, 211, 223, 224, 228, 243, 256, 286

Heriot, George, 167

Heriot Watt University, 151

Hibernian Football Club, 30

Higgs, Peter, 157

High Court (Edinburgh), 59, 281, 282

High School Yards, 84, 158

High Street (Edinburgh), 58–73, 74, 84, 164, 168, 174

High Street (Glasgow), 196, 197, 200, 201, 249, 250–251, 257, 268, 270

Hill, David Octavius, 105, 106, 111, 117, 126, 135–136, 155, 160, 161, 168

Hill House, 247

Hillman Imp, 309

Hirst, Damien, 130

Hogg, James, 79, 164, 175–176

Hole, William Brassey, 115–116

Holmwood House, 288–289

Holy Cross Academy, 148

Holyrood Abbey, 13, 50, 74, 88, 92–93, 94

Holyroodhouse, Palace of, 74, 87–94, 139, 140

Holyrood Park, 88

Holyrood Road, 86

Holy Trinity Church, 126

Home, John, 85, 91

Honeyman, Tom, 265–266, 267, 293

Hooker, William Jackson, 276

Hope, John, 140, 142, 143

Hopkirk, Thomas, 275–276, 298

Hornell, Edward A., 33

Howe Street, 70

Howson, Peter, 131

Hughes, Edith Burnet, 200

Humanity Classroom, 272

Hume, David, 12, 17, 65, 85, 117, 134, 140, 152, 157, 269

Hume, Joseph, 137

Hunter, David, 110

Hunter, Leslie, 129

Hunter, William, 270

Hunterian Art Gallery, 247, 274

Hunterian Museum, 270

Huntly House, 75–76

Hunyman, Alexander, 60

Hutcheson, Francis, 6, 268

Hutcheson, George and Thomas, 190

Hutchesons' Grammar School, 190, 212

Hutchesons' Hospital, 190

Hutchesontown, 212

Hutton, James, 88, 110, 157

Huxley, T. H., 54

Hydro Arena, 309

Ibárruri, Dolores, 300

Ibrox Stadium, 30

Immigration, 30, 147, 210, 211, 214, 259

Independent Labour Party, 185

India Place, 125

Inglis, A. and J., 307

Inglis, John, 282

Ingram, Archibald, 219

Ingram Street, 216, 229, 242, 255

Inverleith, 138–143

Inverleith House, 139

Inverleith Terrace, 68

Irish culture, 30, 172, 179, 201, 210, 211, 227

Italian culture, 147–150, 211, 309

Islamic culture, 216, 240

Jacobites, 64, 91–92

Jacquio, Ponce, 117

Jamaica, 198, 200, 207, 262

Jamaica Bridge, 310

Jamaica Street, 200, 217, 284

James III, King, 10, 100

James IV, King, 88

James V, King, 88

James VI, King, 5, 12, 48, 49, 89, 90, 91, 96, 167, 196

James VII, 46, 81

James, Henry, 283

Jameson, Robert, 155, 159

Jamieson, Mary, 210

Japanese culture, 32, 33, 242, 245, 256–258, 264

Jeffrey, Francis, 63, 126

Jencks, Charles, 131, 132

Jenners, 102

Jewish culture, 191, 211, 213, 240, 241, 259, 267

John Knox Free Church, 211

John Knox's House, 72, 75, 76

Johns Hopkins University, 273

Johnson, Samuel, 169, 270

Johnston, Arthur, 8, 43, 144, 195, 196, 296

Kames, Lord, 31

Kay, Arthur, 291

Kay, Jackie, 138

Kay, John, 15, 49

Keith, Thomas, 170

Kelman, James, 36, 258, 259

Kelvin, Lord, 262, 267, 272–273

Kelvingrove, 33, 232, 261–266, 292, 293

Kelvingrove Park, 254, 261, 263–264, 266–267

Kelvin Hall, 267

Kelvin River, 261, 264, 270, 276, 307

Kelvin Way, 267, 274

Kemp, George Meikle, 103–104

Kennedy, A. L., 36

Kettle, Tony, 316

Kibble, John, 277, 278

Kibble Palace, 233, 277–278

King, Elspeth, 204

King, Jessie M., 236, 258

Kingston Bridge, 37

Kirk, Charles J., 299

Kirkcaldy, 130, 269

Kirkcaldy, Sir William, 48

Kirklee Road, 278

Kirklee Terrace, 252

Kirkwood, David, 185

Knox, John (artist), 298

Knox, John (Reformer), 48, 58, 60, 63, 89, 190–191, 195

Knox, Robert, 136, 159–164

Kokoschka, Oskar, 130, 240

Kuppner, Frank, 258–259

Labour Party, 38, 97

Lady Stair's Close, 56, 84

Laing, Samuel, 52

Lamarck, Jean Baptiste, 155

Lamb's House, 144

Lamont, John, 123

Lancefield Quay, 302

L'Angelier, Pierre Emile, 279–282

Langside, 195

Lavery, John, 32, 183, 291

Law Courts (Edinburgh), 58–59

Lawnmarket, 74, 78

Lean, David, 283

Lee, Chiang, 141–142

Lee, Corlinda, 192

Leith, 10, 15, 20, 89, 127, 128, 136, 143–149

Leith Fort, 118

Leith School of Art, 147

Leith Walk, 145–146, 148

Lennon, John, 305

Leopold Place, 145

Lethaby, W. R., 244–245

Lettice, John, 100

Levi, Joseph, 191

Liberal Democrat Party, 97, 227, 239

Liddell, Faith, 124

Lincoln, Abraham, 80, 138, 207

Linnaeus, 139, 140

Linwood, 309

Lipton, Sir Thomas, 214

Lister, Joseph, 156, 267

Little, Clement, 152

Livingstone, David, 59, 102, 126, 277

Lochhead, Liz, 259

Loch Lomond, 15

Locke, John, 175

Lockerbie, Catherine, 124

Lockhart, George, 64

Lodge, Sara, 107

London, 15, 25, 54, 91, 127, 172, 292
Long, H. Kingsley, 212
Lonsdale, Henry, 161
Lorimer, Sir Robert, 50, 60
Luckenbooths, 60
Lutyens, Edwin, 236
Lynch, Benny, 214

MacAlpin dynasty, 10
Macarthur, Mary, 24
MacCaig, Norman, 86, 101
MacDiarmid, Hugh, 26, 34, 54, 96
MacDonald, Ethel, 300
Macdonald, Flora, 264
Macdonald, Margaret, 33, 236, 244, 247
MacDonald, Ramsay, 186
MacDonald, Robert David, 216
Macdonell, Alastair, 110
Macfarlan, James, 23–24
Macfarlane, Alexander, 198
Macfarlane Observatory, 198–200
Macgillivray, William, 154, 156
Mach, David, 130
Mackenzie, Sir George, 64, 170
Mackenzie, Henry, 123
Mackenzie, Isa, 264
Mackintosh, Charles Rennie, 33, 191, 192, 228,
    236–237, 241, 242–248, 266, 274
Mackintosh, Ewart Alan, 107
MacLaurin, Colin, 198
Maclean, John, 183–186
MacLean, Sorley, 86, 186
MacNicol, Bessie, 234
MacTaggart, William, 113, 123
MacTaggart, Sir William, 111
Madeleine of Valois, 88
Maitland, William, 9–12, 17
Market Street, 70, 105
Martin, John, 287
Martyrs' Monument, 170
Maryhill, 252
Mary King's Close, 37, 70
Mary of Guise, 88, 144

Mary Queen of Scots, 5, 10–11, 12, 46, 47, 49,
    88–91, 93, 117, 144, 152, 153, 158, 163, 195
Masson, Rosaline, 101
Matchboxes, 232–233
Matisse, Henri, 130, 236, 263, 265
Maver, Irene, 29
Maxwell, Catherine, 70
Maxwell, Eglintoune, 70
Maxwell, James Clerk, 109, 272
Maxwell, Jane, 70
Mayne, John, 19, 20
McArthur, Alexander, 212
McDougal, Helen, 162, 163
McGill, James, 272
McGonagall, William, 168, 169
McHattie, John, 108
McInnes, William, 265
McKenzie, Robert Tait, 107–108
McLehose, Agnes, 82, 207–208
McLeish, Robert, 213
McLellan, Archibald, 232, 291
McLellan Galleries, 232, 237, 239, 242
McNeilage, Rev. John, 239
McUre, John, 7–8, 9, 12, 13–14, 26
McWilliam, Candia, 36
Meadows, the, 151
Melrose Abbey, 104
Melville, Andrew, 14, 268
Mendelssohn, Felix, 94
Mercat Cross, 268
Merchant City, 198, 199, 216–220, 241
Merchants' Park, 190, 275
Merchants' Steeple, 196
Metropolitan Museum, New York, 131, 136,
    293
Millar, John, 222
Miller, David Prince, 191
Miller, Hugh, 105, 125, 136
Miller, William, 191–192
Mills, George, 249
Minto, Lord. See Elliot, Gilbert
Miralles, Enric, 94–96
Mitchell, James, 291

Mitchell, John, 23
Mitchell, John Oswald, 256
Mitchell, Stephen, 255, 256
Mitchell Library, 255–260, 261
Mitchell Street, 227, 228
Mitchison, Naomi, 86
Molendinar Burn, 193
Monro, Alexander, 6, 156, 159, 164
Mons Meg, 46–47, 50
Montrose, James, Marquis of, 174–175
Monymusk Reliquary, 175
Moody, Dwight, 277, 278
Moore, Sir John, 179–180
Moray Place (Edinburgh), 125
Moray Place (Glasgow), 287
Morgan, Edwin, 97, 127, 186, 254, 258, 259, 271, 274, 308
Morison, Robert, 139
Morris, William, 283
Mossman, John, 181, 228
Motherwell, 185
Mound, the, 100, 103
Muir, Edwin, 34, 101
Muir, Thomas, 136–137, 201
Mumford, Lewis, 56
Murray, John (archive), 59
Murray, Patrick, 69–70
Murray, Sarah, 67–68, 93, 102
Murray, Stewart, 276
Murrayfield Stadium, 30
Museum of Childhood, 69–70, 71, 72
Museum of Edinburgh, 27, 75–80, 165, 170

Nasmyth, Alexander, 113, 116, 132, 135
National Covenent, 169–170
National Gallery of Scotland, 96, 110, 111–114, 296
National Library of Scotland, 59, 66, 158, 161, 171, 210
National Monument, 133–134
National Museum of Scotland, 27, 172–175, 301
National Theatre of Scotland, 261
National Trust for Scotland, 123, 247, 253, 288

Nelson (publishers), 171
Nelson, Horatio, 204
Nelson, William, 46
Nelson Monument (Edinburgh), 52, 134, 135
Nelson Monument (Glasgow), 204
Netherlee, 288
Newark, 297
Newbery, Francis, 242–243
Newbold, Walton, 185
New Club, 102
New College, 57–58
New Harmony, 296
Newhaven, 124, 136, 168
Newington, 80
Newington Place, 162
New Lanark, 295–296
Newton, Sir Isaac, 128–129, 198
New Town (Edinburgh), 16, 22, 39, 51, 100–125, 135, 144, 157
New York, 78, 127, 130, 131, 259, 262, 283, 293, 310
Nicolson Street, 152, 158
Niven, Frances, 148
North Bridge, 121
North British Locomotive Works, 302
North British Railway Company, 29
North Fort Street, 118
North Loch, 16, 18, 100, 102
North Street, 255, 259
Norton Park Group, 71–72
Norton Park School, 71
Norway, 54
Norwich, John Julius, 293

Oakley, Charles, 240
Ocean Terminal, 146
Old Calton Burial Ground, 134
Old College Bar, 200
Old Town (Edinburgh), 16, 39, 56, 82–85, 119, 120, 121, 165
Old Town Improvement, 74
Oliphant, J., 162
Oliphant, Margaret, 63

Oran Mor, 274
Outlook Tower, 53–56
Owen, Robert, 296
Owen, Wilfred, 34, 35
Oxford, 268

Pacific Quay, 306
Paine, Tom, 137, 201
Paisley, 181
Pandemonium Club, 84
Panmure House, 81
Panoramic Building, 233
Paolozzi, Sir Eduardo, 70, 127–129, 148–150
Paris, 32, 55, 127, 191, 225, 236, 237, 238
Park Circus, 266, 267, 279
Parliament Hall, 58, 63–64, 65
Parliament Square, 60, 64, 66
Paterson, David, 161, 162
Paterson, Mary, 162–163
Paton, Amelia, 126
Patrick, Jenny, 300–301
Patterson, Oscar, 214
Peel, Robert, 181
Pentland Hills, 44
People's Palace, 204–206, 222
People's Story, the, 75
Peploe, Samuel John, 129, 236
Philadelphia, 78
Picardy Place, 150
Pinkerton, Allan, 214
Pirie, Margaret, 232
Pitcairne, Archibald, 158
Plantation Quay, 301, 306
Playfair, William, 109, 126, 133, 134, 144, 152, 153, 154, 158, 169
Pointhouse shipyard, 307
Poker Club, 85
Political Economy Club, 219
Political Martyrs' Memorial, 136–137
Pollock, Jackson, 130
Pollok House, 294
Pollok Park, 293–294
Pollokshields, 253

Porteous Riots, 74–75
Port Glasgow, 15, 290, 297, 302
Portland Street, 184
Portobello, 143
Powell, Sir Francis, 243–244
Prague, 49
Prince's Dock, 305
Princes Square mall, 230
Princes Street, 34, 57, 80, 100–113, 133, 146, 230, 234
Princes Street Gardens, 44, 57, 100, 104–109, 119, 126, 166
Pritchard, Edward William, 232
Professors' Square, 273–274
Prostitution, 84–85, 145, 163
Proust, Marcel, 216
Provand's Lordship, 193–195
Prowse, Philip, 216
Pugin, Augustus, 286
Pugin, P. P. and C. W., 298

Quartermile, 151
Queen Elizabeth, 309
Queen Elizabeth II, 309
Queen Margaret University, 151
Queen Mary, 304, 309
Queensberry House, 96
Queen's Cross Church, 247
Queen's Gallery, 93–94
Queen's Park, 195
Queen's Park Church, 287
Queen's Park Football Club, 29
Queen's Park Terrace, 252
Queen Street (Edinburgh), 100, 114, 117, 122
Queen Street (Glasgow), 193, 194, 220, 221, 227

Raeburn, Henry, 95, 110, 117, 123, 125, 167
Railways, 28–29, 302–303, 309, 311
Ramsay, Allan (Sr., poet), 19, 54, 108, 109–110
Ramsay, Allan (Jr., artist), 110, 111, 117
Ramsay, Dean, 107
Ramsay Gardens, 54, 110, 112

Rangers Football Club, 29–30
Rankin, Ian, 79, 124, 135, 175
Ransford, Tessa, 86
Ray, John, 197
Red Clydeside, 183–186, 205, 304
Red Commune, 300
"Red Flag, The," 239
Reformation, 60, 151, 188, 190–191, 268. *See also* Knox, John
Register House, 121
Reid, Alastair, 38
Reid, Alexander, 33, 265, 292
Reid, Jimmy, 304–305
Reid, McNeill, 265, 274
Reid, Robert (architect), 121, 122, 123
Reid, Robert (benefactor), 152
Rembrandt, 111, 263, 291
Renfrew Street, 241, 242
Rhind, Birnie, 107
Richardson, James, 211
Riddle's Court, 55
Ritchie, James T. R., 72
Riverside Museum, 230, 301, 306–310
Rizzio, David, 89–90, 92
RMJM Architects, 94, 313
Roberts, David, 286
Roberts, Field Marshal, 267
Robertson, E. H., 234
Robertson, William, 85, 157
Robison, William, 85
Rochead, John Thomas, 276
Rock House, 106, 135, 136
Rogers, Richard, 151
Rollock, Robert, 152
Rosebery, Lord, 255
Rose Street, 120
Roslin Institute, 158
Rosner, Lisa, 162
Ross, Daniel, 107
Ross Fountain, 107
Rottenrow, 268
Rowling, J. K., 37, 109, 124, 146
Royal Bank of Scotland, 5, 39, 127

Royal Botanic Garden Edinburgh, 108, 138–143
Royal College of Physicians, 139, 140
Royal College of Surgeons, 158–164
Royal College of Surgeons' Museum, 159–160, 164
Royal Exchange Square, 220, 283
Royal High School, 133, 134
Royal Mile, 10, 12, 15, 37, 44, 49, 50–99, 119, 270
Royal Observatory, 51, 118, 135
Royal Scots Greys, 107
Royal Scottish Academy, 32, 33, 101, 109, 110, 111, 112, 130, 165
Royal Scottish Museum, 172–173
Royal Scottish National Orchestra, 261
Royal Society of Edinburgh, 109, 156, 159, 173
Rugby, 30
Ruskin, John, 118, 285
Ruthven Street, 274

St. Andrews, 10, 135, 136, 139
St. Andrew's Halls, 259, 290
St. Andrews in the Square, 207
St. Andrews University, 151, 152, 268
St. Bernard's Well, 132
St. Cecilia's Hall, 86
St. Cuthbert's Church, 108, 109
St. Enoch, 187, 228
St. Enoch Centre, 187
St. Enoch's Burn, 228
St. Enoch's Station, 182, 302
St. Gaudens, Augustus, 63
St. George's Church, 121, 122, 123
St. George's Cross, 254
St. Giles, 10, 11
St. Giles Cathedral, 58–63, 66, 74, 82, 103, 164, 168
St. Kentigern. *See* St. Mungo
St. Margaret, 46, 49, 88
St. Margaret's Chapel, 45, 49–50
St. Mary's Church, 46
St. Mary's Roman Catholic Cathedral, 127, 150

St. Mary's Street, 74

St. Mungo, 12, 13, 21, 187–188, 189, 195, 228, 254, 262

St. Mungo Museum of Religious Life and Art, 195

St. Rollox works and chimney, 22, 23, 24, 37

St. Serf, 187, 188

St. Thenew. *See* St. Enoch

St. Vincent Place, 186, 227

St. Vincent Street, 191

St. Vincent Street Free Church, 288

Salisbury Crags, 88, 94

Salmond, Alex, 98

Saltire Society, 240

Saltmarket, 196, 248, 296

Sandyford, 275, 276

Sankey, Ira, 277, 278

Sauchiehall Street, 224, 229, 231–242, 251, 260, 265, 275, 280, 301

Saughton Prison, 149

Sayers, Dorothy L., 283

Schiller, Friedrich, 90

Schinkel, Karl Friedrich, 288

Schotz, Benno, 267

Scone, 10

Scotland Street School, 247

Scotsman newspaper, 30, 86, 104, 114, 137, 149, 165, 239, 242, 289

Scots Whisky Centre, 68

Scott, Sir George Gilbert, 270, 271, 273, 286

Scott, John, 63

Scott, Sir Walter, 21, 27, 49, 56, 64, 93, 96, 102–104, 109, 110, 113, 117, 119, 124, 133, 135, 136, 138, 145, 152, 156, 164, 180, 187, 201, 227

Scottish American War Memorial, 107–108

Scottish Chamber Orchestra, 261

Scottish Colourists, 129–130, 265

Scottish Constitutional Convention, 97

Scottish Exhibition and Conference Centre, 301, 305, 309

Scottish Government, 98

Scottish National Gallery of Modern Art, 111, 114, 126–132

Scottish National Party, 97, 98, 239

Scottish National Portrait Gallery, 27, 111, 114–117, 136

Scottish National War Memorial, 50

Scottish Office, 33

Scottish Opera, 261

Scottish Parliament, 38, 74, 86, 87, 94–99, 134, 313

Scottish Poetry Library, 86–87

Scottish Storytelling Centre, 72–73, 75

Scott Monument, 102–106, 166

Scott Street, 245

Seafield, Earl of, 64

Sectarianism, 30, 213

Select Society, 140

Serrent, Duc de, 93

"Shadow" (author), 250–251, 252

Shawfield House, 220

Sheehy, William, 283

Short, Maria Theresa, 51–53

Short, Thomas, 51

Short's Observatory, 51–53

Sibbald, Robert, 139, 140

Signet Library, 59, 64

Simpson, Sir James Young, 102, 156, 166

Simpson, William, 211

Sinclair, Catherine, 122

Sinclair, Sir John, 122

Singing Street, The, 71–72

Skeel, Kenneth, 97

Slater, Oscar, 259

Slavery, 15, 80, 138, 198, 201, 217, 219, 222–223, 255, 269, 306

Slezer, John, 8, 11, 196

Slums, 66–67, 84–85, 211–215, 249–252

Smeaton, John, 21

Smellie, William, 12, 85

Smith, Adam, 6, 19, 81, 85, 140, 157, 218–219, 222, 223, 268–270, 312

Smith, Alexander, 26–27, 29, 37, 104, 298–299

Smith, Alexander McCall, 124

Smith, Duncan, 232

Smith, Horace, 287

Smith, James (architect), 279, 280

Smith, Rev. James, 207

Smith, Dr. John, 159

Smith, Madeleine, 279–284

Smith, Sidney, 211

Smith, Tommy, 271

Smollett, Tobias, 85, 219

Society of Antiquaries, 109

Solicitors' Library, 64

Somerville, Mary, 71

Somerville, Thomas, 120

Sousa, John Philip, 264

South Bridge, 152

South Gray Street, 80

South Lorne Place, 146

Spanish Civil War, 205, 300–301

Spark, Muriel, 34, 69, 70–71, 79, 117, 127, 141, 148

Spence, Sir Basil, 214

Spencer, Stanley, 301

Sport, 29–30, 234

Spottiswoode, John, 12, 14

Spreull's Land, 248–249

Springburn, 252, 302, 309

Stark, John, 154

Steell, Gourlay, 165

Steell, Sir John, 105, 165

Stevenson, D. W., 132

Stevenson, Robert Louis, 8, 47, 56, 63, 64, 66, 68–69, 70, 71, 79, 102, 106, 118, 156, 169, 170

Stewart, Dugald, 134

Stewart's and Macdonald's, 228

Stieglitz, Alfred, 136

Stirling Castle, 10

Stoddart, Alexander, 81, 270

Stothard, Thomas, 64

Strachan, Douglas, 50

Strang, John, 191

Strathaven, 201

Strathclyde University, 256, 270

Suffragettes, 79–80, 137, 203, 237–238

Sugar trade, 15, 198, 222

Surgeons' Hall, 158

Surgeons' Square, 159

Sutherland, James, 139–140, 275

Syme, James, 163

Symons, Jelinger C., 249–250

Tacitus, 115, 311–312

Tagliabue, Benedetta, 94

Tagore, Rabindranath, 55

Tait, William, 84–85

Tall Ship, the, 306–307, 309–310

Tassie, James, 115

Taylor, John, 43, 47

Telford, Thomas, 125

Templeton Business Centre, 207

Tenement House, the, 248, 253–254

Tenements, 84–85, 248–254, 258

Tennyson, Alfred Lord, 167, 280, 285

Thatcher, Margaret, 300

Thistle Street, 120

Thomson, Alexander "Greek," 191, 241, 252, 276, 284–289

Thomson, James, 118–119

Thomson, William. *See* Kelvin, Lord

Titian, 112, 263, 266

Tobacco Exchange, 220

Tobacco Lords, 200–201, 216–222, 269

Tobacco trade, 15, 216–222, 255, 262, 302

Tognieri, Giovanni, 309

Tolbooth (Edinburgh), 58, 78, 174

Tolbooth (Glasgow), 195–196, 197, 248

Tolbooth Kirk (Edinburgh), 58

Tolbooth Steeple (Glasgow), 196, 198, 200

Tollcross, 275

Toward, Agnes, 253–254

Trades Hall, 187, 196

Trades House, 196

Trams, 98, 146, 237

Trench, John Thompson, 259

Treron et Cie., 234, 237–238

Trinity House, 144

Tron Church (Edinburgh), 58

Tron Church (Glasgow), 196

Trongate, 196, 200, 248–250

Tron Theatre, 196, 260
Tucker, Thomas, 197
Turgot, 49
Turnbull, William, 13
Turner, J. M. W., 111, 113, 135, 286, 296
Tweeddale Court, 86

Ubiquitous Chip, 274
UNESCO, 37, 39, 124
Union Canal, 162, 311, 312, 314
Union of the Crowns (1603), 5, 48, 196
Union of Parliaments (1707), 5, 15, 64, 74, 96, 133, 217
Union Street, 286
Universities. *See entries for specific universities*
University Avenue, 270, 274
University Physic Garden, 275
Upper Clyde Shipbuilders, 205, 206, 304–305
Ure, Joan, 304
Usher Hall, 109

Van Gogh, Vincent, 111, 263, 265, 292
Vaughan Bequest, 111
Verse magazine, 86
Victoria, Queen, 93, 105, 124, 179, 181–182, 183, 204, 262, 263
Victoria and Albert Docks, 146
Victoria Bridge, 298
Virginia, 139, 198, 218
Virginia Chambers, 220
Virginia Street, 216, 218, 220
Votadini, 43

Waddell, Helen, 150
Walker, Rev. Robert, 110
Walkinshaw, Clementina, 220
Wallace, William, 45, 202
Walton, E. A., 183
Wardle, Lena, 283. *See also* Smith, Madeleine
Warriston Crescent, 125
Washington, George, 218, 219
Water of Leith, 125, 126, 132, 143
Water of Leith Village, 126

Watson, Bessie, 79, 80
Watson, John, 258
Watt, James, 20, 22, 173, 174, 187, 198–200, 206–207, 208, 289, 297–298, 300, 302
Watt, Robert, 48–49
Watt Brothers, 241
Waverley (paddle steamer), 308
Waverley Railway Station, 18, 139
Weavers, 23, 202, 205, 207, 210
Weir, Jean, 76–78
Weir, Major, 76–78
Welsh, Irvine, 36, 146
Wernerian Society, 159
West, William, 117
West Bow, 76
West Coates, 169
West Nile Street, 283
West Princes Street, 259
Whistler, James McNeill, 32, 265, 274, 291, 292
Whiteford, Kate, 131
Whitehill, 220
Whyte, Hamish, 250, 259
Wigham, Eliza, 80
Wilcox, John, 311, 312, 316
Wilde, Oscar, 259
Wilkie, Sir David, 93, 110
William III, King, 201
William Cunninghame and Co., 219
Williams, Alice Meredith, 50
Williamson, Peter, 65–66
Willow Tea Rooms, 228–229, 236–237
Wilson, Charles, 279
Wilson, Daniel, 45
Wilson, James, 201–203, 204
Wilson, Jean, 79
Wilson, Walter & Co., 234
Wood, Harry Harvey, 34
Woodside, 254
Wordsworth, Dorothy, 298
Wordsworth, William, 244
Wright, Fanny, 296
Wright, Frank Lloyd, 245
Writers' Museum, 56–58, 79

Wylie and Lochhead, 228, 229
Wylie Hill, 229
Wyllie, George, 305

Yamao, Yozo, 256–258
Yeats, William Butler, 96, 244

Yorkhill Quay, 310
York Place, 117
Young, William, 181
Youngson, A. J., 117

Zangwill, Israel, 32